British Music-Hall
1840–1923

An Archon Book on Popular Entertainments

British Music-Hall
1840–1923

A Bibliography and Guide to Sources,
with a Supplement
on European Music-Hall

Laurence Senelick
David F. Cheshire
Ulrich Schneider

Archon Books

1981

© 1981 The Shoe String Press, Inc.

First published 1981 as an Archon Book,
an imprint of The Shoe String Press, Inc.,
Hamden, Connecticut 06514

Library of Congress Cataloging in Publication Data

Senelick, Laurence.
   British music-hall, 1840-1923.

   (An Archon book on popular entertainments)
   Includes index.
   1. Music-halls (Variety-theatres, cabarets, etc.)—Great Britain—Bibliography.
2. Music-halls (Variety-theatres, cabarets, etc.)—Europe—Bibliography.
I. Cheshire, David F.   II. Schneider, Ulrich, 1938-   .   III. Title. IV. Series:
Archon book on popular entertainments.
Z5784.M93S46   [PN1968.G7]   016.7927'0941   81-4996
ISBN 0-208-01840-9   AACR2

CONTENTS

Sydney Fairbrother, 1873–1941
James Fawn, 1849–1923
Sid Field, 1904–50
Happy Fanny Fields, 1881–1961
Dame Gracie Fields, 1898–1979
Bud Flanagan, 1896–1968
Florrie Forde, 1876–1940
George Formby, 1904–61
Harry Fragson, 1866–1913
W[illiam] F. Frame, 1848–1919
Louie Freear, 1873–1939
Will Fyffe, 1885–1947
Gertie Gitana, 1888–1957
Charles Godfrey, 1851–1900
George Gray
The Brothers Griffiths [F. G., 1856–1940; Joe, 1852–1901]
Yvette Guilbert, 1865–1944
Will Hay, 1888–1949
Jenny Hill, 1848–96
Stanley Holloway, 1890–
Percy Honri, 1874–1953
Alec Hurley, 1871–1913
Fred Karno, 1886–1941
Hetty King, 1883–1972
R[ichard] G[eorge] Knowles, 1858–1919
Lupino Lane, 1892–1959
George Lashwood, 1863–1942
Sir Harry Lauder, 1870–1950
John Lawson, 1865–1920
Tom Leamore, 1866–1939
Dan Leno, 1860–1904
Fanny Leslie, 1857–1935
George Leybourne, 1842–84
Harry Liston, 1843–1929
Victor Liston, 1838–1913
Little Tich, 1867–1928
Arthur Lloyd, 1840–1904
Marie Lloyd, 1870–1922
Kitty Lofting
[Marie] Cecilia "Cissie" Loftus, 1876–1943
Marie Loftus, 1857–1940
Arthur Lucan, 1887–1954
Frederic Maccabe, 1831–1904
The Great Macdermott, 1845–1901
E[dmund] W[illiam] Mackney, 1825–1909
Paul Martinetti, 1851–1924

Billy Merson, 1881–1947
Max Miller, 1895–1963
Charles Morton, 1819–1904
George Mozart, 1864–1947
Jolly John Nash, 1830–1901
Jimmy Nervo, 1897–1975
Harry Nicholls, 1852–1926
Renton Nicholson, 1809–61
Harry Pleon, 1856–1911
Sandy Powell, 1900–
Nellie Power, 1854–87
Billy Purvis, 1784–1853
Harry Randall, 1860–1932
Frank Randle, 1902–57
Ada Reeve, 1874–1966
Ella Retford, c. 1886–1962
Harry Rickards, 1841–1911
Arthur Roberts, 1852–1933
Sir George Robey, 1869–1954
Frederick Robson, 1821–64
Clarkson Rose, 1890–1968
Billy Russell, 1893–1971
Henry Russell, 1812–1900
Eugen Sandow, 1867–1925
Ella Shields, 1879–1952
Charles Sloman, 1808–70
Emily Soldene, 1844–1912
Mel[ancthon] B[urton] Spurr, d. 1904
J[ames] H[urst] Stead, 1827–86
Sir Oswald Stoll, 1866–1942
Eugene Stratton, 1861–1918
Harry Tate, 1872–1940
Vesta Tilley, 1864–1952
Alfred Granville "The Great" Vance, 1839–88
Ada Victoria, 1870–
Vesta Victoria, 1874–1951
Nellie Wallace, 1870–1948
Harry Weldon, 1881–1930
Bransby Williams, 1870–1961
Wee Georgie Wood, 1897–1979
Tom Woottwell, 1865–
Zaeo, 1866–1906
Zazel, 1862–

X. PERFORMANCE MATERIAL   241

ABBREVIATIONS

comp.	compiler
DH	Diana Howard, *London Theatres and Music Hall 1850–1950*. London: Library Association, 1970.
dir.	directed by
DNB	*Dictionary of National Biography*.
ed.	editor, edited by, edition
edit.	editorial
EDS	*Enciclopedia dello spettacolo*. Fondata Silvio d'Amico. Roma: Le Maschere, 1962.
ills.	illustrations, illustrated by
L	London, England
M & M	Raymond Mander and Joe Mitchenson. *The Theatres of London*. London: Hart–Davis, 1961. 2d ed. 1963.
M & M, *Lost*	Raymond Mander and Joe Mitchenson. *The Lost Theatres of London*. London: Hart-Davis, 1968.
mgr.	manager
n.s.	new series
N.Y.	New York, New York
obit.	obituary
OCT	*Oxford Companion to the Theatre,* ed. Phyllis Hartnoll. 3rd ed. London: Oxford University Press, 1967.
prop.	proprietor
pseud.	pseudonym
pub.	published
repr.	reprinted

Abbreviations

rev.	reviewed by
S & W	Edwin O. Sachs and Ernest A. E. Woodrow. *Modern Opera Houses and Theatres* . . . . 3 vols. London: Batsford, 1896–98.
TLS	*Times Literary Supplement*
TN	*Theatre Notebook*. London: Society for Theatre Research.
trans.	translated by, translation

INTRODUCTION

"MUSIC-HALL. A term of reproach applied to the chosen nursery of the British drama."

John Hollingshead, *Plain English* (London, 1880) 174

One era's idle pastime becomes a subject for serious inquiry to another. The study of popular entertainments has burgeoned over the last few decades and is now recognized as a distinct branch of theatre history and social science. And just as archaeologists must sift through the refuse of centuries, valuing highly what vanished civilizations discarded or took for granted, so the student of popular theatre finds himself examining inane song lyrics, advertising puffs and stage-manager's time-books to reconstitute from these trifles an important segment of the life of the past, and to speculate on the origins of our present diversions and enthusiasms.

In the last few years, the diggers have been aided by various research tools; the most impressive of these was R. Toole-Stott's massive bibliography of the circus, monumental in every sense. At the other end of the scale is David Mayer's small guide to information sources on pantomime, a slender pamphlet which managed, nonetheless, to be cogent and corrective in scant space. The present work, devoted to the British music-hall in the period 1840–1923, hopes to fall somewhere between these two works, both in size and coverage. There is a slight degree of overlap, for

1

Toole-Stott was considering "circus and allied arts" and therefore gave space to variety entertainments and specialty acts, and as to pantomime, at the turn of the century it was dominated by music-hall comedians. However, the music-hall was so idiosyncratic a form that it deserves separate treatment, all the more so because its span of life was relatively brief. Evolving from the catch-clubs and music houses of eighteenth-century London, passing through a formative stage in the Regency and early Victorian night houses and free-and-easies, it had taken on its characteristic features by 1865 and held the public imagination until competition from other media brought about its obsolescence. Every era has its peculiar form in which variety entertainment is presented, be it the Roman or the three-ring circus, the fair or the *théâtre de la foire*, vaudeville or video. The music-hall essentially presented the same kinds of performers and material as its predecessors had; what made it a distinctive and eloquent expression of the nineteenth century was its organization. It was the first wholly urbanized entertainment to appeal to a large audience of a new kind of proletariat and lower middle class; thanks to cheap printing, and greater literacy on the part of the populace, its means of publicity and self-promotion were widespread. Allied to the liquor interests, its management exercised a more modern form of commercial operation than had the earlier theatrical lessee; associated in agencies and eventually unions, its performers were less independent and more stable than their ancestors had been. In its heyday the music-hall constituted a world separate from and equal to that of the so-called legitimate theatre, with its own press organs, playhouses, backstage traditions and usages, audiences and literature.

The present work is intended primarily for the student exploring this phenomenon. Consequently, it is both more and less than a bibliography in the strict etymological sense: less, because it does not provide extensive bibliographic data on size of volume, illustrations, number of pages and printer's marks, and may disappoint librarians and book-dealers on that account; more, because it lists not only books, but articles in periodicals, caricatures, phonograph records, and information on collections and other holdings, making it a sourcebook for researchers. It cannot pretend to completeness: considering the importance of the music-hall in British culture and the scope of our survey, nothing short of an index to all British periodicals of the last one hundred and fifty years could insure completeness. However, we have attempted to cover every aspect of the music-hall from finances to poetry, and to indicate the breadth of the field and the depth of the material a scholar will encounter. In major instances, we have commented on the value of an item or summarized its contents, but it would have been impractical to attempt that for every entry.

Following standard practice, all sections and subsections are arranged alphabetically, except in the case of periodicals; there we have followed the example of Carl Stratman, believing it important to see at a glance the time-span covered by a magazine or journal. The various rubrics and their headnotes should aid the student to find what he is looking for easily, and to that end the cross-references and indices are copious.

Despite the Londinocentric nature of much writing on the music-hall, space is devoted to the provinces, Scotland, Ireland, and Wales, so the "British" in the title is a true one. In addition, we have provided supplements with brief accounts of the literature of European counterparts to the British music-hall. With the exception of one or two items, we have not touched upon the American variety stage, "vaudeville," in the hope that this work will inspire an American scholar to dedicate to it the full-scale bibliography it deserves.

The dates in the title "1840-1923" refer, of course, not to dates of publication but to that term of the music-hall's life. The music-hall was fundamentally a Victorian institution, which shot up in one final burst of glory in the reign of Edward, but failed to survive the First World War except in a depleted and outmoded manner. The year 1840 is, therefore, a somewhat arbitrary delimitation, halfway between Victoria's coronation in 1838 and the 1843 Theatre Act that distinguished between theatres and those halls which served food and provided only musical entertainment. So-called "music halls" had existed previously, but it was Charles Morton's Canterbury Hall, opened in 1852, that is traditionally considered the first, primarily because of Morton's clever publicity campaigns and the unquestionable respectability of his establishment. In practice and to supply context, we cite books and articles relating to the prehistory of the halls—the pleasure gardens, catch-clubs and so on—but have not felt obliged to be exhaustive in our coverage.

The year 1923 has a more precise rationale. It was the year after the death of Marie Lloyd, arguably the last of the legendary performers, and the year in which the BBC's first variety show, significantly called *Veterans of Variety*, was broadcast. Radio joined cinema and music comedy, ragtime and revue, as potent rivals for the music-hall's audience and performers. Music-hall did not suddenly disappear; it lingered with varying surges of vitality into the 1950s, when television rang its definitive death-knell, and the demolition of the old halls reduced the possibility of resurrection. It may be revived sporadically as a curio or a museum-piece, but it no longer speaks for the public. The date 1923 is thus a *terminus ad quem;* however, halls built before 1923 have their histories traced beyond that time and performers who made their professional music-hall debuts by 1923, even though they may not have reached their greatest fame by then, are included. This explains why there are entries for Gracie Fields, Stanley Holloway, and Max Miller, but not for Max Wall or Jimmy Edwards.

It may be thought that an entire volume devoted to writing about British music-hall in a period of little more than a century suggests that the subject has been thoroughly exhausted. But in fact the opposite is the case. A glance over the listings will show that there are three main types of source: contemporary material, chiefly memoir or journalistic; a handful of well-researched and thoughtful studies, published primarily in the last few decades; and a plethora of redundant, superficial, unreliable accounts. The very wealth of contemporary material should encourage the researcher to consider more profoundly subjects that have barely been glanced at: catalogues and analyses of songs have only been begun, audience studies have hardly been touched on, the economics of the music-hall is still a neglected topic. With rare exceptions, there are no biographies of major music-hall figures that are more than anecdotal. Full-length, interpretive accounts of music-hall censorship, architecture, performance techniques, working conditions, influence on art and literature would prove of value. In short, we hope that the student and scholar will exploit this book as an incentive and an aid to further study. We would appreciate hearing of our omissions and oversights, for inclusion in a possible later edition. Any corrigenda and addenda should be sent to Laurence Senelick, Department of Drama, Tufts University, Medford, Mass. 02155, U.S.A.

The editors would like to acknowledge their thanks to the following persons who gave their assistance by answering questions and appeals, suggesting entries or opening their collections to us: Per Brink Abrahamsen; Tony Barker, editor of *Music Hall*; J. O. Blake, editor of *The Call Boy*; Mary Ellen Brooks of the University of Georgia Libraries; Nina Fenwick of Chadwyck-Healey Ltd.; Barthold Fles; Joe Ging, Keeper of Theatre History, Tyne and Wear County Council; Diana Howard; Tom Munro; Bert Ross; Arthur Saxon; George Speaight; and Martha Vicinus, editor of *Victorian Studies*. As always, the staff of the Harvard Theatre Collection has been unsparing of its cooperation.

Laurence Senelick, Tufts University
David F. Cheshire, Middlesex Polytechnic
Ulrich Schneider, University of Erlangen

Medford, Mass., September 1979.

N.B. This work achieved closure in July 1980. No books or articles printed after that date will be found herein.

I. GENERAL REFERENCE

"There is nothing that should be taken seriously, except, possibly, an income or the music halls . . ."

> Esme, the Oscar Wilde character, in Robert Hichens, *The Green Carnation* (N.Y.: D. Appleton, 1894), 197.

Here we have listed only works which are useful in studying the operation of the halls proper, or understanding the language of their songs and humor. General reference works on the theatre are not given; however, articles that appear in them concerning the music-hall will be found under their authors' names, and can be located by means of the cross-references. Biographical dictionaries and who's whos are cited in Collective Biography, chapter 9.

DIRECTORY OF COLLECTIONS

The following is intended to be a listing of major holdings in British music-hall, primarily in and around London; consequently, it does not include large theatre libraries which may contain scattered but useful material (such as the Lincoln Center Library of the Performing Arts in New York). Researchers should

7

be aware that the central libraries of most cities in the United Kingdom can provide valuable archival material in this field (particularly is this true of Manchester, Liverpool, and Glasgow). Occasionally, the scrapbooks and personal collections of performers are to be found in the locality of their birth or death (for example, there is a great deal of data on Billy Williams in the National Library of Australia). And there are sizeable private collections (such as that of Matthew Murtagh in Dublin) which are often accessible to scholars by application to the owner. For the individual holdings of local London libraries, see Diana Howard, *Directory of Theatre Research Resources in Greater London*. L: Commission for a British Theatre Institute, 1974.

United Kingdom

Two things will be immediately apparent from this list—there have been many changes in both the names and the locations of several famous collections in the last few years, and hours of opening have not been cited. The latter are so frequently varied and amended due to the decrease (or increase) in the number of staff available, the rearrangement or relocation of the material, etc., that those who intend research should always communicate with curators and librarians before arrival to avoid disappointment and delay. If it is known that special arrangements are necessary before admission can be arranged, these are indicated.

ANTONY D. HIPPISLEY COXE CIRCUS COLLECTION
see
THE THEATRE MUSEUM

BRITISH ARCHITECTURAL LIBRARY
Royal Instiute of British Architects, 66 Portland Place, London
W1   01–580–5533

Accredited enquirers may receive permission to use this specialist library, a key feature of which is the very large collection of indexed periodicals.

BRITISH FILM INSTITUTE
81 Dean Street, London W1
Library located at 127/133 Charing Cross Road, London W1
01-437-4355

Much useful information not (as might be expected) only on films, but also on the general careers of those music-hall and variety performers who appeared both on cinema and television screens, is available in this extremely well-organized library of books, periodicals, press cuttings, etc. This is a members-only library but queries from nonmembers are dealt with whenever possible, and students and lecturers of institutions which are full Corporate Members may be given access for reference purposes.

BRITISH LIBRARY
Great Russell St., London WC1   01-636-1544

Department of Manuscripts
All the records of the Lord Chamberlain's Office relating to theatre licensing are now stored here.

Music Library
All English songs printed before 1900 are entered in the Catalogue of Modern Music under the composer's name, with a reference from the first word of the title. Anonymous songs are entered under the first word of the first verse. For certain songs published after 1900 not entered in the catalogue, there is a slip index arranged by title. There is also a title index of songs in song albums from about 1890 onwards. Except for a few which have been lost, most song covers are bound with the music. It is planned to commence publication of the Catalogue of Modern Music and the Music Room Song Title Index in 1980.

Reference Division (formerly British Museum Library)
This is the principal British national copyright library and, therefore, the major collection of books on music-hall and variety. A subject index of works received between 1881 and 1900 was published in 1901. There are supplementary volumes containing accessions received in each succeeding period of five years. The subject index for 1961 onwards is available only on microfilm. Since 1950 the British National Bibliography has listed books published in the U.K. in a Dewey-classified order weekly. The contents of the weekly lists are subsequently cumulated in various, more comprehensive publications.

General Reference

BRITISH LIBRARY
Colindale Avenue, London NW9   01-200-5515

Newspaper Library
The national deposit library for all British newspapers and periodicals, both national and regional, its holdings are indicated in *The British Union Catalogue of Periodicals*, etc.

BRITISH MUSEUM
Bloomsbury, London, WC1   01-636-1555

Department of Prints and Drawings
A random selection of Victorian song covers (with the remainder of music generally removed) is kept in a folder marked "Lithography—English and Foreigners Working in England—Music Titles."

BRITISH MUSIC HALL SOCIETY COLLECTION
all enquiries by post or telephone only to
The General Secretary and Curator
Alan Felton
46 Forsyth House, Tatchbrook Street, London SW1   01-828-5397

The uncatalogued collection contains many costumes, stage properties, posters, bills, autographed photographs, phonograph records, contracts, and books.

BRITISH THEATRE ASSOCIATION
9-10 Fitzroy Square, London W1   01-387-2666

The Library of the Association (formerly The British Drama League) is available strictly to members only, and although it specializes in all subjects relating to the drama and theatre, contains very little on popular entertainment.

BRITISH THEATRE MUSEUM
The collection formerly housed at Leighton House has been transferred to THE THEATRE MUSEUM.

ELLIS ASHTON COLLECTION
1 King Henry Street, London N 16   01-254-4209

This uncatalogued miscellaneous collection of ephemera, photographs, memorabilia, gramophone records, etc. is available to accredited researchers only.

ENTHOVEN COLLECTION
This collection now forms part of THE THEATRE MUSEUM.

GREATER LONDON COUNCIL
County Hall, London SE1 7PB   01-928-5000
Middlesex House, 20 Vauxhall Bridge Road
1 Queen Anne's Gate Buildings, Dartmouth Street, SW1

Architects Department
Serious researchers can make arrangements (through the Record Office) to see the noncurrent plans from 1888 onwards housed in this department.

Library (County Hall)
The library, which comprises about 90,000 books, covers all aspects of London life and history. There are also ancillary collections of prints and drawings (arranged topographically), ephemera (including some playbills, programmes, theatrical portraits) and a photograph library. All these sections of the library contain material on London music-halls but it would not necessarily be distinguished from other theatre material. The library is open to the public for reference purposes.

Record Office (County Hall)
Information on the licensing of music-halls is to be found in the records of the Middlesex Sessions (at present housed in the Middlesex section of the Greater London Record Office) and from 1889 in the minutes and presented papers of the Theatres and Music Halls Committee of the London County Council and its successors (in the London section of the Record Office at County Hall). Collections of theatre plans are held in the Architect's Department (current) and in the Greater London Record (noncurrent).

Record Office (Queen Anne's Gate)
The Search Room of the Middlesex section of the Record Office will close on 29 June 1979 and the London section Search Room at County Hall will close on 31 August 1979. It is hoped that a combined search

room will reopen at County Hall on 2 January 1980.

GUILDHALL LIBRARY
London EC2   01-606-3030

The special London Collection includes not only books on London theatres and music-halls but souvenir pamphlets, etc. as well. The Print Room contains many playbills, programmes, and scrapbooks as well as prints and photographs. Related topics should be consulted: for instance, data on the Coal Hole and Cyder Cellars will be found in the Norman Collection under Inns and Taverns.

HARRY H. BEARD COLLECTION
This collection is now in THE THEATRE MUSEUM.

JOHN JOHNSON COLLECTION
Department of Printed Books
Bodleian Library, Oxford OX1 3RG   0865-44675

This immensely varied collection of printed ephemera contains much of music-hall interest. It is not catalogued. A reader's ticket is required for personal access to the Collection; application forms from Bodleian's Librarian.

LORD CHAMBERLAIN'S OFFICE
Records relating to theatre licensing are now in the Department of Manuscripts in the British Library. All other records are in The Public Record Office, Chancery Lane.

MUSEUM OF LONDON
150 London Wall, London EC 2   01-600-3699

Music-hall material, not on display in the public galleries, may be seen by appointment.

NATIONAL MUSEUM OF MUSIC HALL
This collection was disbanded in 1978.

see

TYNE AND WEAR COUNTY MUSEUM SERVICE

PETER HONRI
32 Complins, Holybourne, Alton, Hants.   0420-83399

This is a well-documented collection on the Honri family and "Lions comiques." Contact by telephone or letter only.

PUBLIC LIBRARIES & RECORD OFFICES
Most local collections in public libraries and most record offices contain information on theatres and music-halls in their areas. Sometimes this information is indexed and catalogued, often it is not. It should be noted that many of these collections are still being sorted out, following the major reorganization of local government responsibilities in 1974; and also that this reorganization produced some less than familiar names for formerly famous areas. Details of all libraries in the U.K. may be found in the following directories: *Aslib Directory*, 2 vols. (London, Aslib—various editions); *Libraries, Museums and Art Galleries Yearbook* (Cambridge, James Clarke, 1897 onwards); and *Libraries in the United Kingdom and the Republic of Ireland* (London: The Library Association, 1960 onwards).
Details of record offices may be found in: *British Records Association: List of Members* (London: The Association, 2nd ed. 1976); *Record Repositories in Great Britain* (London: HMSO, irregularly).

PUBLIC RECORD OFFICE
Ruskin Avenue, Kew, Richmond, Surrey TW9 4DU   01-876-3444
Chancery Lane, London WC2 A ILR   01-405-0741

The new (computerized) Public Record Office at Kew contains records of present and defunct government departments, public offices, etc—as described in the *Guide to the Contents of the Public Record Office*, volumes II and III.
The Chancery Lane building contains legal records, etc., as described in the *Guide*, volume I, certain special collections, census returns for 1841, 1851, 1861, and 1871, and the records of the Lord Chamberlain's Office, excluding those relating to theatre licensing which are in the Department of Manuscripts, British Library. Public records more than thirty years old are available for consultation by holders of valid readers' tickets only

General Reference

in the building in which those records are stored.

RADIO TIMES HULTON PICTURE LIBRARY
35 Marylebone High Street, London W1 M 4AA   01–560–5577

This massive collection of photographs, prints, and drawings is available for commercial use only. As research is undertaken by the Library staff only, detailed written requests must be made in the first instance. An initial search fee is now charged.

RAYMOND MANDER & JOE MITCHENSON THEATRE COLLECTION
5 Venner Road, London SE 26   01–778–6730

In 1977 a trust was formed to administer this famous private collection, currently available for commercial purposes only. It is hoped that by 1981 it will have been transferred to a Georgian mansion in the custody of Lewisham Council—Beckenham Place, Beckenham Place Park, South End Lane, London SE 26—where the collection will be available for public inspection and use.

ROYAL INSTITUTE OF BRITISH ARCHITECTS LIBRARY
see
BRITISH ARCHITECTURAL LIBRARY

SOCIETY FOR THEATRE RESEARCH
103 Ralph Court, Queensway, London W2

The library has now been deposited in THE THEATRE MUSEUM.

THE THEATRE MUSEUM
Victoria & Albert Museum, South Kensington, London SW7
          01–589–6371
N.B. The Theatre Museum is due to be transferred to the basement of the former Flower Market in Covent Garden in the near future.

The Theatre Museum is the name now given to the area formerly known as The Enthoven Collection, for this collection has now been supplemented by the Antony D. Hippisley Coxe Circus Collection, The Harry R. Beard Collection and the Society for Theatre Research Collection to form a major repository of playbills, prints, programmes, photographs, cuttings, etc., some of which have been indexed.

TYNE & WEAR COUNTY MUSEUM SERVICE
Blandford House, West Blandford Street, Newcastle-upon-Tyne

The National Museum of Music Hall at the Empire Theatre, Sunderland, was closed in 1978. [For descriptions of its holdings, see JOE GING, "Music Hall Museum," *Theatre Notebook* XXXI, 3 (1977) 38; and "The National Museum of Music Hall," *Theatre Notebook* XXXI, 2 (1977) 36–37; MICHAEL PARKIN, "Back to the Good Old Days," *Guardian* (20 July 1974) 18; and "Music Hall Hath Charms . . ." *Guardian* (4 July 1974) 13.] Selected items of particular local interest are on permanent display at the Empire and various Tyne & Wear Museums, but the bulk of the collection is stored in the Central Archives at Newcastle where it (and the closely associated Robert Wood ephemera and the Fenwick Circus Collections) may be consulted by accredited scholars. Among the holdings are the Sunderland Empire collection of daybills from 1908 to 1931 and material on Billy Purvis.

VICTORIA AND ALBERT MUSEUM
South Kensington, London SW7   01–589–6371

The Library
All books and periodicals on the theatre arts have been retained here—except those formerly within The Enthoven Collection which are now in THE THEATRE MUSEUM.
Department of Prints & Drawings
All major theatrical paintings, prints, drawings, and objects have been retained at the V & A—except those formerly within The Enthoven Collection study room which are now in THE THEATRE MUSEUM.

WILTON'S GRAND MUSIC HALL RESEARCH CENTRE
Wellclose Square, London E1

When this restored music-hall is reopened in the near future, it will incorporate a small but comprehensive research center and lecture facilities.

United States

THE HARVARD THEATRE COLLECTION
Pusey Library, Cambridge, Massachusetts 02138   617–495–2445

Largest holdings of Victorian sheet music and covers in the U.S., catalogued by performer's name. Particularly strong on playbills and programmes, pictorial material and newspaper clippings, including the indexed Burns M. Kattenburg Collection on Contortion. Open to all accredited scholars; photocopying services available.

THE LILLY LIBRARY
Indiana University Library, Bloomington, Indiana 47401

Major holdings on nineteenth-century London; specifically, its popular entertainment and literature, contemporary histories, surveys and descriptions of the city. Particularly valuable are the Michael Sadleir collection of low-life material, which includes scandal sheets, swell's guides and sensational journalism; and the Virginia Warren collection of street cries. There is also a considerable collection of music-hall sheet music covers. Open to all accredited scholars. For a fuller description see *The Indiana University Bookman* 12 (December, 1977).

MANUSCRIPT COLLECTION. UNIVERSITY OF GEORGIA LIBRARIES
Athens, Georgia 30602

A miscellaneous collection of theatrical memorabilia, including the Harry Tate papers, photographs, playbills and contracts concerning early twentieth century music-hall, the autograph and postcard album of the doorkeeper of the Chelsea Palace Music Hall. The materials are available to qualified scholars and a limited amount of photocopying is done at the discretion of the manuscripts librarian. Sheet music is a separate collection arranged by date and title.

REFERENCE WORKS

Cross-references

See also **114, 115, 390, 392, 408, 416, 424, 425, 432, 433, 456, 1706a, 1808, 1890, 1892, 1896, 1897, 1906, 1910, 1911, 2110, 3488, 3493, 3518, 3558, 3565, 3629, 3738, 3746, 3759.**

See also Collective Biography, chapter 9, and Supplement A.

1. BAUMANN, H. *Londinismen (Slang und Cant). Wörterbuch der Londoner Volkssprache sowie der üblichsten Gauner-, Matrosen- , , Sport und Zunft-Aüsdrucke mit Einleitung und Musterstücken; eine Supplement zu allen englisch-deutschen Wörterbüchern* 2e verbesserte und stark vermehrte Auflage. Berlin: Langenscheidt, 1903
   [on pp. xciv-xcvi, quotes "Wot Cher" and "The Little Nipper" with notes as examples of coster slang.]
2. CHESHIRE, DAVID F. "A Chronology of Music Hall 1819-1923." *Theatre Quarterly* 1, no. 4 (Oct.-Dec. 1971): 41-45.
3. HOWARD, DIANA. *London Theatres and Music Halls 1850 – 1950.*
   L: Library Association, 1970.
   Rev. G. Morice, *Theatre Notebook* 25, no. 3 (spring 1971): 113-115. [The fullest documentation of builders' reports, official surveys and contemporary journalism, arranged chronologically for each hall.]
4. PHILLIPS, BRANDON. *The London Music Hall Artistes' Vade-mecum; or Constant Companion.* L: Sinclair, 1899.
5. SCHOLES, PERCY A. "Music Hall." In *Oxford Companion to Music,* pp. 672-73. 9th ed. L, N.Y.: Oxford University Press, 1955.
6. STUART, C. DOUGLAS, *et al. R. Douglas Cox's Theatrical and C. Douglas Stuart's Variety Directory.* L: Whitton & Smith (1904). (Cover title: *R. Douglas Cox, C. Douglas Stuart and William Martin's Theatrical, Variety & Fit-up Directory.)*
7. TOOLE STOTT, RAYMOND. *Circus and Allied Arts: A World*

Bibliography 1500–1957. 4 vols. Derby: Harpur & Sons, 1958–71.

8. VOYCE, ALBERT, ed. *The Official Music Hall Directory and Variety ABC containing a Three Years Diary . . . a Ready Reference for 1899 . . . No. 1 (March 1899).* L: Barrett, 1899. Rev. *Entr'acte,* 3 Feb. 1899 p. 7. No. 2 was rev. *Entr'acte,* 30 Sept. 1899, p. 11.

9. WARE, J. REDDING. *Passing English of the Victorian Era: A Dictionary of Heterodox English, Slang, and Phrase.* L: George Routledge & Sons [1909].
[A good compendium of music-hall and theatrical slang, though the derivations are occasionally fanciful.]

10. WILMETH, DON B., ed. *History of Popular Entertainment: A Guide to Information Sources.* Detroit: Gale Research Co., 1980.
[A very useful survey of all the fields of popular entertainments in the English-speaking world.]

II. PERIODICALS

Because of its commercial importance, the music-hall was widely covered by the popular press in the late nineteenth century. However, *The Era* was the first journal to develop little footnotes on saloons and concert-rooms into extended accounts of music-hall programmes, with H. Chance Newton a frequent contributor. It spoke primarily to and for the managerial interests. The performer was better represented by the *London Entr'acte,* which attained a weekly circulation of twenty thousand. It featured a sketch of an artiste, usually by Alfred Bryan, and on the facing page the programme of a given hall, so that the paper was sold in lieu of a playbill at that particular hall. Other papers so circulated in the music-halls included *The Music Hall Critic,* which published sketches of prominent professionals with accounts of their lives, and *The Prompter,* owned by Charles Douglas Stuart and profusely illustrated.

Outside of London, the most influential paper was *The Magnet,* a pioneer of the professional penny music-hall press; it included a professional directory of variety halls in the United Kingdom and the artists engaged there for the given week. Its large circulation was almost entirely confined to the provinces.

The first exclusive periodical to survive was *The Music Hall,* with the participation of H.G. Hibbert and Hugh Jay Didcott. Its features included colored plates, a sketch of a celebrity on the front page, alphabetical arrangement of card advertisements, lists of music-hall stocks and shares, monthly catalogues of new songs, and presentation of prizes in competitions. Its letterpress was chatty but accurate.

Other journals devoted space to the music-hall: *The Artiste* contained two relevant wood-block pictures each week; *The Stage* devoted a couple of columns written by Francis Raphael weekly; *The Sketch* and *St. Paul's* included weekly photographs of artistes; and a regular column appeared in *The Topical Times, The Sporting Times* and *The Licensed Victualler's Mirror.*

Of later journals, the most important are *The Encore,* modelled after *The Prompter,* which featured halftone photographs of performers, monographs on suburban stars and managers, and A.J. Park's column "Told by the Chairman" in its first year; *The Referee,* the first general paper to contain a separate article on music-halls, written at the outset by H. Chance Newton and then handed on to Bernard Marks; and *The Performer,* deceased in 1957, the organ of the Variety Artists' Benevolent Fund and Institution, and champion of the artistes' rights.

Currently, *The Call Boy* is the official journal of the British Music Hall Society; and *Music Hall Records,* besides detailed discographies, provides well-researched biographies of Victorian music-hall stars. *The Stage* is similarly useful.

For information on libraries holding files of some of the journals listed below, see Carl J. Stratman, *Britain's Theatrical Periodicals 1720–1967, a Bibliography* (N.Y.: New York Public Library, 1972).

Cross-references

See also **2263, 2521, 2858, 3851, 3863.**

11. *The Era.* L. Vols. 1–103. 30 Sept. 1838–21 Sept. 1939. Weekly. [Extensive music-hall coverage began Easter 1861; regular columns—"The London Music-halls" and "Provincial Theatricals." "Music Hall Gossip" began 23 Mar. 1889.]

12. *Illustrated Sporting News and Theatrical and Musical Review.* L. Nos. 1–186. 15 Mar. 1862–30 Sept. 1865. Weekly. Then *Illustrated Sporting News Theatrical Review.* Nos. 187–193. 7 Oct.–18 Nov. 1865. Weekly. Then *Illustrated Sporting and Theatrical News.* Vols. 4–7, Nos. 194–364. 25 Nov. 1865–20 Feb. 1869. Weekly. Suppl. 13 Oct. 1866. New series vol. 1, nos. 1–441, vol. 10 nos. 2–12, 27 Feb. 1869–19 Mar. 1870. Weekly.

13. *The Sporting Times [The Pink 'Un]. A Chronicle of Racing, Literature, Art and the Drama.* L. Nos. 1–3559. 11 Feb. 1865–5 Dec. 1931. Weekly.

14. *The Glowworm.* L. Nos. 1–1105. 5 June 1865–13 Feb. 1869. Daily. Then, *Glowworm and Evening News.* Nos. 1106–1152. 21 Dec. 1868–13 Feb. 1869. Daily. ["I think I am right in saying that the first little sheet that devoted itself (partly, at least) to music-hall matters towards the late 'six-

ties was a smart thing called the *Glowworm,"* H. Chance Newton.]

15. *The Magnet. A Journal Devoted to the Interests of the Music Hall Professions.* Leeds. No. 1–3628. Sept. 1866–26 June 1926. Weekly.

[Originally four pages, enlarged to eight pages in 1872, enlarged again in 1891. Principal feature: "Professional Directory" of variety halls in U.K. and artists engaged there for present week.]

16. *London Museum Music Hall, Bull Ring, Birmingham. Books of the Words.* Birmingham. 1867. (Vol. 3, No. 80 is only issue extant.)

17. *The Weekly Theatrical Reporter and Music Hall Review.* L. Nos. 1–14. 14 Dec. 1867–14 Mar. 1868. Weekly.

18. *The Theatrical and Musical Review. An Independent Journal of Criticism.* L. Vol. 1, Nos. 1–7. 1868. New series. Apr. 1869. Irregular.

19. *Era Almanack.* Conducted by Edward Ledger. L. Vols. 1–2. 1868–69. Then *The Era Almanack and Annual.* Vols. 3–41. 1870–1919. Annual.

[Ed. Frank Duprez, 1906–13; Alfred Barnard, 1914–18. Records of obituaries and first stage appearances.]

20. *The Music Halls' Gazette. A Journal of Intercommunication between Music Hall Managers, Their Artists at Home and Abroad, and the Public.* L. 1868–? Weekly.

[Vol. 1, Nos. 1–16, 11 Apr. 1868–12 Dec. 1868, all extant.]

21. *London Entr'acte. The Illustrated Theatrical and Musical Critic and Advertiser. A Consulting Paper for All Amusements.* L. Nos. 1–88. Jan. 1869–11 Mar. 1871. Then *London and Provincial Entr'acte.* Nos. 89–1937. 18 Mar. 1871–17 Feb. 1872. Then *Entr'acte Theatrical and Musical Critic and Advertiser.* Nos. 138–1974. 24 Feb. 1872–26 Apr. 1907. Weekly.

[Ed. Samuel Albert Barrow, 1869–May 1870. Reputed in its heyday to have a circulation of twenty thousand.]

22. *Music Hall Critic and Programme of Amusements.* L. Nos. 1–7. 20 June 1870–1 Aug 1870. Weekly.

[Printed by Ralph Augustus Harrison. Included interviews with Vance, Harry Liston, Charles Roberts and Miss Wreghitt.]

23. *The Licensed Victualler's Gazette and Trade Advertiser.* L. Nos. 1–78. 6 July 1872–27 Dec. 1873. Then *Licensed Victualler's Gazette and Hotel Courier.* Nos. 79–3594. 3 Jan. 1874–9 May 1941. Then *Licensed Victualler's Gazette.* Nos. 3595–3691. Oct. 1958–Oct. 1966. Weekly until 1958, then monthly.

[Incorporated with *The Caterer and Hotel Keeper.*]

24. *The Entr'acte Almanack and Theatrical & Music Hall Annual.* L. Vols. 1-34. 1873-1906. Annual.

25. *The Sketch. An Illustrated Miscellany of Art, Music, the Drama, Society and Belles Lettres.* L. Nos. 1-77. 25 Jan. 1879-25 Dec. 1880. Irregular.

26. *Illustrated Sporting and Dramatic News.* L. Vols. 1-80. Nos. 1-3652. 28 Feb. 1874-1945. Weekly.

27. *The Referee.* L. Nos. 1-2662. 19 Aug. 1877-9 Sept. 1928. Then *Sunday Referee.* Nos. 2663- . 16 Sept. 1928-4 June 1939. Weekly.
    [Incorporated with *Sunday Chronicle.*]

28. *The Dramatic and Musical Circular. An Epitome of Dramatic, Operatic and Music Hall Requirements.* L. Nos. 1-29. 27 Mar.-11 Oct. 1879. Then *The London Mirror, in which is incorporated The Dramatic and Musical Mirror.* Nos. 30-31. 18 Oct.-25 Oct. 1879. Weekly.

29. *The Stage Directory.* L. Nos. 1-14. 1 Feb. 1880-1 Mar. 1881. Monthly. Then *The Stage.* L. Nos. 1-in progress. 25 Mar. 1881-. Weekly.
    [Regular music-hall column.]

30. *The Liverpool Entr'acte. A Weekly Journal for Theatre Goers, containing a Complete Programme of the Entertainments at the Principal Places of Amusement in Liverpool.* Liverpool. Dec. 1881-[Mar. ?] 1882. Weekly.

31. *Hague's Minstrel and Dramatic Journal.* Ed. Henry A. Duffy. Liverpool. No. 1. Sept. 1882. Weekly.

32. *Interlude. "The Organ of the Variety Profession."* L. Nos. 1-25. 14 Nov. 1885-8 May 1886. Weekly.

33. *M.H.A.A. Gazette [Music Hall Artistes' Association Gazette].* L. Nos. 1-42. 30 Aug. 1886-15 June 1887. Weekly.

34. *C.H. Ross's Variety Paper. Fact, Fiction & Fancy.* L. Nos. 1-17. 1887.
    [Ills. W.C. Baxter and Archibald Chasemore. Not primarily a show business journal, it does run an illustrated fictional account of early music-hall.]

35. *The Artiste. Music Hall Gossip, Theatrical and General News.* L. Nos. 1-18. 1 Jan. 1887-2 May 1887. Weekly.
    [Published for James Deacon of Deacon's Music Hall, Clerkenwell.]

36. *Licensed Victualler's Mirror. A Trade Sporting and Theatrical Newspaper.* L. Nos. 1-880. 3 Feb. 1888-9 Dec. 1904. Weekly.

37. *The Licensed Victualler's Mirror.* [Published by Speaight & Cox.] L. Nos. 1–222. 6 Feb. 1888–26 Apr. 1892. Weekly. [Became *Sporting and Dramatic Mirror.*]

38. *The Licensed Victualler's Sportsman. A Turf, Athletic, Cycling and Theatrical Journal.* L. Nos. 1–5. 2 Dec. 1888–5 Jan. 1889. Weekly.

39. *The Music Hall.* L. Nos. 1–30. 16 Feb. 1889–7 Sept. 1889. Then *The Music Hall and Theatre.* Nos. 32–42. 27 Sept. 1889–30 Nov. 1889. Then *The Music Hall and Theatre Review.* Nos. 43–1229. 6 Dec. 1889–5 Sept. 1912. Weekly.
[Ed. W. McWilliam, a cycling journalist, with the assistance of Charles Coborn, Sam Torr and Tom Merry. From 1891 ed. Frank Allport and J. Barnes. "Among its particular features at the present time [1898] are the alphabetical arrangement of the card advertisements, its list of music-hall stocks and shares, its monthly catalogue of new songs, and its presentation of prizes in competitions," Stuart & Park. Colored plates.]

40. *The Prompter and the Footlights. A Music Hall and Theatrical Review.* L. Vol. 1, Nos. 1–9. 1 Mar. 1889–28 Apr. 1889. Weekly. [Ed. Charles Douglas Stuart. Profusely illustrated.]

41. *Liverpool Athletic and Dramatic News.* Liverpool. Vols. 1–4, Nos. 1–139. 15 Dec. 1890–26 Jan. 1892. Then *Athletic and Dramatic News.* 2 Feb. 1892–8 Aug. 1893. Weekly.

42. *The Joker.* L. 18 July 1891–29 Oct. 1897. [Column, "Racy Music-hall Gossip."]

43. *The Sporting and Dramatic Mirror.* L. No. 1, new series. 2 May 1892. Then *The Sporting Mirror and Dramatic and Music Hall Record.* New series. Nos. 2–441. 9 May 1892–8 Oct. 1900. Weekly.
[Incorporates *The Licensed Victualler's Mirror.*]

44. *The Encore. A Music Hall and Theatrical Review.* L. Vols. 1–38, Nos. 1–1972. 11 Nov. 1892–9 Oct. 1930. Weekly.
[Ed. Charles Douglas Stuart and Edward Lawrance to Dec. 1893, then Stuart and Fred Lacey to Nov. 1894, then Stuart and T. Murray Ford till 1895, then Ford alone.]

45. *The Encore Annual.* L. Vols. 1–? 1895–? Annual.

46. *The Variety Stage.* L. Nos. 1–2. Nov.–Dec. 1895. Monthly. New series. Vols. 1–3. Nos. 1–54. Jan. 1896–16 Jan. 1897. Weekly.

47. *The Playgoer's Magazine. A Journal for Theatre-goers, Habitués of Music Halls, and Amateur Actors.* L. Vol. 1. Nos. 1–2. 1898.

48. *Variety and "Variety Critic."* L. Vol. 1, Nos. 1–13. 12 Feb. 1898–7 May 1898. Weekly.
   [Ed. Bernard Hounsell.]

49. *Theatrical and Music Hall Life.* L. No. 1. 21 May 1898. [Only issue.]

50. *The Programme and Playbill, illustrated, of all the London Theatres, Music Halls and Entertainments.* L. Vol. 1. Nos. 1–197. 13 Oct. 1898–7 July 1899. Daily.

51. *Showman. An Illustrated Journal for Showmen and All Entertainers.* L. Nos. 1–68. Sept. 1900–21 Mar. 1902. Weekly.
   [Incorporated in *The Music Hall.*]

52. *The Hippodrome. An Illustrated Vaudeville Magazine.* L. 1901–?

53. *The International Entertainer. The Variety Artistes' Illustrated Magazine.* L. Vol. 1, Nos. 1–2. Apr.–May 1902. Monthly.
   [Ed. A. C. Lyster.]

54. *The Stage Souvenir. An Illustrated Monthly Journal, with a Real Photograph as a Supplement.* L. Nos. 1–4. 1903. Monthly.
   [Ed. F. Dangerfield.]

55. *The Theatrical Employees Journal.* L. Oct. 1904–Sept. 1905. Monthly.

56. *The Music Hall Pictorial and Variety Stage.* L. Nos. 1–3. Dec. 1904–Feb. 1905. Monthly.

57. *Variety Stage Illustrated.* L. Nos. 1–3. 16–30 Jan. 1905. Weekly.

58. *Variety Stage and Music Hall Pictorial.* L. No. 1. Feb. 1905.

59. *The Variety Theatre.* L. Vols. 1–3, Nos. 1–33. 12 May 1905–5 Jan. 1906. Weekly.

60. *The Variety Theatre Annual.* L. Vol. 1. 1906–7. Annual.

61. *Variety Time Table and Programme.* L. Nos. 1–44. 26 Feb.–31. Dec. 1906. Weekly.

62. *The Performer. The Official Organ of the Newly Founded Variety Artistes' Federation.* L. Vols. 1–105, Nos. 1–2679. 29 Mar. 1906–26 Sept. 1957. Weekly.

63. *Performer Annual.* L. 1907–32. Annual.

64. *The Stage Year Book.* L. 1908–19, 1921–22, 1926–28, 1949–69. Annual.
   ["The Variety Year," illustrations, obituaries.]

65. *The International Entertainer. The Variety Artistes Illustrated Magazine.* L. Vol. 1, No. 1. Apr. 1910.

66. *The Entertainer. Scotland's Amusements, Weekly, Theatrical, Vaudeville* [etc.]. Glasgow. Vols. 1–7, Nos. 1–285. 4 Oct. 1913–15 Mar. 1919. Weekly.

67. *The Theatre, Music-Hall and Cinema Blue Book. A List of Public Amusement Companies with Full Particulars of Interest to*

Investors. L. Nos. 1–11. 1917–30. Annual.

68. *The Performer Handbook.* L. 1921. Annual.

69. *Variety, Music, Stage and Film News.* L. Vols. 1–5, Nos. 1–106. 2 Sept. 1931–6 Sept. 1933. Then *Variety, Cabaret, Film News.* Vols. 6–8, Nos. 107–251. 13 Sept. 1933–18 Jan. 1936. Weekly.

70. *Amusement World. A Weekly Journal for Amusement Centres, Seaside and Pleasure Proprietors.* L. Vol.1, No. 1. 22 Jan. 1932. Then *Amusement World. Professional Amusement Caterers, Showmen and Public Entertainers.* Vol. 1, Nos. 2–7. 29 Jan.–4 Mar. 1932. Weekly.

71. *Garroway's Directory of Concert and Variety Artistes.* L. 1934. Annual.

72. *Variety Fare.* L. Vol. 1, No. 1–Vol. 3, No. 2. May 1946–Aug. 1947. Then *Night-life.* Vol. 3, No. 3–Vol. 4, No. 2. Sept. 1947–Apr. 1948. Irregular.

73. *Stage and Variety Artistes Guide and Handbook.* L. Vol. 1, 1950. Annual.

74. *Opera, Ballet and Music-hall in the World.* L. No. 1, Oct. 1952. Quarterly.

75. *The Call Boy. Journal of the British Music Hall Society.* L. Vol. 1, No. 1–in progress. Dec. 1963–continuing. Quarterly. [Ed. J. O. Blake.]

76. *Music Hall Organ Record Club. Members' News Bulletin.* Rickmansworth. 1965–?

77. *Music Hall Records.* London. No. 1–8. June 1978–Aug. 1979. Bimonthly. Then *Music Hall.* Continuing. [ed. Tony Barker.]

III. GENERAL STUDIES

"The art of the stage seems to me to be above all the art of France. The music-hall is a more genuinely English institution."

Havelock Ellis, *My Life* (Boston: Houghton Mifflin, 1939), 220.

The interest evoked by the music-hall in its own time was almost matched by the flood of nostalgic reminiscence that accompanied its decadence and obsolescence. But the quality of writing and knowledge diminished as the halls declined. Their earliest chroniclers, Charles Douglas Stuart, H. G. Hibbert and A. J. Park, were reporters and music-hall agents, who knew the field thoroughly and were well aware that the institution was as much a matter of managers and agents, architects and advertisement, as of performers and songs. Their journalistic colleagues, H. Chance Newton, J. B. Booth and Archibald Haddon, were equally familiar with the world of the music-hall, but wrote about it in a style redolent of boozy recollection. A later generation cannibalized these sources indiscriminately and ruthlessly, even to direct quotation without acknowledgment. If one reads the standard works on the subject in chronological order, it soon becomes clear that the same anecdotes, descriptions, value judgements, quotations are constantly recycled, with only the occasional alloy of personal reminiscence. There are exceptions to this practice: Harold Scott's *The Early Doors* relies both on his predecessors and on original research. But only within the last two decades have serious writers returned to original sources (newspapers, builder's plans, committee reports) to amplify and vivify the music-hall's history—although this has not stopped the flow of supererogatory "popularizations" which continue to disseminate misinformation and long-exploded myths.

It has proven difficult to make a more than arbitrary classification among the general works listed below. Roughly, "Historical" refers to works which treat the music-hall as a phenomenon of the past, near or distant as the case may be. "Critical" either concerns evaluation of performances and style contemporary with the writer, or an analysis of music-hall as a genre of performance; this category includes the notices of dramatic critics like Agate, Shaw, and Beerbohm. "Picture Books" is self-explanatory and includes works which, however useful their letterpress, are primarily composed of illustrations. "Reminiscence" alludes to the memoirs and recollections of those who were primarily spectators in the halls; because this commentary is scattered but often highly valuable, we consider this a particularly handy subsection. Our classification is arguable, and one or another book might as readily be transferred to another section, such as "London." For this reason, the cross-references and the index should enable the reader to find what he is looking for with a minimum of frustration.

HISTORICAL

Cross-references

See also **5, 228, 617, 2886, 2887, 3489, 3490, 3491.**

   78. "The Age before Music-Hall." *All the Year Round* 31 (1873): 175.
   79. ALLAN, ANGUS. *The World of People in Shows.* Ills. Gary

Long. L: Young World productions, 1972.
[Pp. 12–15: "Music Hall." A children's book.]

80. ARMSTRONG, ARTHUR COLES. "The Variety Year." *Stage Yearbook* (1916) 23–28; (1917) 23–28; (1919) 316.

81. BAILEY, PETER. *Leisure and Class in Victorian England. Rational Recreation and the Contest for Control.* L: Routledge & Kegan Paul, [Chapter 7, "Rational Recreation and the Entertainment Industry: The Case of the Victorian Music Halls," pp. 147–68. Thorough and well-documented; with very few changes identical to 83. Rev. U. Schneider, *Englisch Amerikanische Studien* (Koln, forthcoming).]

82. ——. *Profit and Morality in a Nineteenth-century Entertainment Industry: The Case of the Music Halls.* The History Workshop Series; ed. R. Samuel. L: Routledge & Kegan Paul [forthcoming].

83. ——. "Rational Recreation and the Entertainment Industry: the Case of the Victorian Music Hall." Abstracted in *The Bulletin of the Society for the Study of Labour History* 32 (spring 1976): 5–18.

84. BEAR GARDENS MUSEUM (London). *An Exhibition: Music Hall: the Early Days.* February 7–March 23, 1975. Arranged by Colin Mabberley for the World Centre for Shakespearean Studies. Bankside, Southwark [L]: Bear Gardens Museum [1975]. [Brief general remarks on S. London halls.]

85. BEAVER, PATRICK. *The Spice of Life: Pleasures of the Victorian Age.* L: Elm Tree Books, 1979. [Chapter 5, "Laughter from the Gods—The Victorian Music Hall."]

86. BELCHAM, HENRY. "The Year in Variety." *Era Annual* (1917) 35–38.

87. BEVAN, IAN. *Royal Performance, the Story of Royal Theatregoing.* L: Hutchinson [1954].

88. BOOTH, JOHN BENNION *The Days We Knew.* With a foreword by Charles B. Cochran. L: Werner Laurie, 1943.
[Chapter 3, "The Old Music Hall," pp. 27–49; Chapter 4, "Dan Leno and Marie Lloyd," pp. 50–64.] [J. B. Booth was a staff member of *The Sporting Times* ("The Pink 'Un," so-called from the color of its pages) under the name "Costs." His many volumes of recollections are anecdotal and repetitious, but reasonably reliable.]

89. ——. "Fifty Years: the Old Music Hall." *Times,* 18 March 1932. Repr. in *Fifty Years. Memories and Contrasts: A Composite Picture of the Period 1882–1932 by Twenty-seven Con-*

tributors to The Times, pp. 77–86. With a foreword by George Macaulay Trevelyan. L: Thornton Butterworth, 1932.

90. ———. *Life, Laughter and Brass Hats.* L: T. Werner Laurie, 1939.
[Chapter 2, "Crises and Choruses," pp. 31–37.]

91. ———. *London Town.* L: T. Werner Laurie, 1929.
[Chapters 6–10.]

92. ———. *"Master" and Men: Pink 'Un Yesterdays.* L: T. Werner Laurie, 1926.
[Chapters 5 and 6.]

93. ———. *Old Pink 'Un Days.* L: Grant Richards, 1924; N.Y.: Dodd, Mead, 1925.
[Chapters 17–19.]

94. ———. *Palmy Days.* L: Grant Richards, 1951.

95. ———. *Pink Parade.* With a foreword by Charles B. Cochran. L: Thornton Butterworth; N.Y.: E. P. Dutton, 1933.
[Chapters 7–9.]

96. ———. *A "Pink 'Un" Remembers.* With a foreword by C. B. Cochran. L: Werner Laurie, 1937.
[Chapter 5, "The Passing of the Halls," pp. 94–117; chapter 6, "The Music-halls at War," pp. 118–33.]

97. BRIDGES-ADAMS, WILLIAM. *British Theatre.* L: N.Y. and Toronto: Longmans, 1944. (British Life and Thought.)

98. BRITANNICA EXTENSION SERVICE. *Music Halls.* Lake Placid [Wis.]: Encyclopaedia Britannica, 1966.
[Contains some errors]

99. "British Royalty at a Music-hall." *Literary Digest* (N.Y.), 25 May 1912, p. 1102.
[Quotes extensively from *The Westminster Gazette* on the first command performance of music-hall.]

99a. BRITTON, A. [pseud.]. "The Old Time Music Hall." N. Y. *Dramatic Mirror,* 29 Dec. 1906, p. 17.

100. BROWN, IVOR. "Music-hall Milestones." *New Statesman* 9 (15 Apr. 1922): 41–42.

101. BROWNE, C. ELLIOTT. "The Origin of Music-hall Entertainment." *Notes & Queries,* 4th ser. 12 (13 Sept. 1873): 205.
[Quotes G. A. Stevens's *Adventures of a Speculatist,* c. 1761.]

102. BURKE, THOMAS. *English Night-life from Norman Curfew to Present Blackout.* L: Batsford, 1941.
["We Won't Go Home Until Morning," pp. 71–132.]

103. CHAPLIN, SID. "The Good Old Days." *Sunday Times,* 4 Apr. 1971, p. 32.

104. CHESHIRE, DAVID F. *Music Hall in Britain*. Newton Abbot: David & Charles, 1974; Cranbury (N.J.): Associate University Presses, 1974. Rev. C. Fox, *New Statesman*, (12 Apr. 1974); L. Senelick, *Nineteenth Century Theatre Research*, 3, no. 2 (autumn 1975): 129–31; M. Vicinus, *Victorian Studies* 18, no. 4 (June 1975) 473.
[A panoramic study using quotations from primary sources.]

105. CLEMART, W. H. "The Variety Stage."*Stage Year Book* (1909) 71–73; (1911) 19–22; (1912) 37–41.

106. COTES, PETER. "The Changing Scene; Music Hall—Yesterday and Today." *What's On in London*, 29 July 1977, pp. 42–44.

107. CROXTON, ARTHUR. *Crowded Nights—and Days: An Unconventional Pageant*. L: Sampson Low, Marston [1934].
[Chapter 2, "The Teens," pp. 9–21 (Dan Leno); chapter 11, "The Variety Theatre," pp. 152–74; chapter 22, "The Great Grock Mystery," pp. 308–11.]

108. DENT, ALAN. "At the Music Hall: The Good Old Days of the Famous Halls." *Strand* 117, no. 705 (Sept. 1949): 56–65.

109. ———. "Those Dear Old Timers." *Illustrated London News*, 26 Feb. 1966, p. 38.

110. DESMOND, SHAW. *The Edwardian Story*. L: Rockcliff, 1950.
[Pp. 313–24.]

111. [DIDCOTT, HUGH J.] "Music Hall History." *Era*, 23 July 1892, p. 14.
[Important testimony to early facts.]

112. DISHER, MAURICE WILLSON. *Clowns & Pantomimes*. L: Constable, 1925. Repr. N.Y.: Benjamin Blom, Arno, 1968.
[Chapter 10, "The Music-hall Comedian," pp.165–84. Willson Disher, a leading authority on popular entertainment, was not averse to embroidering the facts and never footnotes his allegations. His books are highly readable, but must be treated with caution as testimony.]

113. ———. *Fairs, Circuses and Music-halls*. L: Collins, 1942.
[Contains almost nothing on halls.]

114. ———. "Music Hall and Variety." In *Encyclopedia Britannica*, 15:1090–91. Chicago: 1967.

115. ——— and W. MACQUEEN-POPE. "Music-hall." In *Oxford Companion to the Theatre*, ed. Phyllis Hartnoll, pp. 665–67. 3rd ed. Oxford: Oxford University Press, 1967.

115a.———. "The Music-hall." *Quarterly Review* 252 (Apr. 1929): 259–71.

116. ———. *Winkles and Champagne: Comedies and Tragedies of the*

Music Hall. With ills. from photographs, programmes, prints, song covers, song books, bills, and posters, mainly from the author's collection. L: B. T. Batsford, 1938. Repr. Bath: Cedric Chivers, 1974. Pub. in U.S. as: *Music Hall Parade.* N.Y.: Scribner, 1938.

[An entertaining history of performance, enlivened by the author's own memories.]

117. DIXON, STEPHEN. "Music Hall Vets Keep on Truckin'." *Rolling Stone* (N.Y.), 9 Nov. 1972, p. 21.

118. "The Evolution of the Music-hall." *Saturday Review* 77, (27 Jan. 1894): 91–92.

119. FARSON, DANIEL. "The Secret Face of Music Hall." *Men Only*, Apr. 1976, pp. 10–14, 55.

120. FINDLATER, RICHARD. "Posers for the People: Decline and Fall in the Music Halls." *20th Century* 161 (June 1957): 570–76.
[What has passed from the halls.]

121. HADDON, ARCHIBALD. *The Story of the Music Hall from Cave of Harmony to Cabaret.* L: Fleetway Press, 1935.
[Scrappy but informative account by a radio journalist.]

122. HASTINGS, MACDONALD. *The Other Mr Churchill.* L: Harrap, 1963. Paperback ed. L: New English Library, 1966.

123. HIBBERT, HENRY GEORGE. *Fifty Years of a Londoner's Life.* L: Grant Richards, 1916.
[Chapter 5, "Story of the Music Hall," pp. 32–39; chapter 6, "The London Pavilion," pp. 40–45; chapter 7, "The Old Mogul," pp. 46–50; chapter 8, "The Vital Spark," pp. 51–55; chapter 9, "Music Hall Society," pp. 56–62; chapter 12, "Round Leicester Square," pp. 83–90; chapter 13, "Singers Who Are Silent," pp. 91–96; chapter 14, "Half-a-Century of Song," pp. 97–103; chapter 19, "Princes and Palaces," pp. 135–41; chapter 20, "Music Hall Agency," pp. 142–46; chapter 23, "Empire-building," pp. 158–61; chapter 30, "Salaries of Celebrities," pp. 207–14; chapter 32, "A Study in Stoll," pp. 229–32. Hibbert, a music-hall reporter and editor, prided himself on his accuracy and on verifying the facts of the music-hall's youth; consequently, his writings are extremely valuable records. This book has been shamelessly plundered without acknowledgement by most later historians and popularizers.]

123a. ———. "The Story of an English Music-Hall." N. Y. *Dramatic Mirror*, Christmas 1903, pp. xlvii–xlviii.

123b. ———. "The Tea Gardens of Old London." N.Y. *Dramatic Mirror*, Christmas 1907, pp. vii–viii.

124. "History of the Music Hall." *Saturday Review* 72 (1894) 91.

125. HOLLINGSHEAD, JOHN. "Music-hall History." *Entr'acte Annual* (1886): 5–8.

126. ———. "Music Halls." In *Encyclopaedia Britannica*, 19:87–90. N.Y.: Encyclopaedia Britannica Co., 1911.
[According to Hibbert, this was written in Paris from hasty notes sent to Hollingshead by the former.]

127. HUSK, W. H. "The Origin of Music Hall Entertainments." *Notes & Queries*. 4th ser. 12 (18 Oct. 1873).
[The Comus Courts of the eighteenth century.]

128. IRVING, GORDON. *The Good Auld Days: the Story of Scotland's Entertainment from Music Hall to Television.* L: Jupiter Books, 1977.

129. KEATING, PETER. "Gaslight and Greasepaint." *Times Literary Supplement*, 26 Dec. 1975, p. 1534.
[Review of recent books on music-hall by G. Speaight, J. S. Bratton, P. Gammond, M. R. Turner, and H. Stanley.]

130. LAWRENCE, W. J. "Twice-nightly: Early Experiments in London: six till midnight." *Daily Telegraph*, 14 Mar. 1929.

131. LEACH, ROBERT. *The Music Hall.* Brighton: Robert Tyndall, 1974.
[A "ghost" book, announced and given an ISBN, but unpublished.]

132. McKECHNIE, SAMUEL. *Popular Entertainments through the Ages.* L: Sampson, Low, Marston [1931]. Repr. N.Y.: B. Blom, 1973. Rev. Gordon Craig, *News Chronicle*, 11 Nov. 1931.
[One of the best short accounts there is.]

133. MACQUEEN-POPE, WALTER JAMES. *Back Numbers.* L: Hutchinson, 1954.
[A prolific journalist, Macqueen-Pope turned out volumes of writing on the theatre, ranging from encyclopedia articles to romanticized nostalgia and drawing heavily on his precursors.]

134. ———. *Carriages at Eleven: The Story of the Edwardian Theatre.* L: Hutchinson, 1947. [Chapter 13, "From the Palace to the 'Pav,'" pp. 176–93.]

135. ———. *Ghosts and Grease Paint: An Evocation of Yesterday and the Day Before.* L: R. Hale, 1951. [Many references to London halls, managers and artists.]

136. ———. *The Melodies Linger On. The Story of Music Hall.* L: W. H. Allen [1950].
[Chatty, but informative; to be consulted with caution. Whole pages stolen from Stuart and Park's *The Variety Stage*.]

137. MANDLE, W. F. "Music Hall and the Late Victorians." *Teaching History* 7, no. 1 (Mar. 1973) 29–34.

138. MARGETSON, STELLA. "The Age of the Music Hall." *Country Life*, 3 Dec. 1964, pp. 1563–66.

139. ———. *Leisure and Pleasure in the Nineteenth Century*. L: Cassell, 1969.
[Chapter 12, "Fun & Frolic," pp. 173–87.]

140. MILTON, DICK. "The Evolution of the Music-hall: From the 'Sixties to the 'Nineties." *Chambers Journal*, Dec. 1942, 682–85.

141. "The Modern Music-hall, a Review of To-day." *Entr'acte Annual* (1905): 21.

142. "Music-hall Award 1913." *Stage Year Book* (1914) 53–56.

143. "Music-halls Award 1913." *Era Annual* (1914): 68–71.

144. NEWTON, H. CHANCE. *Idols of the 'Halls' being My Music Hall Memories*. With a foreword by Sir Oswald Stoll. L: Heath Cranton, 1928. Repr. East Ardesley: EP Publishing, and N.Y.: British Book Centre, 1975.
[As "Carados" of *The Referee*, Newton was an habitue of greenrooms and stalls' bars; his works are highly informed but maddeningly devoid of dates and supportive material.]

145. ———. "Music Hall Memories." *Performer* Christmas 1923, pp. 71–74; 27 Dec. 1923, p. 9; 2 Jan. 1924, p. 9; 9 Jan. 1924, p. 11; 16 Jan. 1924, p. 9; 23 Jan. 1924, p. 9; 30 Jan. 1924, p. 11; 6 Feb. 1924, p. 9; 13 Feb. 1924, p. 9; 20 Feb. 1924, p. 12; 27 Feb. 1924, p. 10; 5 Mar. 1924, pp. 12–13; 12 Mar. 1924, pp. 10–11; 19 Mar. 1924, pp. 12–13; 26 Mar. 1924, pp. 10–11; 2 Apr. 1924, pp. 10–11; 9 Apr. 1924, p. 11; 16 Apr. 1924, p. 13; 24 Apr. 1924, p. 12; 30 Apr. 1924, p. 11; 7 May 1924, p. 11.

146. NICOLL, ALLARDYCE. *English Drama 1900–1930: The Beginnings of the Modern Period*. Cambridge: Cambridge University Press, 1973.
[Chapter 2.2, "Commercialism, The Music-hall Empire and Trade Unionism," pp. 30–40.]

147. ———. *A History of English Drama 1600–1900*. Late Nineteenth Century Drama 1850–1900, vol. 5. Cambridge: Cambridge University Press, 1959.
["Music Halls," p. 222.]

148. PARKS, JOHN GOWER. "Music-hall." In *Enciclopedia dello Spettacolo*, fondata da Silvio d'Amico, 7:970. Roma: Le Maschere, 1962.

149. PELLING, HENRY MATHISON. *Popular Politics and Society in Late Victorian England, Essays*. L: Macmillan, 1958; N.Y.: St. Martin's Press, 1968.
[On jingoism in music-halls, pp. 87–90.]

150. PENNELL, ELIZABETH ROBINS. "The Pedigree of the Music

Hall.'' *Contemporary Review* 63 (1893): 575–83. Repr. in *Eclectic Magazine* (N.Y.) 120 (June 1893): 792.
[Excellent survey of popular entertainment antecedents.]

151. PRIESTLEY, J. B. *The Edwardians.* L: Heinemann, 1970.
[Part two, 1906–10, chapter 8, ''Music Hall and Vaudeville,'' pp. 172–76.]

152. PURSER, ANN. *Looking Back at Popular Entertainment 1901 – 1939.* East Ardsley, Wakefield: EP Publishing, 1978.

153. REYNOLDS, HARRY. *Minstrel Memories: The Story of Burnt Cork Minstrelsy in Great Britain from 1836 to 1927.* L: Alston Rivers, 1928.
[Firsthand knowledge by a minstrel.]

154. SANSOM, E. M. ''The Variety Year.'' *Stage Year Book* (1913): 27–31; (1914): 48–52; (1915): 21–25; (1917): 25–29; (1921–25) 11–15.

155. SCOTT, HAROLD. *The Early Doors: Origins of the Music Hall.* L: Nicholson & Watson, 1946. Repr. East Ardsley, Wakefield: EP Publishing, 1977.
[Well-researched, authoritative history; indispensable. But in the first edition the index is consistently one page out of step with the text (e.g. page 60 = page 59) and the bibliography contains many mistranscriptions of titles.]

156. SCOTT, W. S. *Bygone Pleasures of London.* L: Marsland Publications, 1948.

157. ———. *Green Retreats: The Story of Vauxhall Gardens 1661 – 1859.* L: Odhams, 1955.

158. SEAMAN, L. C. B. *Life in Victorian London..* L: Batsford, 1973.
[''Theatre and Music Hall,'' p. 170.]

159. ———. *Victorian England: Aspects of English and Imperial History 1837 – 1901.* L: Methuen, 1973. [Music hall, pp. 213, 380, 417, 427, 432–34.]

160. SENELICK, LAURENCE. ''A Brief Life and Times of the Victorian Music-hall.'' *Harvard Library Bulletin* (Cambridge, Mass.) 19, no. 4 (Oct. 1971): 375–98.

161. SHORT, ERNEST. *Fifty Years of Vaudeville.* L: Eyre & Spottiswoode, 1946.
[Chapter 10, ''Palaces of Variety 1910 to 1925''; chapter 11, ''Intimate Revue 1914–1944''; chapter 15, ''The Ladies of Variety.'']

162. ——— and ARTHUR COMPTON-RICKETT. *Ring Up the Curtain: Being a Pageant of English Entertainment Covering Half-a-Century.* L: Jenkins, 1938.

163. ———. *Sixty Years of Theatre.* L: Eyre & Spottiswoode, 1951.

[Chapter 16, "The Palaces of Variety: 1890–1925," pp. 208–34, repr. from *Fifty Years of Vaudeville.*]

164. SOUTHWORTH, J. G. *Vauxhall Gardens: A Chapter in the Social History of England.* N.Y.: Columbia University Press, 1941.

165. STEDMAN-JONES, GARETH. "Working Class Culture and Working Class Politics in London 1870–1900: Notes on the Remaking of a Working Class." *Journal of Social History* 7 (Summer 1974): 460–508.

166. STEVENS, GEORGE ALEXANDER. *The Adventures of a Speculist; or, A Journey through London. . . .* 2 vols. L: printed for the editor, 1788. [Vol. 2, pp. 16–51, "Visit to Comus' Court, with the History of its Stars."]

167. STUART, CHARLES DOUGLAS and A. J. PARK. *The Variety Stage: A History of the Music Halls from the Earliest Period to the Present Time.* L: T. Fisher Unwin [1895]. rev. *Era*, 20 July 1895, p. 14 [with corrigenda]; "Spectator," *Star*, 20 July 1895, p. 1.
[The first, and in many ways the best-informed, history, written by two music-hall editor agents.]

168. TERRY, Sir RICHARD. "Old Music Halls: Their Songs, Singers and Sentiments." Special supplement to *John o' London's Weekly*, 6 Dec. 1924, pp. i–viii.

169. TERRY, WALTER. "The Year in Variety." *Era Annual* (1918): 44–49.

170. "The Variety Year." *Stage Year Book* (1910): 33–36.

171. VICINUS, MARTHA. *The Industrial Muse: a Century of British Working-Class Literature.* L: Croom Helm, 1974.
[Chapter 6, "The Music Hall from a Class to a Mass Entertainment," pp. 238–85; Appendix, pp. 314–20. Rev. G. Stedman-Jones, *Victorian Studies* 20 (1977): 193–95.]

CRITICAL

Cross-references

See also **355, 2850.**

172. "Act Drop Situations; Manners in the Front." *Era,* 9 Feb. 1884, p. 15.
173. AGATE, JAMES. *Alarums and Excursions.* L: Richards, 1922. ["An Evening at Collins,'" "Vesta Ave atque vale."]
174. ———. *Immoment Toys. A Survey of Light Entertainment on the London Stage 1920 – 1943.* L: Cape, 1945. Repr. N.Y.: Benjamin Blom, 1969.
["Fred Emney," pp. 194-98; "The Brothers Griffith and Sir Harry Lauder," pp. 198-202; "George Carney," pp. 202-07; "Vesta Tilley," pp. 207-10; "Marie [Lloyd]," pp. 210-13; "Kate Carney," pp. 216-18; "Nervo and Knox," pp. 218-20; "Toto," pp. 220-22; "Will Fyffe," pp. 224; "Billy Bennett," pp. 225-26; "Gracie Fields," pp. 226-28; "George Robey," pp. 228-30.]
175. ARCHER, WILLIAM. *About the Theatre. Essays and Studies.* L: T. Fisher Unwin, 1886.
[Brief remarks on music-hall.]
176. ———. "The Drama: At a Music-hall." *Nation,* 25 Dec. 1909, pp. 530-31.
177. ———. "The Music-hall, Past and Future." *Fortnightly Review,* n.s., Aug. 1916, pp. 253-62. Repr. *Living Age* (N.Y.), 14 Oct. 1916, pp. 98-105.
178. ———. "Theatre and Music-hall." *Pall Mall Budget,* 28 Mar. 1895. Repr. in *The Theatrical "World" of 1895,* L: Walter Scott, 1896.
[Chapter 15, pp. 96-103. Questions the current fad for praising music-hall over legitimate theatre; prefers acrobats and animal acts to singers.]
178a. "'Arry on 'igh Life." *Punch,* 20 July 1878, p. 24.
["Music-hall fever."]
178b. "'Arry to the Front!" *Punch,* 9 Mar. 1878, p. 100.
[Patriotism in the halls.]
179. BALLANTYNE, EVELYN. "Continental Music Halls." *Theatre,* n.s. 17 (Mar. 1891): 121-25.
[Comments on English music-halls in contrast.]
179a. BARKER, KATHLEEN. "A Middle-class Dissenter's View of Mid-Victorian Music Halls." *Call Boy* 16, no. 4 (winter 1979): 9.
[Samuel Collinson, 1812-95, attending London and Nottingham halls in the 1860s.]
180. BEERBOHM, Sir MAX. *Around Theatres.* 2 vols. Repr. L: Rupert Hart-Davis, 1953.
[Articles from *Saturday Review,* 1898-1910: "Latin and Anglo-Saxon Mimes"; "Dan Leno," pp. 349-52; "Yvette Guilbert and

Albert Chevalier," pp. 436–39; "At the Tivoli," pp. 11–14; "An Object Lesson," pp. 30–4 (on the Empire); "The Older and Better Music-hall," pp. 298–301; "In an Italian Music-hall," pp. 488–91; "Idolum aularum," pp. 414–18.]

181. ———. "The Blight on the Music-Halls." In *More*. L: N.Y.: John Lane, 1899.

182. ———. "Demos' Mirror." *Saturday Review* 90 (1900): 80–81.

183. ———. "The Humour of the Public." In *Yet Again*. L: Chapman & Hall, 1909. [Pp. 247–64.]

184. ———. "In a Music Hall." *Saturday Review* 92 (20 July 1901): 76. [The Oxford.] Repr. in *More Theatres*.

185. ———. *Last Theatres 1904–1910*. With an introduction by Rupert Hart-Davis. L: Rupert Hart-Davis; N.Y.: Taplinger, 1970.
["At the Empire" (31 Oct. 1908), pp. 396–99; "At the Palace Theatre (Maud Allan)," pp. 380–83.]

185a. ———. "The Laughter of the Public." *Living Age* (N.Y.) 233 (5 Apr. 1902): 52–57.

186. ———. *Letters to Reggie Turner*. Ed. Rupert Hart-Davis. L: Rupert Hart-Davis; Philadelphia: J. B. Lippincott, 1965.
[References to Marie Lloyd, Herbert Campbell, Gus Elen, Gracie Fields, R. G. Knowles, George Robey, Zaeo, *et al.*, especially Cissie Loftus (Aug. 1893).]

187. ——— and WILL ROTHENSTEIN. *Max and Will: Max Beerbohm and William Rothenstein, Their Friendship and Letters 1893–1945*. Ed., with an introduction and notes by Mary M. Lago and Karl Beckson. Cambridge, Mass.: Harvard University Press, 1975.
[References to Albert Chevalier, Cissie Loftus, Marie Lloyd, R. G. Knowles, Arthur Roberts, Little Tich. p. 159: Siegfried Sassoon's comments on Beerbohm's "Music Halls of My Youth."]

188. ———. *More Theatres 1898-1903*. L: Rupert Hart-Davis; N.Y. Taplinger, 1969.
["In a Music-hall," pp. 395–98.]

189. ———. "The Older and Better Music Hall." *Saturday Review*, 14 Nov. 1902. Repr. in *Around Theatres* and in George Rowell, ed., *Victorian Dramatic Criticism* (L: Methuen, 1971), pp. 336–38.

190. ———. "The Triumph of the 'Variety Show.'" *Saturday Review* 94 (18 Oct. 1902): 487–90.
[About the Empire.]

191. BEVAN, IAN. "Music Hall." In *Theatre Programme*, ed. J. C.

Trewin. L: Muller, 1954.

192. "Blackmail in the Music Halls." *Era*, 15 Sept. 1883, p. 4; 19 Mar. 1887, p. 13; 3 Mar. 1888, p. 15; 10 Mar. 1888, p. 15.
[On audiences booing.]

193. BLATHWAYT, RAYMOND. "The Re-vulgarising of the Music-hall." *Saturday Review* 111, (14 Jan. 1911): 50.
[A reply to Runciman's article, *infra,* in the 7 January issue. Praises performances at the Palace and the Alhambra.]

194. BRAHMS, CARYL. "Death March of the Music Hall." *Times Saturday Review*, 13 Jan. 1968, p. 17.

195. "The British Music Hall." *Listener*, 30 Jan. 1964, p. 194.

196. BROWN, IVOR. "The English Droll." *Theatre Arts Monthly* (N.Y.), Sept. 1938, pp. 649-62.

197. BROWNE, MATTHEW. "Theatres and Music Halls." *Argosy* 2 (Aug. 1866): 117-28.

198. ———. *Views and Opinions.* L and N.Y.: Strahan, 1866.
[Chapter 21, "Art and Popular Amusement," pp. 252-81.]

199. BURNAND, F. C. "The Music of Bohemia." *Punch*, 15 Feb. 1905, p. 125.
[Series of lectures on the music of the song-and-supper rooms by Sir Alexander Mackenzie.]

200. CAFFIN, CAROLINE. *Vaudeville.* Ills. Marius de Zayas. N.Y.: Mitchell Kennerly, 1914.
[Lauder and Albert Chevalier, pp. 45-55; Yvette Guilbert, pp. 57-60; chapter 8, "Some English Visitors," pp. 151-67 (Marie Lloyd, Vesta Tilley, Vesta Victoria, Alice Lloyd, Ada Reeve.)]

201. CALTHROP, DION CLAYTON. *Music Hall Nights.* L: John Lane, The Bodley Head, 1925.
[Impressionistic study of music-hall stars in their characteristic roles.]

202. CANNAN, GILBERT. *The Joy of the Theatre.* L: Batsford; N.Y.: E. P. Dutton, 1913.
[Appreciation of the music-hall artist as dramatist.]

203. "Capsuloid Comedies (Condensed for Music-hall Consumption) No. I—The School for Scandal." *Punch* 6 Apr. 1904, p. 240.
[Sketch.]

204. "Charlie to 'Arry." *Punch*, 20 Oct. 1877, p. 173.
["There's plenty of spice at the Music 'Alls."]

205. COLLINSON, W. E. *Contemporary English, a Personal Speech Record.* Leipzig and Berlin: Teubner, 1927.
[Influence of music hall on colloquial speech, pp. 68-74.]

206. CRAIG, EDWARD GORDON. "The Vitality of the Music

Hall." *The Mask* [Firenze] 3 (1911):196.

207. CROW, JOHN. "Music Hall: Old Iron, Old Wine." *Spectator* 161 (2 Sept. 1938): 368.
[Compares Fats Waller at the Finsbury Park Empire to Harry Champion at Collins', Islington Green.]

208. DAVIS, RICHARD HARDING. *Our English Cousins.* N.Y.: Harper and Brothers, 1894.
[Good reportage of political songs, pp. 179-84.]

209. [DICKENS, CHARLES?] "Managers and Music Halls." *All the Year Round*, 23 Mar. 1861.
[Excerpted as "Halls in 'Sixty-one,'" *Era*, 22 Apr. 1911, p. 29.]

210. DIRCKS, RUDOLF. "The Apotheosis of the Music Hall." *Theatre,* n.s. 20 (Nov. 1892): 193-97.
[Debunks the romanticizing of the music-hall; sees it as ugly but energetic.]

211. "Distinction between the Music Hall in England and the Theatre." *Spectator* 68 (14 May 1892): 673.

212. "Drama and Music: Music-halls & Theatres." *Nation,* 3 Sept. 1908, p. 218.

213. ELIOT, T[HOMAS] S[TEARNS]. "Music Hall and Revue." ("London Letter"). *Dial* (N.Y.) 70 (June 1921) 687-88.

214. ERVINE, ST. JOHN. "The Glory That was Leno and the Grandeur That was Lloyd." *Observer*, 1 Mar. 1931.

215. FINDLATER, RICHARD. "The Naughty and the Nude." *Observer*, 29 Sept. 1957, p. 12.

216. FITZGERALD, PERCY (HETHERINGTON). *Music-hall Land. An Account of the Natives, Male and Female, Pastimes, Songs, Antics and General Oddities of That Strange Country.* Ills. Alfred Bryan. L: Ward and Downey [1890].

217. ———. "Music Hall Land." *National Review* 15 (1890): 379-91.
[Abridged version of the above.]

218. ———. *The World Behind the Scenes.* L: Chatto & Windus, 1881.

219. GILBERT, DOUGLAS. *American Vaudeville: Its Life & Times.* N.Y.: Whittesley House, 1940. Repr. N.Y.: Dover; L.: Constable, 1968.
["The Foreign Invasion," pp. 135-51.]

220. GRAVES, C. L. and E. V. LUCAS. "Luxury at the Halls." *Punch*, 24 Feb. 1909, p. 131. [Refinement.]

221. GREEN, BENNY. "City Life." *Spectator*, 12 Dec. 1970, p. 784.

222. GREIN, J. T. "The Music Hall Is Not Dead." *Illustrated London News* 179, (3 Oct. 1931): 532.

223. HADDON, ARCHIBALD. "The New Music Hall and the Old." *Theatre World* 19 (Apr. 1933): 202.

224. HALL, STUART and PADDY WHANNEL. *The Popular Arts: A Critical Guide to the Mass Media.* L: Hutchinson; N.Y.: Pantheon Books, 1965; Boston: Beacon Press, 1967.
[Chapter 2, "Minority Art, Folk Art and Popular Art," pp. 45–65.]

225. "Harry Mountford in London; his Views about Vaudeville." *Era*, 29 July 1911, p. 24.
[A performer contrasts English and American variety.]

226. HATTON, JOSEPH. "On Music with a 'K.'" Ills. Dudley Hardy. *Idler* 1 (Apr. 1892): 239–54.
[Strand Musick Hall. Compares old and contemporary halls.]

227. HAYWARD, EDWARD. "Victorian Music Hall." *Arts: A Fourth Level Course. Great Britain 1750 – 1950: Sources and historiography.* L: The Open University, 1974.

228. HIBBERT, HENRY GEORGE. "Music Hall History." *Performer*, 3 Feb. 1916.
[On the inaccuracy of most music-hall writing.]

229. HOLLINGSHEAD, JOHN. "The Century and the Music Hall." *Entr'acte Annual* (1901): 15–16.

230. ———. *Footlights.* L: Chapman & Hall, 1883.
["A Converted Theatre," pp. 154–60 (The Grecian and the Eagle); "Free and Merry England," pp. 296–98 (licensing system).]

231. HOPKINS, TIGHE. "Music Halls." *Dublin University Magazine* (Dublin) n.s. 2 (1878): 192–206.
[Music-hall seen as a symptom of degeneration of modern city life.]

232. IRVING, HENRY. "On Music Halls." *Era*, 3 Nov. 1894, p. 17, repr. from *Daily Chronicle*, 27 Oct. 1894; [follow-ups] 10 Nov. 1894, p. 16 and 15 Dec. 1894, p. 11.

233. JENNINGS, PAUL. "Making Them Laugh." *Saturday Book* 31 (1971) 53–71.

234. JEROME, JEROME KLAPKA. "Variety Patter." *Idler* 1 (Mar. 1892): 120–35. Ills. Dudley Hardy.
[Impressions of several music-hall visits, slanging match at "small hall in the South-East."]

235. JOHNS, ERIC. "Immortalising the Halls." *Theatre World,* Oct. 1963, pp. 17–18.

236. ———. "Musings on Music-halls." *Theatre World,* July 1963, p. 19.

237. JONES, HENRY ARTHUR. "Gargantuan Livery." *Era*, 2 Mar. 1889, p. 11; "Jones on Music Hall" [edit.] p. 15.
[Manchester lecture, on introduction of music-hall style into legitimate theatre.]

238. LAURIE, JOE, Jr. *Vaudeville from the Honky Tonks to the Palace.* N.Y.: Henry Holt, 1953.
["Fair Exchange," pp. 132–38.]

239. LEVEY, ETHEL. "Foreign and American Music Halls." *Green Book Album* (N.Y.) 6 (Aug. 1911): 317–32.
[American singer contrasts experiences in Paris, Berlin, Vienna, London and New York.]

240. LITTLE, G. T. [Music Halls] *London Society* 70 (July 1896): 25.

241. LOUTHER, H. "A Chat about Music-halls." *Tinsley's Magazine* (N.Y.) 27 (1880): 364.

242. LUCAS, E[DWARD] V[ERRALL]. *A Boswell of Baghdad, with Diversions..* L: Methuen, 1917.
["The Two Perkinses" (Harry Clifton and His Songs), pp. 106–17; "The Oldest Joke" (The Face joke in music-hall), pp. 133–39.]

243. MACKAY, C. "Music Hall Literature." *Social Notes*, 1 June 1878.

244. MACKENZIE, COMPTON. "Sidelight." *Spectator* 193 (10 Dec. 1954): 748. [On old music-hall comedians.]

245. MAIR, G. H. "The Music-hall." *English Review* 9 (1911): 122–29.
[Repr. as "The Vitality of the Halls," *Era*, 26 Aug. 1911, p. 24.]

246. "The Making of a Music Hall Artiste." *Era Annual* (1914): 53–54.

247. MATTHEWS, BRANDER. *A Book about the Theatre.* N.Y.: Charles Scribner's Sons, 1916.
["The Ideal of the Acrobat," pp. 201–16; "The Utility of the Variety-show," pp. 235–51; "The Method of Modern Magic," pp. 251–70.]

248. MORRIS, VICTOR. "They're a Rotten Act—Sign 'Em Up." *Weekend*, 21–27 May 1969, p. 24.

249. "The Music-hall." *Cornhill Magazine* 60 (1889): 68–79.

250. "The 'Music-hall' to the Discard." *Literary Digest* (N.Y.), 18 Mar. 1922, pp. 31–32.
[Quotes Gordon Hall of London *Daily Mail* and Manchester *Guardian* on current decadence of halls, dearth of stars.]

251. "Music-halls." *All the Year Round* 25, (Oct. 1880): 520–24.

252. "Music-halls." *All the Year Round* 45 (1888): 520.

253. "Music-halls." *Evening Standard*, 29 Jan. 1883, p. 4.
254. "Music Halls." *Lancet,* 23 July 1870.
254a. "Music-halls. *Tomahawk* 20 (14 Sept. 1867): 201; (21 Sept. 1867): 209.
   [Disappointed that the new phenomenon does not uplift public taste but is stupid and worthless.]
255. "Music Halls and Theatres." *Nation* 87 (3 Sept. 1908): 218.
   [Improvements over the years; presentation of tabloid drama; old music-hall nonexistent, nowadays replaced by 'variety'; getting closer to legitimate drama.]
256. "Music Halls and Their Effects." *Meliora: A Quarterly Review of the Social Sciences* 10 (1867): 246-56.
   [On Select Committee on Theatrical Licences and Regulations, *infra* 1593.]
257. "The Old Music Halls." *Times* [edit.], 18 Mar. 1932.
258. OSBORNE, JOHN. "The Brave Old World of Music Hall." *Observer Magazine*, 20 Apr. 1975, pp. 20-24.
259. "Our Music Halls." *Tinsley's Magazine* 4 (1869): 216-33.
   [Low character of music-halls.]
260. PALMER, JOHN. *The Future of the Theatre*. L: Bell, 1913.
   [Chapter 1, "Competitors," pp. 1-17.]
261. "PATERSON, PETER" [pseud. of James Glass Bertram]. *Glimpses of Real Life as Seen in the Theatrical World and in Bohemia*. Edinburgh: William P. Nimmo, 1864. Repr. Hamden, Conn: Archon Books, 1980.
   [Unfavorable comments on saloon theatres.]
262. "PILGRIM, THE." "Variety on the Up-grade," *Era Almanack & Annual* (1912): 61-67.
263. POEL, WILLIAM. "Variety Stage." In *Monthly Letters: Selected and arranged by A.M.T.* L: Werner Laurie, 1929.
264. PRIESTLEY, J.B. *Particular Pleasures, being a Personal Record of Some Varied Arts and Many Different Artists*. L. Heinemann; N.Y.: Stein & Day, 1975.
   [Sid Field, p. 161; George Robey and Robb Wilton, p. 184; Harry Tate, p. 185; Little Tich, p. 187.]
265. ———. "Pathway to Theatrical Reflection," *Saturday Review,* repr. in Boston *Transcript,* 24 Apr. 1926.
266. ———. "Variety," *Saturday Review* 144 (29 Oct. 1927): 578-79.
267. ———. "Variety: The Grand Manner," *Saturday Review* 146 (27 Oct. 1928): 534-35.
268. RIGBY, REGINALD. "Music Hall Notes," *Punch,* 30 Oct. 1912, p. 360.

269. [RUNCIMAN, JOHN F.] "At the Music-halls." *Saturday Review* 81 (25 Jan. 1896): 97–98.
[Vivacity of music-halls in contrast with dull concert halls.]

270. ———. "The De-vulgarising of the Music-hall," *Saturday Review* 111 (14 Jan. 1911): 43–44.

271. ———. "The Music-halls Again," *Saturday Review* 81 (21 Mar. 1896): 299–300.
[Refinement of music-halls.]

272. ———. "The Re-vulgarising of the Music-hall," *Saturday Review* 111 (7 Jan. 1911): 9–10.
[Edyth Walker at the Palladium lost amid vulgarity; deplores "super stars."]

273. ———. "The Re-vulgarising of the Music-hall," *Saturday Review* 111 (21 Jan. 1911): 82.

274. ———. "A Use for Music Halls," *Saturday Review* 87 (15 Apr. 1899): 460–61.
[Composers and musicians should seize their chance and work for the music-hall.]

275. SCOTT, CLEMENT. "The Modern Music-hall," *Contemporary Review* 56 (1889): 683–90.
[On the new London County Council which in 1889 succeeded the magistrates in licencing music-halls.]

276. SHAND, JOHN. "Music Halls." *Nineteenth Century* 127 (May 1940): 615–22. Repr. in *Theater and Song*. Literary Taste, Culture and Mass Communication, ed. P. Davison, R. Meyersohn, E. Shils, vol. 8. Teaneck, N.J.: Somerset House, 1978.
[Signs of renewed interest; the provincialism of the old halls.]

277. SHAW, GEORGE BERNARD. "Do I Mind Having My Play Performed in a Variety Theatre? *Daily Graphic,* 2 Dec. 1911 p. 4.

278. ———. *London Music in 1888 – 89.* L: Constable, 1935. [Pp. 231–35, 316.]

279. ———. *Music in London 1890 – 1894.* 3 vols. rev. ed. L: Constable, 1950.
[1:42–47; 2:61–66, 89–90, 168–70, 239–44, 270–71; 3:68–69, 137–40, 212–16.]

280. ———. *Our Theatre in the 'Nineties.* 3 vols. L: Constable, 1933. Repr. 1948.

281. ———. *Shaw on Music, a Selection from the Music Criticism of Bernard Shaw Made by Eric Bentley.* Garden City, N.Y.: Doubleday Anchor Books, 1955.
["Music Hall," pp. 224–25 (first appeared in *The Star,* 18 October 1889); "Yvette Guilbert," pp. 239–43 (first appeared in *The*

World, 16 May 1894).]

282. " 'Sir Oracle' on the Music Hall." *Era,* 9 Jan. 1885, p. 10.
[Reply to "The New Music Hall."]

283. SLAPKINS, Rev. JOSEPH [pseud. of Alfred Allinson]. *The Parson and the Painter: Their Wanderings and Excursions among Men and Women. . . .* Ills. Charlie Summers [pseud. of Phil May.] L: Central Publishing and Advertising Co., 1891.

284. SMITH, BESSIE. "Music Hall Matinees." *Entr'acte Annual* (1899): 36.

285. "Songs and Suppers." *Era,* 29 Oct. 1887, p. 13.
[Important edit. on attractions of music-halls.]

286. SPECTATOR, A. *The Music Hall as It Is, as It Might Be.* L: Smart & Allen, 1880.

287. SWINGLER, RANDALL. "English Music Hall. I. Its Psychology." *Theatre Today,* Dec. 1947, pp. 16–19.

288. SYMONS, ARTHUR. *Cities and Sea-coasts and Islands.* L: W. Collins Sons, 1918.
["A Spanish Music-hall" (1892), pp. 145–57; "London Music Hall", p. 206; "Yvette Guilbert," pp. 207–8.]

289. "Tabloid Tragedies. (Bovrilised from the Best British Bards for Music-hall Purposes.) Tabloid No. I. —Hamlet, Prince of Denmark." *Punch,* 23 Mar. 1904, pp. 205–7.

290. "The Theatre of Varieties." *Times,* 24 Jan. 1910.

291. "Theatres and Music Halls." *Saturday Review* 83 (7 May 1892): 533.
[Against their assimilation into one another.]

292. TITTERTON, W.R. *From Theatre to Music Hall.* L: Stephen Swift, 1912.
[Part 2, "The Halls," pp. 109–231.]

293. "Up in the Gallery." *All the Year Round,* 29 July 1882.

294. "The Variety Entertainment." *Punch,* 30 Mar. 1904, p. 226.

295. WALLIS, DOROTHY. "At the Music Hall." *Longman's Magazine* (22 June 1893): 163–69.

296. WEDMORE, FREDERICK. "The Music-halls." *Nineteenth Century* 40 (July 1896): 128–36.
[Concerns tableaux vivants and dance, Albert Chevalier and the kinetophone; music-hall on the upgrade.]

297. "Where the Music Hall Holds Its Own." *Times,* 10 Apr. 1963, p. 15.

298. WHITE, R.F. "The Hall-mark." *Punch,* 25 Dec. 1912, p. 360.
[Critique of halls.]

299. WILLIAMS, RAYMOND. *The Long Revolution.* L: Chatto &

Windus, 1961.
[Pp. 264–66: music-hall as a product of the Industrial "Revolution."]

300. WILSON, ANDREW E. "Influence of the Music Halls." *Contemporary Review* 78 (July 1900): 134–41.

301. [WRIGHT, THOMAS]. *Some Habits and Customs of the Working Classes.* L: 1867.
[Penny readings in Boughtborough Music Hall, p. 169; music-halls as expensive amusements, p. 199.]

302. Y.Y. "Enchantment in the Music Hall." *New Statesman* 20, no. 511 (27 Jan. 1923): 478–79.
[Loving memories of thirty years before preferable to seeing Veterans of Variety; music-hall atmosphere conducive to genius.]

PICTURE BOOKS

Cross-references

See also **2219**

303. CLARK, G[EORGE] F[REDERICK] SCOTSON-. *The "Halls."* L: T. Fisher Unwin [1899].
["Chiefly concerning the Music Halls," by George Gamble. 24 colored plates.]

304. DELGADO, ALAN. *Victorian Entertainment.* Newton Abbot: David & Charles, 1971.

305. DOYLE, RICHARD. *Bird's Eye View of Society.* L: Smith, Elder, 1864.
[Originally appeared in *Punch* as "Manners and Customs of Ye Englyshe," with letterpress by Percival Leigh; first published as *Mr. Pips His Diary*, L: Bradbury & Evans, 1849. Picture of Cyder Cellars with Ross singing 'Sam Hall.']

306. GAMMOND, PETER, comp. *Your Own, Your Very Own! A Music Hall Scrapbook.* L: Ian Allan, 1971.

307. [GATTY, TED] *Memories of Music Hall: A Pictorial Glimpse down Memory Lane.* Margate: Margate Estates [1966].

308. HOLT, HAZEL. *The Music Hall.* L: Theatre Museum, 1976.
[Theatre Museum card 1.]
309. ———. *Music Hall Portraits.* L: Theatre Museum, 1976.
[Theatre Museum card 7.]
310. HUDD, ROY. *Music-hall.* L: Methuen, 1976.
[Unusual and outstanding selection of portraits of performers.]
311. MANDER, RAYMOND and JOE MITCHENSON. *British Music Hall, a Story in Pictures.* Foreword by John Betjeman. L: Studio Vista, 1965. Rev. ed. L: Gentry books, 1974. Rev. R. Mackender, *Theatre Notebook,* 20 (summer 1966): 163–65; C. Davison, *Times Literary Supplement,* 21 Mar. 1975.
312. ———. *Victorian and Edwardian Entertainment from old photographs.* L: B. T. Batsford, 1978.
[No. 37–39, 91–100, 147–151.]
313. MAY, PHIL. *Songs and Their Singers.* L: Bradbury, Agnew, 1898.
[Fifteen "Japanese" proofs.]
314. NERMAN, EINAR. *Darlings of the Gods in Music Hall, Revue and Musical Comedy as Seen by Nerman.* Introduction by Ivor Novello. L: Alston Rivers [1929].
[Caricatures.]
315. WOOD, ROBERT. *Entertainments 1800 – 1900.* L: Evans, 1971.
[Advertising material.]

REMINISCENCE, MEMOIRS, DIARIES, AND OBSERVATIONS OF SPECTATORS AND THEATRE-GOERS

Cross-references

See also **435, 463, 532, 662, 1001, 1159, 2769, 2887, 3490.**

316. À BECKETT, ARTHUR WILLIAM. *Green-Room Recollec-*

tions. Arrowsmith's 3/6 Series, vol. 25. Bristol: J. W. Arrowsmith; L: Simpkin, Marshall, Hamilton, Kent [1896].
["Dwelling in Marble Halls," pp. 184–90 (The Oxford); "Boatrace Night at Evans'," pp. 199–205; "Supper Time at Evans'," pp. 206–15.]

317. AGATE, JAMES. *Ego. The Autobiography of James Agate.* L: Hamish Hamilton, 1935.
[References to C. B. Cochran, Marie Lloyd, George Robey, Vesta Tilley, *et al.*]

318. ———. *Ego 2, being More of the Autobiography of James Agate.* L: Victor Gollancz, 1936.
[References to Albert Chevalier, C. B. Cochran, Gus Elen, Gracie Fields, Marie Lloyd, Arthur Roberts, George Robey, Frederick Robson, Vesta Tilley, Nellie Wallace, *et al.*]

319. ———. *Ego 3, being Still More of the Autobiography of James Agate.* L: George G. Harrap, 1938.
[References to C. B. Cochran, Little Tich, Ada Reeve, George Robey, Harry Tate, Vesta Tilley, *et al.*]

320. ———. *Ego 4. Yet More of the Autobiography of James Agate.* L: George G. Harrap, 1940.
[References to Wilkie Bard, Maurice Chevalier, C. B. Cochran, G. H. Elliott, Gracie Fields, Jay Laurier, Marie Lloyd, George Robey, Harry Lauder, Harry Tate, Vesta Tilley, *et al.*]

321. ———. *Ego 5. Again More of the Autobiography of James Agate.* L: George G. Harrap, 1942.
[References to Flanagan and Allen, C. B. Cochran, Mrs. Sam Cowell, Fred Emney, George Formby, Will Fyffe, Marie Lloyd, Lupino Lane, Arthur Roberts, George Robey, Harry Tate, Little Tich, Vesta Tilley, *et al.*]

322. ———. *Ego 6. Once More the Autobiography of James Agate.* L: George G. Harrap, 1944.
[References to Fred Emney, C. B. Cochran, Sid Field, Bud Flanagan, Will Hay, George Robey, Harry Tate, Max Wall, *et al.*]

323. ———. *Ego 7. Even More of the Autobiography of James Agate.* L: George G. Harrap, 1945.
[References to Belle Elmore, Sid Field, Gracie Fields, George Robey, Vesta Tilley, *et al.*]

324. ———. *Ego 8, continuing the Autobiography of James Agate.*
[References to Billy Bennett, C. B. Cochran, Sid Field, George Robey, *et al.*]

325. ———. *Ego 9, concluding the Autobiography of James Agate.* L: George G. Harrap, 1948.

[References to Wilkie Bard, Albert Chevalier, C. B. Cochran, Lottie Collins, Tom Costello, Leo Dryden, T. E. Dunville, Gus Elen, Sid Field, Bud Flanagan, George Formby, Will Fyffe, Dan Leno, Little Tich, Marie Lloyd, Harry Randall, George Robey, Eugene Stratton, Harry Tate, Vesta Tilley, and Harriet Vernon.]

326. BALLANTINE, Mr Serjeant WILLIAM. *Some Experiences of a Barrister's Life.* 2 vols. L: Richard Bentley & Sons, 1882.
[Vol. 1, chapter 23, "Evan's": Evan's, Paddy Green, Herr von Joel, Habitues at Evan's, Thackeray, Dickens, etc.]

327. BAMBERGER, LOUIS. *Bow Bell Memories.* L: Sampson, Low, Marston [*n.d.*]
["London Entertainment," pp. 139–51; "Music Halls," pp. 152–66.]

327a. BASON, FRED. "Music Hall Memories." In *Saturday Book 30*, ed. John Hadfield. NY: Clarkson N. Potter, 1970. Pp. 121–24.

328. BEDFORD, PAUL. *Recollections and Wanderings. Facts, not Fancies.* L: Routledge, Warne and Routledge, 1864.

329. BEERBOHM, Sir MAX. "Music Halls of My Youth." *Listener*, 22 Jan. 1943. Repr. in *Listener*, 14 Jan. 1954, pp. 92–95; and in *Mainly on the Air* (N.Y.: Alfred A. Knopf, 1958).
[Radio talks on "Music Halls of My Youth" and "Marie Lloyd."]

330. BEHRMAN, S[AMUEL] N[ATHANIEL]. *Conversations with Max.* L: Hamish Hamilton, 1960.
[Beerbohm reminiscing about music-hall artistes.]

331. BENNETT, ARNOLD. *The Journal of Arnold Bennett 1896 – 1910.* N.Y.: Viking Press, 1932.
[24 Oct. 1897, Folies-Bergere; 14 Feb. 1905, Bal Tabarin; 4 Mar. 1905, Alhambra (Paris); 2 Jan. 1910, Tivoli (Little Tich, George Formby, Marie Lloyd on the bill).]

332. BLOW, SYDNEY. *Sydney Blow Presents Through Stage Doors, or Memories of Two in the Theatre.* Ills. J. S. Goodall. Edinburgh & L: W. & R. Chambers, 1958.
[Chapter 19, "When Theatre Stars Shone on the Halls," pp. 202–14.]

333. BOYD, FRANK M. *A Pelican's Tale: Fifty Years in London & Elsewhere.* L: Herbert Jenkins, 1919.
[Journalist's memoirs with scattered references to music-hall.]

334. BROADBENT, R. J. *Stage Whispers.* L: Simkin, 1901.

335. BROOKFIELD, C[HARLES] H. E. *Random Reminiscences.* L: Arnold, 1902. Repr. L: Nelson [1911].
[Chapter 12, "Music halls . . . ," pp. 271–91.]

336. BURNAND, Sir FRANCIS C. *Records and Reminiscences. Personal and General.* 2 vols. L: Methuen, 1903. Repr. in one vol., 1905.
[Chapter 8, reminiscences of Cyder Cellar, Evans's, Judge and Jury Society.]

337. BUSSEY, HARRY FINDLATER. *Sixty Years of Journalism.* Bristol: J. W. Arrowsmith, 1906.

338. "A Chat with Jack Camp." *Era*, 17 July 1897, p. 17.
[Important testimony of a veteran of the free-and-easies.]

339. CRAIG, EDWARD GORDON. *Index to the Story of My Days.* L: Hulton Press, 1957.
[Pp. 115–17, Albert Chevalier; p. 185, Little Tich and music-hall comedy.]

340. DAREWSKI, HERMAN. *Musical Memories.* Ills. Mac. L: Jarrolds [1937].

341. DARK, SIDNEY. *Mainly about Other People.* L: Hodder & Stoughton, 1925.

342. ELLIOT, WILLIAM GEORGE. *In My Anecdotage.* L: P. Allan, 1925.

343. "Fifty Years: Memories of Music Halls." *Times*, 18 Mar. 1932, p. 18.

344. FOSTER, GEORGE. *The Spice of Life: 65 Years in the Glamour World.* L: Hurst & Blackett, 1939.
[Chapters on Marie Lloyd, Harry Lauder, business aspect of variety.]

345. FURNISS, HARRY. *Some Victorian Men.* L: John Lane; N.Y.: Dodd, Mead, 1924.
["The Music-hall," pp. 155–62.]

346. GANTHONY, ROBERT. *Random Recollections.* L: Henry J. Drane [c. 1918].
["How I Became a Lightning Cartoonist," pp. 156–57; "Moore & Burgess," pp. 161–63; "Music Halls," pp. 195–204.]

347. GARDINER, ALFRED GEORGE. *Pillars of Society.* L: James Nisbet, 1913.

348. GIELGUD, Sir JOHN. *Distinguished Company.* L: Heinemann, 1972.
["Music-halls," pp. 103–15.]

349. GIFFORD, DENIS. *Fifty Years of Radio Comedy.* L: New English Library, 1972.
["Ladies and Gentlemen, Music Hall," pp. 7–8.]

350. GLOVER, JAMES. [Master of Music at Drury Lane]. *Hims Ancient and Modern, being the Third Book of Jimmy Glover.* L:

Fisher Unwin, 1926. [Chapter 12, "The Old Mogul," pp. 149–63.]

351. ———. *Jimmy Glover and His Friends.* L: Chatto & Windus, 1913.
[Chapter 7, "My Friend 'Leicester Square,'" pp. 133–50 (The Alhambra, Mrs Ormiston Chant); chapter 11, "My Friend 'The Comic Song,'" 196–219 (much on Alfred Concanen).]

352. ———. *Jimmy Glover His Book.* L: Methuen, 1911.
[On Dan Leno, Arthur Collins, Mascagni conducting at music-halls. See especially chapters 9, 10, 15.]

353. GREENWALL, HARRY J. *The Strange Life of Willy Clarkson.* L: Long, 1936.
[Memoirs of theatrical wigmaker.]

354. HADDON, ARCHIBALD. *Green Room Gossip.* L: Stanley Paul, 1922.

355. HATTON, JOSEPH. *In Jest and Earnest. A Book of Gossip.* L: Leadenhall Press, 1893. ["Music with a 'K'," pp. 11–14 (Strand Musick Hall, in support of music-halls); "From East to West," pp. 14–16 (on Chirgwin and Marie Lloyd); "Realism," pp. 16–18 (on realism in performances old and new); "Colonel Newcome and the Cave of Harmony," pp. 18–20; "Evans'," pp. 20–23.]

356. ———. *Reminiscences of J. L. Toole.* L: Hurst & Blackett, 1889.

357. HIBBERT, H. G. *A Playgoer's Memories.* Prefatory Note by William Archer. L: Grant Richards, 1920.
[Chapter 26, "A Pageant of Principal Boys"; chapter 27, "A Dwarf, Some Monsters and a Magician"; chapter 28, "Frenzied Finance"; chapter 29, "Theatrical Fortunes"; chapter 30, "Everlasting Flowers"; chapter 31, "The Passing of the Music Hall."]

358. HOLLINGSHEAD, JOHN. *My Lifetime.* 2 vols. 2d ed. L: Sampson, Low, Marston, 1895.
[1:18–29 (penny-gaffs, saloon theatres, the Grecian, Robson, a refined music-hall); 30–37 (Albert & Britannia saloons, licencing acts); 151–60 (Evans', Cyder Cellars, "Sam Hall"); 209–20 (Alhambra, Great Theatre of Variety, Canterbury and Oxford Halls); 221–29 (Can-can); 2:66–74; (Macdermott); 93–97 (Paddy Green, Charles Morton); 98–103 (Jenny Hill, drawing from the music-hall); chapter 22 (Coffee Palace association); 203–8 (Hollingshead as champion of music-hall); 227–36 (music-hall directorship, Alhambra in 1892).

359. HUDSON, DEREK, ed. *Munby, Man of Two Worlds.* L: John

Murray, 1972. [Creole Serenaders, p. 27; Evans' Song and Supper Rooms, p. 55; the can-can, p. 92; Leotard at the Alhambra, p. 97; Ethiopian Serenaders, p. 57; Margaret Douglas the Walker at the Alhambra, p. 200; female acrobats, p. 252; Zuleilah the acrobat, p. 254; temperance music-hall, p. 255; female acrobats at the Oxford, p. 285; Zazel at the Aquarium, p. 389.]

360. JACOB, NAOMI ELLINGTON. *Me, a Chronicle about Other People.* L: Hutchinson, 1933, 1936.

361. ———. *Me Again.* L: Hutchinson, 1937, 1939.

362. ———. *Me and the Stage.* L: Kimber, 1964.

363. ———. *Me—Likes and Dislikes.* L: Hutchinson, 1954. [Chapter 13, The Sisters Adair, Bransby Williams, Robb Wilton, pp. 182–95.]

364. ———. *Me—Yesterday and Today.* L: Hutchinson, 1957. [Chapter 3, Music halls, Marie Lloyd, Dan Leno, Marie Kendal, Gus Elen, Albert Chevalier, Gracie Fields, pp. 40–53.]

365. JEPSON, EDGAR. *Memories of a Victorian.* Vol 1. L: Victor Gollancz, 1933.
[London music-hall in 1890s, pp. 229–34; against the cult of the music-hall.]

366. LEATHAM, J. *Shows and Showfolk I Have Known North and South of the Tweed.* Turriff: Deveron Press, 1936.

367. LINDO, R. H. *From Stage to Bar.* Margate: Perrett, 1928.
[Memoirs of small-time music-hall and panto performer.]

368. MACKAY, CHARLES. *Forty Years Recollections of Life, Literature and Public Affairs from 1830 to 1870.* 2 vols. L: 1877.

369. MACKAY, WILLIAM. *Bohemian Days in Fleet Street.* L: John Long, 1913.
[Chapter 15, "The 'Alls," used extensively by Willson Disher in *Winkles and Champagne.*]

370. MACQUEEN-POPE, W. *Back Numbers.* L: Hutchinson, 1954.

371. ———. *Shirtfronts and Sables. A Story of the Days When Money Could be Spent.* L: Robert Hale, 1953.

372. ———. *Twenty Shillings in the Pound.* L: Hutchinson, 1948.
[Chapter 17, "The Theatre, the Halls and the Cinema," pp. 264–78.]

373. NEWTON, H. CHANCE. *Cues and Curtain Calls being the Theatrical Reminiscences of H. Chance Newton ("Carados" of The Referee).* With an introduction by Sir Johnston Forbes-Robertson. L: John Lane, The Bodley Head, 1927.
[Chapter 8, "Kosher Comedians and Froom Friends."]

374. PAXTON, SYDNEY. *Stage See-saws or The Ups and Downs of* *an Actor's Life, being Some Experiences of Sydney Paxton.* L: Mills & Boon [c. 1918].

[Chapter 16, "The Zancigs," pp. 168-75; chapter 17, "Cyril Maude, Sir Herbert Tree, Laurence Irving, Miss Millard and the Halls," pp. 176-81; chapter 19, "Anecdotes Concerning Some of the Men I Have Met and Known" (George Beauchamp, Arthur Lloyd).]

375. PAYNE, JACK. *Signature Tune.* L: Stanley Paul [n.d.].
["By Royal Command," pp. 14-22.]

376. PRIESTLEY, J.B. "Music Halls." *New Statesman* 71 (28 Jan. 1966): 117.
[Reminiscences of music-hall 1909-14; incongruity and general daftness, ambience.]

377. RENDLE, THOMAS MACDONALD. *Swings and Round-abouts: a Yokel in London.* L: Chapman & Hall, 1919.
[Chapters 9, 10, 13-18.]

378. RICHARDS, GRANT. *Memories of a Misspent Youth 1872 – 1896.* L: Heinemann, 1932.
["The Empire and Mrs. Chant," pp. 323-26.]

379. RICHARDSON, JOHN. *Recollections Political, Literary, Dramatic and Miscellaneous of the Last Half-century.* 2 vols. L: the author, 1855.

380. RIDGE, W. PETT. *I Like to Remember.* N.Y.: George H. Doran [n.d.].
[On Dan Leno, pp. 26-27; on music-halls, pp. 272-73.]

381. ———. *A Story-teller: Forty Years in London.* L: Hodder & Stoughton; N.Y.: George H. Doran [n.d.].
[Chapter 10, "Through the Galleries," pp. 119-30 (information on difference in gallery audiences and music-hall sketches); chapter 22, "Songs of the Street," pp. 262-69.]

382. ROTHENSTEIN, WILLIAM. *Men and Memories: Recollections 1872 – 1900.* N.Y.: Coward, McCann, 1931.
[Parisian music-halls and cabarets, pp. 61-67; the Empire promenade, p. 237; London music-halls, pp. 275-76; Richard Le Gallienne at a music-hall, drawn by Max, p. 238.]
Abridged ed., ed. Mary Lago. L: Chatto & Windus, 1978.

383. SCOTT, CLEMENT. *The Drama of Yesterday & To-day.* 2 vols. L: Macmillan, 1899.
[Chapter 10, "Bohemia in Days of Old," pp. 307-53 (Cyder Cellars, Coal Hole, Evans', Charles Sloman, Judge and Jury Society).]

384. SCOTT, MARGARET [Mrs. CLEMENT]. *Old Days in Bohe-*

mian London. *Recollections of Clement Scott.* L: Hutchinson, 1918.
[References to Wiry Sal and Lottie Collins.]

384a. SECOMBE, HARRY. "I Dreamt I Dwelt in Music Halls." *Punch,* 28 Nov. 1979. [Memories of youth in variety at Grand Theatre, Bolton.]

385. SIMS, GEORGE ROBERT. *My Life: Sixty Years' Recollections of Bohemian London.* L: Eveleigh Nash, 1917.
[Pp. 310–13 (Moore & Burgess, Maskelyne, etc.); 314–19 (song-and-supper rooms, early music-hall performers).]

386. WODEHOUSE, P.G. "The 'alls," *Theatre Arts Monthly* (N.Y.) 33, no. 1 (Jan. 1949): 22–23.
[Affectionate but generalized remembrance.]

387. WOOLF, VIRGINIA. *The Diary of Virginia Woolf.* Ed. Anne Olivier Bell. N.Y. and L: Harcourt Brace Jovanovich, 1977.
[1:19–20, visit to Coliseum in 1915; 144, visit to Hippodrome to see Harry Tate in 1918.]

IV. LONDON

"There is in them [the London music-halls] a certain satirical or sceptical attitude towards the commonplace, there is an attempt to turn it inside-out, to distort it somewhat, to point up the illogicality of the everyday. Abstruse, but—interesting."

V.I. Lenin to Maksim Gorky, 1907,
in *Collected Works* (Moscow, 1952)
XVII, 16.

Lenin may seem an unexpected visitor to the music-halls, especially at a time when they represented the epitome of capitalist enterprise: not long before the London Coliseum Ltd. had consolidated with a capital of £196,000. But he is not unrepresentative of the breadth of audience to which the music-hall in London was making its appeal by the turn of the century. In 1900 the sixty-three theatres in London were on the way to being equalled in number by the forty music-halls: every neighborhood seemed to have its local, with a tone, a clientele, and an atmosphere of its own, while the West End boasted Stoll's and Moss's massive palaces of entertainment. This exceptional growth had occurred in fifty years' time, despite constant attack from licensing boards and proprietors of legitimate theatres. As it was the hub of the straight theatre, so London was the center of music-hall agencies, stock companies, music publishing, trade papers. However varied and individual the provincial halls, when the average commentator says music-hall he means London.

Diana Howard's *London Theatres & Music Halls 1850–1960*

provides the fullest documentation of the careers of all such places of entertainment erected during that time span; she gives the location of builder's plans, relevant legislation, management tenures and other valuable data for each. However, her focus is on the music-halls as *buildings*. We have sought not to supplant but to supplement her; in a few cases we cite the same references but in every case have added new information, particularly on occurrences within the halls—fires, thefts, presentations to managers, special performances.

The first section concerns London in general: guidebooks, surveys, panoramas of the municipal scene. The next section is broken down into districts, often rather broad, such as the East End, which had a fatal fascination for the inquiring journalist and sensation-seeker; and finally, individual halls. We follow Howard's practice of calling the hall by its last operative title, but other names it boasted during its lifetime are listed and can also be found in the cross-index of halls.

GENERAL

Cross-references

See also: **3, 4, 179a, 2764.**

388. ANDERSON, A.B. "Old London Music-halls." *Notes & Queries* 180 (1941).

389. ANSTEY, F. (pseud. of Thomas Anstey Guthrie). "London Music Halls." *Harper's Monthly Magazine* (N.Y.) 21 (1891): 190–202. [An important article, classifying halls into three main types.]

390. BAEDEKER, KARL. *London and its Environs . . . Handbook for Travellers.* Leipsic: Karl Baedeker; L: Dulau, 1878. ["Music Halls, Public Gardens, Concerts, and Comic Operas, and Circuses," pp. 37–38 (gives times, addresses, admission fees).] 1890 ed., "Music-halls," p. 45. 1894 ed., "Music-halls, and Variety Entertainments, Public Gardens," pp. 42–43. 1923 ed., "Music Halls," p. 33.

391. BARNES, HORACE. "A Glimpse at the London Music-halls, the Typical Amusement-resorts of the British Metropolis," *Munsey's Magazine* (N.Y.), Mar. 1902, pp. 732–46.

392. *Black's Guide to London, and its Environs.* Edinburgh: Adam and Charles Black, 1863. [Chapter 16, "Theatres, Concert Rooms, and Places of Public Amusement," pp. 211–18.]

393. BOOTH, CHARLES. *Life and Labour of the People in London.* 1st ser.: Poverty, East, Central & South London. L: Macmillan, 1902. [On entertainment, pp. 101–98.] 3rd ser.: Religious Influences. L: Macmillan, 1902. [On music-halls converted to mission halls.] Final vol.: Notes on Social Influences and Conclusion. L: Macmillan, 1903. [On entertainment, 52–53.]

394. ———. *Life and Labour of the People in London.* Final vol., 3rd ed. L: Macmillan, 1903.
["Music-halls," pp. 41–91.]
2nd ser. L: Macmillan, 1903.
["Theatre and Music Halls," pp. 119–120, 137–39.]

395. BOURDON, GEORGES. *Les Théâtres anglais* . . . . Paris: Bibliothèque-Charpentier, 1903.
[Appendix: music-halls functioning in 1903.]

396. BOWLEY, RUTH. "Amusements and Entertainments." In *Life and Leisure,"* pp. 41–56. The New Survey of London Life and Labour, vol. 9. L: P.S. King & Son, 1935.
[Contrasts previous forty years with 1935. Music-hall trying to compete with continuous showings of cinema.]

397. BURKE, THOMAS. *London in My Time.* L: Rich & Cowan; N.Y.: Loring & Mussey, 1934. [Pp. 131–200.]

398. ———. *Nights in Town: a London Autobiography.* L: G. Allen & Unwin, 1915. Pub. in U.S. as: *Nights in London.* N.Y.: Henry Holt, 1915.
["An Entertainment Night (Round the Halls)," pp. 25–26 (concentrates on the Oxford).]

399. ———. *The Real East End.* L: Constable, 1932.

400. CHANCELLOR, EDWIN BERESFORD. *The Pleasure Haunts of London during Four Centuries.* L: Constable; Boston: Houghton Mifflin, 1925.

401. *Chromatic Programmes of London Amusements.* 2 vols. [L: 1886–89.]

402. CLUNN, HAROLD P. and E.R. WETHERSETT. *The Face of London.* Completely new ed. L: Spring Books [n.d.].
[Many music-halls and history of their sites.]

403. COVENEY, MICHAEL. *London's Theatreland.* Hove (Sussex): Wayland, 1978.
["Music Hall," pp. 24–25.]

404. *Dens & Sinks of London Laid Open.* L: Duncombe, 1845. Repr. East Ardesley (Yorks) S.R., 1971.
[Chapter 12, "One Noise Substituted for Another—The Clamours of Strife Exchanged for Songs of Peace," pp. 81–87.]

405. DESMOND, SHAW. *London Nights of Long Ago.* L: Duckworth, 1927. Pub. in U.S. as: *London Nights in the Gay Nineties.* N.Y.: Robert M. McBridge, 1928.
[With many illustrations from contemporary sources. Chapters 23–27.]

406. DICKENS, CHARLES. *Sketches by Boz: Illustrative of Everyday Life and Every-day People.* Ills. George Cruikshank. L: Oxford University Press, 1957, etc.
[First pub. 1839. See especially "Vauxhall Gardens by Day," "Miss Evans and the Eagle," and "The Parlour Orator" for proto-music-hall amusements.]

407. DICKENS, CHARLES the Younger. *Dickens's Dictionary of London 1879. An Unconventional Handbook.* L: Charles Dickens, "All the Year Round" Office [1879].
["Music Halls," pp. 151–52, a pungent summing-up of the music-hall scene of the time. Later eds. annually to 1894.]

408. DIPROSE, JOHN. *Diprose's Book about London and London Life.* L: Diprose, 1872.
[Chapter 10; "London Amusements."]

409. DISHER, MAURICE WILLSON. *Pleasures of London.* L: Robert Hale, 1950.

410. DORÉ, GUSTAVE and BLANCHARD JERROLD. *London: A Pilgrimage.* L: Grant, 1872. Repr. N.Y.: Benjamin Blom, 1968; Dover Books, 1970.
[Chapter 20, "London at Play."]

411. DOUGLAS, JAMES. *Adventures in London.* L: Cassell, 1909.

412. EAST, JOHN M. *'Neath the Mask: the Story of the East Family.* L: Geo. Allen & Unwin, 1967.

413. ELKIN, ROBERT. *The Old Concert Rooms of London.* L: Edward Arnold, 1955.

414. FISKE, STEPHEN. *English Photographs by an American.* L: 1869.

[Pp. 130–34: music-hall management, atmosphere, topical songs, etc.]

415. FLETCHER, GEOFFREY SCOWCROFT. "The Magic of the Halls." In *London Overlooked*, pp. 9–37. L: Hutchinson, 1964.
416. FORSYTH, GERALD. *Historical Notes on London Theatres, Music Halls and Places of Entertainment made (by permission) from L.C.C. Records*. October, 1948.
[In Greater London Council, Architects Department.]
417. FRANKLYN, JULIAN. *The Cockney: A Survey of London Life and Language*. L: André Deutsch, 1953.
[Chapter 21, "Early Doors This Way," pp. 118–25; chapter 22, "Words and Music," pp. 126–39. Relies heavily on Booth and Mayhew. Very good section on language.]
418. G., The Hon. F. L. [pseud.] *The Swell's Night Guide through the Metropolis*. L: printed for private circulation by Roger Funnyman [c. 1840].
[Three Tuns, p. 5; Joy's Hotel, pp. 5–6; Coal Hole, pp. 7–8; Cyder Cellars, p. 8; The Mogul, p. 12. 2nd ed. 1846.]
419. GEORGE, W. L. *A London Mosaic*. L: W. Collins, 1921. [Pp. 21–30.]
420. HARDING, FRANK. "A Visit to the London Music Halls." N. Y. *Clipper* 29 Aug. 1885, p. 380.
421. HOLDEN, W. H. *They Startled Grandfather. Gay Ladies and Merry Mashers of Victorian Times*. L: British Technical and General Press, 1950.
[Chapter 4, "Bob Bignell and the Argyll Rooms"; chapter 5, "Some Forgotten Night Haunts."]
422. JAGGARD, WILLIAM. "Old London Theatres and Music Halls." *Notes & Queries* 171 (12 July 1941): 28.
[Responses in 183:329, 183:383, 184 (11 Jan. 1943): 57–58.]
423. JONES, A. G. E. "The London Music-hall at the Beginning of the Century." *Notes & Queries* 217 (1972): 327–28.
[Memories of R. J. Cyriax: interesting information on prices, etc.]
424. KENT, WILLIAM. *An Encyclopedia of London*. Revised by Godfrey Thompson. 3rd ed. L: Dent, 1970.
["Music Hall and Pantomime," pp. 377–80.]
425. KNIGHT, CHARLES, ed. *London*. 6 vols. L: Charles Knight, 1843. Repr. 1851.
["Music," by J. Saunders, 6:177–92 (Catch clubs).]
426. *The Life and Adventures of C. H. Simpson, Master of the Ceremonies at the Royal Gardens, Vauxhall*. L: Strange [1835].

427. *London by Night.* L: E. Rozez [n.d.].
[By the author of "Skittles," "Anonyma," "Agnes Willoughby," etc.]
428. "The London Music Halls." *Era*, 3 May 1874, p. 4.
[An important defense, in reply to libels.]
429. MACCULLOCH, JAMES RAMSAY. *London in 1850–1851. From the Geographical Dictionary of J. R. Macculloch.* L: The Traveller, 1856.
430. MACHRAY, ROBERT. *The Night Side of London.* Ills. Tom Browne. L: John MacQueen, 1902. [Chapter 7, "An East End Music-hall," pp. 112–24.]
431. MacINNES, COLIN. "Up and Down the City Road." In *The Complete Imbiber*, pp. 115–27. L: Vista Books, 1962.
432. MANDER, RAYMOND and JOE MITCHENSON. *The Lost Theatres of London.* L: Rupert Hart-Davis; N.Y.: Taplinger, 1968.
[The Alhambra, The Empire, The Gaiety, The Holborn Empire *et al.*]
433. ———. *The Theatres of London.* L: Rupert Hart-Davis, 1961. 2nd ed., 1963. Rev. ed. L: New English Library, 1975.
[The Coliseum, London Palladium, Victoria Palace, Middlesex, Metropolitan Theatre, Player's Theatre, London Pavilion.]
434. MARSHALL, ERNEST. "The London 'Halls' Pass." N.Y. *Times*, 2 Feb. 1930.
435. MASSON, DAVID. *Memories of London in the 'Forties.* Edinburgh & L: William Blackwood & Sons, 1908.
[Arranged for publication and annotated by his daughter Flora Masson. Song-and-supper rooms, pp. 148–56: *Sam Hall*, Herr von Joel, etc.]
436. MATTHEWS, WILLIAM. *Cockney Past and Present, a Short History of the Dialect of London.* L: G. Routledge & Sons, 1938. Repr. L: Routledge, Kegan Paul, 1972.
[Chapter 4, "Cockney in the Music-hall," pp. 82–104: on music-hall songs as linguistic evidence; catch phrases.]
437. "Minor Music Halls." *Music Hall*, 18 May 1889, pp. 6–7.
438. MORICE, GERALD. "A Record of Some XIX-Century London Theatres." *Notes & Queries* 185 (9 Oct. 1943): 223–24.
[Responses from Patty Ceil, 185 (6 Nov. 1943): 295; Michael Gardner, 185 (20 Nov. 1943): 326; Charles D. Williams, 185 (4 Dec. 1943): 354; and E. A. Freeman, 186 (15 Jan. 1944): 56.]
439. ———. "A Further Record of Some XIX-Century London Theatres." *Notes & Queries* 186 (26 Feb. 1944): 108–10.

[Responses from Hugh Harting (8 Apr. 1944): 175–76; and Charles D. Williams (22 Apr. 1944): 212.]

440. "The Music Hall." *Standard*, 20 Oct. 1894, pp. 73 *et seq.*
[Mentions White Lion (Metropolitan); Salmon and Compasses, Penton St.; King's Head, Knightsbridge; Grapes (Winchester); Britannia Theatre; Yorkshire Stingo; Grecian; Canterbury; Weston's; Oxford; Marylebone; Collins'; Raglan; Alhambra; Paragon; and Empire.]

441. "The Music Halls of the Metropolis." *Era*, 26 June 1879, p. 4.

442. NEVILL, RALPH. *Night Life London and Paris—Past and Present.* L: Cassell, 1926.
[Chapter 2, "Pleasure Haunts and Night Houses," pp. 24–45; chapter 3, "London in the 'Eighties—the Empire Lounge," pp. 46–61; chapter 4, "Bohemian Clubs," pp. 62–81; chapter 5, "The Music-hall and its Stars," pp. 82–109.]

443. ——— and CHARLES EDWARD JERNINGHAM. *Piccadilly to Pall Mall: Manners, Morals & Men.* L: Duckworth, 1908.
[Music-hall, pp. 111–27.]

444. NEWTON, H. CHANCE. "Music-hall London." In *Living London: its Work and Play, its Humour and its Pathos, its Sights and its Scenes*, ed. George R. Sims, 2:222–28. L: Cassell, 1892.

445. O'MALLEY, F. W. "In the 'Appy London 'Alls." *Saturday Evening Post* (Philadelphia), 17 Mar. 1923, pp. 195–215.

446. "ONE OF THE OLD BRIGADE" [pseud.]. *London in the Sixties (with a Few Digressions).* L: Everett, 1908.
[Chapter 4, "Kate Hamilton's and Leicester Square"; chapter 5, "The Night Houses of the Haymarket"; chapter 6, "Evans' and the Dials."]

447. *Rambles after Dark; or, A Peep behind the Scenes. Containing a full description of all places of entertainment, amusement, etc., open "after dark," including many of the so-called "Naughty Places" in London.* [L?: 1865?]
[Chapters on the Alhambra, poses plastiques, Judge and Jury Society, music halls, Evans', the Oxford, etc.]

448. RAY, TREVOR. "London's Lost Theatres." *Illustrated London News*, June 1972, pp. 33–38.

449. RITCHIE, J. EWING. *Days and Nights in London; or, Studies in Black and Grey.* L: Tinsley Brothers, 1880.
["Our Music-halls," pp. 39–53; "More about Music-halls," pp. 54–89.]

450. ———. *The Night Side of London.* L: William Tweedie, 1857.
["The Canterbury Hall," pp. 58–65; "The Music Hall, Hunger-

ford Market," pp. 144–51; "The Costermonger's Free-and-Easy," pp. 192–200. The 1858 ed. has "The Canterbury Hall," pp. 67–74; "The Judge and Jury Club," pp. 85–91; "Cave of Harmony," pp. 92–98; "The Eagle Tavern," pp. 218–20; "The Southwark Music Hall," pp. 220–26. Important firsthand reportage by a moralist.]

451. "Rowdies at Music Halls." *Era*, 19 Apr. 1890, p. 13.
[Edit. condemning the conditions that led to the murder of Thomas Marten.]

452. SCHLESINGER, MAX. *Saunterings In and About London.* English ed. by Otto Wenckstern. L: Nathaniel Cooke, 1853.
[Chapter 9, "The Theatrical Quarters," pp. 265–86.]

453. SHERSON, ERROLL. *London's Lost Theatres of the Nineteenth Century, with notes on the plays and players seen there.* With a foreword by Mrs. Kendal. L: John Lane, The Bodley Head. [1925].
[Basic source.]

454. "The State of the London Theatre." *Saturday Review*, 11 June 1887, pp. 841–42; 18 June 1887, pp. 866–67.
[On fire safety. I: The Alhambra, Comedy, St. James's, Drury Lane; II: Gaiety, Olympic, Strand, Globe, Opera Comique.]

455. SYMONS, ARTHUR. *The Cafe Royal and Other Essays.* L: C. W. Beaumont, 1923.

456. TIMBS, JOHN. *Curiosities of London exhibiting the most Rare and Remarkable Objects of Interest in the Metropolis with nearly Sixty Years' Personal Recollections.* A new ed., corrected and enlarged. L: Virtue [1867].
[First ed. 1855. "Music Halls," pp. 608–10 provides costs of buildings and fittings, number of persons accommodated daily as well as descriptions of Canterbury Hall, Oxford, Alhambra, Philharmonic, Weston's, St. James', St. Martin's, Evans', Strand, Highbury Barn, Grecian, Hanover Square, Surrey, and Agricultural Hall.]

457. *Views of Pleasure Gardens of London.* L: 1896.

458. WAKEMAN, EDGAR L. "With London Actors . . . Music Halls of London . . . " Chicago *News Record*, 3 June 1892.

459. WHEATLEY, HENRY B. *London Past and Present, its History, Associations and Traditions.* 3 vols. L: John Murray; N.Y.: Scribner & Welford, 1891.

460. WILLIS, FREDERICK. *101 Jubilee Road: A Book of London Yesterdays.* L: Phoenix House, 1948.
[Chapter 20, "The Halls," pp. 156–67.]

461. WROTH, WARWICK WILLIAM. *Cremorne and the Later London Gardens.* L: Elliot Stock, 1907.
462. ———. *The London Pleasure Gardens of the XVIII Century.* Reprint. Hamden, Conn. Archon, 1979.
463. YATES, EDMUND. *Recollections and Experiences.* L: Richard Bentley, 1884. Pub. in U.S. as: *Fifty Years of London Life: Memoirs of a Man of the World.* N.Y.: Harper & Brothers, 1885. [Vol. 1, chapter 4, "The Amusements of My Youth 1847–1852" (pleasure gardens, nighthouses, song-and-supper-rooms).]

INDIVIDUAL REGIONS AND HALLS

Districts

Cross-references

See also East End **393, 399, 430, 1434, 3326.** Leicester Square **123, 371, 446.**

BETHNAL GREEN

464. SNAITH, STANLEY. *Bethnal Green's Music Halls.* L: 1951. [Typescript in Central Library of Tower Hamlets, London.]

EAST END

465. ARCHER, THOMAS. *The Pauper, the Thief and the Convict: Sketches of Some of Their Homes, Haunts & Habitations.* L: Groombridge & Sons, 1865. [Ratcliffe Highway.]
466. "East End Music Halls," *Era*, 25 Oct. 1890, p. 17. [On their family appeal.]
467. GRAHAM, STEPHEN. *London Nights: Studies and Sketches of*

London at Night. L: John Lane, The Bodley Head, 1925; N.Y.: George H. Doran, 1926.

[Chapter 29, "In the Fourpenny Gallery," pp. 194–203 (an East India Dock Road hall on a Saturday night).]

468. MELLING, JOHN KENNEDY. "100 Years of East London Theatres and Music Halls," *East London Paper* 13 (1970): 41–44.

469. "The Penny Gaffs of London: Boxing Night in the East. An Artist's Sketch," N. Y. *Clipper Annual for 1874,* pp. 7–8.

470. PHILLIPS, WATTS. *The Wild Tribes of London.* L: Ward and Lock, 1855.

[Chapter 4, "The East London Music Hall," Ratcliffe Highway.]

471. ROSE, MILLICENT. *The East End of London.* L: Cresset press, 1951.

[Chapter 15, "Victorian Entertainments and Customs," pp. 215–35.]

472. SIMS, G.R. *How the Poor Live.* L: Chatto & Windus, 1883.

[Chapter 10: visit to a music hall.]

473. WILSON, ALBERT EDWARD. *East End Entertainment.* L: Barker, 1954.

[Chapter 17, "From Tea-gardens to Music-halls," pp. 208–21.]

ISLINGTON

474. MORLEY, MALCOLM. "Islington's Dramatic Past," L: Islington Public Library.

[Transcript of a speech.]

475. WILLATS, E.A. "A Cradle of the Music Hall," *Islington Gazette,* 2 May 1958.

LAMBETH

476. O'ROUKE, EVA. *Lambeth and Music Hall.* L: London Borough of Lambeth, Directorate of Amenity Services, 1977.

[Portfolio containing illustrations, reference aids, and quotations.]

LEICESTER SQUARE

477. HOLLINGSHEAD, JOHN. *The Story of Leicester Square . . . .* Ills. M. Faustin, Howell Russell, Phil May and others. Art ed. Mons. Charles Allais. L: Simpkin, Marshall, Hamilton, Kent, 1892.

["Public Amusements," pp. 40–76.]

478. LUCAS, EDWARD VERRALL. *A Wanderer in London.* L:

Methuen, 1906.
[Chapter 5, "Leicester Square and the Halls," pp. 59–74. Evaluates skills of performers with emphasis on Leno and Cinquevalli.]

TOTTENHAM COURT ROAD

479. CHANCELLOR, EDWIN BERESFORD. *London's Old Latin Quarter.* L: Jonathan Cape, 1930.

WALTHAMSTOW

480. TOMKIN, W.G.S. *Show Time in Walthamstow.* L: Walthamstow Antiquarian Society, 1967.

Individual Halls

Cross-references

See also Alhambra **122, 193, 351, 358, 359, 432, 440, 447, 454, 456, 1397, 1444, 1640, 1647, 1654, 1696, 2652, 2730, 3318, 3339, 3376, 3380.**
Bedford **3373–76.**
Canterbury **358, 440, 450, 456, 2737, 2739, 2928, 3083, 3097.**
Coal Hole **383, 418, 1434, 3098.**
Collins's **173, 207, 440, 1708.**
Cremorne Gardens **461.**
Eagle **230, 406, 450, 657–63.**
Empire **180, 185, 190, 378, 382, 432, 440, 442, 1397, 1412, 1480, 1640, 1647, 1711, 3356.**
Evans's **316, 326, 336, 355, 358, 359, 383, 406, 446–47, 456, 3109–10.**
Finsbury Park **207.**
Gaiety **226, 355, 1403.**
Gatti's in the Road **1890.**
Grecian **230, 358, 440, 456, 588–89.**

Holborn (Weston's) **432, 440, 456.**
Islington Empire **474–75.**
Islington Palace **474–75.**
London Coliseum **387–433.**
London Hippodrome **387, 2378.**
London Palladium **272, 433.**
London Pavilion, Piccadilly **123, 433, 2032, 2151.**
Lord Raglan **440, 689.**
Metropolitan **433, 2292.**
Mile End Empire (Paragon) **440.**
Oxford **184, 316, 358–59, 398, 440, 447, 1397, 2857, 3196.**
Palace **185, 193, 1750, 1914, 2102, 3402.**
Player's **433, 3472.**
Queen's **2028.**
Royal Albert **358.**
Royal Victoria **358, 1418.**
South London **1777.**
Tivoli **180, 2026, 2423.**
Trocadero **2171.**
Victoria Palace **433.**
West London **440.**
Winter Garden **123, 350, 418, 433, 2536, 3097.**

ALHAMBRA PALACE

27, Leicester Square, and 23–25, Charing Cross Road, Westminster
Also known as: Royal Alhambra Palace/Theatre; Theatre Royal,
Alhambra; Alhambra Theatre of Varieties; Alhambra Theatre.
[DH, pp. 8–11; M & M, *Lost,* 1st ed., pp. 15–50 and 2d ed. pp.
11–25; OCT, p. 21 (W. Macqueen-Pope, revised); S & W 1:42–43,
vol. 3, plans and plates.]

481. "The Alhambra." *Era,* 12 Apr. 1872, p. 12.
482. "The Alhambra." *Licensed Victualler's Gazette and Hotel
Courier,* 27 May 1898, p. 352.
483. [Alhambra] *Pall Mall Gazette,* 9 June 1870.
484. [Alhambra Additions] *Architectural Review* 12 (1895).
485. *The Alhambra Alterations and Decorations.* L: Sept. 1892.
[Broadside.]
485a. "The Alhambra as a Theatre." *London Figaro,* 29 Apr. 1871,
p. 13.

486. "The Alhambra Company, Ltd." *Era,* 8 Aug. 1885, p. 10; 11 Feb. 1888, p. 14; 9 Feb. 1889, p. 17; 5 Feb. 1890, p. 17; 9 Aug. 1890, p. 16; 14 Feb. 1891, p. 17; 15 Aug. 1891, p. 15; 6 Feb. 1892, p. 17; 6 Aug. 1892, p. 14; 10 Feb. 1894, p. 16; 17 Feb. 1894, p. 17; 6 Feb. 1897, p. 21; 5 Feb. 1898, p. 18.

487. "Alhambra 'Popular Pictures.' " *Era,* 7 Apr. 1894, p. 16.

488. [Alhambra Theatre] *Builder,* 24 Feb. 1883.

489. "The Alhambra Theatre Company." *Era,* 18 Feb. 1882.

490. [Alhambra Theatre Reconstructed] *Builder,* 6 June 1892.

491. "The Canteen at the Alhambra." *The Ferret: An Inquisitive, Quizzical, Satirical and Theatrical Censor of the Age,* 29 Jan. 1870, p. 2.

492. "CARADOS" [pseud. of H. Chance Newton]. "Au Revoir to the Alhambra." *Referee,* 16 Aug. 1912.

493. "Decorations at the Alhambra." *Era,* 16 June 1894, p. 16.

494. "Destruction of a Music Hall by Fire." *Era,* 3 June 1882, p. 18.

495. "Destruction of the Alhambra Theatre." N.Y. *Clipper,* 16 Dec. 1882.

496. DISHER, MAURICE WILLSON and SIR MICHAEL W. S. BRUCE. *The Personality of the Alhambra; and, The History of the Odeon.* Birmingham: Odeon Theatres, 1937.

497. ELLIS, S. M. "Passing of the Alhambra. Early Memories." *Observer,* 13 Aug. 1933.

498. "The History of the Alhambra." *Era,* 11 July 1908, p. 24; 5 Oct. 1912, p. 19.

499. *The London Lounger's Album. A Series of Illustrations Depicting Life As It Is.* L: Rozez [c. 1870]. [No. 1, The Pretty Girls of London; no. 2, Alhambra Palace (1st series), no. 3, Alhambra Palace (2d series).]

500. "Mr. Alfred Maul and the Alhambra." *Daily Chronicle,* 30 Mar. 1912.

501. "Mr. John Maltby's Farewell." *Era,* 6 May 1897, p. 18. [Mgr.]

502. "Mr. William Bailey." *Era,* 3 Oct. 1891, p. 16. [Mgr.]

503. "The New Alhambra Theatre." *Era,* 10 Nov. 1883, p. 6.

504. "Our Representative Man." *Punch,* 28 Sept. 1878, p. 141. [*Genevieve de Brabant* at the Alhambra.]

505. "Our Representative Man." *Punch,* 18 Oct. 1879, pp. 171–72. [Lecocq's *La Petite Mademoiselle* at the Alhambra.]

506. "Our Representative Man." *Punch,* 10 Jan. 1880, p. 3. [A visit to the Alhambra.]

507. "Our Representative Man." *Punch,* 15 May 1880.

508. "The Police and the Alhambra." *Era,* 8 Oct. 1892, p. 16.

509. SIMS, GEORGE R. "The Early Days of the Alhambra." *Referee,* 23 July 1917, p. 2.

510. "Tales of the Alhambra." *Punch,* 29 Apr. 1882, pp. 202–3. [*Babil and Bijou.*]

511. "Theatres vs Music Halls." *Era,* 17 Jan. 1875. [Theatre Royal v. Alhambra.]

512. WALBROOK, H.M. "Passing of the Alhambra." *Observer,* 23 July 1933. Repr. in Boston *Transcript,* 21 Oct. 1933.

513. [WHITE, W.] *The Illustrated Handbook of the Royal Alhambra Palace Leicester Square.* [L] Nicholls Brothers [1869].

ARCADIA, ISLINGTON

514. "Arcadia, Islington." *Era,* 13 Sept. 1890, p. 15.

BALHAM EMPIRE

75, High Road, Balham
Also known as: Balham Music Hall. [DH, pp. 17–18.]

515. "Balham Varieties." *Era,* 29 Dec. 1900, p. 21.

516. "New Balham Varieties." *Era,* 28 July 1900, p. 17.

BATTERSEA PALACE

32, York Road, Battersea
Also known as: Royal Standard Music Hall; Washington Music Hall; Standard (Washington) Music Hall; Battersea Palace of Varieties; New Battersea Empire; Palace Theatre of Varieties. [DH, pp. 19–20.]

517. "Fraud on a Music Hall Proprietor." *Era,* 12 May 1888, p. 16.

518. GREEN, RICHARD JUDD, and JOHN DAMER. *Clapham Junction and Its People: A Peep Show.* L: 1889. [Pp. 53–57.]

519. "A New Music Hall." *Era,* 3 July 1886, p. 10; 13 Nov. 1886, p. 10.

520. "Sale of the Washington." *Era,* 11 Dec. 1897, p. 20.

521. "Tony Pastor at the Washington." *Era,* 19 July 1890, p. 15.

BEDFORD THEATRE

93–95 Camden High Street
Also known as: Bedford Arms Tavern and Tea Garden; Bedford Music Hall; New Bedford Palace of Varieties; New Bedford Theatre. [DH, pp. 21–22.]

522. "Action against a Music Hall Proprietor." *Era,* 1 Aug. 1875, p. 4.

523. "The Bedford Music Hall." *Era,* 3 Oct. 1875, p. 4.

524. "The Bedford Music Hall Band." *Era,* 24 Jan. 1875, p. 7; 31 Jan. 1875, p. 9.

525. [Bedford Theatre Rebuilt] *Builder,* 11 Feb. 1899.

526. "Charge against a Music Hall Waiter." *Era,* 15 Mar. 1884, p. 5.

527. COLLIER, JOHN W. "A Visit to the 'Bedford.'" *Theatre Newsletter,* (13 Dec. 1947).

528. "Disturbance at a Music Hall." *Era,* 24 Mar. 1878, p. 3.

529. FLETCHER, GEOFFREY. "Cupid in the Gallery." *Camden Journal,* Dec. 1970–Jan. 1971, pp. 3–7.

530. "Narrow Escape of the Bedford Music Hall." *Era,* 17 Nov. 1872, p. 4.

531. "The New Bedford." *Era,* 4 Feb. 1899, p. 23; 11 Feb. 1899, p. 21.

BOW PALACE

156–58, Bow Road, Bow

Also known as: Three Cups Public House and Music Hall; Bow Music Hall, Marlow's Music Hall, Eastern Empire; Palace Theatre; Bow; Tivoli Theatre Bow. [DH, pp 28–29.]

532. "East London Palace." *Era,* 26 Nov. 1910, p. 29.

533. "Eastern Empire Improvements." *Era,* 2 Feb. 1895, p. 16.

534. "The Eastern Empire Music Hall." *Music Hall,* 17 May 1895, p. 14.

535. "Two Music Halls Sold." *Era,* 17 Apr. 1897, p. 16.

BOWER THEATRE

Stangate Street, Lambeth

Also known as: Bower Music Hall; Bower Saloon; Bower Operetta House; Stangate Music Hall/Theatre. [DH, pp. 29–30.]

536. [History of Bower Theatre] *Illustrated Sporting and Dramatic News,* 20 Oct. 1877.

CAMBERWELL PALACE

23–31, Denmark Hill, Camberwell

Also Known as: Oriental Palace of Varieties. [DH, pp. 37–38.]

537. "Camberwell Palace of Varieties." *Era,* 8 July 1899, p. 20; 18 Nov. 1899, p. 20; 25 Nov. 1899, p. 18; 2 Dec. 1899, p. 9.

538. DYOS, HAROLD JAMES. *Victorian Suburb: A Study of the Growth of Camberwell.* Leicester: University Press, 1973. [Pp. 153–54.]

539. "Oriental Palace of Varieties." *Era,* 4 Dec. 1897, p. 20.

Canterbury Music Hall

143, Westminster Bridge Road, Lambeth

Also known as: Canterbury Arms Public House; Canterbury Hall; Royal Canterbury Theatre of Varieties. [DH, pp. 40–41; OCT (W. Macqueen-Pope), p. 155.]

540. "Alarm of fire at the Canterbury." *Era,* 5 Nov. 1887, p. 10.

541. "Alterations at the Canterbury." *Era,* 26 July 1890, p. 15.

542. "Assault at a Music Hall." *Era,* 2 July 1892, p. 14.

543. "The Canterbury." *Music Hall and Theatre,* 16 Nov. 1889, pp. 9–10.

544. "Canterbury and Paragon." *Era,* 2 Mar. 1889, p. 17; 13 Sept. 1890, p. 14; 12 Sept. 1891, p. 17; 10 Sept. 1892, p. 14; 17 Sept. 1892, p. 16; 8 Sept. 1894, p. 16; 15 Sept. 1894, p. 17; 14 Sept. 1895, p. 16; 5 Sept. 1896, p. 18; 19 Sept. 1896, p. 18; 25 Sept. 1897, p.19.

545. "The Canterbury and Winchester Licences." *Era,* 1 Apr. 1882, p. 4.

546. "The Canterbury Anniversary." *Era,* 1 Dec. 1900, p. 20.

547. "The Canterbury Gasman." *Era,* 2 July 1887, p. 17.

548. [The Canterbury Hall] *Sketch,* 3 May 1879.

549. "The Canterbury—Old and New." *Era,* 8 June 1912.

550. *The Canterbury Theatre of Varieties and Its Associations.* With *Some Account of Lambeth and Its Vicinity.* [Half title reads: *The Canterbury Album.*] [L: 1876?]
[Thirteen lithographed plates of theatres and artistes, signed portrait frontispiece of Edwin Villiers, engraving of Canterbury Cathedral. Title and half title printed in red, gold and black. Cover embossed green cloth, stamped *Canterbury Theatre of Varieties.* "This luxurious production was presumably published shortly after the opening of the theatre in 1876 as part of the campaign to establish the ultra-respectability of the establishment," George Speaight.]

550a. *Canterbury Theatre of Varieties. Souvenir 1200 – 1907. (55th Anniversary Commemoration of the Canterbury, 5 December 1907.)* L: Canterbury Theatre, 1907.

551. [Description of the Canterbury] *Builder,* 6 Nov. 1858, p. 746.

552. "Disgraceful Sensation at a Music Hall." *Era,* 4 July 1885, p. 10.

553. "Disturbance at the Canterbury Hall." *Era,* 31 Mar. 1878, p. 4.

554. EARL, JOHN and JOHN STANTON. *The Canterbury Hall.* Cambridge: Chadwyck-Healey, 1980.

[To accompany slides. "Theatre in Focus, a Pictorial History of World Theatre."]

555. "Heroes at the Canterbury." *Era,* 5 Nov. 1898, p. 18.
556. "A Music Hall Case." *Era,* 24 Sept. 1887, p. 10.
557. "A Music Hall in Danger." *Era,* 24 Oct. 1885, p. 10.
558. "Our Representative Man." *Punch,* 26 Jan. 1878, pp. 30, 33. [Panorama "Plevna."]
559. "A Pleasant Scene at the Canterbury." *Era,* 8 Dec. 1883, p. 4.
560. RICHARDSON, Sir BENJAMIN WARD. *Thomas Sopwith . . . with excerpts from his diary.* L: Longmans, 1891. [Pp. 273-74.]
561. "Robbery from the Canterbury." *Era,* 11 Apr. 1891, p. 17.
562. "What is a Stage Play?" *Era,* 10 Oct. 1884, p. 10.

COAL HOLE PUBLIC HOUSE
Fountain Court, Strand

[DH, p. 48.]
563. "The Last of 'The Coal Hole.'" *Era,* 2 Apr. 1887, p. 10.

COLLINS' MUSIC HALL
10–11, Islington Green, Islington

Also known as: Lansdowne Arms Public House; Lansdowne Music Hall; Collins' Theatre of Varieties; Islington Hippodrome. [DH, pp. 49-50; TN, 17:38.]

564. "A Chat with Herbert Sprake." *Era,* 1 Sept. 1894, p. 14.
565. "Collins' Company in the Workhouse." *Era,* 23 Jan. 1886, p. 10.
566. [Collins' Music Hall Rebuilt] *Builder.* 15 Jan. 1898, p. 66.
567. CURTIS, C.V. "Going Down to Collins's." *Everybody's,* 4 Dec. 1948.
568. "Disturbance at a Music Hall." *Era,* 10 Sept. 1876, p. 4.
569. "Fire Benefit at Collins's." *Era,* 14 Apr. 1900, p. 17.
570. MEYER, L. "The Chapel on the Green: Collins' Music Hall." (Typescript read at the Central Library, 20 Nov. 1948. Islington Public Library.)
571. "Mr. H. Sprake's Benefit." *Era,* 18 Jan. 1896, p. 16.
572. "The New 'Collins's'." *Era,* 7 Nov. 1885, p. 10.
573. NICHOLSON, HERBERT. "A Night at Collins'." *Theatre Today,* winter 1947.
574. "Paupers and Professionals." *Era,* 10 Jan. 1891, p. 16.
575. "Presentation to Mrs. H. Sprake." *Era,* 16 Oct. 1897, p. 20.

CREMORNE GARDENS
Chelsea

[DH, p. 57.]

576. "Cremorne and the Middlesex Magistrates." *Era,* 22 Oct. 1871, p. 9.

577. "Cremorne Gardens." *Era,* 24 Mar. 1872, p. 8; 5 May 1872, p. 12.

578. "Cremorne Gardens and the Licensed Victualler's Asylum." *Era,* 18 Aug. 1872, p. 12.

DALSTON THEATRE
12, Dalston Lane, Hackney

Also known as: Dalston Circus; North London Colosseum Theatre; London Colosseum and National Amphitheatre; Dalston Theatre of Varieties. [DH, p. 62.]

579. [Theatre of Varieties, Dalston] *Builder,,* 5 June 1897, p. 516; 12 Feb. 1898.

DEACON'S MUSIC HALL
Sir Hugh Myddelton Public House, Myddelton Place, Finsbury

[DH, p. 64.]

580. [Capt. H. E. Davis demonstrates Fire Brigade] *Illustrated Sporting and Dramatic News,* 7 Mar. 1891.

581. "Deacon's vs. Sadler's Wells." *Era,* 18 June 1887, p. 17.

582. "A Music Hall Action." *Era,* 17 Jan. 1891, p. 16.

583. "Music Hall Litigation." *Era,* 11 Feb. 1888, p. 15.

584. [Obituary of H.E. Davis, mgr at Deacon's closing in 1891] *Era,* 5 July 1933.

585. [Obituary of H.E. Davis, mgr at Deacon's closing in 1891] *Stage,* 29 June 1933.

586. "Soiree at Deacon's." *Era,* 14 Sept. 1889, p. 15.

587. WARD, H.B. "A Memory of the 'Eighties.'" *Finsbury Star,* May 1925, p. 4.

EAGLE TAVERN MUSIC HALL
Shepherdess Walk, City Road

Also known as: Royal Eagle Music Hall. [DH, p. 74.]

588. ROUSE, T. "Chapters of Old Shoreditch, No. VII." *Shoreditch Observer,* 22 Jan. 1898.

589. "Royal Eagle." *Entr'acte,* 13 Dec. 1884.

EMPIRE THEATRE
5-6 Leicester Square, Westminster

[DH, pp. 79-81; M & M *Lost*, 1st ed., pp. 58-79, 2d ed. pp. 30-39; OCT (W. Macqueen-Pope), p. 275; S & W, 2:39-40.]

590. "The Case of the Empire." *Saturday Review* 88 (10 Nov. 1894):501-02.
[On the Promenade.]

591. CHURCHILL, Sir WINSTON. *My Early Life: A Roving Commission.* L: MacMillan, 1944.
[1st ed. 1930. Pp. 65-73: attack on the screens at the Empire.]

592. "Death of Mr Harry Hitchins." *Era*, 11 Feb. 1911, p. 25; 18 Feb. 1911, p. 25. [Mgr.]

593. [Empire Alterations] *Builder*, 1 Apr. 1905, p. 350.

594. "The Empire Is Piece, or Rather, Ballet." *Punch*, 16 Aug. 1890, p. 77.

595. "The Empire Licence." *Era,* 27 Oct. 1894, p. 17.

596. "The Empire Palace." *Era*, 24 Dec. 1887, p. 16.

597. "The Empire Palace." *Era*, 4 March 1899, p. 20.

598. "The Empire Palace Ltd." *Era,* 27 Feb. 1892, p. 17; 30 Mar. 1895, p. l6.

599. "Empire Palace Meeting." *Era*, 26 Feb. 1898, p. 19.

600. "The End of the Empire." *Times*, 21 Jan. 1927.

601. "For the Sake of the Empire." *Punch*, 25 Jan. 1890, p. 41.
[Programme review.]

602. "The History of the Empire." *Era*, 27 Oct. 1894, p. 17; 11 Feb. 1911, p. 26.

603. "Last Days of the Empire: Dan Leno to Ben Hur." *Times*, 27 May 1961.

604. "Living Pictures at the Empire." *Era*, 10 Feb. 1894, p. 16; 2 June 1894, p. 17; 16 June 1894, p. 16.

605. MARSH, JANET. "Night at the Empire." *Financial Times*, 27 July 1974, p. 12.

606. "Mr Arthur Aldin." *Era*, 4 Mar. 1911, p. 25. [Mgr.]

607. "Music Hall Employee's Agitation." *Era*, 20 Oct. 1894, p. 17.

608. [Opposition to the Empire Licence] *Daily Telegraph*, 11 Oct. 1894; 15 Oct. 1894; 18 Oct. 1894; 27 Oct. 1894.

609. "Patriotism at the Empire." *Era*, 4 Mar. 1899, p. 20.

610. "Piping Times for the Empire." *Punch*, 22 Mar. 1890, p. 137.
[Boucicault's *The Relief of Lucknow*.]

611. [Re-opening of the Empire] *Pall Mall Gazette*, 5 Nov. 1894.

612. [Re-opening of the Empire] *Star*, 27 Oct. 1894.

613. ROSS, BERT. "The Empire, Leicester Square." *Call Boy*, 15, no. 4 (winter 1978): 8–9; 16, no. 1. (spring 1979): 8–9; no. 2 (summer 1979): 8–9; no. 4 (autumn 1979): 8–9.

614. "The Shah at the Empire." *Era*, 24 Dec. 1887, p. 16.

615. STREET, G. S. "Court and Empire." *Punch*, 9 Oct. 1907, pp. 268–69.
    [Evening's bill.]

616. ———. "From Court and Empire." *Punch*, 15 May 1907, p. 350.
    [Evening's bill.]

617. SUMMERFIELD, PENNY. "The Effingham Arms and the Empire: Working Class Culture and the Evolution of the Music Hall." Unpublished thesis abstracted in *Bulletin of the Society for the Study of Labour History* 32 (spring 1976): 5–18.

EMPRESS THEATRE OF VARIETIES

Carlton Grove (Brighton Terrace), Brixton
Also known as: Empress Music-Hall   [DH, p. 81.]

618. *An Account of the 'Empress' Theatre of Varieties, Brixton.* Ills. [L: Wilkes & Co., printers] 26 Dec. 1898.

619. "A Chat with Charles Dundee Slatler." *Era*, 10 Nov. 1900, p. 21.
    [Mgr.]

620. [Empress Music Hall] *Builder*, 8 May 1897, p. 426; 23 Dec. 1898, p. 823.

621. "The Empress Theatre of Varieties, Brixton." *Era*, 17 Dec. 1898, p. 22; 24 Dec. 1898, p. 18; 31 Dec. 1898, p. 22.

622. "STAGE REPORTER." "Redevelopment Threat to historic Empress, Brixton." *Stage*, 9 Nov. 1978, p. 3.

EVANS' MUSIC-AND-SUPPER ROOMS

43, King Street, Covent Garden
Also known as: Grand Hotel; Falstaff Club.   [DH, p. 82.]

622a. [Description of Evans' singing room] *Builder*, 22 Dec. 1855, pp. 622–23.

623. EMERY, RONGY. "Early Variety: Evans Supper Rooms." *Call Boy* 14, no. 2 (summer 1977): 6–7.

624. "Evans's Hotel." *Art Journal*, (Apr. 1856) p. 127.

625. "Evans' Music and Supper Rooms." *Era*, 8 June 1873, p. 14.

626. "Evans' Music Hall." *Era*, 25 Jan. 1880, p. 3.

627. "Evans Supper Rooms." *Era*, 14 Dec. 1879, p. 4.
    [Charged with harboring prostitutes.]

627a. "An Hour at Evans's." *London Figaro*, 15 Apr. 1871, p. 13.

628. "Our Captious Critic." *Illustrated Sporting and Dramatic News*,

27 Nov. 1875.

629. "The Riot at Evans's." *Era*, 11 Apr. 1875, p. 4.

630. SALA, GEORGE AUGUSTUS. *Twice Round the Clock, or The Hours of the Day and Night in London.* With an introduction by Philip Collins. Leicester: Leicester University Press, 1971. [First pub. L: Houlston & Wright, 1858-59. "One A.M.—Evans's Supper-Rooms, and a Fire," pp. 330-56.]

631. [TOWNSEND, GEORGE HENRY] *Evans' Music and Supper Rooms, Covent Garden. Odds and Ends about Covent Garden and its Vicinity, the Ancient Drama, the Early English Divinity and Controversial Plays, &c.; compiled from Various Sources. . . Also, a Selection of Madrigals, Glees, Songs, Choruses, &c., sung every Evening in the above Room.* [L: privately printed for John Green, 1866?]

Finsbury Park Empire

St. Thomas's Road and Prah Road, Finsbury Park
[DH, p. 84; TN, 15:78, 16.]

632. "Finsbury Park Empire." *Era*, 3 Sept. 1910, p. 25; 10 Sept. 1910, p. 25.

633. [Finsbury Park Empire] *Islington Gazette,* 9 May 1958.

634. "New Variety Theatres." *Builder*, 24 Sept. 1910, p. 351.

635. ROSS, BERT. "The Finsbury Park Empire Story." *North London Press*, 13 May 1960.

Foresters Music Hall

93-95 Cambridge Road, Bethnal Green
Also known as: Artichoke Public House; Royal Foresters Music Hall; New Lyric Music Hall, New Lyric Theatre. [DH, pp. 85-86.]

636. "Action against a Music Hall Proprietor." *Era*, 19 May 1872, p. 13.

637. "Alterations at the Foresters." *Era*, 1 Oct. 1892, p. 16.

638. "The Foresters." *Era*, 23 June 1888, p. 16; 31 May 1890, p. 15.

639. RULE, LEONARD G. "'Foresters' Lives Again . . . ." *The Circle,* n.s. 1 (Nov. 1949).

Gaiety Theatre

354, Strand, Westminster
Also known as: Strand Musick Hall. [DH, pp. 88-89; M & M, Lost, pp. 80-119.]

640. [Building of the Strand] *Builder,* 25 Oct. 1862, p. 768; 22 Oct. 1864, pp. 771-72.

641. CURL, JAMES STEVENS. *Victorian Architecture*. Newton
 Abbot: David & Charles, 1973.
 [Pp. 47–55; Bassett Keeling.]
642. [Description of the Gaiety] *Building News,* 21 Oct. 1864; 4 Nov.
 1864.
643. "Prohibited Hours at a Music Hall." *Era*, 5 Dec. 1885, p. 10.
644. *The Strand Musick Hall: Historie of ye Bylding*. L: Strand
 Musick Hall, 1879.

GATTI'S PALACE OF VARIETIES

214–16, Westminster Bridge Road, Lambeth
Also known as: Gatti-in-the-Road; Gatti's-over-the-Water; Gatti's
Music Hall.   [DH, pp. 92–93; OCT, p. 365.]
645. "Carlo Gatti" [Obit.] *Era*, 15 Sept. 1878, p. 4.
646. [Gatti's Music Hall Rebuilt] *Builder*, 24 Mar. 1883, pp. 394–95.]
647. "Gatti's (Road)." *Era,* 2 Aug. 1902.
 [Description of bill.]
648. "Gatti's, Westminster." *Era*, 5 June 1886, p. 10.

GRAND THEATRE

21, St John's Hill, Clapham Junction
Also known as: New Grand Theatre of Varieties; Grand Theatre of
Varieties. [DH, pp. 98–99.]
649. "A Chat with J. Sparrow." *Era*, 1 May 1897, p. 19. [Mgr.]
650. [Description of the Grand] *Builder*, 1 Dec. 1900, pp. 495–96.
651. "Mr J. Sparrow's Benefit." *Era*, 27 Oct. 1900, p. 19.
652. "The New Grand, Clapham." *Era*, 19 May 1900, p. 19; 1 Dec.
 1900, p. 21.
653. "New Grand Varieties, Clapham." *Era*, 17 Mar. 1900, p. 19.

GRANVILLE THEATRE OF VARIETIES

Fulham Broadway, Walham Green
[DH, p. 100.]
654. [Granville Theatre] *Building News,* 9 Sept. 1898, pp. 375–76.
655. "Granville Theatre of Varieties." *Era*, 5 Mar. 1898, p. 18; 3 Sept.
 1898, p. 18; 24 Sept. 1898, p. 18.
656. "The Granville, Walham Green." *Era*, 28 July 1900, p. 17.

GRECIAN THEATRE

City Road, Shoreditch
Also known as: Shepherd and Shepherdess Gardens; Grecian
Saloon; Coronation Pleasure Ground. [DH, pp. 100–102.]

657. BLIGH, N. M. "Lost London Theatres No. 15: The Story of the Eagle or Grecian." *Theatre World*, Jan.-Feb., 1961.
658. "Echoes of the Past No. 53: End of the Grecian." *Hackney Gazette*, 26 Jan. 1951.
659. "The Last of the Grecian." *Era*, 30 Sept. 1899, p. 11.
660. "The New Grecian." *Touchstone*, 3 Nov. 1877.
661. "Panic at the New Grecian Theatre." *Daily Telegraph*, 28 Dec. 1881.
662. "Reminiscences of 'The Grecian.'" *Era*, 19 Aug. 1882, p. 5.
663. "The Stage in the Suburbs No. 3." *Observer*, 29 Sept. 1872.

GREENWICH HIPPODROME

Stockwell Street and Nevada Street, Greenwich

Also known as: Rose and Crown Public House; Crowder's Music Hall; Rose and Crown Palace of Varieties; Greenwich Palace of Varieties; Parthenon Palace of Varieties. [DH, 103; M & M, 3rd ed., pp. 246-48.]

664. "Crowder's Music Hall." *Era*, 26 May 1872, p. 13.
665. "Music Hall and the Stage Play." *Era*, 28 Jan. 1872, p. 13. [C. S. Crowder charged with staging plays.]
666. "Opening of the New Parthenon." *Era*, 17 Dec. 1898, p. 20.
667. "Opening of the Parthenon." *Era*, 2 Sept. 1885, p. 10.
668. "Parthenon, Greenwich." *Era*, 20 Apr. 1889, p. 15.

GUN PUBLIC HOUSE

97, New Road, Woolwich

[DH, pp. 105-06.]

669. "Alleged Assault on Music Hall Chairman." *Era*, 20 June 1885, p. 10.

HAMMERSMITH PALACE OF VARIETIES

82, King Street, Hammersmith

Also known as: Town Hall, Hammersmith; Town Hall and Temple of Varieties. [DH, pp. 107-8.]

670. "Hammersmith Varieties." *Era*, 16 Mar. 1889, p. 17.
671. [Variety Theatre, Hammersmith] *Builder*, 26 Nov. 1898, pp. 490-91.

HOLBORN EMPIRE

242-45, High Holborn, Holborn

Also known as: Seven Tankards and Punch Bowl Public House; National Hall; Weston's Music Hall; Royal Music Hall; Royal

Holborn Empire; Royal Holborn Theatre of Varieties. [DH, pp. 113–14; M & M, *Lost*, 1st ed., pp. 168–85; OCT (W. Macqueen-Pope, revised), p. 447.]

672. "Disorder at a Music Hall." *Era,* 3 Jan. 1885, p. 10.

673. "Disturbance at the Royal Music Hall." *Era,* 17 Oct. 1875., p. 4.

674. "The Electric Light at 'The Royal.'" *Era,* 8 July 1882, p. 4.

675. [Empire, Holborn] *Builder,* 3 Feb. 1896.

676. "'Here Stands a Post!'" *Era,* 5 May 1878, p.4. (Suit against Royal Music Hall.]

677. MAYES, RONALD. "The Romance of London Theatres. No. 92. The New Amphitheatre, Holborn." *Prince of Wales Theatre Programme,* 2 May 1930.

678. "Music Hall Litigation." *Era,* 13 June 1885, p. 10.

679. [Rebuilding] *Era,* 27 Jan. 1906.

680. [Reconstruction] *Builder,* 9 Aug. 1905, p. 213.

681. "The Right to Hiss." *Era,* 22 Aug. 1880, p. 4.

682. "The Royal Music Hall." *Daily Telegraph,* 10 Sept. 1887.

683. "The 'Royal' Music Hall." *Era,* 1 Oct. 1881, p. 4; 3 Sept. 1887, p. 10.

684. "Royal Music Hall Opens." *Era,* 17 Sept. 1887.

685. "'The Scamp' at the Royal Music Hall." *Era,* 16 Aug. 1874, p. 4.

686. [Theatre Opens] *Era,* 17 Nov. 1857.

687. "Weston's Music Hall." *Era,* 23 Nov. 1889, p. 17; 28 Feb. 1891, p. 16.

688. "Weston's Music Hall Company." *Era,* 25 Feb. 1888, p. 15; 15 Dec. 1888, p. 17; 29 Dec. 1888, p. 17; 24 Aug. 1889, p. 15; 31 Aug. 1889, p. 15; 7 Sept. 1889, p. 15.

689. YATES, EDMUND. "Soothing the Savage Breast." *Train,* Jan. 1858, pp. 38–43. [Easton's and Lord Somerset used as pseuds. for Weston's and the Lord Raglan.]

HOLLOWAY EMPIRE
564, Holloway Road, Islington

Also known as: Empire Theatre of Varieties. [DH, p. 116.]

690. [Holloway Empire] *Builder,* 6 Dec. 1899, p. 565.

691. [Holloway Empire] *Islington Gazette,* 5 May 1958.

692. "New Empire, Holloway." *Era,* 2 Dec. 1899, p. 21; 9 Dec. 1899, p. 19.

693. [Opening of Empire] *Building News,* 8 Dec. 1899, p. 762.

694. [Programme of Holloway Empire] *Grand Matinee. Thursday,*

Oct. 22nd, 1903.
[With brief description of the theatre.]

HOPE MUSIC HALL

Hope Public House, 63 Banner Street, Finsbury

[DH, p. 117.]

695. "A Music Hall Proprietor Fined." *Era,* 30 July 1887, p. 10.

ISLINGTON EMPIRE

40, Islington High Street, Islington

Also known as: Philharmonic Hall; Grand Theatre; Empire; Islington; Islington Palace. [DH, p. 121; S & W, 1:41 (plans and sections).]

696. "Burning of the Grand." *Graphic,* 7 Jan. 1888.

697. "Destruction of the Grand Theatre at Islington." *Daily Telegraph,* 29, 30, and 31 Dec. 1887.

ISLINGTON PALACE

Royal Agricultural Hall; Upper Street, Islington

Also known as: Berners Hall; New Concert Hall; Mohawkes Hall; Empire Music Hall. [DH, p. 123.]

698. FEEST, LEONARD, J. "A Playgoer Looks Back." *Islington Gazette,* 1 Dec. 1947.
[On Mohawk Minstrels.]

699. LOSACK, CLAUDE. "History of Berners Hall, Islington, North London, 1869–1969." *Call Boy,* 6 (1969): 10–12.

700. "Our Representative Man: A Visit to the Horse Show at the Agricultural Hall . . . ." *Punch,* 16 June 1877, p. 273.
[Pantomime.]

KILBURN EMPIRE

9–11, The Parade, Kilburn High Road, Kilburn, Hampstead

Also known as: New Kilburn Empire; Kilburn Vaudeville Theatre. [DH, p. 126.]

701. "Empire of Varieties, Kilburn." *Era,* 18 Sept. 1900, p. 18.

702. [Palace of Varieties, Kilburn.] *Builder,* 11 Feb. 1899.

LEICESTER SQUARE THEATRE OF VARIETIES

39–41, Leicester Square, Westminster

[DH, p. 136; M & M, 2d ed. pp. 271–72.]

703. [Leicester Square Theatre] *Builder,* 8 Oct. 1892, p. 287; 10 Dec. 1930, pp. 1040, 1042–44.

LEWISHAM HIPPODROME
135 and 139, Rushey Green, Catford

[DH, pp. 136–37.]
704. "Lewisham Hippodrome Opened." *Era,* 18 Feb. 1911, p. 26.

LONDON COLISEUM
St. Martin's Lane, Westminster

Also known as: Coliseum Theatre. [DH, pp. 138–39; M & M, 2d ed. pp. 41–46, 3rd ed. pp. 38–44; OCT (W. Macqueen-Pope, revised), p. 188.]

705. BARKER, FELIX. *The House that Stoll Built: The Story of the Coliseum Theatre.* L: Muller, 1957.

706. "Coliseums Old and New." *Notes & Queries,* 10th ser. 2:485–529; 2 (21 Jan. 1905): 51–54; (11 Mar. 1905): 189–90.

707. "Fifty Years at the Coliseum." *Times,* 25 Dec. 1954.

708. GLASSTONE, VICTOR. *The London Coliseum.* L: Chadwyck-Healey, 1979.
[Letterpress to accompany slide set "Theatre in Focus: A Pictorial History of World Theatre."]

709. GRAVES, C.L. and E.V. LUCAS. "New Departure at the Halls." *Punch,* 22 Feb. 1905, p. 135. [The four daily performances at the Coliseum.]

710. GREIN, J.T. "Behind the Scenes at the Coliseum." In *The New World of the Theatre 1923–1924.* L: Martin Hopkinson, 1924. [Pp. 144–48. First pub. *Illustrated London News,* 27 Oct. 1923.]

711. "Half a Century of the London Coliseum." *Sphere,* 25 Dec. 1954.

712. "The London Coliseum." *Christian Science Monitor* (Boston), 16 Dec. 1924.
[With caricature of Harry Tate in "Motoring."]

713. "The London Coliseum." *Stage,* 8 Dec. 1904.

714. "The London Coliseum. Opening Performance." *Stage,* 29 Dec. 1904.

715. MOODY, FREDERICK. "London in Pen and Ink No. 74: The Coliseum." *What's On in London,* 18 June 1971, p. 4.

716. STANLEY, HARRY. *The Greatest Music Hall in the World.* L: Hutchinson, forthcoming.

LONDON HIPPODROME

Cranbourne Street, Westminster

Also known as: Hippodrome Theatre. [DH, pp. 139–40; M & M, 2d ed. pp. 269–70; 3rd ed. pp. 119–22; OCT (W. Macqueen-Pope, revised), p. 444.]

717. BENNETT, WILLIAM A. *London Hippodrome. 25th Birthday Souvenir.* L: London Hippodrome, 1924.

718. "The L.C.C. and the Hippodrome." *Era,* 24 Mar. 1900, p. 17. [Edit.]

719. "The London Hippodrome." *Era,* 30 Dec. 1899, p. 9; 17 Feb. 1900, p. 18.

720. MORTON, TURNER. "Running a Great Variety Show." *Pearson's Magazine,* Sept. 1904, pp. 254–63.

721. "Robbery at the Hippodrome." *Era,* 7 Sept. 1911, p. 23.

LONDON PALLADIUM

Argyll Street, Westminster

Also known as: Corinthian Bazaar; Hengler's Grand Cirque; National Skating Palace; Palladium Theatre. [DH, pp. 140–41; M & M, 2d ed. pp. 126–29; OCT, p. 586.]

722. BEVAN, IAN. *Top of the Bill: The Story of the London Palladium.* L: Frederick Muller, 1952.

723. COVENEY, MICHAEL. "More Palladium Nights." *Plays and Players* 22 (Nov. 1974): 19.

724. [Description] *Building News,* 23 Dec. 1910, pp. 896–97.

725. GREEN, BENNY. "Survival of a Legend." *What's On in London,* 14 July 1978, p. 41.

726. "Hengler's Circus in Auction Market." *Builder,* 21 July 1883, p. 95.

727. *[London Palladium] Jubilee, 1899 – 1949.* L: Moss' Empires Ltd., 1949.

728. *London's Theatres. 2—The Palladium.* L: House of Whitbread, 1937.

729. "The New Palladium." *Era,* 14 Dec. 1910, p. 23.

730. "The Palladium." *Era,* 3 Dec. 1910, p. 27.

731. "The Palladium Penalized." *Era,* 18 Mar. 1911, p. 27.

732. PILTON, PATRICK. *Every Night at the London Palladium.* L: Hobson Books, 1976.
[Concentrates on the postwar period.]

733. RUTHERFORD, MAURICE. "Every Night at the Palladium."

Spectator 213 (16 Oct. 1964): 505.

[Review of the show *Startime at the Palladium,* inquiring into the theatre's 'secret.']

734. TREWIN, J. C. "Business as Usual." *Illustrated London News* 238 (13 May 1961): 812.

LONDON PAVILION

3 and 4, Tichborne Street, Westminster

[DH, p. 141.]

735. "Action by Music Hall Singer." *Era,* 8 Dec. 1878, p. 4.

736. "Assault at a Music Hall." *Era,* 23 July 1881, p. 4.

737. "Causing a Disturbance in a Music Hall." *Era,* 19 May 1878, p. 4.

738. "Illegal Lottery at a Music Hall." *Era,* 2 Feb. 1879, p. 4.

739. "The London Pavilion Music Hall." *Era,* 29 Mar. 1874, p. 4.

LONDON PAVILION

3-5, Piccadilly

[DH, p. 142; M & M, 2d ed. pp. 277-79; 3rd ed. pp. 316-18; OCT (W. Macqueen-Pope), p. 586.]

740. "About the Halls." *Sketch,* 12 Feb. 1913.

741. "Come to Our Pavilion." *Punch,* 4 June 1898, p. 262. [Dan Leno and other attractions.]

742. EARL, MICHAEL. "The Centre of the World, the London Pavilion—a Monument to Glamour." *Stage,* 16 Oct. 1978, p. 28.

743. FERGUSSON, Sir LOUIS. "An Evening at the Pav in 1898." *Call Boy,* Mar. 1969, pp. 8-9.

744. [Entry deleted.]

745. FORSTER, PAT. "An Act of Vandalism?" *Country Life,* 6 July 1978, p. 30.

746. "London Pavilion." *Era,* 13 Feb. 1892, p. 18.

747. "The London Pavilion and Mr. Varley." *Era,* 20 Aug. 1887, pp. 7, 8, 11.

748. [London Pavilion Interiors] *Architectural Review* 8 (1900).

749. "The London Pavilion Ltd." *Era,* 8 Feb. 1890, p. 17; 4 Feb. 1891, p. 17.

750. "London Pavilion Meeting." *Era,* 10 Feb. 1894, p. 17; 9 Feb. 1895, p. 16; 6 Feb. 1897, p. 20; 5 Feb. 1898, p. 19.

751. "London Pavilion v. the Tivoli." *Era,* 24 May 1890, p. 15.

752. "Mr. Frank Glenister." *Era,* 27 Aug. 1898, p. 19. [Mgr.]

753. "A Music Hall Artist's Action." *Era,* 17 July 1897, p. 16; 14 Aug. 1897, p. 17; 19 Feb. 1898, p. 22.

[Kelly vs. the London Pavilion.]

754. "The New London Pavilion." *Era,* 21 Nov. 1885, p. 10; 28 Nov. 1885, p. 10; 5 Dec. 1885, p. 10.

755. "The New London Pavilion." *Era,* 10 Nov. 1900, p. 21; 17 Nov. 1900, p. 20.

756. NORTHEDGE, RICHARD. "Live Shows Plea for the Pavilion." *Evening Standard,* 13 Nov. 1978.

757. "The Passing of the Pavilion." *Observer,* 1 Apr. 1934, p. 18.

758. "The Pavilion." *Christian Science Monitor* (Boston), 21 Apr. 1934.

759. PEVSNER, NIKOLAUS. *The Buildings of England. London.* Harmondsworth: Penguin Books, 1974.

760. "PINCE-NEZ." [Pavilion License renewed.] *Age,* 28 Oct. 1882.

761. "STAGE REPORTER." "GLC Plans for London Pavilion Will Dash Hope for Any Theatre Revival." *Stage,* 16 Nov. 1978, p. 40.

762. "Variety is Charming." *Punch,* 19 Nov. 1902, p. 359.
   [Lord Mayor's Night at the Pavilion; high praise for Dan Leno.]

LORD RAGLAN MUSIC HALL AND PUBLIC HOUSE

26, Theobalds Road, Holborn

Also known as: The Golden Horse Public House; Raglan Music Hall. [DH, p. 143.]

763. "Action against the proprietor of the Raglan Music Hall." *Era,* 8 June 1873, p. 7.

764. "Destruction of the Raglan Music Hall." *Era,* 17 Nov. 1883, p. 4.

LORD RAGLAN PUBLIC HOUSE

St. Anne's Road, Burdett Road, Stepney

[DH, pp. 143–44.]

765. "A Music Hall Proprietor in Court." *Era,* 20 Dec. 1890, p. 16; 7 May 1892, p. 16.

766. "The Raglan Music Hall Licence." *Era,* 9 Aug. 1890, p. 16.

METROPOLITAN THEATRE

267, Edgware Road, Paddington

[DH, p. 151.]

767. "Action by a Music Hall Proprietor." *Era,* 11 Jan. 1874, p. 4.
   [Against the South Coast Railway.]

768. "At the Met." *Sketch,* 12 Feb. 1913.

769. B.M. "The Metropolitan Music Hall." *Sketch,* 1 June 1898. Repr. in *Music Hall Records* 1 (1978): 14–16.

770. BEAVAN, JOHN. "Music Hall." *20th Century* 159 (Mar. 1956): 283–85.
[Theatre decaying because of TV.]

771. "David Max Trytel, the Metropolitan's Dutch Musical Director." *Era,* 21 May 1910, p. 20.

772. "Disturbances at a Music Hall." *Era,* 6 Sept. 1874, p. 4.

773. " 'Life' at the Metropolitan." *Era,* 21 Feb. 1875, p. 4.

774. [Metropolitan, Edgware Road, Rebuilt] *Builder,* 1 Jan. 1898, p. 24.

775. "The Metropolitan Music Hall." *Era,* 19 May 1888, p. 16; 26 May 1888, p. 16.

776. "The Metropolitan Music Hall Company." *Era,* 9 June 1888, p. 16; 12 Jan. 1889, p. 14.

777. "Metropolitan Theatre of Varieties." *Advertiser,* 18 Dec. 1897.

778. "Music Hall Litigation." *Era,* 30 Apr. 1887, p. 16.

779. "Music Halls and Stage Plays." *Era,* 27 Jan. 1883, p. 4; 3 Feb. 1883, p. 4.

780. "The New Metropolitan." *Era,* 24 Aug. 1897, p. 16.

781. [Obit. of George Speedy, mgr] *Era,* 12 Sept. 1880, p. 4.

782. "Robbery from the Metropolitan Music Hall." *Era,* 18 Nov. 1877, p. 4.

783. ROSS, BERT. "The Good Old 'Met.' " *Call Boy* 11, no. 3 (autumn 1974): 12–13; 11, no. 4 (winter 1974): 12–14; 12, no. 1 (spring 1975): 12–15; 12, no. 2 (summer 1975): 14–17; 12, no. 3 (autumn 1975): 12–15; 12, no. 4 (winter 1975): 12–16; 13, no. 1 (spring 1976): 12–14; 13, no. 2 (summer 1976): 12–15.

784. *Some Account of the New Metropolitan Theatre of Varieties and Early History of Its Site and Associations.* Ills. [L] 267, Edgware Road, January 1898.

785. [Summons of H.S. Lake, prop., for presenting a stage play.] *Times,* 22 Jan. 1883; *Pall Mall Gazette,* 25 Jan. 1883.

786. "Theatre and Music Hall." *Era,* 1 Sept. 1878, p. 4.
[Management and Building Acts Amendment.]

MILE END EMPIRE

95, Mile End Road, Stepney

Also known as: Eagle Public House; Lusby's Summer and Winter Garden; Lusby's Music Hall; Paragon Music Hall. [DH, pp. 151–52; S & W, Vol. 3 (plans and section).]

787. "A Chat with Mr. Adney Payne." *Era,* 11 Aug. 1894, p. 14. [Mgr.]
788. "A Chat with William Lusby." *Era,* 20 Feb. 1897, p. 21.
789. "An East End Music Hall." *P.T.O.,* 22 Dec. 1902, p. 905.
790. "George Adney Payne's Jubilee." *Era,* 30 June 1897, p. 19.
791. "Lusby's." *Era,* 21 Feb. 1875, p. 4.
792. "Marriage of George Adney Payne." *Era.* 10 Nov. 1898, p. 21.
793. "Mr. Charrington and 'Lusby.' " *Era,* 30 May 1885, p. 10.
794. "Mr. Lusby's Benefit." *Era,* 2 Nov. 1889, p. 15.
795. "Music Hall Litigation. Crowder vs. Charrington." *Era,* 14 Feb. 1885, p. 9; 21 Feb. 1885, p. 10; 28 Feb. 1885, p. 10; 7 Mar. 1885, p. 10.
796. "The Paragon." *The Music Hall,* 17 May 1893, p. 14.
797. "The Paragon and Eastern Empire." *Era,* 3 Feb. 1894, p. 17.
798. "The Paragon Reopened." *Era,* 10 June 1911, p. 24.
799. "The Paragon Theatre of Varieties." *Era,* 9 May 1885, p. 10; 23 May 1885, p. 10.
800. *Paragon Theatre of Varieties. Souvenir . . . 21st Anniversary . . .* [L] F.F.W. Oldfield, 1906.
801. "Presentation at Lusby's Music Hall." *Era,* 18 Mar. 1882, p. 5.
802. "Presentation to a Music Hall Manager" [Crowder]. *Era,* 19 Sept. 1885, p. 15.
803. "Stabbing at a Music Hall." *Era,* 27 Oct. 1894, p. 17.

MONTPELIER PALACE

18, Montpelier Street, Newington

Also known as: Montpelier Tavern; Montpelier Music Hall; Empire Music Hall; Walworth Empire. [DH, p. 154.]
804. "Destruction of a Music Hall." *Standard,* 14 Sept. 1891.
805. "A Music Hall Burned." *Era,* 19 Sept. 1891, p. 16.

NEW CROSS EMPIRE

New Cross Road and Watson Street, New Cross

Also known as: Deptford Empire Theatre of Varieties; New Cross Empire Theatre of Varieties. [DH, pp. 157–58.]
806. [Empire, New Cross] *Builder,* 19 Aug. 1899, p. 182.
807. "The New-Cross Empire." *Era,* 5 Aug. 1899, p. 16.

OLD VIC, *See*
ROYAL VICTORIA HALL AND COFFEE TAVERN

OXFORD THEATRE
26–32, Oxford Street, St. Marylebone

Also known as: Boar and Castle Public House; Oxford Music Hall;
New Oxford Theatre. [DH, p. 168; M & M, *Lost*, 1st ed. pp.
299–321; OCT (W. Macqueen-Pope, revised), p. 712; S & W vols. 2
and 3 for plans and elevations.]

808. "Action against a Music Hall Proprietor." *Era*, 1 June 1879,
p. 4.
[To recover an acrobat's apparatus.]

809. "A Chat with Harry Lundy." *Era*, 28 Sept. 1895, p. 17. [Mgr.]

810. "A Chat with Mr. J.H. Jennings." *Era*, 7 July 1894, p. 15; 14
July 1894, p. 14. [Mgr.]

811. [Destruction by fire] *Building News*, 14 Feb. 1868, p. 110.

812. "Destruction by Fire of the Oxford Music Hall." *Era*, 3 Nov.
1872, p. 4.

813. "Disturbance at the Oxford Music Hall." *Era*, 31 Oct. 1875, p. 4;
7 Nov. 1875, p. 4.

814. JINGLE [pseud.] "The Oxford Music Hall." *Pick-Me-Up*, 30
June 1893. Repr. in *Music Hall Records* 2 (Aug. 1978): 16–19.

815. "The Management of the Oxford Music Hall." *Era*, 13 Aug.
1876, p. 4.

816. "The New Oxford Music Hall." *Sketch*, 15 Feb. 1893. p. 15.

817. "Our Representative Man." *Punch*, 26 Oct. 1878, pp. 184–85.
[Visit to Oxford.]

818. [The Oxford] *Builder*, 17 Nov. 1860; 30 Mar. 1861.

819. "The Oxford." *Era*, 3 June 1899, p. 18; 17 June 1899, p. 18.

820. *The Oxford: Annals of Old and New.* L: Oxford Musick Hall,
1893.
[Souvenir of the reopening.]

821. "The Oxford Annual Meeting." *Era*, 6 June 1896, p. 16; 6 Feb.
1897, p. 19; 29 May 1897, p. 18; 17 June 1899, p. 18.

822. [Oxford appointments] *Building News*, 22 March 1861, p. 241.

823. "The Oxford Ltd." *Era*, 23 July 1892, p. 14; 26 May 1894, p. 16;
2 June 1894, p. 16; 8 June 1895, p. 16; 11 June 1898, p. 18.

824. "The Oxford Music Hall." *Era*, 5 March 1876, p. 9.
[Syers vs. Syers.]

825. "The Oxford Music Hall." *Era*, 12 Dec. 1880, p. 4.

826. "The Oxford Music Hall and Stage Plays." *Era*, 5 Nov. 1871,
p. 12.

827. "Presentation to J.H. Jennings." *Era*, 24 Mar. 1900, p. 18.

828. "Re-opening of the Oxford Music Hall." *Era*, 23 Mar. 1873,
p. 7.

829. "Riot at the Oxford." *Era*, 26 Dec. 1875, p. 4.

830. "Sale of the Oxford." *Era,* 1 Nov. 1890, p. 16.
831. [Sale of the Oxford] *Builder,* 4 Oct. 1890, p. 276.
832. "Saturday Morning at the Oxford." *Era,* 1 Sept. 1872, p 12.

PALACE THEATRE
Cambridge Circus, Westminster

Also known as: D'Oyly Carte's New Theatre; Royal English Opera House; Palace Theatre of Varieties. [DH, pp. 169-70; M & M, 2d ed. pp. 122-25, 3rd ed. pp. 141-45; S & W 1:35-37, 3:30-32.]

833. BLATHWAYT, RAYMOND. "The Control of a Great Music-Hall. Mr. Alfred Butt and the Palace Theatre." *World's Work* 17 (Feb. 1911): 248, 251-53.
834. "Druriolanus in (Music) Aulis." *Punch,* 6 Aug. 1892, p. 49. [Augustus Harris, mgr.]
835. [HIBBERT, H.G.] *London. Palace Theatre. Souvenir Presented on the Occasion of the Royal Performance Given for His Majesty the King, July 1st 1912.* [Includes "The Story of Music Hall," foreward by Malcolm Watson, text by Hibbert.]
836. "The Music Hall Licences." *Punch,* 24 Oct. 1896, p. 201. [Opposition to licences.]
837. "The Palace Anniversary." *Era,* 15 Dec. 1900, p. 20.
838. "The Palace Theatre." *Era,* 7 Sept. 1895, p. 16.
839. "The Palace Theatre Co." *Era,* 25 Aug. 1895, p. 14.
840. "The Palace Theatre Licence." *Era,* 2 Nov. 1895, p. 15. [Edit.]
841. "The Palace Theatre Ltd." *Era,* 26 Nov. 1892, p. 16.
842. "Palace Theatre Meeting." *Era,* 16 Oct. 1897, p. 22; 1 Oct. 1898, p. 18.
843. *Souvenir of the Opening of the Palace Theatre Dec. 10th 1892.* Sir Augustus Harris, Managing Director. [L: 1892.]
844. "Tableaux vivants at the Palace." *Era,* 3 Mar. 1894, p. 17.

PAVILION THEATRE
191-93, Whitechapel Road, Stepney

Also known as: Eastern Opera House. [DH, pp. 171-72.]

845. MERION, CHARLES. *Pavilion Theatre of Varieties, Whitechapel Road . . . The Grand Comic Pantomime, entitled Valentine and Orson.* L: Williams & Strahan, 1869.
846. "New Royal Pavilion Theatre." *Illustrated London News,* 6 Nov. 1858.
847. "Old Whitechapel and its Theatres." *Sketch,* 16 Jan. 1895.

PHOENIX PUBLIC HOUSE
Phoenix Place, Ratcliff Cross, Ratcliff

[DH, pp. 176–77.]
848. "A Music Hall Dispute." *Era,* 1 June 1873, p. 7.
[Sisters Laurie v. prop.]

PLAYER'S THEATRE
173–74, Villier's Street, Westminster

Also known as: The Arches; Hungerford Music Hall; "Gatti's Under the Arches"; Charing Cross Music Hall; Gatti's Charing Cross Music Hall. [DH, p. 179; M & M, 2d ed. pp. 260–64, 3rd ed. pp. 299–303; OCT, p. 744.]
849. [ANDERSON, JEAN, ed.] *Late Joys at the Player's Theatre.* L: T.V. Boardman, 1943.
850. "Gatti's Hungerford Palace." *Era,* 20 Mar. 1886, p. 10.
851. KIPLING, RUDYARD. *Something of Myself for My Friends Known and Unknown.* Garden City, N.Y.: Doubleday, Doran, 1927. [Living across from Gatti's in the 1880s. pp. 87–90.]
852. "The Late Tom Tinsley." *Era,* 7 Jan. 1911, p. 26. [Chairman of Gatti's Under the Arches.]
853. *Player's Theatre. 'Late Joy's' Past and Present, including special photographs reproduced by kind permission of Picture Post.* L: Player's Theatre, 1951, [Pamphlet.]
854. SHERIDAN, PAUL *Late and Early Joys at the Player's Theatre.* Ills. Reginald Woolley, with a foreword by Dame Sybil Thorndike. L: T.V. Boardman, 1952.
855. STEWART, HAL D. *Player's Joys: A Record of the First Twenty Five Years of the Player's Theatre Club.* [L] The Theatre, 1962.

POPLAR HIPPODROME
East India Dock Road, Poplar

Also known as: New Eldorado; New Prince's Theatre; Prince's Theatre; Hippodrome, Poplar. [DH, pp. 180–81.]
856. [Hippodrome, Tooting] *Builder,* 6 Jan. 1906, p. 25.
857. "Poplar's New Theatre." *East End News,* 15 Dec. 1905.

QUEEN'S THEATRE
275–79, Poplar High Street, Poplar

Also known as: Queen's Arms Palace of Varieties and Public

House; Apollo Music Hall; Albion Theatre; Oriental Theatre; Queen's Music Hall; Queen's Theatre of Varieties. [DH, p. 190.]

858. "Managing the Queen's Theatre, Poplar." *Times,* 24 Aug. 1955.

859. "A Music Hall Dispute." *Era,* 9 Feb. 1884, p. 7.

860. "Palace of Varieties, Ltd." *Era,* 9 July 1892, p. 15.

861. "Queen's Palace of Varieties." *Era,* 22 Aug. 1885, p. 10.

862. "Queens' Poplar." *Era,* 1 Sept. 1888, p. 10; 15 Oct. 1892, p. 16.

863. "The Queen's Theatre, Poplar; a Victorian Music Hall." *Times,* 3 Jan. 1950.

864. "Two Music Halls Sold." *Era,* 17 Apr. 1897, p. 16.

REGENT MUSIC HALL AND PUBLIC HOUSE

21, Regent Street St. John the Evangelist, Westminster

[DH, p. 196.]

865. "The Regent Music Hall." *Era,* 29 Oct. 1871, p 13. [Reopening.]

866. "Re-opening of the Regent Palace of Varieties." *Era,* 5 Oct. 1873.

REGENT THEATRE

Euston Road and Tonbridge Street, Kings Cross

Also known as: Euston Palace of Varieties; Euston Theatre; Euston Music Hall. [DH, pp. 196–97.]

867. [Euston Theatre of Varieties] *Builder,* 5 Jan. 1901, p. 23.

868. "Euston Theatre of Varieties." *Era*, 19 June 1900, p. 19; 22 Dec. 1900, p. 19; 29 Dec. 1900, p. 21.

ROYAL ALBERT PUBLIC HOUSE

Wandsworth Road

[DH, p. 200.]

869. "The Passing of 'the Chairman.'" *Era*, 4 Aug. 1906, p. 24. [On the retirement of Walter Leaver, and history of the hall.]

ROYAL CAMBRIDGE MUSIC HALL

136, Commercial Street, Shoreditch

Also known as: Cambridge Music Hall. [DH, p. 201.]

870. "Burning of the Cambridge." *Era,* 1 Feb. 1896, p. 20; 15 Feb. 1896, p. 19.

871. "The Cambridge." *Era*, 3 Oct. 1896, p. 18.

872. [Cambridge Music Hall] *Builder,* 23 Jan. 1897, p. 83; 10 Apr. 1897, p. 344; 4 Dec. 1897, p. 476; 15 Jan. 1898, p. 65.

873. "Chappell's Concert Company." *Era*, 2 Sept. 1899, p. 19.
874. "Death of Mr Will Riley." *Era*, 13 Feb. 1897, p. 19. [Mgr.]
875. "Mr James Chappell." *Era*, 17 June 1899, p. 19. [Mgr.]
876. "The New Cambridge." *Era*, 3 Apr. 1897, p. 18; 1 June 1898, p. 22.

ROYAL VICTORIA HALL AND COFFEE TAVERN

The Cut, Lambeth

Also known as: Royal Coburg Theatre; Royal Victoria Theatre; Victoria Theatre; "Old Vic"; New Victoria Palace. [DH, pp. 164–66; M & M, 2d ed. pp. 237–43, 3rd ed. pp. 260–66; OCT, pp. 694–96.]

877. BARKE, ELLEN. *Pantomime Waifs; or A Plea for Our City Children*. L: S. W. Partridge, 1884.
    [Chapter 10, "The Victoria Coffee Music-hall," pp. 192–224.]
878. DENT, EDWARD. *A Theatre for Everybody. The Story of Old Vic and Sadlers Wells*. L & N.Y.: T. V. Boardman, 1945.
    [Chapter 2, "The Royal Victoria Hall."]
879. HAMILTON, CICELY and LILIAN BAYLIS. *The Old Vic*. L: Jonathan Cape, 1926. [Pp. 176–88.]
880. *The History of the Royal Victoria Hall and Morley Memorial College, Waterloo Road*. Reprinted from *The Morley College Magazine*. [L: Morley College, 1894.]
881. HODDER, ERWIN. *The Life of Samuel Morley*. 2d ed. L: Hodder & Stoughton, 1887.
    [On the transformation of the 'Old Vic' into the 'Victoria Temperance Music Hall.']
882. "Music for the Million." *Era*, 19 Mar. 1881, p. 4.
883. "Philanthropic Music-halls." *Punch*, 3 Dec. 1881.
884. RICHARDS, DENIS. *Offspring of the Vic: A History of Morley College*. L: Routledge & Kegan Paul, 1928. [Chapter 3, on music-hall, pp. 37–65.]
885. ROBERTS, PETER. *The Old Vic Story*. L: W. H. Allen, 1976.
886. *The Royal Victoria Coffee Hall*. [L] For private circulation only [1881].
    [Further reports were issued in 1882, 1883, 1884, 1885, and 1886.]

SEBRIGHT MUSIC HALL

Coate Street, Hackney

Also known as: Sebright Arms Public House; Belmont's Sebright; Regent Theatre of Varieties; English's Music Hall. [DH, p. 217.]

887. "A Chat with George Belmont." *Era*, 13 Oct. 1894, p. 17.
    [Prop.]

888. "A Chat with George English." *Era*, 10 Nov. 1894, p. 16. [Mgr.]
889. "The Sebright." *Era*, 31 July 1886, p. 8.

SHOREDITCH OLYMPIA

203–4, Shoreditch High Street, Shoreditch
Also known as: Royal Standard Public House and Pleasure Gardens; Royal Standard Theatre; New Standard Theatre; Olympia; Shoreditch. [DH, pp. 222–24.]
890. "Destruction by Fire of the Standard Theatre." *Illustrated Sporting and Dramatic News*, 27 Oct. 1866.
891. DOUGLASS, ALBERT. *Memories of Mummers and the Old Standard Theatre*. L: *Era*, 1925.
892. "The New Standard, Shoreditch." *Era*, 18 Dec. 1897, p. 18.
893. "New Standard Theatre." *Illustrated London News*, May 1845.

SOUTH LONDON PALACE OF VARIETIES

92, London Road, Lambeth
Also known as: South London Music Hall. [DH, pp. 225–26; OCT (W. Macqueen-Pope), p. 899.]
894. "Alleged Libel on the South London Palace of Amusements." *Era*, 24 May 1874, p. 4; 31 May 1874, p. 4.
895. "A Chat with Frank Egerton." *Era*, 28 Mar. 1896, p. 18. [Mgr.]
896. "Palace where a 'Baron' Glittered is Coming Down for Shops." *Evening News*, 21 Jan. 1955.
897. "Refusal of Licence to the Proposed Music Hall in the London Road at the General Licensing Meeting." *South London Chronicle*, 17 Mar. 1860.
898. "Robbery at the South London Palace." *Era*, 5 Dec. 1891, p. 16.
899. "Sale of the South London." *Era*, 17 Aug. 1895, p. 14.
900. "A Scene at a Music Hall." *Era*, 31 Jan. 1875, p. 8.
901. "South London Palace." *Era*, 16 Feb. 1889, p. 17.

STAR MUSIC HALL

Star and Garter Public House, 189, Abbey Street, Bermondsey [DH, p. 228; TN, 14:141.]
902. "A Music Hall Case." *Era*, 17 Feb. 1883, p. 4.
903. "A Music Hall Proprietor in Court." *Era*, 2 June 1888, p. 16.

SUN MUSIC HALL

26, Knightsbridge High Street, Knightsbridge
Also known as: Rising Sun Public House. [DH, p. 232.]
904. [Obit. of E. Williams, prop.] *Era*, 12 Sept. 1880, p. 4.

SURREY MUSIC HALL

Surrey Zoological Gardens,
between Kennington Park and Walworth Roads, Southwark
Also known as: Royal Surrey Gardens Music Hall; Surrey Gardens
Theatre. [DH, p. 233; OCT (W. Macqueen-Pope), p. 899.]

905. "Destruction of the Surrey Music Hall by Fire." *Illustrated London News*, 22 June 1861.

906. "The Music Hall at the Surrey Gardens." *Builder*, 19 June 1856.

907. "PENSIVE SHAREHOLDER, A." *Facts and Documents Relating to the Surrey Gardens Company.* L: 1857.

908. "The Surrey Gardens." *Era*, 21 Apr. 1872, p. 12.

909. "The Surrey Theatre." *Stage*, 30 Apr. 1904.

TIVOLI MUSIC HALL

65–70 1/2 Strand, Westminster
[DH, 242–43; M & M, *Lost*, pp. 518–29; OCT, p. 948.]

910. "The Art of the Music Hall." *Times,* 31 Jan. 1914. [On closing.]

911. BEERBOHM, MAX. "At the Tivoli." *Saturday Review* 86 (3 Dec. 1898): 730–31.

912. "Cigar Ends at Music Halls." *Era*, 8 Oct. 1892, p. 16.

913. GALSWORTHY, ARNOLD. "At the Tivoli." *Tatler*, 18 Feb. 1903. Repr. in *Music Hall Records* 1 (June 1978): 8–9.

914. "A Music Hall Action." *Era*, 6 June 1891, p. 15. [Tivoli v. *The Hawk*.]

915. "The New Tivoli." *Era*, 3 Aug. 1895, p. 14.

916. "The New Tivoli." *Era*, 30 July 1910, p. 15.

917. "The New Tivoli." *Stage*, 1 Aug. 1908.

918. "The New Tivoli: A Committee of Investigation Proposed but Ruled Out of Order." *Music Hall*, 7 Aug. 1896, pp. 13–15.

919. "The New Tivoli and the Old. Evolution of a Picture Palace." *Observer*, 8 Sept. 1923.

920. "The New Tivoli Ltd." *Era*, 19 Sept. 1891, p. 17; 30 July 1892, p. 15; 7 Aug. 1897, p. 16; 5 Aug. 1899, p. 16.

921. "Opening of the Tivoli." *Era*, 31 May 1890, p. 15.

922. "The Revue at the Tivoli Music-Hall." *Tatler* 3 (2 July 1902): 28.

923. ROSS, BERT . "The Tivoli Never Had a Chairman." *Call Boy* 9, no. 1 (Mar. 1972): 16–18; 9, no. 2 (June 1972): 12–14; 9, no. 3 (Sept. 1972); 9, no. 4 (Dec. 1972): 16–20; 10, no. 1 (Mar. 1973): 16–18, 24.

924. "Threatening a Music Hall Manager." *Era*, 29 Jan. 1898, p. 20.

925. "The Tivoli." *Era*, 11 Oct. 1890, p. 16; 25 Oct. 1890, p. 16; 1 Nov. 1890, p. 17.

926. "The Tivoli. An Historic House." *Daily Telegraph*, 5 Sept. 1923.
927. "The Tivoli Anniversary." *Era*, 13 Sept. 1902.
928. "The Tivoli Anniversary." *Stage*, 23 Sept. 1905, p. 22.
929. "The Tivoli Directorate." *Era*, 17 Dec. 1898, p. 20.
930. "The Tivoli in Liquidation." *Era*, 22 Nov. 1890, p. 16.
931. "The Tivoli Ltd." *Era*, 4 Aug. 1894, p. 14.
932. "The Tivoli Meeting." *Era*, 20 Aug. 1898, p. 17; 4 Aug. 1900, p. 16.
933. [Tivoli Music Hall] *Builder*, 31 May 1890, p. 398; 1 Sept. 1900, p. 199.
934. "Tivoli Restaurant." *Era*, 28 June 1890, p. 15.
935. "Tivoli Shares." *Era*, 1 June 1889, p. 15.
936. "Tivoli Theatre of Varieties." *Era*, 4 July 1891, p. 14.

TROCADERO MUSIC HALL

7-8, Great Windmill Street, Piccadilly
Also known as: Royal Albion Theatre; New Queen's Theatre; Theatre of the Arts; Royal Albion Subscription Theatre; Dubourg's Theatre of the Arts; Ancient Hall of Rome; Argyll Rooms; Royal Trocadero Palace of Varieties; Royal Trocadero Music Hall; Royal Trocadero and Eden Theatre. [DH, p. 245; M & M, *Lost*, pp. 551-59.]

937. "Assault in the Trocadero." *Era*, 11 Apr. 1885, p. 10.
938. "Death of Mr Robert R. Bignell." *Era*, 21 July 1888, p. 16. [Mgr.]
939. "Decorations at the Trocadero." *Era*, 7 Feb. 1891, p. 17.
940. "Mr Sam Adams." *Era*, 27 Dec. 1890, p. 15. [Interview with mgr.]
941. "A Night at the Trocadero." *Era*, 20 May 1899, p. 18.
942. "Nights of Other Days: IV. The Argyll Rooms and the Middlesex." *King*, 6 Aug. 1906.
943. "Riot at the Trocadero." *Era*, 9 Apr. 1885, p. 16.
944. "A Row at the Trocadero." *Era*, 23 Mar. 1889, p. 17.
945. [Trocadero licences] *Age*, 28 Oct. 1882.

VARIETY THEATRE

18-20, Pitfield Street, Hoxton, Shoreditch
Also known as: Theatre of Varieties; Varieties Music Hall; Harwood's Music Hall; New King's Theatre; Bromwich Theatre; Mortimer's Theatre; Hoxton Variety Theatre. [DH, p. 247.]

946. GOODFELLOW, T. *Hoxton Hall. A Short History.* L: Hoxton Hall and the London Borough of Hackney, 1977.
947. "Important Music Hall Action." *Era*, 7 Dec. 1889, p. 17.

948. "Mr. Leonard Mortimer . . . ." *Mercury*, 18 Mar. 1905. [Mgr.]
949. "Mr Will Thompson (Acting Manager)." *Shoreditch Mail*, 2 Sept. 1905.
950. "Seat in the Stalls for Sixpence: Recollections of Harwood's Music Hall. Building Now for Sale." *Star*, 15 Aug. 1923.
951. "Tales of the Old Halls: Hoxton Varieties to Make Way for Cinema Shows." *Star*, 29 Nov. 1913.

VICTORIA PALACE

126, Victoria Street, Victoria
Also known as: Royal Standard Hotel; Moy's Music Hall; Royal Standard Music Hall; Victoria Palace Theatre. [DH, pp. 249–50; M & M, 2d ed., pp. 199–202.]

952. AUTOLYCUS [pseud.] "The Puppet-show: A Night at the Victoria Palace." *Passing Show*, 25 Aug. 1917, p. 23. [Sketches by O. A.]
953. "A Chat with Mr Richard Wake." *Era*, 26 Jan. 1895, p. 18. [Mgr.]
954. "A Chat with Mr. T. S. Dickie." *Era*, 22 Feb. 1896, p. 18. [Mgr.]
955. "Mr. R. Wake's Retirement." *Era*, 14 Dec. 1895, p. 16; 21 Dec. 1895, p. 17.
956. "Mr. T. S. Dickie." *Music Hall*, 3 Jan. 1896, p. 13.
957. [The Victoria Palace] *Era*, 4 Nov. 1901.

WEST LONDON THEATRE

69, Church Street, Edgware Road, St. Marylebone
Also known as: Royal Pavilion West; Portman Theatre; Royal Marylebone Theatre; Royal Alfred Theatre; Royal West London Theatre; West London Stadium.

958. BLIGH, N. M. "Lost London Theatres. No. 2. The Story of the Marylebone Theatre." *Theatre World*, June 1954.
959. MORLEY, MALCOLM. *The Old Marylebone Theatre.* L: St. Marylebone Society, 1960. (Publication No. 2.)
960. ———. *Royal West London Theatre.* L: St. Marylebone Society, 1962. (Publication No. 6.)
961. "West London Theatre." *Era*, 14 Apr. 1894, p. 16.

WILTON'S MUSIC HALL

Prince of Denmark Public House, 1, Grace's Alley, Wellclose Square
Also known as: Albion Saloon; Old Mahogany Bar; Frederick's Royal Palace of Varieties. [DH, p. 261.]

962. AUBREY, CRISPIN and STEVE HAYWOOD. "Half Moon

Upstaged." *Time Out*, 23–29 Sept. 1977, p. 5.

963. "Boomps-a-daisy back in East End." *Evening Standard*, 22 Nov. 1977, p. 5.

964. BRATTON, JACQUELINE S. *Wilton's Music Hall*. Cambridge: Chadwyck-Healey, 1979.
[Text to accompany slide set. "Theatre in Focus: a Pictorial History of World Theatre."]

965. ———. *Wilton's Music Hall, a Set of Slides with Notes*. L: Consortium for Drama and Media in Higher Education, 1975. Rev. G. Speaight, *Theatre Notebook* 21, no. 2 (1977): 48.

966. BUCKMAN, DAVID. "Will Wilton's Music Hall Live Again?" *Outlook* 2 (summer 1971): 13–17.

967. CHAILLET, NED. "Move to Music Hall for Half Moon Theatre." *Times*, 16 Apr. 1977.

968. CHURCH, MICHAEL. "Waiting in the Wings." *Times Educational Supplement*, 8 Mar. 1974, p. 69.

969. DAY-LEWIS, JAN. "When Wilton's Came Back to Life." *Daily Telegraph Magazine*, 18 Dec. 1970, pp. 50–54.

970. [Description] *Building News*, 15 Apr. 1859, p. 348; 22 Apr. 1859, p. 388.

971. "Destruction of Wilton's." *Era*, 2 Sept. 1877, p. 4.

972. DOBSON, CARLA. "Behind the Scenes." *Building*, 23 June 1978, pp. 80–81.

973. FREEMAN, SIMON. "Eclipse of the Half Moon's Theatre Hope." *Evening Standard*, 18 Aug. 1977, p. 8.

974. GIBB, FRANCES. "New Life for World's Oldest Music Hall." *Daily Telegraph*, 23 Nov. 1977, p. 15.

975. "Half Moon Launch Wilton's Demo." *Stage*, 22 Sept. 1977, p. 1.

976. HONRI, PETER. "What Happened to John Wilton?" *Call Boy* 15, no. 3 (summer 1978): 3.

977. KINGSLEY, MADELEINE. "Wilton's." *Radio Times*, 17/24 Dec. 1970, p. 11.

978. KNIGHT, PETER. "Saga of Colehan's Foresight." *Daily Telegraph*, 8 Jan. 1973, p. 9.

979. MANDER, RAY and JOE MITCHENSON. "Wilton's." *Stage*, 12 Jan. 1978, p. 9.

980. MAY, DAVID. "Tug-of-war over Oldest Music Hall." *Sunday Times*, 25 Sept. 1977, p. 6.

981. MERION, CAROLYN. "Wilton's for the East End." *Greater London Arts* 95 (Sept./Oct. 1976): 6–8.

982. MOYNIHAN, MICHAEL. "Reviving Music Hall without Taking the Mike." *Sunday Times*, 21 Oct. 1973, p. 13.

983. "Music Hall Plan." *Times*, 25 May 1978.

984. MYERSON, JEREMY. "Wilton's: an Attractive Proposition but Still a Long Way to Go." *Stage*, 19 Oct. 1978, p. 6.
985. "National Theatre of Music Hall." *Stage*, 1 Dec. 1977, p. 3.
986. "Record Company to Take Over Historic Music Hall." *Stage*, 13 June 1974, p. 1.
987. ROBINSON, DAVID. "Wilton's." *Financial Times*, 6 Dec. 1964.
988. SANDFORD, HERBERT H. "Wilton's." *Stage*, 19 Jan. 1978, p. 8.
989. ———. "Wilton's Will Live Again." *Stage*, 22 Dec. 1977, p. 3.
990. "To let: Victorian Music Hall." *Evening Standard*, 22 Oct. 1973, p. 10.
991. WAINWRIGHT, MARTIN. "Music Hall at Risk." *Evening Standard*, 14 April 1977.
992. WALSH, GEORGINA. "The Old Music Hall Awaits Revival." *Evening Standard*, 25 Jan. 1973, p. 13.
993. WAYMARK, PETER. "New Life for an Old Hall." *Times*, 19 Aug. 1972.
993a. "What Kind of Wilton's?" *Theatre Quarterly* 9, no. 36 (winter 1980): 89–96.
   [Debate between Peter Honri, arguing that the theatre should become a music hall, and Jacqueline S. Bratton, arguing that it should become a museum.]
994. *Wilton's Grand Music Hall Needs Friends*. L: London Music Hall Protection Society [1978].
   [Fund-raising appeal.]
995. *Wilton's Grand Music Hall Newsletter*. Oct. 1978, No. 1–Continuing. Irregular.
   [Ed. Peter Honri.]
996. "Wilton's Lives Again." *Stage*, 1 June 1978.
997. "Wilton's New Music Hall." *Peeping Tom: a Journal of Town Life* 5 (1859).

WINCHESTER MUSIC HALL

Southwark Bridge Road, Southwark
Also known as: Grapes Public House; British Saloon; Grand Harmonic Hall; Surrey Music Hall. [DH, pp. 261–62.]
998. "Gulling the Public." *Era*, 7 Apr. 1878, p. 6; 14 Apr. 1878, p. 4; 21 Apr. 1878, p. 4; 28 Apr. 1878, p. 4.
999. "The Winchester Music Hall Litigation." *Era*, 10 Oct. 1880, p. 4;

17 Oct. 1880, p. 4.

WINDSOR CASTLE MUSIC HALL AND PUBLIC HOUSE

Coopers Road, Camberwell
Also known as: Turners's Music Hall. [DH, pp. 262–63.]
1000. "Affray in a Music Hall." *Era*, 12 Nov. 1881, p. 4; 19 Nov. 1881, p. 5.

WINTER GARDEN THEATRE

167, Drury Lane, Holborn
Also known as: Great Mogul; Mogul Saloon; Mogul Music Hall;
Middlesex Music Hall; New Middlesex Theatre of Varieties. [DH,
pp. 264–65; M & M, 2d ed. pp. 211–16, 3rd ed. pp. 133–40; OCT
(W. Macqueen-Pope, revised; under Middlesex), p. 712.
1001. "London's Oldest Music Hall: some Middlesex Reminiscences."
Pall Mall Gazette, 18 Oct. 1906, p. 10.
1002. *The Middlesex Drury Lane; Souvenir of the 31st Anniversary* [of
J. L. Graydon's Management and Proprietorship]. [L: Artistic
Stationery Co.] Thursday, 20 Nov. 1902.
1003. "The Middlesex Enlargement." *Era*, 5 Sept. 1891, p. 14.
1004. "Nestor of the Halls. The Graydon Banquet." *Era*, 4 Feb. 1911,
p. 21.
[J. L. Graydon, mgr.]
1005. "The New Middlesex." *Morning Post*, 30 Oct. 1911.
1006. "The Nights of Other Days IV. The Argyll Rooms and the Middlesex." *King*, 6 Aug. 1904.
1007. " 'The Old Mogul' a Famous Music Hall in a New Guise: Mr
Stoll's Scheme." *Evening Standard*, 30 Oct. 1911.
1008. "Reopening of the Middlesex." *Era*, 16 Dec. 1891, p. 16.
1009. "Under the Hammer: Sale of the Middlesex Music Hall." *Globe*,
6 Nov. 1909.

WOOD GREEN EMPIRE

High Road, Wood Green
1010. BLAKE, J. O. "Portrait of a Theatre." *Call Boy* 5, no. 2 (Mar.
1968); 5, no. 2a (June 1968): 6–8, 10.
1011. "Memories of Wood Green Empire." *Haringay Advertiser*, 2
Nov. 1978.
1012. "The Wood Green Empire." *Era*, 14 Sept. 1912, p. 22.

WOOLWICH EMPIRE

Beresford Street, Woolwich

Also known as: New Portable Theatre; West Kent Theatre; Duchess of Kent's Theatre; Barnard's Theatre; Woolwich; Theatre Royal; Empire Theatre, Woolwich. [DH, p. 266.]

1013. "Barnard's Theatre, Woolwich." *Era*, 26 Nov. 1898, p. 18; 3 Feb. 1900, p. 20.

1014. "I Was There When a Music Hall Died." *Daily Mail*, 31 Mar. 1958.

V. PROVINCIAL HALLS

"We exchange the farm, or the county fair for the gallery of
the city music-hall, where the cutler sits armed with stones,
red herrings, 'flat-backs,' and other missiles ready to be
hurled at the performers 'if they don't play "Nancy's Fancy"
or onay tune we fix.' "
　　　F. W. Moorman, *Yorkshire Dialect Poems (1673 – 1915)
　　　　and Traditional Poems* (London: Sidgwick and
　　　　　　　　　　　　　　Jackson, 1916) xxxi.

The bulk of writing on British music-hall has been devoted to London, and this is deceptive for the provincial circuits were soon as
active as the capital. Leeds was the home of a leading music-hall
journal, *The Magnet*, and Glasgow, Dublin, Manchester and
Liverpool had nearly as many halls in proportion to population as
London itself. To date, the only full-length works devoted to the
subject have been G. J. Mellor's *The Northern Music Hall*, which
is packed with information, none of it annotated or documented,
and Kathleen Barker's more scholarly but brief books on Bristol.
Without examining the clippings and newspaper files of major
provincial, Scottish, Irish and Welsh centers, we could hardly provide a full account of extra-Londinian activity; but we have
combed *The Era* and *The Builder* for references to principal halls,
and hope that our preliminary researches will inspire local
historians to turn their attention to neglected sources and subjects.
　　Our arrangement is alphabetical by counties and shires for
England, by cities for Scotland, Ireland and Wales.

GENERAL

Cross-references

See also **171, 1813, 1876, 2781–86, 3351a.**

1015. BRERETON, CHRISTOPHER. "Act now to save provincial theatres." *Architectural Review,* Oct. 1976, pp. 216–222.
1016. "The Cost of Amusing the Public." *London Society* 1 (Apr. 1862): 193–98.
[Estimate of 119 halls outside of London.]
1017. LEWTHWAITE, C. "Music Hall in the North-east." *Bulletin of the Durham County Local History Society,* Apr. 1978, pp. 18–35.
1018. MELLOR, G. J. *The Northern Music Hall. A Century of Popular Entertainment.* Newcastle-upon-Tyne: Frank Graham, 1970.
[Introduced by Ken Dodd and with a foreword by George Wood, O.B.E. ("Wee Georgie Wood").]
1019. ———. *Pom-poms and Ruffles: The Story of Northern Seaside Entertainment.* Clapham (Yorks): Dalesman, 1966. Rev. V. C. Clinton-Baddeley, *Theatre Notebook* 22, no. 4 (summer 1968): 174.
1020. "Ned Corvan." *Monthly Chronicle of North-country Lore and Legend* 5 (Nov. 1891): 522–23.

ENGLISH INDIVIDUAL TOWNS

Cross-references

See also Sunderland **1776.**
Bristol **1968, 2149, 2353, 2663.**
Bolton **81, 384a.**
Liverpool **2021, 2666, 2674, 3010.**
Manchester **2021, 2665, 2676.**
Leicester **1951.**

Newport **2662.**
Newcastle-upon-Tyne **2050, 3092a, 3464.**
Nottingham **179a, 2166, 2667, 3328.**
Wolverhampton **1952.**
Brighton **2885.**
Birmingham **1973, 2172, 2175, 2700, 3008, 3072.**
Yorkshire **1392.**
Bradford **2143, 2613, 2706.**

Cheshire

CHESTER

1021. "Extraordinary Scene at a Music Hall." *Era*, 4 Jan. 1880, p. 4.

Cumberland

MARYPORT

1022. "Panic in a Music Hall." *Era*, 30 Mar. 1889, p. 16. [Russell's Theatre of Varieties.]

WHITEHAVEN

1023. "Disastrous Fire at a Music Hall." *Era*, 6 June 1885, p. 10. [Royal Standard Palace of Varieties.]

Derbyshire

DERBY

1024. "Destruction of the Star Theatre and Music Hall by Fire." *Era*, 1 June 1873, p. 7.
1025. "A Row at a Music Hall." *Era*, 27 Oct. 1888, p. 10. [Scarsdale Arms.]

Devonshire

DEVONPORT

1026. [Hippodrome] *Builder*, 29 Aug. 1908.

PLYMOUTH

1027. "Accident and Panic in a Music Hall." *Era*, 8 Apr. 1882, p. 4. [St. James' Hall.]

1028. "Burning of the Palace." *Era*, 24 Dec. 1898, p. 19.

1029. "Palace Theatre." *Era*, 29 Jan. 1898, p. 21; 3 Sept. 1898, p. 18; 10 Sept. 1898, p. 19.

1030. [Theatre of Varieties] *Builder*, 17 Apr. 1897.

Durham

GATESHEAD

1031. "Queen's Variety." *Era*, 27 Aug. 1898, p. 18.

JARROW

1032. "Accident at a Music Hall." *Era*, 27 Apr. 1889, p. 15. [Albert Hall.]

SOUTH SHIELDS

1033. [Empire] *Builder*, 18 Feb. 1899.

1034. "Mr. R. Thornton interviewed." *Era*, 30 Aug. 1890, p. 15. [Mgr.]

1035. "New Empire Palace." *Era*, 5 Mar. 1898, p. 18; 4 Feb. 1899, p. 16; 18 Feb. 1899, p. 21.

1036. "New South Shields Variety Theatre." *Era*, 28 May 1898, p. 21.

STOCKTON-ON-TEES

1037. [Hippodrome] *Builder*, 30 Dec. 1905.

SUNDERLAND

1038. [Bijou Variety] *Builder*, 11 June 1898.

1039. [Empire] *Builder*, 13 June 1908.

1040. "Music Hall Enterprise." *Era*, 30 Nov. 1889, p. 17.

1041. "A New Variety Theatre." *Era*, 8 Aug. 1891, p. 15. [People's Palace.]

1042. "Thornton's Variety." *Era*, 8 Sept. 1888, p. 10.

WEST HARTLEPOOL

1043. [Music Hall] *Builder*, 24 Apr. 1909.

1044. "West Hartlepool Alhambra." *Era*, 16 Aug. 1890, p. 15.
1045. "West Hartlepool Alhambra Licence." *Era*, 3 Oct. 1891, p. 17.

WINGATE

1046. "Row in a Music Hall." *Era*, 13 Sept. 1890, p. 13. [Queen's Hotel.]

Essex

SOUTHEND-ON-SEA

1047. "Burning of the Empire." *Era*, 12 Jan. 1895, p. 17.

Gloucestershire

BOURNEMOUTH

1048. "Backward Bournemouth." *Era*, 14 May 1898, p. 17. [Edit.]
1049. "Bournemouth Licences." *Era*, 14 Sept. 1912, p. 23.

BRISTOL

1050. "Alleged Breach of Contract." *Era*, 23 Feb. 1884, p. 10. [Alhambra.]
1051. BARKER, KATHLEEN. *Bristol at Play: Five Centuries of Live Entertainment.* Bradford-on-Avon: Moonraker Press, 1976. [Chapter 4, "From Music Hall to Movies 1853-1901," pp. 31-43.]
1052. ———. *Early Music Hall in Bristol.* Bristol: Bristol Branch of the Historical Association, 1979.
1053. ———. *Entertainment in the Nineties.* Bristol: Bristol Branch of the Historical Association, 1973. ["Music-hall," pp. 11-16.]
1054. "Bristol Empire Varieties." *Era*, 16 June 1894, p. 16; 3 Nov. 1894, p. 17.
1055. "Destruction of Another Music Hall." *Era*, 28 June 1874, p. 7; 5 July 1874, p. 7. [Alhambra.]
1056. "The Empire." *Era*, 19 May 1894, p. 17; 25 Aug. 1894, p. 14.
1057. [Empire] S & W 1:46, 3:29-30, 62-70.
1058. MACRAE, F. G. H. "Bristol Hippodrome Stage: Its Machinery & Mechanical Equipment." *Stage Year Book* (1916): 37-39.
1059. "Music Hall Engagements." *Era*, 6 Mar. 1886, p. 10; 13 Mar.

1886, p. 10.
[Tom Gannon, mgr of Grand Palace of Varieties.]
1060. "The People's Palace." *Era*, 31 Dec. 1892, p. 18.

Hampshire

PORTSMOUTH

1061. "Burning of a Music Hall." *Era*, 27 Dec. 1890, p. 10. [Amphitheatre.]
1062. "Central Music Hall." *Era*, 30 Aug. 1890, p. 14.
1063. "Destruction of a Music Hall." *Era*, 22 Sept. 1878, p. 4. [South of England.]
1064. "The Empire at Portsmouth." *Era*, 3 Oct. 1891, p. 17.
1065. [Hippodrome] *Builder*, 11 Apr. 1903.
1066. "A Music Hall Convict." *Era*, 15 July 1882, p. 4. [Amphitheatre.]
1067. "Music Hall Litigation." *Era*, 19 Dec. 1891, p. 17. [Vento's Theatre of Varieties.]
1068. "A Music Hall Proprietor in Court." *Era*, 7 Nov. 1891, p. 16. [Alhambra.]
1069. "Opening of Portsmouth Empire." *Era*, 7 Nov. 1891, p. 16.
1070. "Opening of the New Music Hall at Portsmouth." *Era*, 5 Oct. 1879, p. 4.
1071. "Portsmouth Empire Palace." *Era*, 27 Jan. 1894, p. 16.
1072. SARGEANT, H. A. *A History of Portsmouth Theatres*. Portsmouth: Portsmouth City Council, 1971. (The Portsmouth Papers, No. 13.)

SOUTHAMPTON

1073. "Destruction of a Music Hall." *Era*, 22 Nov. 1884, p. 10. [Rainbow.]
1074. "Fracas at a Music Hall." *Era*, 27 Aug. 1887, p. 8. [Gaiety.]
1075. "Music Hall Disagreement." *Era*, 12 Mar. 1887, p. 10. [Royal York.]
1076. "A Music Hall Dispute." *Era*, 29 Sept. 1883, p. 4. [Gaiety Theatre of Varieties.]
1077. "Royal York." *Era*, 29 May 1897, p. 18; 12 Mar. 1898, p. 21; 2 Apr. 1898, p. 22.

Kent

CHATHAM

1078. "Burning of a Music Hall." *Era*, 16 May 1885, p. 10. [Barnard's.]

1079. MOAD, M. *Victorian and Edwardian Medway.* Rochester: Medway Borough Council, Directorate of Leisure Services, 1978. [pp. 23–24]

1080. ———. *Yesterday's Medway: Public Entertainments.* Chatham: Medway Borough Council, Directorate of Leisure Services, [1978]. [Data on the Empire, Barnard's Palace of Varieties, Gaiety.]

1081. "Music Hall Action." *Era*, 6 Feb. 1892, p. 17. [Gaiety.]

1082. "A New Music Hall." *Era*, 6 Sept. 1890, p. 14; 20 Sept. 1890, p. 15. [Gaiety.]

DOVER

1083. "Royal Hippodrome Gone, but Memory Lingers On." *Kent Messenger,* 13 June 1956.

1084. "The Tivoli Theatre." *Era*, 8 May 1897, p. 18; 19 June 1897, p. 17.

GRAVESEND

1085. "The Grand [Theatre of Varieties]." *Era*, 3 Nov. 1894, p. 16.

1086. "Mr. A. A. Thiodon's Affairs." *Era*, 11 May 1895, p. 16. [Grand Theatre of Varieties.]

1087. "Music Hall Litigation." *Era*, 28 Nov. 1885, p. 10. [Palace of Varieties.]

1088. "The New Grand." *Era*, 10 Nov. 1894, p. 16.

MAIDSTONE

1089. WILTSHIRE, SONIA. "Reminder of Great Music Hall Days." *Gazette,* 28 Feb. 1978, p. 63.

MARGATE

1090. "The Bigots and the Hall-by-the-sea." *Era*, 6 Sept. 1874, p. 4.

1091. "The Hall-by-the-sea." *Era*, 30 July 1898, p. 17.

1092. "Halls by the Sea." *Era*, 4 Oct. 1874, p. 14.

RAMSGATE

1093. "Action by a Music Hall Proprietor." *Era*, 11 Nov. 1877, p. 4. [Hart v. Braithwaite, Alexandra.]

SANDGATE

1094. "The Alhambra." *Era*, 7 Nov. 1896, p. 18.
1095. FOLEY, VICTOR. "Music Hall Days at Sandgate." *Folkestone Herald*, 6 Oct. 1956. [A letter about the Alhambra Theatre of Varieties.]
1096. "The New Alhambra." *Era*, 10 Nov. 1894, p. 16.

Lancashire

1097. RUSSELL, C. E. B. and E. T. CAMPAGNAC. "Poor People's Music-halls in Lancashire." *Economic Review*, July 1900, pp. 290–308.
1098. SMITH, MORRIS. "Victorian Music Hall Entertainment in the Lancashire Cotton Towns." *Local Historian* 9 (Nov. 1971): 379–86.

ASHTON-UNDER-LYNE

1099. "Harte's Grand Palace [and Fairyland]." *Era*, 8 Aug. 1896, p. 17.

BLACKBURN

1100. "Opening of the New Palace." *Era*, 9 Dec. 1899, p. 9; 16 Dec. 1899, p. 20.
1101. "A Theatre Destroyed at Blackburn." *Era*, 6 Oct. 1878, p. 4. [Star Theatre of Varieties.]

BLACKPOOL

1102. "The Alhambra." *Era*, 11 Dec. 1897, p. 20; 8 July 1899, p. 22.
1103. "The Empire Theatre." *Era*, 13 July 1895, p. 15.
1104. "Music Hall Litigation." *Era*, 5 June 1886, p. 10. [Clarence Music Hall.]

BOLTON

1105. [Museum Music Hall] *Bolton Chronicle*, 18 Jan.–22 Feb. 1873; 29 Jan. 1876.

1106. [Star Museum and Concert Hall] *Bolton Chronicle*, 17 July 1852; 14 Aug.–9 Oct. 1852.

1107. [Star Museum and Concert Hall] *Era*, 29 Aug.–9 Oct. 1852.

LANCASTER

1108. "New Palace of Varieties." *Era*, 1 Oct. 1898, p. 18.

LIVERPOOL

1109. "Another 'Scene' in a Liverpool Concert Hall." *Era*, 17 Nov. 1878, p. 4. [Gaiety Temperance Theatre of Varieties.]

1110. BROADBENT, R. J. *Annals of the Liverpool Stage from the Earliest Period to the Present Time*. Liverpool: Edward Howell, 1908. Repr. N.Y.: Benjamin Blom, 1969. ["The Variety Stage," pp. 338–44, 346–55.]

1111. C.J.S.T. "The Music Halls of Liverpool and Those Who Frequent Them." *Liverpool Review*, 15 Oct. 1892, p. 74.

1112. "Charles Johnson, Chairman of the New Star Music Hall." *Era*, 29 June 1879, p. 4. [Obit.]

1113. "City Theatre of Varieties." *Liverpool Review*, 3 Nov. 1883, pp. 101.

1114. ELLIS, DON. "The History of the Liverpool Theatres." *Call Boy* 6, no. 2 (June 1969): 13–15.

1115. "Fearful Catastrophe in a Music Hall." *Era*, 20 Oct. 1878, p. 4; 27 Oct. 1878, p. 5; 19 Jan. 1879, p. 4.
[People's Palace or Colosseum.]

1116. "The Licence of the Liverpool Grand." *Era*, 19 Nov. 1892, p. 12; 26 Nov. 1892, p. 17.

1117. "Liverpool Licensing." *Era*, 24 Dec. 1892, p. 17.

1118. "Liverpool Music and Dancing Licences." *Era*, 25 Oct. 1890, p. 18.

1119. "A Low Music Hall." *Wasp and Liverpool Punch* 39 (16 July 1880): 5, 8.

1120. "Magistrates and Music Halls." *Era*, 30 Apr. 1892, p. 16.

1121. "Mr. Jas. Kiernan and his Palaces." *Liverpool Review,* 10 Dec. 1896, p. 5.

1122. "A Music Hall Action." *Era*, 21 May 1892, p. 16. [Paddington Palace.]

1123. "A Music Hall and its Licences." *Era*, 19 Sept. 1891, p. 17. [Palace of Varieties.]

1124. "Music Hall Litigation." *Era*, 8 Nov. 1884.

1125. "Music Hall Litigation." *Era*, 19 May 1894, p. 17. [Westminster Music Hall.]

1126. "New Proposed Variety Theatre in Liverpool." *Era*, 4 Sept. 1886, p. 7. [Pavilion.]
1127. "New Star Music Hall." *Era*, 3 Dec. 1871, p. 10.
1128. "New Star Theatre of Varieties." *Era*, 2 Jan. 1897, p. 20.
1129. "New Tivoli." *Era*, 7 Mar. 1896, p. 18.
1130. "New Variety Theatre near Liverpool." *Era*, 13 Jan. 1900, p. 18.
1131. "ONE OF THE AUDIENCE." "The People's Amusements: The Parthenon, Great Charlotte St." *Liverpool Review*, 17 Nov. 1883, pp. 10–11.
1132. "A Plum for the Public." *Liverpool Review* 5 Dec. 1896. [Kiernan's Palaces of Variety.]
1133. *Publicity the True Cure of Social Evils. Liverpool Life: Its Pleasures, Practices and Pastimes. . . .* Repr. from the Liverpool *Mercury* by Hugh Shimmin. [Liverpool: 1856.]
1134. [Royal Hippodrome Rebuilt] *Builder*, 9 Aug. 1902.
1135. "Singular Scenes at a Theatre." *Era*, 4 May 1895, p. 16. [Alexandra.]
1136. WADDINGTON, JAMES. [Music-hall sketch book for Liverpool and Birkenhead halls, 1900–1953. Owned by Harry Powell of Totley, Sheffield.]

Manchester

1137. "Action against Music Hall Lessees." *Era*, 4 Aug. 1872, p. 10. [Alexandra.]
1138. "Alleged Music Hall Impropriety." *Era*, 1 Mar. 1890, p. 17. [Folly.]
1139. [Alteration to Palace] *Builder*, 11 Aug. 1900.
1140. "The Deeper Deeps of the Music Halls." *Free Lance* (Manchester), 8 Feb. 1868, pp. 41–42.
1141. "The Good Old Days." *Manchester Evening News* 30, no. 338 (19 June 1976). [Pp. 1–23. Owen French, "The Great Golden and Silver Ages," p. 2; Roy Hudd, "When They Did the Same Act for Forty Years!" p. 3. (Manchester theatre in Victorian and Edwardian eras.)]
1142. "How Manchester is Amused. I: At a Music Hall. *Free Lance* (Manchester), 22 Dec. 1866, pp. 5–6.
1143. LEARY, FRANK. "Low Singing Rooms." [Unpub. manuscript c. 1892. Manchester Central Reference Library.]
1144. "Licences in Manchester." *Era*, 1 Oct. 1892, p. 17; 28 Apr. 1894, p. 16; 19 Sept. 1896, p. 19.
1145. "Licensing at Manchester." *Era*, 22 Sept. 1900, p. 17; 29 Sept. 1900, p. 17.

1146. "Manchester and Music Halls." *Era*, 12 Oct. 1889, p. 13.
1147. MANCHESTER CENTRAL LIBRARY. *Two Hundred Years of Theatre in Manchester. . .an Exhibition. . .October 6th to October 25th, 1952.* Manchester: Society for Theatre Research (Manchester Group), 1952. [Includes check-list of Manchester theatres and music-halls 1753–1952.]
1148. "The Manchester Empire Licence." *Era*, 11 Apr. 1891, p. 17.
1149. "The Manchester Palace Licence Appeal." *Era*, 8 Jan. 1898, p. 16; 7 May 1898, p. 18.
1150. "Manchester Palace of Varieties." *Era*, 28 Sept. 1889, p. 15; 16 May 1891, p. 18; 23 May 1891, p. 14; [licence refused] 21 Feb. 1891, p. 17; [licence granted] 28 Mar. 1891, p. 15; [benefit and presentation to Mr. Scott] 12 Mar. 1892, p. 17; 2 Apr. 1892, p. 16; 6 Apr. 1892, p. 16; [liquor licence refused] 3 Oct. 1891, p. 17; 27 Aug. 1892, p. 14; 3 Sept. 1892, p. 14; 3 Dec. 1892, p. 17; 7 July 1894, p. 14; 11 Aug. 1900, p. 18.
1151. [Music Hall, Bridge Street] *Builder*, 3 Jan. 1863.
1152. "A Music Hall Licence Refused." *Era*, 12 Sept. 1885, p. 7. [Folly.]
1153. "New Music Hall in Manchester. *Era*, 20 Jan. 1878, p. 4. [New Star.]
1154. "The New Tivoli." *Era*, 11 Dec. 1897, p. 21.
1155. [The Palace] S & W 1:45, 67; vol. 3, passim.
1156. "The Round of the Music Halls." *Free Lance* (Manchester), 25 Jan. 1868, pp. 236–37.
1157. "Sale of a Manchester Music Hall." *Era*, 3 Oct. 1880, p. 4. [Britannia.]
1158. "Stage Play or Sketch?" *Era*, 15 Oct. 1892, p. 19; 29 Oct. 1892, p. 17. [Palace of Varieties.]
1159. [WELDON, CHARLES]. *Reminiscences of Music Hall and Variety Entertainments, Manchester 1864 – 5 – 6.* Leeds; Charles Weldon, 1907. 2d ed., 1908. [Engagement lists for the London Grand Music Hall, Bridge St., with introduction.]
1160. WEWIORA, GEORGE E. "Manchester Music-hall Audiences in the 1880s." *Manchester Review* 12, no. 4 (autumn 1973): 124–28.
1161. WILLIAMSON, ROBERT J. R. "The Manchester Theatre." Lecture for The Society for Theatre Research, London, 25 Jan. 1966. [Abstract in *Reports of Lectures Given During 1965 – 1966.* L: STR, 1966.]

MORECAMBE

1162. "Victoria Pavilion." *Era*, 24 July 1897, p. 17.

OLDHAM

1163. "The Empire." *Era*, 18 Sept. 1897, p. 20; 2 Oct. 1897, p. 20.

1164. "Sad Accident at a Music Hall." *Era*, 13 July 1889, p. 15; 20 July 1889, p. 15. [People's Concert Hall.]

1165. [Theatre of Varieties] *Builder*, 29 May 1897.

PRESTON

1166. "Opening of the New Empire." *Era*, 27 May 1911, p. 10.

1167. "Preston's New Empire Licence." *Era*, 29 Oct. 1910, p. 27; 3 June 1911, p. 28.

ROCHDALE

1168. CUTTS, RANDLE S. "Portrait of a Theatre. . . The Hippodrome, Rochdale, 1908–1970." *Call Boy* 7, no. 1 (Mar. 1970): 8–9.

1169. "Joe Smith of Rochdale." *Era*, 28 Nov. 1896, p. 18.

1170. "Manager and Steeplejack." *Era*, 16 Mar. 1895, p. 16. [J. Smith.]

WIGAN

1171. [Music Hall] *Builder*, 30 Jan. 1909.

Leicestershire

LEICESTER

1172. "Destruction of a Music Hall." *Era*, 2 Mar. 1889, p. 17. [Paul's.]

1173. "A New Music Hall." *Era*, 2 Aug. 1890, p. 16. [Prince of Wales' Theatre of Varieties.]

1174. "New Music Hall for Leicester." *Era*, 1 Oct. 1892, p. 16. [Gaiety Theatre of Varieties.]

1175. [Theatre of Varieties] *Builder*, 29 June 1901.

1176. WADDINGTON, R. W. "Victorian Entertainment." *Leicester Mercury*, 25 Feb. 1938.

Lincolnshire

GREAT GRIMSBY

1177. "Suicide of a Music Hall Proprietor." *Era*, 15 Oct. 1887, p. 10. [Frederick Hoffman of the Victoria.]

LINCOLN

1178. "Opposition to a Theatrical Licence in Lincoln." *Era*, 5 May 1878, p. 4.

Middlesex

CHISWICK

1179. "Chiswick Empire Opened." *Era*, 7 Sept. 1911, p. 22.

WILLESDEN

1180. [Empire] *Builder*, 28 Sept. 1907.

Monmouthshire

NEWPORT

1181. [Empire] *Builder*, 15 July 1899.
1182. "Extraordinary Refusal of a Music Hall Licence." *Era*, 30 Sept. 1877, p. 4.

Norfolk

NORWICH

1183. [Empire] *Builder*, 16 Dec. 1893.

YARMOUTH

1184. "Death of Mr. W. J. Nightingale." *Era*, 1 July 1911, p. 16; 15 July 1911, p. 15. [Mgr, Yarmouth Aquarium.]

Northamptonshire

NORTHAMPTON

1185. [New Theatre] *Northampton Independent*, 18 Nov. 1911.
1186. WARWICK, LOU. *Death of a Theatre*. Northampton: The Author, 1960. Rev. ed., 1978. [New Theatre.]

Northumberland
BLYTH

1187. "New Music Hall at Blyth." *Era*, 10 Aug. 1895, p. 14.

NEWCASTLE-UPON-TYNE

1188. [Empire] *Builder*, 6 Dec. 1890.
1189. [Empire Rebuilt] *Builder*, 10 May 1902.
1190. "Fire at the Empire." *Era*, 15 Jan. 1898, p. 18.
1191. "The New Empire at Newcastle." *Era*, 6 Dec. 1890, p. 16.
1192. [Pavilion Theatre of Varieties] *Builder*, 16 Jan. 1904.

NORTH SHIELDS

1193. [Central Hall of Varieties] *Builder*, 26 Oct. 1901.
1194. "Destruction of the Northumberland Music Hall." *Era*, 22 Dec. 1878, p. 4.

TYNEMOUTH

1195. "The Tynemouth Palace." *Era*, 25 June 1898, p. 18.

Nottinghamshire
NOTTINGHAM

1196. "Alleged Assault by a Music Hall Manager." *Era*, 31 Oct. 1875, p. 14. [Alhambra.]
1197. "Disturbance at a Music Hall." *Era*, 5 Dec. 1880, p. 4. [Royal Alhambra.]
1198. [Empire Palace] *Builder*, 12 Mar. 1899.
1199. "The Gaiety." *Era*, 7 Jan. 1899, p. 19.
1200. ILIFFE, RICHARD and WILFRED BAGUELEY. *Victorian Nottingham: A Story in Pictures*. Nottingham: 1974. [Vol. 12 covers music-hall 1837–1901, with introductory remarks on earlier periods.]
1201. [Music Hall, Goldsmith Street] *Builder*, 1 Feb. 1908.
1202. "The Nottingham Empire." *Era*, 5 Mar. 1898, p. 20.

Shropshire
SHREWSBURY

1203. "New Theatre." *Era*, 17 Dec. 1898, p. 22.

Staffordshire
HANLEY

1204. "The Empire Varieties." *Era*, 20 Feb. 1892, p. 17.
1205. "The New Grand Theatre." *Era*, 27 Aug. 1898, p. 18.
1206. "Theatrical Prosecution at Hanley." *Era*, 11 Mar. 1877, p. 4. [People's Music Hall.]

TAMWORTH

1207. "A Music Hall Proprietor in Court." *Era*, 22 Oct. 1887, p. 10. [George Rose of Rose's.]

WALSALL

1208. "The People's Music Hall." *Era*, 2 Apr. 1892, p. 16.

WOLVERHAMPTON

1209. "Empire Palace." *Era*, 3 Dec. 1898, p. 18.
1210. "New Empire." *Era*, 23 Oct. 1897, p. 21.

Suffolk
IPSWICH

1211. [Theatre of Varieties] *Builder*, 22 May, 1897.

Surrey
CROYDON

1212. [Empire] *Builder*, 16 Dec. 1905.
1213. "National Palace of Varieties." *Era*, 10 Oct. 1896, p. 18.
1214. "Opening of the Empire." *Era*, 25 Sept. 1897, p. 18.

KINGSTON-ON-THAMES

1215. "Kingston Empire Opened." *Era*, 29 Oct. 1910, p. 27.

Sussex
BRIGHTON

1216. "The Brighton Alhambra." *Era*, 25 Aug. 1888, p. 7; 6 Oct. 1888,

p. 15; 3 Nov. 1888, p. 15.

1217. "The Brighton Empire." *Era*, 26 Mar. 1898, p. 19.
1218. "The Cancan in Brighton." *Era*, 3 Nov. 1888, p. 13.
1219. "Fatal Accident in a Music Hall." *Era*, 31 Dec. 1881, p. 13; 7 Jan. 1882, p. 5. [Long Look at the Oxford.]
1220. [Hippodrome] *Builder*, 7 Sept. 1901.
1221. "A Music Hall Company's Bankruptcy." *Era*, 28 May 1887, p. 17; 18 June 1887, p. 17.
1222. "A Music Hall Licence Refused." *Era*, 3 Oct. 1880, p. 4; 10 Oct. 1880, p. 5. [Gaiety.]
1223. "Opening of the Brighton 'Empire.'" *Era*, 27 Aug. 1892, p. 14.
1224. "Time Has All Things." *Sussex County Magazine* 28:410–414. [Gaiety Royal Hippodrome.]

HASTINGS

1225. "The Empire." *Era*, 8 Apr. 1899, p. 19.
1226. "Farewell to a Theatre." *Hastings Observer*, 25 Feb. 1970. [Hippodrome.]

Warwickshire

BIRMINGHAM

1227. "Birmingham Empire Jubilee." *Era*, 14 Sept. 1911, p. 21.
1228. "Birmingham Empire, Ltd." *Era*, 30 July 1898, p. 17.
1229. "Birmingham Empire Palace." *Era*, 28 Apr. 1894, p. 17; 5 May 1894, p. 16.
1230. "Birmingham Star Music Hall Meeting of the Creditors." *Era*, 27 Mar. 1886, p. 10.
1231. "Brown, Newland and Le Clerq." *Era*, 27 Jan. 1894, p. 16.
1232. "A Chat with Charles Barnard." *Era*, 2 Mar. 1895, p. 16. [Prop. Gaiety.]
1233. "Death of a Music Hall Manager." *Era*, 22 Dec. 1883, p. 4. [Dan Saunders of Day's and New Star.]
1234. "Empire Anniversary." *Era*, 11 May 1895, p. 17.
1235. "Fatal Outrage at a Music Hall." *Era*, 12 Apr. 1890, p. 15 [Murder of mgr. of Canterbury Concert Hall.] "Rowdies at Music Halls" [edit.], p. 13; 19 Apr. 1890, p. 14; 16 Aug. 1890, p. 15.
1236. FLANAGAN, CHRIS and TOM HITCH HOUGH. "Brummagem Nights." *Call Boy* 14, no. 3 (autumn 1977): 10–11; no. 4

(winter 1977): 10–11; 15, no. 1 (spring 1978): 10–11; no. 2 (summer 1978): 10–11.
1237. "The Gaiety Palace." *Era*, 24 Oct. 1896, p. 20; 6 Nov. 1897, p. 16; 13 Nov. 1897, p. 18.
1238. [Inge Street Music Hall] *Builder*, 12 Mar. 1898.
1239. [James Day, prop. Day's Music Hall, obit.] *Era*, 27 Feb. 1876.
1240. "The Major and the Music Hall." *Era*, 18 June 1881, p. 4; 20 Aug. 1881, p. 4. [Major Bond v. Props. of Day's Concert Halls.]
1241. MANNING, HAROLD. "Heyday of the Music Hall." *Birmingham Post Midland Magazine*, 22 Aug. 1968, p. 1.
1242. "Music Hall Action." *Era*, 25 Jan. 1890, p. 16. [Crystal Palace Concert Hall.]
1243. "New Tivoli." *Era*, 18 Aug. 1900, p. 16.
1244. "Presentation to A. W. Matcham." *Era*, 15 Jan. 1898, p. 19. [Mgr Empire.]
1245. "Presentation to a Music Hall Manager." *Era*, 11 Feb. 1882, p. 4. [R. G. Goldsmith.]
1246. [Reconstruction of the Empire] *Builder*, 18 Nov. 1893.
1247. WILLIAMSON, RICHARD. *Those Good Old Theatre Days*. Birmingham: *Sunday Mercury & Weekly Post*, 1978. [A Sunday Mercury Special.]

LEAMINGTON

1248. "Suicide of a Music Hall Manager." *Era*, 15 Aug. 1885, p. 10. [Edwin Holmes.]

STRATFORD-UPON-AVON

1249. "The New Empire." *Era*, 25 Mar. 1899, p. 21; 8 Apr. 1899, p. 18.

Wiltshire

SALISBURY
1250. [Palace Theatre] *Builder*, 3 Aug. 1888.

Worcestershire

DUDLEY
1251. [Music Hall, Hall Street] *Builder*, 29 Mar. 1902.

Kidderminster

1252. BIVEN, THOMAS. "Troubles of a Provincial Music Hall Proprietor." *Era*, 3 Dec. 1876, p. 3. [Oxford Theatre of Varieties.]

Worcester

1253. "Destruction of Worcester Music Hall." *Era*, 12 Feb. 1881, p. 5.

Yorkshire

Attercliffe

1254. "The Alhambra." *Era*, 8 Jan. 1898, p. 21.

Barnsley

1255. "A Music Hall Case." *Era*, 27 Oct. 1890, p. 10. [Lewis's.]

Bradford

1256. "The Alhambra Theatre." *Bradford Pictorial*, Nov. 1965, p. 23.
1257. BURNLEY, JAMES. *Phases of Bradford Life: A Series of Pen & Ink Sketches.* L: Simpkin, Marshal, 1871. L, Bradford: T. Brear, 1875. ["Music Hall Life," pp. 54–63. Unfavorable account, discusses rapport between audience and entertainer.]
1258. "Destruction of a Bradford Theatre." *Era*, 21 July 1878, p. 4. [Star Music Hall]
1259. [Empire] *Builder*, 11 Mar. 1899.
1260. "Empire Palace." *Era*, 23 Oct. 1897, p. 18; 22 Jan. 1898, p. 19.
1261. "King of Pantomimes Became Mecca of North." *Bradford Telegraph*, 21 Mar. 1964. [Alhambra.]
1262. MELLOR, GEOFF J. *et al. Theatres of Bradford. A Review by Mr. Geoff Mellor, with an introduction by Mr. Roger W. Suddard, and a Theatrical Portrait by Mr. Peter Holdworth.* Bingley; The Bookworm, 1978.
1263. "New Empire." *Era*, 28 Jan. 1899; 4 Feb. 1899, p. 22.
1264. "The People's Palace." *Era*, 1 Aug. 1896, p. 17.
1265. "Star Music Hall." *Era*, 8 Sept. 1894, p. 16.

Clapham

1266. "The New Grand Hall of Varieties." *Era*, 20 Oct. 1894, p. 16.

Dewsbury

1267. [Music Hall] *Builder*, 16 Jan. 1909.

DONCASTER

1268. "Doncaster's New Palace of Varieties." *Era*, 26 Aug. 1911, p. 23.

HUDDERSFIELD

1269. [Music Hall] *Builder*, 5 June 1909.

HULL

1270. "The Alhambra Palace at Hull." *Era*, 13 Oct. 1872, p. 12.
1271. "Assault on a Music Hall Proprietor." *Era*, 30 Mar. 1889, p. 15.
1272. "Hull Palace Anniversary." *Era*, 10 Dec. 1898, p. 20.
1273. "Licensing at Hull." *Era*, 27 Aug. 1898, p. 20.
1274. "The New Palace Theatre." *Era*, 4 Dec. 1897, p. 20; 11 Dec. 1897, p. 21.
1275. [Palace] *Builder*, 18 Dec. 1897.
1276. SHEPPARD, THOMAS. *Evolution of the Drama in Hull and District*. Hull: A Brown & Sons, 1927. [Pp. 65-66, 71.]

LEEDS

1277. "Assault by a Music Hall Proprietor." *Era*, 4 Oct. 1874, p. 4. [Varieties.]
1278. "Death of Mr. Frank Hall." *Era*, 29 Oct. 1898, p. 20. [Mgr. Alhambra.]
1279. *The Famous City Varieties Music Hall, Leeds, Souvenir Brochure*. Leeds: Roberts [c. 1955].
1280. HOLE, J. *The Working Classes of Leeds*. L, Leeds: 1863. [Music halls more attractive than Mechanics' Institutes.]
1281. "Music Hall Union at Leeds." *Era*, 10 Nov. 1872, p. 4.
1282. "New Empire Palace." *Era*, 6 June 1896, p. 16; 13 Aug. 1898, p. 17.
1283. "The New Princess's Palace." *Era*, 10 Nov. 1888, p. 18.
1284. "Opening of the Empire." *Era*, 3 Sept. 1898, p. 18.
1285. "A Row in a Music Hall." *Era*, 23 Feb. 1889, p. 16. [Varieties.]

MEXBOROUGH

1286. HILLERBY, BRIAN. *A History of the Hippodrome Theatre, Mexborough*. Mexborough: Hillerby, 1978.

MIDDLESBOROUGH

1287. [Empire] *Builder*, 4 Mar. 1899.
1288. "The Empire." *Era*, 6 Nov. 1897, p. 16.

1289. "Empire Palace." *Era*, 11 Mar. 1899, p. 18.
1290. *The Empire Palace of Varieties Limited, Middlesborough, Yorks: Souvenir presented upon the Occasion of the Laying of the Foundation Stone by His Worship the Mayor, Col. S. A. Sadler, Middlesborough 4th November 1897.* [Middlesborough: 1897.]
1291. "The Middlesborough Lock-out." *Stage Year Book* (1910): 175–76.

SCARBOROUGH

1292. PRESCOTT, CYRIL. "The Opera House, Scarborough." *Call Boy* 10, p. 4. (winter, 1973–74): 18–20.

SHEFFIELD

1293. [Alterations to Music Hall] *Builder*, 8 Apr. 1865.
1294, [Empire Palace] *Builder*, 5 Oct. 1895.
1295. "New Empire Palace." *Era*, 26 Oct. 1895, p. 19; 9 Nov. 1895, p. 18.
1296. "Sheffield Music Hall Company." *Era*, 9 Feb. 1895, p. 16.
1297. "Sheffield Palace of Varieties." *Era*, 8 Sept. 1894, p. 16; 6 Oct. 1894, p. 16.

WHITBY

1298. "Action by a Music Hall Artiste." *Era*, 7 Nov. 1885, p. 10. [Stella de Vere v. Star Theatre.]

SCOTLAND

Cross-references

See also General **128, 366, 1948, 2271–72, 2276–78, 2390–2489, 2668, 3300, 3303.**
Aberdeen **1948.**
Edinburgh **2173, 2435, 2580.**
Falkirk **1951.**
Glasgow **2152, 2658, 2664–65.**

General

1298a. "Death of Tom Maclagan." *Era,* 16 Aug. 1902. [Relates career of popular Scottish comedian.]

1299. IRVING, GORDON. *The Good Auld Days. The Story of Scotland's Entertainment from Music Hall to Television.* L: Jupiter, 1977.
[Appendix ("Theatres and Halls in Scotland") lists every music-hall.]

1300. ———. "Music Hall in Scotland." *Call Boy* 7, no. 1 (Mar. 1970): 5.

1301. "Last of the Halls." *Economist* 205 (3 Nov. 1962): 468–70.
["A Theatrical Correspondent" reports on Glasgow and Edinburgh.]

1302. "The Theatre Committee." *Era,* 21 May 1892, p. 7.

Specific Towns

ABERDEEN

1303. "Burning of a Music Hall." *Era,* 3 Oct. 1896, p. 20; 10 Oct. 1896, p. 19.
[Palace of Varieties.]

1304. [Empire Palace Rebuilt] *Builder,* 25 Dec. 1897.

1305. "The Palace Theatre." *Era,* 29 Oct. 1898, p. 22.

1306. "Panic in a Music Hall." *Era,* 26 Aug. 1877, p. 4.
[M'Farland's.]

ARGYLE

1307. "D. J. Clarke of Birkenhead." *Era,* 24 June 1911, p. 23.
[Prop., Argyle Theatre of Varieties.]

AYR

1308. MOORE, JOHN. *Ayr Gaiety: The Theatre Made Famous by the Popplewells.* Edinburgh: Albyn Press, 1975.

1309. ———. "Britain's Last Twice-nightly Theatre." *Call Boy* 14 (winter 1977): 5. [Gaiety.]

DUNDEE

1310. "Burning of a Music Hall." *Era,* 13 Oct. 1888, p. 15.
[M'Farland's Theatre of Varieties.]

119

1311. "Death of Mr. William M'Farland." *Era*, 23 Apr. 1898, p. 22.
[Mgr, Dundee Music Hall.]
1312. "New Variety Hall." *Era*, 21 Feb. 1891, p. 17.
[People's Palace of Amusements.]
1313. "Presentation to Mr. W. M'Farland." *Era*, 11 May 1889, p. 15.
1314. [Variety Theatre] *Builder*, 18 Apr. 1903.

EDINBURGH

1315. "The Edinburgh Calamity." *Era*, 13 May 1911, p. 28.
[Palace of Varieties.]
1316. "Edinburgh Empire Reopened." *Era*, 12 Aug. 1911, p. 21.
1317. "An 'Empire' Palace for Edinburgh." *Era*, 27 Apr. 1889, p. 18.
1318. "Music Hall Litigation." *Era*, 13 Mar. 1886, p. 10; 18 July 1886,
p. 10.
[Theatre of Varieties.]
1319. "New Empire Palace." *Era*, 12 Nov. 1892, p. 16.

FALKIRK

1320. [Music Hall] *Builder*, 10 Apr. 1909.

GLASGOW

1321. "The Alexandra." *Era*, 22 Oct. 1898, p. 18.
1322. "Arthur Lloyd's Music Hall." *Era*, 15 Oct. 1881, p. 4.
1323. "Bankruptcy of a Music Hall Lessee." *Era*, 26 Mar. 1876, p. 5.
[Alexandra.]
1324. [Cambridge Music Hall] *Builder*, 13 Feb. 1909.
1325. "Comic Songs." *Era*, 10 Oct. 1885, p. 10.
1326. "Death of Mr. R. McKean." *Era*, 16 May 1885, p. 10.
[Prop., Britannia.]
1327. "Death of Mrs. Baylis." *Era*, 8 Jan. 1898, p. 22. [Mgr.]
1328. [Empire Reconstructed] *Builder*, 17 Apr. 1897.
1329. "The Gaiety Theatre." *Music Hall*, 23 Aug. 1895, p. 15.
1330. "The Glasgow Alhambra." *Era*, 17 Dec. 1910, p. 29; 24 Dec.
1910, p. 16; 27 June 1911, p. 24.
1331. "The Glasgow Gaiety." *Era*, 7 Feb. 1891, p. 16.
1332. "The Glasgow Gaiety Licence." *Era*, 28 Feb. 1891, p. 18.
1333. "The Glasgow Music Hall Scandal." *Era*, 22 Nov. 1884, p. 18.
[Alexandra.]
1334. "The Glasgow 'Scotia.'" *Era*, 18 June 1892, p. 14.
1335. "The Glasgow Singing Saloons." *Era*, 7 Mar. 1875, p. 4.
1336. IRVING, GORDON. "Theatre of a Thousand and One
Glamourous Nights. The Story of the Glasgow Alhambra." *Call*

Boy 7, no. 2 (June 1970): 8–9; no. 3 (Sept. 1970): 8–10; no. 4 (Dec. 1970): 8–10.

1337. "The New Albert Music Hall." *Era*, 7 Sept. 1879, p. 4.
1338. "New Empire Palace, Glasgow." *Era*, 3 Apr. 1897, p. 19; 10 Apr. 1897, p. 19.
1339. "Old Glasgow Halls." *Era*, 7 June 1911, p. 26.
1340. "Opening of a New Music Hall in Glasgow." *Era*, 20 Dec. 1874, p. 7. [Royal Albert.]
1341. "Panic in a Music Hall." *Era*, 8 Nov. 1884, p. 10. [Star Theatre of Varieties.]
1342. "Robbery from the Britannia Music Hall." *Era*, 3 Nov. 1878, p. 4.
1343. [Scotia Music Hall Rebuilt] *Builder*, 1 Jan. 1898.
1344. "Two Glasgow Music Halls on Fire." *Era*, 10 May 1874, p. 4; 17 May 1874, p. 4. [Scotia and Brown's Royal.]
1345. WILLIAMS, ELLIOT. "The Old Britannia of the Trongate, Glasgow." *Call Boy*, 15, no. 3 (summer 1978): 3.

GREENOCK

1346. [Music Hall] *Builder*, 24 May 1902.
1347. "A Scotch Squabble over Music Hall Morality." *Era*, 20 July 1873, p. 13.

INVERNESS

1348. [Music Hall] *Builder*, 4 Mar. 1899.

LEITH

1349. "Riot in a Music Hall." *Era*, 15 Dec. 1878, p. 4. [Star.]

IRELAND

Cross-references

See also General **3042**.
Dublin **2143, 3026**.

General

1350. LAWRENCE, W. J. "The Old Music Hall: Successor to the 'Free and Easy': Favourites of 50 Years Ago; Audiences Then Largely Male." *Ireland Saturday Night* (Dublin), 14 June 1930.

Specific Towns

BELFAST

1351. "The Alhambra. Refusal of licence." *Era*, 21 Jan. 1872, p. 13.

1352. "The Belfast Empire of Varieties." *Era*, 24 Apr. 1897, p. 19.

1353. BELFAST PUBLIC LIBRARIES. Irish and Local Studies Department. *Theatres and Cinemas in Belfast — a Retrospective View: Catalogue of an Exhibition held at the Central Library, Belfast, 12 May – 30 June 1979.* Belfast: Belfast Public Libraries, Irish and Local Studies Department, 1979.
[Summary of ephemeral and archival material held by agencies in Belfast.]

1354. "Empire Theatre." *Era*, 5 Oct. 1895, p. 16.

1355. "Funeral of J. J. Stamford." *Era*, 3 June 1899, p. 19.
[Mgr, Royal Alhambra.]

1356. GILBERT, LOUIS. *The Solid Man: The Life of Willie John Ashcroft.* Belfast: Blackstaff Press, 1979.
[Biography of American entertainer who was mgr of Belfast Alhambra Theatre 1878-1900.]

1357. "A Mad Music Hall Proprietor." *Era*, 1 Nov. 1884, p. 14; 6 Dec. 1884, p. 14.
[W. J. Ashcroft of Alhambra.]

1358. "Music Hall Litigations." *Era*, 14 Nov. 1885, p. 10; 14 June 1890, p. 15. [Buffalo.]

1359. "A New Music Hall." *Era*, 12 Dec. 1891, p. 16. [Empire.]

1360. "Opening of Empire." *Era*, 5 Oct. 1895, p. 16.

CORK

1361. "Cork Palace of Varieties." *Era*, 24 Apr. 1897, p. 18; 6 May 1899, p. 19.

1362. "The Munster Music Hall." *Era*, 8 June 1873, p. 7.

DUBLIN

1363. "A Dublin Music Hall License." *Era*, 15 Oct. 1892, p. 16. [Dublin Music Hall.]

1364. "Empire Palace." *Era*, 3 Sept. 1898, p. 19.

1365. [Empire Palace Rebuilt] *Builder*, 4 Dec. 1897.
1366. "Empire Palace Theatre." *Era*, 20 Nov. 1897, p. 20.
1367. "Funeral of Mr. Dan Lowrey." *Era*, 28 Aug. 1897, p. 18.
1368. "Grand Lyric Hall." *Era*, 20 Nov. 1897, p. 20.
1369. [Grand Lyric Music Hall Rebuilt] *Builder*, 13 Nov. 1897.
1370. "A Jump from the Gallery." *Era*, 25 Aug. 1888, p. 12. [Lowrey's Star.]
1371. "The Late Mr. Dan Lowrey." *Era*, 13 July 1889, p. 15.
1372. "The Lyric Theatre." *Era*, 17 Dec. 1898, p. 20.
1373. "Music Hall Action." *Era*, 20 June 1885, p. 10; 27 June 1885, p. 10. [Star]
1374. "The New Empire." *Era*, 30 Oct. 1897, p. 18.
1375. "New Music Hall for Dublin." *Era*, 9 Apr. 1892, p. 17.
1376. "New Star Varieties." *Era*, 27 Aug. 1892, p. 14.
1377. "Presentation to Mr. Dan Lowrey." *Era*, 6 Oct. 1894, p. 16.
1378. "Star Theatre of Varieties." *Era*, 4 Sept. 1897, p. 18; 25 Sept. 1897, p. 20.
1379. WATTERS, EUGENE and MATTHEW MURTAGH. *Infinite Variety: Dan Lowrey's Music Hall 1878 – 97*. Dublin: Gill and Macmillan, 1975.

WALES

Cross-references

See also Cardiff **1969**.

CARDIFF
1380. "The Cardiff Empire Fire." *Era*, 4 Nov. 1899, p. 19.
1381. [Cardiff Empire Rebuilt] *Builder*, 9 May 1896.
1382. "Licences at Cardiff." *Era*, 24 Sept. 1887, p. 10.
1383. "The New Empire Palace." *Era*, 3 Apr. 1896, p. 16; 9 May 1896, p. 18.

CAERNARVON
1384. "A Comedian from Caernarvon. A Chat with Tom Jones." *Era*, 1 Oct. 1910, p. 27.

SWANSEA

1385. [Empire] *Builder*, 20 Dec. 1900.
1386. "A Music Hall Licence refused." *Era*, 6 Feb. 1892, p. 17. [Pavilion.]
1387. "Swansea New Empire." *Era*, 15 Dec. 1900, p. 20.

ISLE OF MAN

DOUGLAS

1388. GREY, JOHN. "Frank Matcham's Gaiety, Douglas, up to Complete Renovation." *Stage*, 2 Feb. 1978, p. 10.

VI. ARCHITECTURE

"The Canterbury has an arrangement for ventilation peculiar
to itself. A large portion of the roof is so arranged as to admit
of its easy and rapid removal and replacement."

*Dickens's Dictionary of
London,* 1890–1891.

The ingenuity in the Canterbury arrangements reflects the part
played by the music-hall in English playhouse architecture of the
nineteenth century. In its inceptive phases the music-hall had no
distinctive building of its own. Backrooms of taverns, wine-vaults,
rectangular chambers with platforms barely fitting a piano and a
performer were the makeshifts that accommodated song-and-
supper entertainments. The saloon theatres that abounded after
the 1843 Act may have varied in atmosphere from the club-like ap-
pointments of Evans' to the *gemütlich* festivity of the Canterbury
to the seedy ambience of the Argyll Rooms, but what they all had in
common was a stage at one end for performance and a bar at the
other for refreshment. At first, the latter was the more important
imposing feature of the arrangement, but by the 1870s there was less
of restaurant and more of theatre in the disposition of the halls.

Gradually with the music-hall's growing popularity and atten-
dant respectability, the influence of the concert hall could be
detected in new buildings and those remodelled to suit variety bills.
Overhanging balconies and galleries and a regular amount of
decorative hardware and plasterwork became regular features of
these theatres. Lavish eclecticism was the keynote of the more

125

elegant houses, and by the end of the century, with the rise of the "Palaces of Variety," gilt and plush were standard hallmarks of decorum and audience comfort as were, less ostentatiously, new means of ventilation and fire safety. Architects like Frank Matcham and Bassett Keeling specialized in the Imperial styles of Moorish-Hindu, Flemish Renaissance and Alhambran that wafted the spectator to a fantasy world, remote from his reality and equally at odds with the homelier references on the stage. Nazi bombing, thoughtless redevelopment, and "urban renewal" have all played a part in the demolition of many prime examples of this idiosyncratic, highly characteristic school of British design and construction. But of late the rescue and preservation of major extant halls, such as Wilton's, have proved successful.

The location of existing architect's plans for London music-halls can be found in Diana Howard; the most important contemporary source for ground-plans, blueprints and detailed reportage of music-hall architecture is the journal *The Builder*. We have given a number of specific references in the listings for individual halls and cities. The following enumerates some works of general interest on the subject.

Cross-references

See also 3, 432–33, 484–85, 488, 490, 493, 503, 513, 525, 533, 537, 541, 551, 554, 566, 572, 579, 593, 622, 632, 637–38, 640–42, 644, 646, 650, 654–55, 671, 675, 679–80, 690, 692–93, 701–3, 708, 729, 748, 759, 774, 780, 799, 806, 816, 818, 820, 822, 867–68, 872, 876, 901, 906, 915–16, 918, 933, 939, 964, 970, 972, 994, 1015, 1026, 1029, 1030, 1033, 1035, 1037–39, 1041, 1043, 1056, 1064–65, 1069, 1070–71, 1082, 1084–85, 1088, 1096, 1099, 1102–3, 1127–28, 1130, 1151, 1153–55, 1165–66, 1171, 1173, 1175, 1179, 1180–81, 1188–89, 1192–93, 1198, 1200–1201, 1203, 1209–17, 1220, 1223, 1229, 1237–38, 1246, 1249–51, 1254, 1267, 1269, 1275, 1287, 1289, 1290, 1293–94, 1304, 1312, 1314, 1320, 1324, 1328, 1337, 1340, 1343, 1346, 1348, 1352, 1354, 1359–62, 1364–66, 1368–69, 1372, 1374–76, 1378, 1381, 1385, 1387, 1388.

1389. GIROUARD, MARK. *Victorian Pubs*. L: Studio Vista, 1975.

1390. GLASSTONE, VICTOR. *Victorian and Edwardian Theatres: An Architectural and Social Survey.* L: Thames & Hudson, 1975. ["The Rise of Music Hall," pp. 45–57.]

1391. HONRI, PERCY, and BAYNHAM HONRI. "The Matchless Matcham." *Call Boy* 9, no. 4 (Dec. 1972): 12–14; 10, no. 1 (Mar. 1973): 12–14. [Music-halls designed by Frank Matcham.]

1392. LINSTRUM, DEREK. *West Yorkshire Architects and Architecture.* L: Lund Humphries, 1978. [Chapter 9, "Theatres and Music Halls." pp. 269–80.]

1393. McCARTHY, SEAN. "Frank Matcham's Early Career." *Theatre Notebook* 25, no. 3 (spring 1971): 103–8; no. 4 (summer 1971):152–57; 26, no. 2 (winter 1971/72):64–72.

1394. McNAMARA, BROOKS. "The Scenography of Popular Entertainment." *The Drama Review* (N.Y. University), 18, no. 1 (Mar. 1974): 16–24.

1395. "Obituary of Frank Matcham." *Builder,* 28 May 1920.

1396. RENTON, E. *Vaudeville Theatres: Building, Operation, Management.* N.Y.: Gotham Press, 1918.

1397. SACHS, EDWIN O. and ERNEST A. S. WOODROW. *Modern Opera Houses and Theatres.* 3 vols. L: Batsford, 1896–98. Repr. N.Y.: Benjamin Blom, 1968. [Vol. 1, Alhambra, pp. 42–43; vol. 2, Empire, pp. 39–40; Oxford, p. 41; vol. 3, various.]

1398. SPAIN, GEOFFREY and NICHOLAS DROMGOOL. "Theatre Architects in the British Isles." *Architectural History* 13 (1970):77–89.

1399. SPILLER, BRIAN. *Victorian Public Houses.* Newton Abbot: David & Charles, 1972. ["Going Out," pp. 48–53.]

1400. STATHAM, H. H. "Architecture of Music Halls." *Eclectic Engineering Magazine (Van Nostrand's)* (N.Y.) 8 (1877):345.

1401. ———. "Planning of Music Halls." *American Architect and Building News* (Boston) 64 (1898):37.

1402. THOMPSON, PAUL. *William Butterfield.* L: Routledge & Kegan Paul, 1971. [On Bassett Keeling, architect of the Strand Musick Hall.]

VII. REGULATION

"As to your notion that music halls are an unmitigated evil, I think that *is* sweeping, in your own sense of the term. I am convinced that music halls, when they are freed from the censorship of Middlesex magistrates and their like, will do more to educate the people artistically than all the nimminy-pimminy concerts in the world."

George Bernard Shaw to Francis Hueffer, 19 Jan. 1883. [*G. B. Shaw, Collected Letters 1874-1897*, ed. Dan Laurence (London: Max Reinhardt, 1965) 58.]

Almost from its inception, the music-hall was subject to external interference. The Theatre Act of 1843, which allowed minor theatres to play straight drama so long as they did not serve food and drink, at the same time doomed the saloon theatres, which became the music-halls, to be regarded as species of public houses, subject to the same regulation. Later in the century, when music-hall bills included dramatic sketches, the managers ran afoul of the same law which forbade them to stage plays. Regularly Parliament appointed Select Committees to investigate places of entertainment from the point of view of morality, tax revenues and public safety; the most important of these were named in 1852, 1866, and 1892 to recommend changes in the prevailing laws.

In addition to parliamentary control, the music-hall was subject to local regulation by Boards of Works and County Councils;

licenses had to be renewed annually at which time anyone could register a complaint and try to prevent the reissuance of the license. Many did, particularly those who saw the halls as sinks of corruption and nests of crime. The most famous of these moralists was the brewery heir turned missionary Frederick Charrington, whose well-publicized attacks on East End halls made him a laughingstock to some, a hero to others. However, the most notorious of these attacks came in 1894 from the reformer Mrs. Ormiston Chant, whose insistence that the Empire Music Hall shut down its Promenade, the haunt of expensive prostitutes, before its license was renewed, provoked a flurry of controversy. The moralists were seldom strong enough to carry the day in the nineteenth century, although conservative opinion was capable of having the Rev. Stewart Duckworth Headlam relieved of his curacy when he preached that attendance at music-halls was harmless. Pharisaism received a boost, however, in the twentieth century, during the Great War, when the music-halls were rigorously policed to prevent the corruption of service-men, and barmaids were replaced by barmen.

Although magistrates often prosecuted on moral grounds as well as strictly legal ones, we have in the following pages distinguished between morality and censorship, and civic and parliamentary legislation, with a special subsection in the latter devoted to the sketch controversy of the 1890s, when it was argued whether a ten-minute playlet constituted a drama. There are, as well, sections devoted to a list of relevant public bills and reports of select committees, and articles concerning music copyright, for songs were regularly pirated throughout the nineteenth century.

MORALITY AND CENSORSHIP

Cross-references

See also **82, 122, 256, 351, 378, 590–91, 627, 793, 877–86, 1090, 1138, 1347, 1643, 1744–46, 1748–50, 2084, 2480, 2629, 3497, 3653.**

1403. "Alleged Music Hall Impropriety." *Era*, 1 Mar. 1890, p. 17.

1404. "Ash Wednesday and Music Halls." *Era*, 14 Feb. 1875, p. 6; 24 Oct. 1875, p. 4.

1405. BETTANY, FREDERICK GEORGE. *Stewart Headlam: a Biography.* L: John Murray, 1926.
[On the Church and Stage Guild.]

1406. "Canon Barfield on Music Halls." *Era*, 11 Jan. 1880, p. 4.

1407. [Censorship] *Times*, 12 Nov. 1909, p. 4e.

1408. [Censorship. Appeal of the National British Women's Temperance Association.] *Times*, 27 Nov. 1913, p. 12a.

1409. "The Censorship of Music Halls." *Saturday Review* 68 (26 Oct. 1910):446.

1410. "The Censorship of the Halls." *Era Annual* (1917): 36.

1411. CENTRAL VIGILANCE COMMITTEE, L. *First Annual Report.* L: 1884. [All pub.]

1412. CHANT, Mrs. LAURA ORMISTON. *Why We Attacked The Empire* L: Marshall & Son, 1895.

1413. CHARRINGTON, FREDERICK M. *The Battle of the Music Halls.* L: Dyer Brothers [1885].

1414. [Church and Music Halls] *Times*, 3 Oct. 1912, p. 5d.

1415. "Church and Stage." *Music Hall and Theatre*, 26 Oct. 1889, p. 12.

1416. "The Church and the Music Halls." *Era*, 19 Oct. 1889, p. 15.

1417. "Clerical Intolerance." *Era*, 20 Jan. 1878, p. 4.
[On Headlam's dismissal.]

1418. "The Coffee Music Halls Movements." *Era*, 12 Dec. 1880, p. 4; 23 July 1881, p. 4.

1419. *Coffee Tavern Protection Society: Objects, Rules and Officers 1889.* L: 1889.

1420. [Cooperation between L.C.C. and Lord Chamberlain's Office] *Times,* 22 Jan. 1912, p. 13.

1421. CORDEROY, E. *Popular Amusements. A Lecture before the Young Men's Christian Association.* [L: James Nisbet, 1857.]

1422. COWEN, JOHN. "Music Halls and Morals." *Contemporary Review* 110 (Nov. 1916): 611–20.

1423. CRAIG, EDWARD GORDON. *The Music Hall & The Church. A Letter reprinted from "The Mask" January 1914.* Florence [Italy]: The Mask, 1914.
[Addressed to the Bishops of London and Kensington "who have lately been interesting themselves so actively in the Music-hall."]

1424. CURWEN, J. SPENCER. "The Progress of Popular Music." *Contemporary Review* 52 (Aug. 1887): 236–48.

1425. "The Dancer and the Vigilantes." *B[ritish] F[ilm] I[nstitute] News* 30 (Oct. 1977): 3.

1426. [Defence of music halls] *Church Reformer*, June 1892.

1427. DICKENS, CHARLES, the Younger. "Magistrates and Music Halls." *Theatre* 2 (1879): 87–90.
[Do away with improper songs and you do away with the need to supervise audience.]

1428. FRYER, PETER. *Mrs. Grundy: Studies in English Prudery.* L: Dobson Books, 1963. Paperback ed. L: Corgi books, 1965.
[Chapter 25, "Kicking against the High-kicks" (Cancan in London); Chapter 26, "Shocking History of Strip-tease."]

1429. "'Gagging' by Comic Vocalists." *London and Provincial Entr'acte*, 17 Feb. 1872, p. 3.

1430. GREENWOOD, JAMES. *In Strange Company, being the Experiences of a Roving Correspondent.* Edinburgh: 1873. 2d ed. L: H. S. King, 1874.

1431. ———. *Low Life Deeps.* L: Chatto & Windus, 1876.
[Ills. Alfred Concanen.]

1432. ———. "Music Hall Morality." *London Society* 14 (Dec. 1868): 486–91.

1433. ———. *The Seven Curses of London.* L: Stanley Rivers; N.Y.: Harper & Row, 1869.
[Section 4, chapters 16, 18, pp. 271–330, on prostitution in the halls.]

1434. ———. *The Wilds of London.* Guildford & L: Chatto & Windus, 1874.
[Ills. Alfred Concanen. "An Evening at a Whitechapel 'Gaff,'" pp. 12–20; "Amongst the Music-hall luminaries," pp. 90–98; "At the Death-bed of a London Dragon" (The Coal Hole), pp. 99–106; "An 'Anti-idiotic-entertainment Company,'" pp. 303–9.]

1435. HALL, EDWARD HEPPLE. *Coffee Taverns, Cocoa Houses, and Coffee Palaces: Their Rise, Progress and Prospects, with a Directory.* L: 1878.

1436. HANDS, CHARLES E. "A Common Person's Complaint. Music Halls Improved out of Existence." *Daily Mail*, 25 Nov. 1913, p. 8.

1436a [Harcourt's Theatre and Music Halls Bill] *Times*, 26 Apr. 1909, p. 10a; 7 June 1909, p. 10a.

1437. HARRISON, BRIAN. *Drink and the Victorians: the Temperance Question in England 1815-1872.* L: Faber & Faber; Pittsburgh, Pa.: University of Pittsburgh Press, 1971.
[Pp. 27, 47, 324–25, 347. Important in indicating relation be-

tween music-hall management and drink manufacturers.]
1438. ———. "Pubs." In *The Victorian City: Images and Realities* ed. H. J. Dyos and Michael Wolff, 1:174–75. L. & Boston: Routledge and Kegan Paul, 1973.
1439. HAWEIS, H. R. *Music and Morals.* L: W. H. Allen, 1871. ["Music Halls and Negro Music," pp. 498–501; "Vocal Street Music," pp. 547–48. Pro music-hall.]
1440. HEADLAM, STEWART DUCKWORTH. *The Function of the Stage.* L: F. Verinder, 1899.
[Lecture before the Church and Stage Guild, in defence of stage, dancing and ballet.]
1441. ———. "Theatres and Music Halls." *Era,* 18 Nov. 1877, p. 12. [Follow-up correspondence, 27 Jan. 1878, pp. 4–5.]
1442. ———. *Theatres & Music Halls: a Lecture given at the Commonwealth Club, Bethnal Green on Sunday, October 7, 1877... with a Letter to the Bishop of London and Other Correspondence.* 2d ed. Westminster: Women's Printing Society [1877].
[First pub. in the *Era,* led to the end of Headlam's curacy at St Matthew's, Bethnal Green.]
1442a HOLE, DONALD. *The Church and the Stage: the Early History of the Actors' Church Union.* L: Faith Press, 1934.
1443. "The Hooligan and the Music Halls." *Era,* 10 Nov. 1900, p. 20. [Letter from *Daily Chronicle* with reply by Edgar Bateman; follow-up 17 Nov. 1900, p. 20.]
1444. IMAGE, SELWYN. "Miss Annie Abbott at the Alhambra." *Church Reformer,* Jan. 1892, p. 277.
["Quaedam miscellanae."]
1445. ———. "The New Puritanism." *Church Reformer,* Nov. 1894, p. 246; Dec. 1894, p. 270; Jan. 1895, pp. 7–11.
1446. [Improper Music-hall Dialogue] *Times,* 26 Feb. 1914, p. 4d.
1447. [Improper Songs] *Times,* 21 Dec. 1915.
1448. [Impropriety: Lord Chamberlain's Warning to Music-Hall Managers] *Times,* 7 May 1915, p. 5d; 8 May 1915, p. 5b.
1449. "The Indictment of the Music-hall." *New Statesman* 8, no. 89 (18 Nov. 1916): 153–55. Repr. in *Living Age* (N.Y.) 292 (3 Feb. 1917): 313–16.
[Question of indecency. Value of music-hall's ribaldry and its growing improvement.]
1450. "Irresponsible Puritans." *Era,* 20 Jan. 1897, p. 17. [Edit.]
1451. JEVONS, W. STANLEY. "Methods of Social Reform: Amusement of the People." *Contemporary Review* 33 (Oct. 1878): 498–513.

1452. KINGHONE, J. "Music Hall Censorship." *Era*, 13 Feb. 1876, p. 9.

1453. KITCHNER, TOM W. "The Moral Music Hall." *Music Hall and Theatre Review*, Christmas no. 1894, pp. 7–13.
[Ills. Will Bray. Comic story of a fraudulent "moral" music-hall.]

1454. MANTON, HENRY. *Letters on Theatres and Music-halls: Especially Intended for Sunday School Teachers and Senior Scholars.* Birmingham: C. Caswell [1888].

1455. MERION, CHARLES. *The Music Hall Stage and its Relation to the Dramatic Stage and the Church.* [L? c. 1881.]

1456. "The 'Missionary' and the Music Hall." *Era*, 5 Aug. 1882, p. 4; 12 Aug. 1882, p. 4.
[About Frederick Charrington.]

1457. "Morals and Music Halls." *Punch*, 23 Aug. 1862, p. 3. ("A Confidential Letter to Tom Turniptoppe, Esquire, late of Greenley Bottom, Blankshire, and now of Blackstone Buildings, Temple," pp. 79–80.)
[Quotes from an *Observer* piece against music-hall. Better to go to Evans' than to music-halls. Accompanied by a cartoon: SWEEP: "Shall I see you at the Music Hall to-night, William?" DUSTMAN: "No, Joseph, that's a cut below me."]

1458. "Mrs Chant on Music Halls." *Era*, 17 Nov. 1894, p. 16.

1459. "A Music Hall Artist's Defence." *Era*, 23 June 1894, p. 17.
[Dora Langlois riposting to Grant Allen's "New Hedonism" in *The Fortnightly Review.*]

1460. "Music-hall Morality." *Spectator* 63, 12 Oct. 1889): 461.

1461. "Music Hall Morals." *Era*, 28 Feb. 1875; 7 Mar. 1875, p. 6; 30 Mar. 1879, p. 4.

1462. "Music Halls and Mission Halls." *Era*, 21 Oct. 1882, p. 4.
[About Frederick Charrington.]

1463. "The Music Halls as Others Would See It." *Punch,* 2 Nov. 1895, p. 210.
[Reformed music-halls.]

1464. "Music Halls for the Millions." *Punch*, 13 Sept. 1879, p. 110.
[Coffee music-halls.]

1465. NEWTON, H. CHANCE. "A Terrible Outlook." *Entr'acte Annual* (1903): 30–31.
[Poem about a reformed music-hall.]

1465a. ORENS, JOHN RICHARD. "Lewis Carroll and the Dancing Priest." *Jabberwocky The Journal of the Lewis Carroll Society* (1978): 31–36.

[On Stewart Headlam, whose biography the author is writing.]
1466. "Our Popular Amusements." *Dublin University Magazine* 84 (1874):233–44.
[Expectation of elevating influence of music-hall disappointed.]
1467. "Pharisaism and Music-halls." *Saturday Review* 88 (13 Oct. 1894): 405; 17 Nov. 1894, p. 534; 24 Nov. 1894, p. 557.
1468. [Promenades] *Times*, 19 Apr. 1916, p. 5c; 24 July 1916, p. 8b; 13 Sept. 1916, p. 5a; 16 Sept. 1916, p. 5b; 30 Oct. 1916, p. 5a.
1469. [Promotion of Public Morality] *Times*, 25 Jan. 1915, p. 5c.
1470. [Purification of Music Halls] *Times*, 24 Jan. 1910, p. 2d.
1471. REECE, R. "The Pious Music Hall by a Converted Proprietor." *Entr'acte Annual* (1890): 10.
1472. "Sadler's Wells as a Music Hall. The Vicar and Churchwarden Speak." *Era*, 10 Sept. 1892, p. 15; 8 Oct. 1892, p. 16.
1473. [SCOTT, CLEMENT] "Prudes on the Prowl." *Daily Telegraph*, 14 Oct. 1894.
1474. "Slighting the Variety Profession." *Era*, 22 July 1911, p. 19. [Edit.]
1475. "'Smut' at the Music Halls." *Era*, 26 Jan. 1879, p. 4.
1476. [Stage Play Prosecutions] *Times*, 20 May 1910, p. 2d.
1477. "Temperance Music Halls." *Era*, 20 July 1879, p. 4.
1478. *Tempted London: Young Men.* L: Hodder & Stoughton, 1888. [Chapter 9, "Music-halls," pp. 172–91; chapter 10, "The Variety Theatres of London," pp. 192–200.]
1479. THORNE, GUY. *The Great Acceptance: the Life Story of F. N. Charrington.* L: Hodder & Stoughton, 1913. [Chapter 5, "The Battle of the Music Halls," pp. 104–34; chapter 6, "The Fight on the London County Council," pp. 135–52. Charrington's moral crusade against East End halls.]
1480. TURNER, E. S. *Roads to Ruin.* L: Michael Joseph, 1950. Repr. 1966. Paperback ed. Harmondsworth: Penguin Books, 1966. [Chapter 9, "A Flourish of Strumpets," is the best account, based on contemporary newspapers, of the Empire Promenade controversy.]
1481. "A Vicar on Music Halls." *Era*, 19 Oct. 1889, p. 15. [H. B. Chapman.]
1482. ["Vulgar Innuendo" in Songs] *London and Provincial Entr'acte*, 17 Feb. 1872, p. 3.
1483. "Vulgarity on the Stage." *Era*, 24 Nov. 1900, p. 18.
1484. WILLIAMS, H. L. "Coffee Palace Failures." *Social Notes and Club News*, 16 July 1881.

MUNICIPAL LICENSING AND PARLIAMENTARY LEGISLATION

Cross-references

See also **General 230, 256, 275, 358, 545, 576, 595, 608, 718, 766, 786, 836, 840, 897, 921, 945, 1045, 1049, 1116–17, 1120, 1123, 1144, 1148, 1149, 1152, 1167, 1177–78, 1182, 1222, 1273, 1332, 1363, 1382, 1386, 1803.**

"Sketch" Controversy **232, 562, 665, 826, 1158, 1486, 1556, 2079.**

General

1485. "Alleged Infringement of Music Licensing Act." *Era*, 21 Feb. 1875, p. 7.
1486. "Alleged Stage Plays in Music Halls." *Era*, 14 Mar. 1880, p. 4; 29 Mar. 1880, p. 4.
1487. "The Anti-gagging Clause." *Era*, 22 Mar. 1890, p. 13. [Edit.]
1488. ARCHER, WILLIAM. "The County Council and the Music Halls." *Contemporary Review*, 67 (Mar. 1895): 317–27.
1489. "The Battle of the Music Halls; (Meeting about Licencing)." *Era*, 19 Oct. 1889, p. 15.
1490. BIRMINGHAM (Borough of). *Report of the Committee of Justices appointed on the Subject of the Protection of the Public from Fire in the Theatres and Music Halls within the Borough.* Birmingham: Geo. Jones and Son [1888]. [Dated 28 Dec. 1887, approved by the justices 4 Jan. 1888.]
1491. "The Board of Works and Music Halls." *Era*, 13 Feb. 1886, p. 10; 9 Apr. 1887, p. 16.
1492. BRAYDON, J. L. [Mgr of Middlesex]. "Theatres and Music Halls." *Era*, 7 Mar. 1891, p. 16; 14 Mar. 1891, p. 11 [follow-ups]; p. 15 [edit.]; 28 Mar. 1891, p. 15.
1493. "Child Labour in Music Halls." *Era*, 12 July 1890, p. 15.
1494. COBORN, CHARLES. "The Magistrates and the Music Halls." *Era*, 7 Oct. 1877, p. 4.

1495. "County Council and Early Opening." *Era*, 9 Apr. 1898, p. 17.
1496. "The County Council and Licenses." *Era*, 1 Dec. 1900, p. 19.
1497. "The County Council and Music Halls." *Era*, 27 Apr. 1889, pp.15, 17 [edit.]; 14 May 1889, pp. 14–15; 22 Feb. 1890, p. 15 [edit.]; 28 June 1890, p. 15; 11 Oct. 1890, p. 15 [edit.]; 29 Nov. 1890, p. 17; 6 Dec. 1890, p. 15 [edit.] 8 Aug. 1891, p. 14; 17 Feb. 1894, p. 15 [edit.]
1498. "County Council Licensing." *Era*, 17 Oct. 1896, pp. 19, 20.
1499. "A County Councillor on Music Halls." *Era*, 31 Aug. 1889, p. 15.
1500. "County Councils and Amusements." *Era*, 21 June 1890, p. 9.
1501. "Dangerous Performances Bill." N.Y. *Clipper*, 3 Apr. 1880, p. 16.
1502. D'OYLY CARTE, RICHARD. "Mr. D'Oyly Carte and Music Halls." *Era*, 16 Apr. 1892, p. 14.
1503. "Exits and Improprieties." *Era*, 16 Aug. 1890, p. 13. [Edit.]
1504. [For the Music Halls] "The Theatre Committee." *Era*, 28 May 1892, p. 8; 4 June 1892, p. 10; 25 June 1892, p. 15.
1505. GEARY, Sir WILLIAM NEVILL MONTGOMERIE. *The Law of Theatres and Music-halls including Contracts and Precedents of Contracts*. L: Stevens & Sons, 1885.
[With appendix of statutes, and London and provincial acts and regulations. Local regulations, pp. 161–212.]
1506. GRAHAM, H. A. "The Regulation of Music Halls." *Era*, 10 Feb. 1883, p. 5.
1506a. HADDON, ARCHIBALD. *The Story of the Music Hall from Cave of Harmony to Cabaret*. With a foreword by Henry Arthur Jones. L: Cecil Palmer, 1924.
[A pamphlet, not to be confused with No. 121. Protests the "unjust discrimination of the London County Council" in refusing to grant refreshment licences to music-halls.]
1507. "History of Legislation for Regulation of Theatres and Music-halls." *Builder*, 5 Apr. 1884, p. 493.
1508. HOLLINGSHEAD, JOHN. "Molly-coddling Legislation." *Entr'acte Annual* (1904): 15–16.
1509. ———. *Plain English*. L: Chatto & Windus, 1880.
["Music and Dancing Licenses," pp. 65–69; "Theatrical Licenses," pp. 70–104.]
1510. ———. *Theatrical Licenses*. Repr. from "The Daily Telegraph" and "Times." L: Chatto & Windus, 1875.
1511. "Important to Music Hall Proprietors: Licensed or Not Licensed?" *Era*, 5 Oct. 1873, p. 7.

1512. ISAACS, SIDNEY CHARLES. *The Law Relating to Theatres, Music-halls, & Other Public Entertainments, & to the Performers therein, including the Law of Musical and Dramatic Copyright, etc.* L: Stevens & Sons, 1927.
1513. JONES, HENRY ARTHUR. *The Foundations of a National Drama: a Lecture.* L: Chiswick Press, 1904.
["The Licensing Chaos in Theatres and Music-halls."]
1514. ———. "One License for All." *Era*, 5 Mar. 1910, p. 15.
1515. ———. *An Open Letter to the Right Honourable Winston Churchill, M.P.* L: Chiswick Press, 1910.
[Advocates measures to legalize the production of plays at music-halls.]
1516. "The Licensing Question." *Era*, 2 Oct. 1897, p. 17. [Edit.]
1517. "Liquor Licenses in Music Halls and Theatres." *Era*, 13 June 1896, p. 16.
1518. "London County Council and the Music Halls." *Theatre*, n.s. 24 (Dec. 1894): 277.
1519. "The Lord Chamberlain and licensing." *Era*, 19 Nov. 1894, p. 15.
1520. "The Magistrates and Music Halls." *Era*, 16 Feb. 1879, p. 7; 27 Apr. 1879, p. 4; 30 Apr. 1881, p. 5; 20 Aug. 1881, p. 5.
1521. "Magistrates and Music Halls." *Era*, 10 Feb. 1883, p. 4; 17 Feb. 1883, p. 4 [reply].
[Important exchange.]
1522. "The Magistrates' Muddle." *Era*, 15 Oct. 1871, p. 9.
1523. "M'Dougall [of the LCC] on Music Halls." *Era*, 21 Feb. 1891, p. 17; 19 Mar. 1892, p. 16.
1524. "The Middlesex Licensing Muddle." *Era*, 22 Oct. 1881, p. 5.
1525. "Middlesex Music and Dancing Licenses." *Era*, 15 Oct. 1881, p. 5; 11 Oct. 1884, p. 9.
1526. "Minutes of Theatres and Music Halls Committee." 8 Nov. 1911. Greater London Record Office [unpub.]
1527. Mr M'Dougall [of the LCC] on Music Halls." *Era*, 15 Mar. 1890, p. 14.
1528. "Music and Dancing and Stage Play Licences for Music Halls and Theatres." *Report by the Clerk of the Council.* 28 Oct. 1911. Greater London Record Office [unpub.].
1529. "Music and Dancing Licences." *Era*, 15 Oct. 1871, p. 12; 19 Oct. 1879, p. 3; 24 Oct. 1880, p. 5; 14 Oct. 1882, p. 5; 4 Oct. 1890, p. 8; 11 Oct. 1890, p. 17; 25 Oct. 1890, p. 17.
1530. "Music and Dancing Licences in Middlesex." *Era*, 6 Oct. 1878,

p. 4; 13 Oct. 1878, p. 3.

1531. "Music and Dancing Licenses Bill." *Stage Yearbook* (1913): 85–86.

1532. "A Music Hall County Council Candidate." *Era*, 2 July 1892, p. 14 [Philip J. Rutland.]

1533. "Music Hall Inspection." *Era*, 2 Aug. 1890, p. 15; 9 Aug. 1890, p. 15 [edit.]

1534. "Music Hall Licenses." *Era*, 14 July 1894, p. 14.

1535. "Music Hall Licensing." *Era*, 10 Sept. 1887, p. 10.

1536. [MUSIC HALL PROPRIETORS' PROTECTION ASSOCIA-TION] *The Regulation of Music Halls. A Summary of the Attempts made by Music Hall Proprietors to Obtain an Improvement of the Law Regulating Places of Public Entertainment; with Some Opinions of the Press on the Subject.* L: F. Chiffenel and Co. [1883].

1537. "[Music Hall Statistics before] The Theatre Committee." *Era*, 14 May 1892, p. 8.

1538. "Music Hall versus Theatre. Mr. George Dance's Resolve." *Era*, 1 Oct. 1910, p. 15; 8 Oct. 1910, p. 15.

1539. "Music Halls and Stage Plays." *Era*, 17 Mar. 1872, p. 7.

1540. "Music Halls and the Board of Works." *Era*, 20 May 1882.

1541. "Music Halls and the Licensing Act." *Era*, 20 Jan. 1883, p. 2.

1542. "Music Halls and the Theatre Bill." *Era*, 9 May 1891, p. 17; 30 May 1891, p. 15.

1543. "Music Halls Municipalised." *Era*, 10 Sept. 1910, p. 25. [Quoted from P. P. Howe in *Socialist Review*.]

1544. "Music-halls versus the Drama." *Cornhill Magazine* 15 (1867): 119–28. [On Select Committee on Theatrical Licenses, 1866.]

1545. "The New County Council Bill." *Era*, 1 Mar. 1890, p. 15.

1546. "New Legislation for the Prevention of Fires in Music Halls." *Era*, 28 Apr. 1878, p. 4.

1547. NICHOLSON, WATSON. *The Struggle for a Free Stage in London.* Boston & N.Y.: Houghton Mifflin, 1906. Rev. *Academy*, 25 May 1907, pp. 503–4. [History of theatrical licensing.]

1548. "Penny Theatres and Wise Magistrates." *Era*, 27 Oct. 1878, p. 7.

1549. "The Police and the Music Halls." *Era*, 21 Apr. 1872, p. 12.

1550. RALEIGH, CECIL. "Music Hall Law." *Era*, 14 Jan. 1911, p. 23.

1551. REYNOLDS, WALTER. "The Double Licence." *Era*, 11 Mar.

1911, p. 23; 1 July 1911, p. 22.

1552. ROWLEY, J. W. "Muzzling the Comedian." *Era*, 15 Mar. 1890, p. 14.
[The anti-gagging clause.]

1553. [Scrapbook of Clippings from London newspapers 8 Mar. 1890 to 28 Mar. 1892, covering the London County Council's proposed Bill of 1891 for licensing theatres and music halls, including protests by Henry Irving, Edward Terry, Sir Arthur Pinero, Herbert Beerbohm Tree, and others. N.p., c. 1892.] N.Y. Public Library [call no. NCOM +]

1554. SHAW, GEORGE BERNARD. Preface to *The Shewing-Up of Blanco Posnet: A Melodrama*. L: Constable, 1918.
[Pp. 297–373. First pub. 1909.]

1555. "Skating on Dangerous Ground." *Era*, 12 Mar. 1876, p. 10.

1556. "Stage Plays at Music Halls." *Era*, 13 May 1877, p. 4; 15 Feb. 1880, p. 5; 29 Aug. 1880, p. 4.

1557. *"The State of the London Theatre and Music Hall 1886."* Repr. from the *Saturday Review*. L: Frederick Warne, 1887.
[Concerning fire safety.]

1558. STRONG, ALBERT AMBROSE. *Dramatic and Musical Law being a Digest of the Law Relating to Theatres and Music Halls, and containing Chapters on Theatrical Contracts, Theatrical, Music and Dancing and Excise Licences, Dramatic and Musical Copyright, &c. with an Appendix containing the Acts of Parliament relating thereto and the Regulations of the London County Council and the Lord Chamberlain*. L: "The Era" Publishing Office, 1898. [Dedicated to Edward Ledger.] 2d ed. 1901; 3rd ed. 1910.

1559. STUMP, WALTER RAY. *British Parliamentary Hearings on the Theatre between 1843 and 1909: the Struggle for a Free Stage in London Revisited*. Ph.D. dissertation, Indiana University, 1973.

1560. "Sunday Amusements. A Chat with Mr Charles Jesson, L.C.C." *Era*, 4 June 1910, p. 22.

1561. "Sunday Opening." *Stage Yearbook* (1913): 92–93.

1562. "Theatre and Music-hall." *Spectator*, 14 May 1892, pp. 673–74.
[Parliamentary committee: two separate audiences for halls and theatres; music-hall audience likes to smoke and drink.]

1563. "Theatres and Music Halls." *Era*, 14 May 1892, p. 15. [Edit.]

1564. "Theatres and Music Halls." *Era*, 10 Sept. 1898, p. 20; 16 Sept. 1899.
[Committee Report.]

1565. "Theatres and Music Halls." *Saturday Review* 81 (14 Mar. 1891): 320.

[Legal status.]
1566. "Theatres and Music Halls Commission." *Punch*, 9 Apr. 1892, p. 173.
1567. "Theatres and Music Halls; Deputation to the Home Secretary." *Era*, 13 Mar. 1886; 20 Mar. 1886, pp. 9, 15.
1568. "Theatres and Music Halls Report." *Era*, 27 Aug. 1894, p. 14.
1569. "Theatres *v.* Music Halls. 'How are Women Going to Regard the Question of Smoking in Theatres?' asks the Daily Mirror of Nov. 17." *Punch*, 25 Nov. 1903, p. 367.
1570. "The Two Licences." *Era*, 10 Dec. 1910, p. 21. [Edit.]
1571. VALENTINE, J. "A Plea for Music in Common Life." *Good Words* 7 (July 1866): 473-76. [On report of Select Committee of 1866.]
1572. "What is a Stage Play? Important to Music Hall Proprietors." *Era*, 16 Jan. 1870, p. 4.

The "Sketch" Controversy

1572a HARDY, HAROLD. "Stage Plays in Music Halls." N.Y. *Dramatic Mirror*, 2 Apr. 1904, p. 17.
1573. IRVING, HENRY and J. L. TOOLE. "The Drama at the Music Halls." *Era*, 23 Apr. 1892, p. 15.
1574. MACKAY, W. S. "Sketches at the Halls." *Era*, 11 Feb. 1899, p. 21.
1575. "The Music Hall Sketch." *Era*, 7 Dec. 1889, p. 16.
1576. "Music Hall Sketches." *Era*, 12 Oct. 1889, p. 16 [long piece]; 19 Oct. 1889, p. 15.
1577. "Music Hall 'Sketches.'" *Saturday Review* 81 (6 June 1891): 672. [On their legal status.]
1578. PIGGOTT, EDWARD F. S. "Sketches in Music Halls." *Era*, 2 June 1894, p. 17; 9 June 1894, p. 16 [replies].
1579. "The Sketch Question." *Era*, 8 Apr. 1911, p. 21; 19 Nov. 1892 [edit.]; 26 Nov. 1892, p. 16; 3 Dec. 1892, p. 17; 27 Aug. 1910, p. 16.
1580. "The Sketch Question Again." *Era*, 10 May 1890, p. 15; 19 Nov. 1892 [edit.]; 26 Nov. 1892, p. 16; 3 Dec. 1892, p. 17; 27 Aug. 1910, p. 16.
1581. "Sketches at Music Halls." *Era*, 9 May 1891, p. 15 [edit.]; 16 May 1891, p. 17; 9 Apr. 1892, p. 15 [edit.]
1582. "Stage Plays in Music Halls." *Era*, 19 Nov. 1892, pp. 16, 17.
1583. "Still the Sketch Question." *Era*, 31 Dec. 1910, p. 23 [edit.]

PUBLIC BILLS, SELECT COMMITTEES, DEBATE PROCEEDINGS

Cross-references

See also **1490**

[To be found in the State Paper Room of the British Library.]

1584. A Bill for the better regulation of theatres and music halls in the metropolis. [Public bills 1886 VI, 35 (69 sess. 1).]

1585. A Bill for the better regulation of theatres and music halls in the metropolis. [Public bills 1888 VIII, 415 (37).]

1586. A Bill for the better regulation of theatres and music halls in the metropolitan area. [Public bills 1887 VI, 327 (15).]

1587. A Bill for the better regulation of theatres and music hall within the Metropolitan area. [Public bills 1884 VII, 257 (6).]

1588. A Bill to amend and extend the law relating to theatres, music halls, and places of public entertainment or resort in the administrative County of London (not printed). [Public bills 1890 IX, 95 (159).]

1589. A Bill to confer further powers upon the Metropolitan Board of Works for inspecting theatres and music halls and granting certificates. [Public Bills 1886 IV, 119 (44 sess. 1).]

1590. A Bill to confer further powers upon the Metropolitan Board of Works for inspecting theatres and music halls and granting certificates. [Public Bills 1887 IV, 227 (117).]

1591. A Bill to make better provision for the requisition of theatres in London (not printed). [Public Bills 1890 IX, 93 (133).]

1592. A Bill to provide for the control and regulation of theatres, music halls, and places of public entertainment in the administrative County of London; and for other purposes. [Public Bills 1890–91 X, 329 (106).]

1593. Select Committee appointed to examine into the system under which public houses, hotels, beer-shops, dancing saloons, coffee

houses, theatres, temperance hotels, and places of public entertainment are sanctioned and regulated, with a view of reporting
whether any alteration of the law can be made for the better preservation of public morals, the protection of the revenue, and for
the proper accommodation of the public. Report with proceedings, minutes of evidence, appendix and index. *British Sessional
Papers: House of Commons* 1852–53 (855) xxxvii, 1.

1594. Select Committee appointed to inquire into the constitution, effi-
ciency, emoluments, and finances of the Metropolitan Fire
Brigade, and into the most efficient means of providing for secur-
ity from loss of life and property by fire in the metropolis. Report
with proceedings, evidence, appendix and index. *British Sessional
Papers: House of Commons, 1876 . . . (&c), British Sessional
Papers: House of Commons,* 1877 (Sessional Papers, Vol. 14,
p. 37) Appendix 3: Metropolitan theatres, licensed by the Lord
Chamberlain. Appendix 4: List of music halls (&c) licensed by the
magistrates, and lists of theatres licensed by the Lord Chamberlain (&) by the magistrates. (Short title: Select Committee on the
Metropolitan Fire Brigade.)

1595. Select Committee appointed to inquire into the working of the
Acts of Parliament for licensing and regulating theatres and
places of entertainment in Great Britain. Report together with the
proceedings of the Committee, minutes of evidence, and appendix. *British Sessional Papers: House of Commons,* 1866, XVI, 1.
(375). [Short title: Select Committee on Theatrical Licenses and
Regulations.] [Includes: Capacities of various parts of house,
295; estimated cost of buildings and fittings and numbers of people accommodated daily in London halls.]

1596. Select Committee on theatres and places of entertainment. PP
1892, XVIII, appendix 15.

1597. Select Committee on theatrical licenses and regulations. PP 1866,
XVI, appendix 3.

1598. "Stage Play Performances in Music Halls." *Minutes of the
Theatres and Music Halls Committee* (15 May 1912), Greater
London Record Office.

1959. "Stage Plays (Theatres and Music Halls) Motion," *Parliamentary Debates* L: 1928. [LI (16 April 1913) 2036–66.]

1600. *Stage and Theatre.* 3 vols. Shannon: Irish University Press, 1971.
[Three nineteenth-century reports of Select Committees of House
of Commons 1831–92.]

1601. "Theatre and Music hall Licences." *Parliamentary Debates.* L:
1928. [DCCLIX, 1019.]

COPYRIGHT

Cross-references

See also **1512, 1558, 2076.**

1602. "Copyright in Comic Songs." *Era,* 12 Nov. 1871, p. 10.
1603. "Copyright in Songs." *Era,* 13 Mar. 1897, p. 20.
1604. "Copyright of 'Daisy Bell.'" *Era,* 2 Mar. 1895, p. 16; 29 June 1895, p. 14.
1605. "Copyright of Songs." *Era,* 18 June 1887, p. 17.
1606. "Is a Comic Song a Dramatic Representation?" *Era,* 14 Jan. 1872, p. 7. [Case of Clark v. Bishop involving copyright of song sung publicly.]
1607. M'GLENNON, FELIX. "Copyright Music Hall Songs." *Era,* 16 Jan. 1886, p. 10; 23 Jan. 1886, p. 10 [follow-up by Hubert Cole and F. V. St. Clair]; 30 Jan. 1886, p. 10 [others]; 6 Feb. 1886, p. 10; 13 Feb. 1886, p. 10.
1608. "The Musical Copyright Agitation." *Era,* 25 Feb. 1876, p. 4. [Hopwood & Crew.]
1609. [Performing Rights Society, formed 1875, Cases brought by] *Times,* 10 June 1882.
1610. "Song Piracy." *Era,* 20 June 1888, p. 16; 14 July 1888, p. 16.
1611. "Song Writers and Song Stealers." *Era,* 15 Dec. 1878, p. 14; 22 Dec. 1878, p. 4; 5 Jan. 1879, p. 4; 12 Jan. 1879, p. 3; 26 Jan. 1879, p. 9.

VIII. OPERATION

"What I like in Halls are 'turns'—comic singers, or men imitating Prima Donna's, or Jugglers. I don't like one act plays . . . the humour of Harry Tate, though a low grade was still the queer English humour; something natural to the race, which makes us all laugh; why I don't know; & you can't help feeling its the real thing, as, in Athens one might have felt that poetry was."

> Virginia Woolf, *Diaries 1915–1919*, ed. A. O. Bell (N.Y. and London: Harcourt Brace Jovanovich, 1977) 19, 144. [16 Jan. 1915, 1 May 1918.]

Under the somewhat catch-all title "Operation" the reader will find comic singers, men imitating prima donnas, jugglers and no one-act plays. Essentially this section is devoted to performance, management, and the concerns of those who worked within the halls. The first two subsections concern singing, dancing, and general performance techniques, as well as sidelights on the artistes' working lives. The subsection on specialty acts has its own headnote, explaining the principles of selection there. The section on management and agency relates to economics from the lessees' point of view; music halls were businesses as well as places of amusement, and questions of incorporation, contracts, and monopoly were as lively there as in the stock exchange. The final section concerns labor's point of view and the various friendly societies and benevolent organizations created to protect the music-hall worker, culminating in the formation of the Variety Artists' Federation in 1906 and the ensuing strike of 1907, the so-called "Music Hall War," that followed the refusal of the manager Walter Gibbons to sign a VAF charter.

N.B. The most important or interesting legal cases were summarised annually in *The Stage Year Book* 1908–28.

GENERAL PERFORMANCE TECHNIQUES AND WAY OF LIFE

Cross-references

See also **4, 112, 246, 248, 1298, 1384, 1429, 1822, 1830, 1909, 2036–37, 2297, 2301.**

1612. " A Chat with a Comic Singer." *Era,* 18 July 1891, p. 15. [J. H. Milburn.]
1613. "A Chat with Theo. Gordon [baritone]." *Era,* 23 Jan. 1897, p. 16.
1614. COMBES, WILLIAMS H. "Truest to Nature—a Music Hall Legend." *Entr'acte Almanack* (1878): 18–20.
1615. ———. "Two of a Trade Seldom Agree." *Entr'acte Annual* (1898): 22–23.
1616. "A Comical Comic Vocalist in Court." N. Y. *Clipper,* 25 July 1872, p. 132. [Frederick Deuters v. Metropolitan District Railway. Much information on salary and work routines.]
1617. CONNOLLY, CHARLES. "English, You Know." N.Y. *Clipper,* 21 Nov. 1885, p. 568. [On publicity sobriquets of performers.]
1618. KENNICK, THOMAS. *Comic Singing Made Easy: with Useful and Practical Hints Suitable Alike for Artist & Amateur. Notes and Comments on Celebrated Singers, Past and Present: with Arguments Illustrative of Excellence in the above Art, and How to Obtain It.* L: William Challoner, 1869. [Discusses Vance,

Arthur Lloyd, Harry Clifton, Ford, Sam Collins, and Mrs. F. R. Philips.]

1618a. KITCHNER, TOM W. *Music Hall and Theatre Guide and How to Get on the Stage. . .a Complete Treatise for Every Amateur and Beginner.* [L: c. 1890.] [Brief pamphlet.]

1619. LANE, LUPINO. *How to Become a Comedian.* L: Muller, 1945.

1620. LAWRENSON, HELEN. "Inconsistency of Music Hall Performances." *Era,* 18 Apr. 1891, p. 17.

1621. LUCAS, MAY F. "A Movin' on." *Era Annual* (1910): 92-93. [American vaudevillian's memoirs of British music-hall tour as "Poor Jo."]

1622. "Music Hall Broughams." *Era,* 17 Sept. 1892, p. 16.

1623. REYNOLDS, FRANK. "The 'Halls' from the Stalls. VI.—The Comedian." *Sketch,* 22 Feb. 1905, p. 212.

1624. "The Risks of a Topical Singer." *Era,* 17 Mar. 1878, p. 4.

1625. "Rival Comic Vocalists." *Era,* 19 Sept. 1880, p. 4.

1627. SMITH, ARTHUR. "Recollections of Billy Randall [comic singer]." *Era,* 18 June 1898, p. 16.

1627. VICINUS, MARTHA. "Happy Times. . .If You Can Stand It: Women Entertainers during the Interwar Years in England." *Theatre Journal* (Washington, D.C.) 33, no. 3 (Oct. 1979): 357-69. [Material on minor careers gleaned from interviews with stage veterans.]

1628. WILLIAMSON, JOHN. "Vicar of Mirth." And VIVIAN FOSTER. "Music Hall Eloquence and Wit." *Stage,* 15 Feb. 1979, p. 8. [On John Foster-Hall who performed under the stage name Vivian Foster, 1868-1945.]

DANCE

Cross-references

See also **296, 358, 594, 1218, 1425, 1428, 1912-17, 2121, 2132, 2528, 2541-42, 3377, 3506-7, 3599, 3650, 3662, 3829-30.**

1629. "The Ballet at the Alhambra." *Era,* 16 Jan. 1876, p. 14.

1630. BELMONT, GEORGE E. "Clog-dance Reminiscences." *Era,* 23 Oct. 1897, p. 18.

1631. "The Can-can." *Era,* 13 Dec. 1874, p. 11.

1632. "The Clang of the Wooden Shoon." *Era,* 21 May 1898, p. 20. [Clog-dancing.]

1633. "Clog-dancing Contest." *Era,* 2 July 1898, p. 20.

1634. "Do the Clodoches Dance?" *Era,* 28 Apr. 1872, p. 7; 5 May 1872, p. 13.[Cambridge music-hall prop. sued for allowing dancing.]

1635. DUNCAN, ISADORA. *My Life.* L: Victor Gollancz, 1928.

1636. "An English Dancer [Ida Heath]." *Era,* 19 May 1894, p. 17.

1637. FROST, HELEN. *Clog and Character Dances.* N.Y.: A. S. Barnes, 1924.

1638. ———. *The Clog Dance Book.* N.Y.: A. S. Barnes, 1921.

1639. [FULLER, LOIE] "Loie Fuller on Dancing." *Era,* 3 Sept. 1910, p. 24.

1640. GUEST, IVOR FORBES. *The Alhambra Ballet.* Brooklyn, N.Y.: Dance Perspectives, 1959. [Dance Perspectives, 4.]

1641. ———. *The Empire Ballet.* L: Society for Theatre Research, 1962.

1642. ———. "Hey-day of the Can-can." In *Second Empire Medley,* ed. W. H. Holden. L: British Technical & General Press, 1952.

1643. "Indecent Dancing." *Era,* 26 Oct. 1873, p. 12.

1644. "Juvenile Clog-dancing." *Era,* 24 Apr. 1897, p. 19.

1645. "My Fancy." *Era,* 10 Dec. 1898, p. 20. [Soft-shoe performer.]

1646. PARKER, DEREK and JULIA. *The Natural History of the Chorus Girl.* Newton Abbot: David & Charles, 1975.

1647. PERUGINI, MARK EDWARD. *A Pageant of Dance and Ballet.* L: Jarrolds, 1935. [Chapter 26, "Ballet at the Alhambra Theatre, 1854–1894," pp. 219–26; Chapter 27, "Ballet at the Alhambra Theatre, 1894–1914," pp. 227–36; Chapter 28, "Ballet at the Empire Theatre, 1884–1902," pp. 237–46; Chapter 29, "Ballet at the Empire Theatre, 1903–1914," pp. 247–61,]

1648. PILLEN, JULIAN. *Lancashire Clog Dance.* L: English Folk Dance & Song Society, 1967. [Repr. from *Journal of EFDSS.*]

1649. "The Question of Dancing in Music Halls." *Era,* 2 June 1872, p. 13.

1649a. SHERRY, SAM. "'Actual Stepdancing,' an Autobiography." *Call Boy* 17, no. 1 (spring 1980): 12–14. [repr. from *English Dance & Song.* Transcribed and ed. by Ann-Marie Hulme and Peter Clifton.]

1650. "Skirt Dancing." *Saturday Review* 83 (25 June 1892): 741–42. [Introduced on the halls by John D'Auban.]

1651. THOMPSON, LYDIA. "Boot-blacks as Chorus Girls." *Era Almanack* (1900): 22–23.

1652. TILLER, JOHN. "Stage Dancing." *Performer,* 10 Apr. 1919, p. 19.

1653. TUCKER, HENRY. *Clog Dancing Made Easy.* N.Y.: R. M. de Witt, 1874.

1654. WALKER, KATHRINE SORLEY. "Georges Jacobi and Alhambra Ballet." *Theatre Notebook* 1 (1945–47): 82–83. [Jacobi was musical director 1871–97.]

SPECIALTY ACTS

"There is a story told of an earnest and conscientious young man who was instructed by a firm of theatrical publishers to compile a directory of music-hall artistes, with a special section for each line of business. It took him a long time to master the nice distinctions existing between 'vocal' comedians, 'characteristic' artistes, and 'actor' vocalists, and when he had overcome that difficulty, he had to contend with a whole host of bewildering 'specialities,' including 'funambulists,' 'eccentrics,' 'knockabouts,' 'high-kickers,' and others, who in very despair of acquiring a suitable designation, styled themselves 'nondescripts.' He struggled on manfully with the work, however, until a professor of legerdemain whom he had inadvertantly described as a conjurer, instead of 'prestidigitateur and illusionist' withdrew his advertisement. Then the publishers wrote a snubbing letter to the compiler, who finally threw up the work in despair."

C. D. Stuart and A. J. Park,
The Variety Stage (London, 1895) 216.

The editors of the present work, laboring under similar difficulties, here present only a sampling of the kinds of acts which filled the music-hall in its later career as it became known as "variety." To pursue much further studies of acrobats, animal acts, and jugglers would be to invade the province of the circus and the fairground, and the investigation of conjurers, pugilists and mind readers deserves separate and full-scale treatment. We have been content to indicate certain major figures and important books and articles relating their skills to the music-hall. The student can supplement these references by referring to Toole-Stott's bibliographies of conjuring and circus arts. Various branches of the profession have their own journals, such as *Acrobatics* (1954–76; then *Acrobatics Magazine*), which should be consulted. Separate data on Walford Bodie, Paul Cinquevalli, and Eugen Sandow will be found under Personalia, and the cross-references are provided.

Cross-references

See also Acrobats, Trapeze Artists, and Wire Walkers **359, 808, 1718b, 1816, 3075–92, 3315, 3496, 3506, 3533, 3557, 3592, 3752.**
Animal Acts **1791, 2863, 3057, 3662.**
Animal Impersonators **2293–95.**
Conjuring and Magic **247, 357, 1816, 1945–54, 3726, 3752.**
Contortionists and Gymnasts **3496.**
Female and Male Impersonators **1955–64, 2362–69, 2922–26, 2974–3020, 3313, 3533, 3592.**
Jugglers **247, 2052–71.**
Living Pictures **296, 487, 604, 844.**
Mentalists, Memory Experts, and Mind Readers **374.**
Mimicry **1909.**
Strong Men and Women **1444, 2902–21, 3073a.**
Ventriloquists **1909, 2684–85.**
Wrestlers and Boxers **2766.**

Acrobats, Trapeze Artists, and Wire Walkers

1655. "An Acrobat Interviewed [Herbert Lenton]." *Era,* 15 Aug. 1891, p. 15.
1656. "Alarming Accident to Lulu." *Era,* 13 Aug. 1876, p. 4.
1656a. "Amusement for the People." *Tomahawk* 63 (18 July 1868): 24. [Attack on spectators' reactions to female gymnasts.]
1657. BARRET-ZEMGANNO, JEAN. "Léotard, le premier." *Le Cirque dans l'univers* (Paris) 35 (4e trimestre 1959): 7–9.

1658. BERNARD, LÉO DE. "Léotard." *Le Cirque dans l'univers* (Paris) 35 (4e trimestre 1959): 10. [Contemporary description.]
1659. "The Brothers Rizarelli." *Era,* 21 Apr. 1872, p. 10. [Accident.]
1660. "A Chat with Beautiful Geraldine." *Era,* 4 May 1895, p. 16. [Trapezist.]
1661. "A Chat with G. A. Farini [Lulu]." *Era,* 30 June 1894, p. 14.
1662. "A Chat with John Higgins." *Era,* 11 Sept. 1897, p. 20.
1663. "A Chat with the Leopolds." *Era,* 14 Sept. 1895, p. 17.
1664. COUDERC, PIERRE. "Les Jeux icariens ou le travail 'à la Risley.'" *Le Cirque dans l'univers* 58 (3e trimestre 1965): 7–11.
1665. COURT, ALFRED. "Mes Débuts comme professionel." *Le Cirque dans l'univers* 28 (4e trimestre 1957): 9–13. [Debut in a Nice music-hall in 1899 as a barre artist.]
1666. "Death of Blondin." *Era,* 27 Feb. 1897, p. 18.
1667. "Death of Ethardo." *Era,* 1 July 1911, p. 25. [Steve Ethair, ascensionist.]
1668. "A Famous Acrobat [Nathan Jackley]." *Era,* 5 Jan. 1895, p. 19.
1669. [George Letine obit.] N.Y. *Clipper,* 6 July 1889, p. 275.
1670. "Interview with an Acrobat" *Era,* 27 Apr. 1889, p. 18. [Herbert Lenton.]
1671. LÉOTARD, JULES. *Mémoires de L'eotard.* Paris: Chez tous les libraires, 1860.
1671a. PFENING, FRED D., JR. "Human Cannonballs, Part One." *Bandwagon* (Baraboo, Wisc.), Nov.-Dec. 1976, pp. 4–15. [George Farini, Zazel, Lulu, etc.]
1672. RAYMOND, J. "Comment Léotard se brouilla avec Dejean." *Le Cirque dans l'univers* 35 (3e trimestre 1959): 9–10. [Article of 1860.]
1673. RÉMY, TRISTAN. "De Miss Ellen à Barbette." *Le Cirque dans l'univers* 111 (4e trimestre 1978): 5–8.
1674. "The Schaffer Troupe." *Era,* 6 Apr. 1889, p. 17.
1674a. STREHLY, GEORGES. *L'Acrobatie et les Acrobates.* Texte et dessins par G. Strehly. Paris: Librairie Ch. Delagrave [1903]. Repr. Paris: Zlatin, 1977. [The classic work on the subject.]
1675. "The Three Delevines." *Era,* 4 Aug. 1894, p. 16.
1676. "[Victor Julien] A Flying Trapezist in Court." *Era,* 12 May 1872, p. 12.

Animal Acts

1677. "The Alleged Animal Torturing." *Era,* 9 May 1896, pp. 17, 19. [Edit.]

1678. "A Chat with Julius Seeth." *Era,* 10 Feb. 1900, p. 19. [Lion-tamer.]
1679. "Death of J. E. Jimson ('Roscoe')." *Era,* 21 May 1910, p. 21. [Trainer.]
1680. DOLMAN, F. "Four Footed Actors." *English Illustrated Magazine,* Sept. 1899. [Mlle. Erna and her dogs; F. Victor and his dogs; Joe Woodward and his sea lions; Sam Lockhart and his elephants.]
1681. FONT-RÉAULX, P.-L. de. "Un Banquiste-née: l'otarie." *Le Cirque dans l'univers* 36 (1er trimestre 1960): 9–10. [Training of sea lions.]
1682. "The Great Lafayette." *Era,* 13 May 1911, p. 28. [Exhibitor of Sigmund Neuberger's dogs.]
1683. LAFAYETTE. "What's Wrong with the Halls." *Era,* 20 May 1911, p. 28.
1684. MAY, BETTY. *Tiger Woman: My Story.* L: Duckworth, 1929.
1685. "Mr Leslie's Dogs." *Era,* 7 Nov. 1896, p. 18.
1686. OHARD, Professor. "Are Trained Animals Tortured?" *Era,* 2 May 1896, p. 16.
1687. "Sharman's Dog Troupe in China." *Era,* 18 Aug. 1900, p. 17.
1688. WALKER, HARRY "WHIMSICAL." "Cats, a Man and Donkeys." *Era Almanack* (1900): 35–36.

Animal Impersonators

1689. "C. Lauri the Animal Impersonator." *Era,* 9 Mar. 1889, p. 17. [Interview.]
1690. "Charles Lauri at Home." *Era,* 20 Mar. 1892, p. 17.
1691. "Charles Lauri's First Collie Dog Impersonation." *Era,* 12 May 1900, p. 18.
1692. " A Famed Animal Impersonator, a Chat with George Ali." *Era,* 22 July 1911, p. 23.
1693. "The Garrick of Animal Mimics." *Era,* 9 Mar. 1895, p. 19. [Lauri.]
1694. LAURI, CHARLES. "Light on the Road." *Era,* 5 Mar. 1898, p. 14.
1695. "A Pantomime Favorite. A Chat with Mr. Charles Lauri." *Era,* 26 Feb. 1898, p. 14.

Conjuring and Magic

1695a. "A Talk with Houdini." N.Y. *Dramatic Mirror,* 25 June 1904, p. 18.

1696. "Carl Hertz at the Alhambra." *Era,* 12 May 1894, p. 16.

1697. "Carter the Magician." *Era,* 8 Oct. 1910, p. 26.

1698. "The 'Catch the Bullet' Act that Tragically Misfired." Haringey *Star,* Dec. 1974–Jan. 1975, p. 2. [Chung Ling Soo.]

1699. "Chat with a Wizard." *Era,* 5 Mar. 1892, p. 19. [Hercat.]

1700. "A Chat with Hercat." *Era,* 14 Apr. 1894, p. 16.

1701. "A Chat with Imro Fox." *Era,* 2 Aug. 1890, p. 15.

1702. "A Chat with Professor Alberto." *Era,* 20 Oct. 1894, p. 16.

1703. "A Conjurer's Experiences." *Era,* 12 Sept. 1891, p. 17. [Interview with Carl Hertz.]

1703a. DAWES, EDWIN A. *The Great Illusionists.* Newton Abbot: David & Charles, 1979. [A well-researched but selective historical account of stage conjurers.]

1704. DEVANT, DAVID. *My Magic Life.* L: Supreme Magic, 1971.

1705. ———. *Secrets of My Magic.* L: Supreme Magic, 1971.

1706. DEXTER, WILL. *The Riddle of Chung Ling Soo.* L: Arco, 1955. Paperback repr.: N.Y.: Arco, 1976.

1706a. GILL, ROBERT. *Magic as a Performing Art: A Bibliography of Conjuring.* L and N.Y.: Bowker, 1976.

1707. "Hercat at the Imperial." *Era,* 5 Mar. 1892, p. 18.

1708. HERTZ, CARL. *A Modern Mystery Merchant. Trials, Tricks and Travels of the Famous American Illusionist.* L: Hutchinson, 1924.

1709. "Hertz, Magician and Globe-trotter." *Era,* 18 Mar. 1899, p. 19.

1710. LAMB, GEOFFREY. *Victorian Magic.* L. & N.Y.: Routledge & Kegan Paul, 1976.

1711. "Mr Carl Hertz, New Illusion 'Iris' at the Empire Theatre." *Era,* 27 June 1900, p. 19.

1712. REYNOLDS, CHARLES and REGINA. *100 Years of Magic Posters.* N.Y.: Grosset & Dunlap, 1976. [Much information compactly conveyed.]

1713. SELDOW, MICHEL. *Les Illusionistes et leurs secrets.* Paris: Fayard, 1959.

1714. TOOLE STOTT, RAYMOND. *A Bibliography of English Conjuring 1581–1876.* Derby: Harpur & Sons, 1976.

1715. WADE, JOHN. "Magic Can Misfire." *Observer Magazine,* 6 Apr. 1975. [Chung Ling Soo.]

1715a. "A Wonderful Conjuror." N.Y. *Dramatic Mirror,* 3 June 1899, p. 16. [Ching Ling Foo.]

Contortionists and Gymnasts

1716. "Bertolde." *Era,* 3 June 1899, p. 21.

1717. "A Chat with Hector and Lauraine." *Era,* 7 Sept. 1895, p. 16.
1717a. DWIGHT, THOMAS. "The Anatomy of the Contortionist." *Scribner's Magazine* (N.Y.), Apr. 1889, pp. 493–505. [Medical account of what happens to the vital organs during the contortionist's performance.]
1718. "A Female Contortionist." *Era,* 31 Oct. 1891, p. 17. [Interview with Emily Sells.]
1718a. FITZGERALD, WILLIAM G. "A Human Alphabet" [The Three Delevines]. *Strand,* Jan. 1898, pp. 659–64.
1718b. HILEY, MICHAEL. *Victorian Working Women: Portraits from Life.* L: Gordon Fraser, 1979. [Pp. 115–19, "Female Gymnasts." Excerpts from Munby's diary and photographs from his collection of women working as gymnasts and acrobats in music-halls in the 1860's and 1870's.]
1719. SHEȦ ᴾˢ E. M. "'Benders' et 'Posturers.'" *Le Cirque dans l'univers* 38 (3e trimestre 1960): 13–15. [History of famous contortionists by a music-hall performer who retired in 1937.]
1719a. STEVENS, C. L. M'CLURE. "A Human Telescope." *Strand,* Sept. 1915, pp. 277–78. [Carlton, pseud. of the clown-contortionist Arthur Carlton Phelps.]

Cyclists

1720. "Murder at a Music Hall." *Era,* 29 June 1889, p. 15 [Of Letine the bicyclist.]; p. 13 [Edit.] 6 July 1889, p. 15; 13 July 1889, p. 15.
1721. "Walter Emerson." *Era,* 26 Aug. 1911, p. 23.

Female and Male Impersonators

1722. BAKER, ROGER. *Drag: a History of Female Impersonation on the Stage.* L: Triton Books, 1968.
1722a. CHESHIRE, DAVID. "Male Impersonators." In *Saturday Book 29,* ed. J. Hadfield. N.Y.: Clarkson N. Potter, 1969. Pp. 245–52.
1723. LIECHTI, ROBERT. "Male Impersonation on the Stage." *Call Boy* 5 no. 4 (Dec. 1968): 16–19.
1724. SHAW, CHRIS and ARTHUR OATES. *A Pictorial History of the Art of Female Impersonation.* L: King-Shaw Productions, 1966.
1725. SUTCLIFFE, TOM. "That's No Lady, That's My Life." *Guardian Extra,* 2 Jan. 1976, p. 14.
1725a. TRUSSLER, SIMON. "That's no lady. . . ." *Plays & Players,*

July 1966, pp. 52–57. [Brief history of stage male and female impersonation.]

Fire Eaters

1726. "Death of a Fire Prince." *Era,* 24 Feb. 1900, p. 19. [Eugene Rivalli.]

Jugglers

1727. BAUDEZ, JEAN. "Un Jongleur 'classique': Nino Frediani." *Le Cirque dans l'univers* 81 (2e trimestre 1971): 9–15.

1728. "A Chat with 'Chinko.'" *Era,* 28 July 1900, p. 17.

1729. [Dalvine, obit.] N.Y. *Clipper,* 13 July 1889, p. 297.

1730. DISHER, MAURICE WILLSON. "Juggler." OCT, p. 526.

1731. FRÉJAVILLE, GUSTAVE. "Un Artiste inspiré: Rastelli." *Comoedia* (Paris), 15 Dec. 1931.

1732. LEGRAND-CHABRIER. "La Vie et l'art d'un jongleur: Rastelli." *L'Illustration* (Paris), 18 Oct. 1930.

1733. NUTKINS, HARRY. "L'Art aimable de jongleur." *Le Cirque dans l'univers* (Paris) 93 (2e trimestre 1974): 5–7.

1734. RÉMY, TRISTAN. "Le Jonglage aux bilboquets." *Le Cirque dans l'univers* (Paris) 43 (4e trimestre 1961): 23–24.

1735. ROST, NICO. "Rastelli." *Variétés* (Bruxelles), Oct. 1929.

1736. SHEARS, E. M. "Jongleurs d'hier et d'aujourd'hui." *Le Cirque dans l'univers* (Paris) 31 (3e trimestre 1958): 20–21.

1737. SILVA, MARIO DE. "Rastelli." *Scenario* (Roma-Milano), Feb. 1932.

1737a. TRUZZI, MARCELLO, with MASSIMILIANO TRUZZI. "Notes toward a history of juggling." *Bandwagon,* Mar.-Apr. 1974, pp. 4–7.

1738. "The Zanetto Troupe." *Encore,* 31 Dec. 1896, p. 9.

1739. "Zarmo the Juggler." *Era,* 6 Oct. 1894, p. 16.

Knockabout

1740. "Famous Knockabouts." *Era,* 30 May 1891, p. 15. [Interview of J. P. MacNally and Frederick M. Maccabe.]

1741. HOYLAND, ERIC. *"Tickey": The Story of Eric Hoyland as Told by Him to T. V. Bulpin.* Cape Town, S.A.: T. V. Bulpin, 1978. [Ills. Penny Miller. Autobiography of a knockabout dwarf.]

1742. "The Two Macs." *Era,* 19 May 1888, p. 16. [Frederick Michael Maccabe and Patrick Joseph Maccabe.]

Living Pictures

1743. "Death of Herr Kilanyi." *Era,* 21 Dec. 1895, p. 17. [Inventor of living pictures.]
1744. "The 'Living Picture' Case." *Era,* 24 Feb. 1894, p. 16; 24 Mar. 1894, p. 16; 22 Dec. 1894, p. 17; 30 Mar. 1895, p. 16.
1745. "Living Pictures." *Saturday Review* 89 (6 Apr. 1895): 443–44.
1746. "'Living Pictures' in the Lords." *Era,* 8 Dec. 1894, p. 16.
1747. MILLER, NORBERT. "Mutmassungen über Lebende Bilder: Attitüde und 'Tableau vivant' als Anschauungsformen des 19. Jahrhunderts." In *Das Triviale in Literatur, Musik und Bildender Kunst,* ed. Helga de la Motte-Haber. Frankfurt: Klosterman, 1972. [Pp. 106–30. On their origin.]
1748. "The Other Side of the Pictures." *Daily Graphic,* 15 May 1894, p. 70.
1749. SOMERSET, Lady HENRY. "Living Pictures." *Sentinel,* Sept. 1894, p. 164.
1750. "Tableaux vivants at the Palace." *Era,* 25 Jan. 1896, p. 18.

Mentalists, Memory Experts, and Mind Readers

1751. "Charles N. Steen and Martha E. Steen." *Era,* 9 Apr. 1898, p. 19.
1752. "A Chat with Professor Steen." *Era,* 15 Sept. 1894, p. 17.
1753. "'Is That Right, Sir?' A Chat with Datas." *Era,* 3 Dec. 1910, p. 27.
1754. "The Secret of the Zancigs." *Royal Magazine,* May 1909.

Mimicry

1755. BLEACKLEY, J. ARTHUR. *The Art of Mimicry.* N.Y. & L.: Samuel French [1914].

Pedestrians

1756. "Music Hall Pedestrians." *Era,* 16 Nov. 1879, p. 4; 23 Nov. 1879, p. 3.

Quick-change Artists

1757. "A Chat with Ugo Biondi." *Era,* 27 Feb. 1897, p. 20.

1758. GASCH, SEBASTIAN. "Fregoli, Brossa i el 'music-hall.'" *Estudios escenicos* (Barcelona) no. 16.
1759. "Huit cent acteurs et un." *Les Lectures pour tous* (Paris) (1905–06): 393. [Fregoli.]
1760. JARRO [pseud. of Giulio Piccini]. "Vita di L. Fregoli." In *Il Naso di Ermete, novelli.* Firenze: R. Bemporad, 1900.
1761. NOHAIN, JEAN MARIE [pseud. Jaboune] and FRANCOIS CARADEC [pseud. Alphonse de Crac]. *Fregoli 1867–1936. Sa vie et ses sécrets.* Paris: La Jeune Parque [1968]. [Ills. René Dazy.]
1762. "The Proteus of the Stage. A Chat with Ugo Biondi." *Era,* 1 Sept. 1900, p. 19.
1763. RÉMY, TRISTAN. "Leopold Fregoli, l'homme aux cent personnages." *Vaillant* (Paris), 15 Feb. 1959.
1764. [ROBERTS, R. A.] "A Quick-change Artist's Experiences." *Era,* 3 Dec. 1910, p. 29. [Repr. from *The Strand.*]
1765. "Ugo Biondi. World Press Opinions." *Era,* 14 July 1900, p. 18.

Solo Instrumentalists

1766. "A Chat with a Harpist." *Era,* 1 Oct. 1892, p. 17. [Charles Clifford.]
1767. CLIFFORD, CHARLES. "A Harpist's Reminiscences." *Era Annual* (1910): 100–101.
1768. "Hermann Unthan, the Pedal Paganini, at the London Pavilion Music Hall." *Penny Illustrated Paper,* 21 May 1870.
1769. "Mr Charles Clifford." *Era,* 30 Sept. 1899, p. 19.
1770. PULLING, CHRISTOPHER. "At the Piano." *Call Boy* 5 no. 4 (Dec. 1968): 12–14. [Piano entertainments.]
1770a. UNTHAN, CARL HERMANN. *The Armless Man. A Pediscript being the Life Story of a Vaudeville Man.* Preface by J. Malcolm Forbes. L: G. Allen & Unwin, 1935.

Strong Men and Women

1771. "The Little Georgia Magnet." *Era,* 16 Nov. 1891, p. 16; 28 Nov. 1891, p. 15. [Edit.] [Annie Abbott.]
1772. "A Modern Samson." *Era,* 31 Aug. 1889, p. 15. [Samson.]
1773. "More Strong Men." *Era,* 6 Feb. 1892, p. 17.
1774. "Sampson's [sic] Feats." *Era,* 22 Apr. 1899, p. 18.
1775. "Samson in Court." *Era,* 14 Dec. 1889, p. 15.
1776. "Strong man in Sunderland." *Era,* 29 Jan. 1898, p. 21.
1777. "Strong Men at South London." *Era,* 21 Nov. 1891, p. 16.

Ventriloquists

1778. BROUGH, PETER. *Educating Archie.* L: S. Paul, 1955. [For details of his father Arthur Brough.]

1779. CARDUS, NEVILLE. "Obituary: Russ Carr." *Stage,* 17 May 1973.

1780. "Celebrated Ventriloquists." *Boy's Own Paper* 3 (1881): 372, 406, 423.

1781. "A Chat with Fred Millis." *Era,* 24 Aug. 1895, p. 14.

1782. COLE, WALTER. *Ventriloqual Vagaries in Variety Stars.* L [c. 1895].

1783. "Death of Mr. Fred Newman." *Era,* 31 Dec. 1910, p. 29.

1784. GARNAULT, PAUL. *History of Ventriloquism.* Brooklyn, N.Y.: 1900.

1785. McINTYRE, GEORGE. *George McIntyre's Bibliography on Ventriloquism.* Seattle, Wash.: Gregory & Walter Berlin, 1970.

1786. PRINCE, ARTHUR. *The Whole Art of Ventriloquism.* 2d ed. L: Goldston [n.d.].

1787. RUSSELL, FRED. *Ventriloquism and Kindred Arts. . . .* L: Keith, Prowse [c. 1898].

1788. "Ventriloquists." *Penny Cyclopaedia.* L: 1833–43.

Whistlers

1789. "Miss Florrie Behrens." *Era,* 7 Apr. 1900, p. 19. [Souffleuse.]

Wrestlers and Boxers

1790. KENT, GRAEME. *A Pictorial History of Wrestling.* L: Spring Books, 1968. [Chapter 7, "The Golden Age," pp. 146–72.]

MANAGEMENT AND AGENCY (SALARIES, CONTRACTS, ECONOMICS)

Cross-references

See also **6, 8, 123, 209, 344, 357, 423, 436, 438, 440, 443, 501-2,**

517, 522, 544, 564, 571, 575, 584, 592, 598–99, 606, 619, 636, 645, 649, 651, 688, 695, 720, 749, 750, 752, 763, 765, 767, 781, 787–88, 790, 792, 794, 802, 808–10, 815, 821, 823, 827, 833, 839, 841–42, 848, 858, 873–75, 887–88, 895, 903–4, 907, 920, 924, 929, 931–32, 935, 938, 940, 948–49, 953, 956, 976, 1004, 1016, 1034, 1050, 1068, 1081, 1093, 1121, 1137, 1169–70, 1184, 1196, 1207, 1232–33, 1239–40, 1244–45, 1248, 1252, 1271, 1277–78, 1307, 1311, 1313, 1326–27, 1355–57, 1367, 1371, 1377, 1396, 1437, 1505, 1511, 1536, 1558, 1616, 2081, 2158–59, 2285, 2288, 2356–61, 2544, 2810, 2867, 2959–64.

1791. "Action by a Music Hall Agent." *Era,* 12 Feb. 1887, p. 9. [Frank Albert v. troupe of trained dogs.]
1792. ADAIR, PETER. "Music Hall Salaries." *Era,* 8 Oct. 1892, p. 16. [Valuable source of information.]
1793. "Alleged Libel on an Agent." *Era,* 10 Oct. 1880, p. 4. [Hugh J. Didcott.]
1794. ALLTREE, GEORGE W. *Footlight Memories. Recollections of Music Hall and Stage Life.* L: Sampson Low, Marston [1932]. [With a foreword by Edward Knoblock. Memoirs of an agent.]
1795. ASKWITH, GEORGE. "Music Halls Award 1913. New Model Contract." *Era Annual* (1914): 68–71.
1796. "Attempted Fraud on Music Hall Proprietors." *Era,* 3 Nov. 1878, p. 4.
1797. BOOTH, CHARLES. " On the Economics of Music Hall." *Theatre Quarterly* 1 no. 4 (Oct.–Dec. 1971): 46.
1798. BURTON, PERCY. "How a Variety Theatre is Run." *Strand Magazine* (May 1909): 501–9.
1799. BUTT, ALFRED. "Double Dummy." *Era Annual* (1908): 46–47.
1800. "A Chat with George Foster." *Era,* 15 May 1897, p. 18. [Agent.]
1801. "A Chat with Mr Worland S. Wheeler." *Era,* 1 Oct. 1910, p. 27. [Agent.]
1802. "A Chat with Perceval Hyatt." *Era,* 20 Oct. 1900, p. 21. [Agent.]
1803. "Conference between Managers of Music Halls and Theatres." *Licensing Committee of the London County Council Report of Proceedings.* Great London Record Office (20 Nov. 1889). [Unpub.]
1804. COTES, PETER. *J.P.—the Man called Mitch.* L: Paul Elek, 1977. [Biography of J. P. Mitchelhill, prop. of Collins' Music Hall 1911–19.]

1805. "Death of H. Newson-Smith." *Era,* 30 Apr. 1898, p. 19; 7 May 1898, p. 18. [Founder of The Syndicate.]
1806. "Didcott v. the Rev. S. Marten and another." *Era,* 28 Feb. 1885, p. 10.
1807. "Frauds on Music Hall Proprietors." *Era,* 10 Sept. 1876, p. 5; 26 Oct. 1876, p. 4.
1808. GLOVER, JAMES M., ed. and comp. *The Theatre Managers' Handbook: A Useful Compendium of All the Necessary Legal Requirements, Many Stated Cases, Copyright Provisions, Accepted Customs, and General Practices Obtaining in Theatrical Management, with a List of the Theatres and Houses of Amusement of the United Kingdom, their Lessees, Managers, and Such General Information as May be Useful for Daily Reference.* L: The Editor, 1928. [With annotations and additions by P. M. Selby. Includes listings of theatrical tradesmen, bill-posters, variety theatres and music-halls in London, its suburbs, the provinces, LCC regulations, booking agents, sample contracts, etc.]
1809. HAND, CHARLES [impresario]. *I Was After Money.* L: Partridge, 1949.
1810. "Harry Starr 'The Power of the Press.'" *Era,* 1 Nov. 1899, p. 9.
1811. HIBBERT, HENRY GEORGE. "Magnates of the English Music Halls." N.Y. *Dramatic Mirror,* 2 July 1904, p. 3.
1812. "High Salaries Paid to Variety Artistes." *Daily News,* 25 Mar. 1892.
1813. "A Hustler from the North: a Chat with Mr Harry Burns." *Era,* 15 Oct. 1910, p. 25. [Agent.]
1814. "Important to Proprietors." *Era,* 1 June 1879, p. 4.
1815. "In an Agent's Office." *Era,* 29 Nov. 1890, p. 18.
1816. LEAVITT, M[ICHAEL] B[ENNETT]. *Fifty Years in Theatrical Management.* N.Y.: Broadway Publishing Co., 1912. [Chapter 16: Meteoric Rise of Moss and Stoll—Vaudeville Palaces of London—When I First met Oswald Stoll—Dissolution of Moss and Stoll Empires—Stoll's Recent Combine with Walter Gibbons—Prominent English Vaudeville Managers—J. L. Graydon, the Dean of Music Hall Proprietors—The Late Charles Morton—Alfred Butt, his Successor—Walter de Frece and the Butt Combine—Frank Macnaghten Vaudeville Circuit—Parisian Theatres des Variétés—The Seguin Tour of South America—Vaudeville in the Antipodes—South Africa's Limited Field—Potnoy's "Tivoli," Calcutta—Mooser Bros. and Vaudeville in China and Japan—Levy and Jones Controlling Vaudeville in the Philippines—J. C. Cohen Vaudeville Promoter in Honolulu, pp.

211–20. Other chapters have references to Eugen Sandow, Emily Soldene, Frederic Maccabe, Great Magicians, Yvette Guilbert, English Aid Societies, the Zancigs, etc.]

1817. "Mr Hugh J. Didcott." *Era,* 29 June 1895, p. 14.

1818. "Mr Hugh J. Didcott's Bureau." *Era,* 13 Apr. 1889, p. 18.

1819. "Music Hall Agency." *Era,* 8 Nov. 1890, p. 16.

1820. "A Music Hall Agent." *Era,* 13 Feb. 1892, p. 19. [John James Taylor v. Henry Labouchére.]

1821. "Music Hall Amalgamation." *Era,* 21 Oct. 1899, p. 17. [Edit.]

1822. "Music Hall Artistes' Trials." *Era,* 2 Oct. 1897, p. 19. [Important article on touring expenses.]

1823. "Music Hall Artists and Agents." *Era,* 19 June 1895, p. 16.

1824. "The Music-hall Business." *St. James's Gazette,* 21 and 27 Apr. 1892.

1825. "Music Hall Contracts." *Era,* 19 Apr. 1890, p. 14; 21 Nov. 1891, p. 17.

1826. "Music Hall Finance." *Era,* 11 June 1892, p. 14.

1827. "Music Hall Frauds." *Era,* 25 Feb. 1877, p. 4; 4 Mar. 1877 p. 7.

1828. "Music Hall Investment." *Financial News* 15 (Feb. 1887).

1829. "The Music Hall Profession and Railway Rates." *Era,* 14 Nov. 1896, p. 18; 21 Nov. 1896, p. 19; 28 Nov. 1896, p. 19; 5 Dec. 1896, p 19; 12 Dec. 1896, p. 19; 19 Dec. 1896, p. 19; 26 Dec. 1896, p. 17; 2 Jan. 1897, p. 20; 16 Jan. 1897, p. 19; 23 Jan. 1897, p. 20; 6 Feb. 1897, p. 21; 20 Feb. 1897, p. 21; 27 Feb. 1897, p. 20; 6 Mar. 1897, p. 19; 13 Mar. 1897, p. 19; 20 Mar. 1897, p. 19; 27 Mar. 1897, p. 19; 3 Apr. 1897, p. 19; 10 Apr. 1897, p. 14; 17 Apr. 1897, p. 17; 8 May 1897, p. 19; 15 May 1897, p. 19; 14 Aug. 1897, p. 17; 11 Sept. 1897, p. 18; 2 Oct. 1897, p. 21; 23 Oct. 1897, p. 19; 15 Jan. 1898, p. 17; 26 Feb. 1898, p. 20.

1830. "Music Hall Professionals and Their Agents." *Era,* 25 Aug. 1872, p. 13; 1 Sept. 1872, p. 4; 8 Sept. 1872, p. 4.

1831. "Music Hall Profits." *Times,* 27 Feb. 1914, p. 15c.

1832. "Music Hall Proprietor's Action." *Era,* 17 Dec. 1910, p. 18. [Frank MacNaghten v. *The Stage.*]

1833. "Music Hall Proprietors' Petition." *Era,* 30 Mar. 1879, p. 4; 6 Apr. 1879, p. 4; 13 Apr. 1879, p. 4; 20 Apr. 1879, p. 4.

1834. "Music Hall Proprietors' Protection Association." *Era,* 23 Mar. 1878, p. 7; 23 Mar. 1879, p. 7.

1835. "Obituary: Robert Burton." *Era,* 15 June 1879, p. 4. [Mgr.]

1836. "Our Variety Knights: A Quartet of Music Hall Magnates." *Era Annual* (1919): 33–34.

1837. "Rival Music Hall Proprietors." *Era,* 2 May 1880, p. 4.

1838. "Selling Music Hall Tickets." *Era,* 17 Sept. 1876, p. 4.
1839. SHEREK, HENRY. *Not in Front of the Children.* L: Heinemann, 1959. [Memoirs of a variety agent; earlier chapters most relevant.]
1840. "Sketch Managers and Railway Charges." *Era,* 21 Sept. 1912, p. 23.
1841. "The Syndicate Hall." *Era,* 23 Apr. 1898, p. 21.
1842. "Testimonial to Hugh J. Didcott." *Era,* 23 July 1887, p. 14; 4 June 1892, p. 14.
1843. "Theatre and Music Hall (Limited) Companies." *Stage Year-book* (1917): 65–73.
1844. "Theatre and Music Hall (Limited) Companies." *Stage Year-book* (1918): 46–54.
1845. "Variety Theatre Catering." *Era,* 17 May 1890, p. 15.
1846. WALLIS. A. "The Variety Managers of London." *Sketch,* 10 Feb. 1897, p. 121; 3 Mar. 1897, p. 250.
1847. WARNER, RICHARD. "An Episode in a Music Hall Agent's Career." *Entr'acte Annual* (1902): 34–35.
1848. "A Warning to Music Hall Proprietors." *Era,* 14 Feb. 1878, p. 4.

UNIONS, FRIENDLY SOCIETIES, AND STRIKES

Cross-references

See also **146, 607, 994–95, 1816, 2082–83, 2608, 3067.**

1849. BARON, ALEC. "The Artists Strike! Lessons from 1907." *Stage,* 15 July 1974, p. 74.
1849a. [CASEY, pseud.] *The Music Hall War and the Musicians' Living Wage.* Stockport: For the Author [c. 1907]. ["This little book is dedicated to the Theatre proprietor who excused low salaries by saying musicians could work in the daytime. I have taken his advice. I hope this little labour of love, which I have done in the

daytime as he suggested, will please him.''']

1850. [Combination of Variety Agencies] *Times,* 4 Mar. 1910, p. 18a.

1851. [Contracts between Music Hall Managers and Artistes; threatened dispute in De Frece Circuit] *Times,* 2 Nov. 1908, p. 12d.

1852. "Dramatic and Music Hall Trades Unions." *Era,* 28 Feb. 1891, p. 12; 12 Sept. 1891, p. 17.

1853. "Frauds on Music Hall Professionals." *Era,* 15 Oct. 1876, p. 5.

1854. FYFFE, H. HAMILTON. "The Music Hall War, What It Is All About." *Daily Mail* (1907).

1855. GOLDEN, GEORGE FULLER. *My Lady Vaudeville and Her White Rats.* N.Y.: White Rats of America, 1909. Rev. *Performer,* 20 May 1909, p. 14. [History of American variety artists' union.]

1856. "The Halls and the War." *Era,* 9 Dec. 1899, p. 19; 23 Dec. 1899, p. 20; 30 Dec. 1899, p. 20; 13 Jan. 1900, p. 18 *et seq.* [Organized support of Boer War.]

1857. "History of the Music-hall War." *Stage Yearbook* (1908): 54-72.

1858. HONRI, PETER. "When Elephants were Blacklegs." *Call-Boy* 2 (June 1972): 4-5. [1907 strike. Repr. from *Equity.*]

1859. "Important to Music Hall Artistes." *Era,* 21 Apr. 1878, p. 4. [On recovering salaries.]

1860. KITCHNER, TOM. "The Great Song Syndicate." *Music Hall,* 26 Apr. 1896, p. 14. [Organization of songwriters.]

1861. LE ROY, GEORGE. *The Golden Jubilee Book of Show Business 1906-1956: A Literary Panorama of the Theatrical Scene Marking the Fifty Years Existence of the Profession's Oldest Organization. . .the V.A.F. . . .* L: Variety Artistes' Federation [1956].

1862. "Music Hall Artistes' Protection Society." *Era,* 15 Sept. 1872, p. 12; 6 Oct. 1872, p. 7; 13 Oct. 1872, p. 4; 3 Nov. 1872, p. 4.

1863. "Music Hall Artists and Benefits." *Era,* 10 Feb. 1894, p. 17.

1864. "Music Hall Artists' Cricket and Recreation Club." *Era,* 9 Feb. 1873, p. 7; 10 Aug. 1873, p 12 [the 'Canterbury' versus the 'Oxford']; 2 Aug. 1874, p. 4, *et seq.*

1865. "Music Hall Benevolent Fund." *Era,* 17 Jan. 1891, pp. 15, 16 [edit.]; 26 Sept. 1891, p. 17; 3 Oct. 1891, p. 17; 13 Feb. 1892, p. 20; 27 Feb. 1892, p. 17 [letter by Charles Coborn]; 5 Mar. 1892, p. 18; 12 Mar. 1892, p. 16; 24 Sept. 1892, p. 17; 1 Oct. 1892, p. 17; 3 Mar. 1894, p. 16; 17 Mar. 1894, p. 16; 15 Sept. 1894, p. 16; 29 Feb. 1896, p. 16; 12 Sept. 1896, p. 18; 11 Sept. 1897, p. 19; 12 Mar. 1898, p. 21; 10 Sept. 1898, p. 19.

1866. "Music Hall Co-operative and Anti-agency Union." *Era,* 1 Sept. 1872, p. 4.

1867. "Music Hall Mutual Benefit and Protection Society." *Era,* 26 Sept. 1885, p. 10; 3 Oct. 1885, p. 10; 17 Oct. 1885, p. 10; 7 Nov. 1885, p. 10.

1868. "Music Hall Protection Association." *Era,* 26 Mar. 1876, p. 5; 12 Dec. 1885, p. 10; 26 Apr. 1890, p. 18; 17 May 1890, p. 15.

1869. "Music Hall Sick Fund." *Era,* 15 Feb. 1874, p. 4; 31 Jan. 1875, p. 4.

1870. "Music Hall Sick Fund Benefit." *Era,* 20 July 1879, p. 4; 3 Dec. 1892, p. 16.

1871. "Music Hall Sick Fund Fete." *Era,* 10 Sept. 1876, p. 5.

1872. "Music Hall Sick Fund Society." *Era,* 12 Sept. 1880, p. 4.

1873. "Music Hall Trades' Exhibition." *Era,* 9 May 1891, p. 16.

1874. "Music Halls and the Jubilee." *Era,* 29 May 1897, p. 19; 5 June 1897, p. 19; 12 June 1897, p. 17.

1875. "Perils of the Profession." *Era,* 21 Dec. 1895, p. 15. [Edit.]

1876. "The Provincial Music Hall Artistes' Anti-agency and Sick Fund." *Era,* 8 Sept. 1872, p. 4; 15 Sept. 1872, p. 12; 3 Nov. 1872, p. 4.

1877. "'Rats' and the War Fund." *Era,* 9 Dec. 1899, p. 18.

1878. "The Rights of Music Hall Artistes." *Era,* 23 Jan. 1876, p. 4.

1879. RUSSELL, FRED. *The History of the Grand Order of Water Rats.* L: Grand Order of Water Rats, 1947.

1880. "Song-writers and their Sufferings." *Era,* 19 Oct. 1895, p. 15. [Edit.]

1881. "The Song-writers' Union." *Era,* 28 Sept. 1895, p. 16; 5 Oct. 1895, p. 16; 19 Oct. 1895, p. 16; 26 Oct. 1895, p. 20; 16 Nov. 1895, p. 16.

1882. [Strike of 1907] *Daily Telegraph,* 23 Jan., 24 Jan., 25 Jan., 28 Jan., 30 Jan., 5 Feb., 12 Feb., 15 Feb., 15 June 1907.

1883. [Strike of 1907] *Era,* 26 Jan. 1907, *et seq.*

1884. [Strike of 1907] *Stage,* 24 Jan. 1907. [Edit.]

1885. [Strike of 1907] *Times,* 23 Jan. 1907, p. 8d; 24 Jan. 1907, p. 9f; 25 Jan. 1907, p. 7e; 30 Jan. 1907, p. 6f; 1 Feb. 1907, p. 4f; 2 Feb. 1907, p. 8f; 4 Feb. 1907, p. 6d; 5 Feb. 1907, p. 8c; 6 Feb. 1907, p. 10e; 7 Feb. 1907, p. 4e; 8 Feb. 1907, p. 10a; 9 Feb. 1907, p. 13a; 28 Mar. 1907, p. 4f.

1886. [Syndicate Halls: operative working arrangements made] *Times,* 8 Sept. 1908, p. 9d.

1887. "Theatre and Music Hall Operatives." *Era,* 16 Aug. 1890, p. 15; 23 Aug. 1890, p. 13; 30 Aug. 1890, p. 15; 20 Sept. 1890, p. 10.

IX. PERSONALIA

"A mass of corruption—long front teeth—a crapulous way
of saying 'desire', and yet a born artist."

> Virginia Woolf on Marie
> Lloyd, after a visit to the Old
> Bedford, April 1921. [Quoted
> in Quentin Bell, *Virginia Woolf
> a Biography* (N.Y.: Harcourt
> Brace Jovanovich, 1972) II,
> 77.]

This comment of one great technician on another sums up the difficulties in researching the stars and celebrities of popular entertainments. The division between private life and personality and
creative achievement is often keen; the accounts of marriages,
divorces, liaisons, alcoholism, and suicide may or may not be
related to the talents which make an individual worth studying in
the first place. But "show biz" biographies tend to play up the
former aspect and generally ignore the latter. The exceptions—
Richard Findlater's biography of Grimaldi the clown, Tristan
Rémy's of Deburau the mime, and Arthur Saxon's of Ducrow the
equestrian—are the more outstanding because of their rarity, and
little solid work of that quality has been performed for the music-
hall artiste. Moreover, the show business *auto*biography is seldom
trustworthy and often ghostwritten. Nothing is more frustrating
than the usual hodgepodge of undated, unattested anecdotes
followed by a travelogue, with never a word about the subject's
skills, materials, or audiences. The whole matter of extricating
solid fact from the accretions of legend is complicated by theatrical

publicity; the music-hall was the first performing art to benefit (if that is the word) from modern methods of promotion and press-agentry. Thus, one is dealing not only with the normal processes of distortion and rumor, but with a wilful rearrangement or glamorization of the truth. Merely ascertaining the data on a performer's birth, debut, or real name becomes a challenge.

The following section lists the basic biographical reference works and then enumerates a number of outstanding individuals, both performers and managers, with a sampling of the kind of material available concerning them. When possible, we have given full birth and death data to enable searches of parish registers and newspaper obituaries. We have also listed a subject's appearance in the *Oxford Companion to the Theatre,* the *Dictionary of National Biography,* the *Enciclopedia dello spettacolo* and (on a lesser scale) George Le Roy's *Music Hall Stars of the Nineties* as useful surveys to begin with. (Roy Busby's who's who *British Music Hall* is also helpful, but must be used with great caution, especially for earlier figures.) But in addition to the standard biographies, we have provided a record of contemporary interviews and remembrances which are generally more accurate and more revelatory than later accounts. In particular, the "Chats" series in *The Era* was managed by H. G. Hibbert, who prided himself on his precision in matters of fact.

Each entry begins with the individual's own writings (or those attributed to him) and then proceeds to so-called "secondary materials," the writings of others. If such material is available, the entry is concluded with "Repertoire," a collection of songs or jokes used by a performer. Cross-references will indicate further repertoire material in other sections. To save space, an acronym of the individual's name is used throughout.

COLLECTIVE BIOGRAPHY

Cross-references

See also **3514, 3656, 3746.**

1888. BARRETT, VERNON. E. *Clown Land.* L: Dean & Son [c. 1910].

1889. BOARDMAN, WILLIAM H. ("Billy"). *Vaudeville Days.* L: Jarrold, 1935. [Ed. David Whitelaw. Foreword by Andrew Soutar. Chapters on Dan Leno, Marie Lloyd, Bransby Williams, Billy Merson, etc.]

1890. BOASE, FREDERICK. *Modern English Biography, containing many thousand concise memoirs of persons who have died between the years 1851–1900, with an index of the most interesting matter.* 6 vols. Truro: Netherton & Worth, 1892–1921. Repr. L: Frank Cass & co. [1965]. [Vol. 1: Paul Bedford, p. 219; Henry Clifton, p. 649; Sam Collins, p. 679; Patrick Corri, p. 722; Sam Cowell, p. 735; Frederick Coyne, p. 744; Charles Du Val, p. 944; Patrick Feeney, p. 1031; Carlo Gatti, p. 1130; John Green, p. 1224; William Hyles, 1612. Vol. 2: John Jolly, p. 121; Sir Horace Jones, p. 128; F. Jonghmans, p. 147; Kate King, p. 226; Frederick Kingsburg, p. 233; Benjamin Lacy, p. 272; George Leybourne, p. 421; Ambrose Maynard, p. 816; John Moody, p. 941; James Moss, p. 999; George Nugent, p. 1187; J. H. Ogden, p. 1217; George Parkes, p. 1352; Stefano Parraviccini, p. 1359; J. O. Parry, p. 1364; Elizabeth Pearce, p. 1415; Frederick C. Perry, p. 1470; Philip Phillips, p. 1510; Ellen Poole (Nellie Desmond), p. 1581; John Poole, p. 1583. Vol. 3: William Riley, p. 178; Charles Ross, p. 293; H. T. Rossborough, p. 305; John W. Sharp, p. 517; James Hurst Stead, p. 718; Harry Sydney, p. 852; James Taylor, p. 893; Alfred Vance, p. 1073; John Ward, p. 1197; Edward Weston, p. 1288; Thomas Youdan, p. 1568. Vol. 4: Samuel Adams, p. 35; Frederick Albert, p. 62; Bessie Bellwood, p. 355; R. R. Bignell, p. 399; Deane Brand, p. 484; Mrs J. F. Brian, p. 491; Edward Clark, p. 667; Henry Collard, p. 713; Chas. S. Crowder, p. 815. Vol. 5: Edward Dunbar, p. 166; William C. Evans, p. 251; Frederick Frampton, p. 343; George A. Hodson, p. 679. Vol. 6: William Thomas Purkiss, p. 439; Henry Russell, p. 516; George Ware, p. 787; Richard Weighell, p. 818; Zazel, p. 985.]

1891. BREWER, CHARLES. *The Spice of Variety.* L: Frederick Muller, 1948. [Chapter 12, "Figures of Mirth," pp. 160–74.]

1892. BUSBY, ROY. *British Music Hall: an Illustrated Who's Who from 1850 to the Present Day.* L: Paul Elek, 1976. [Inconsistent, incomplete and occasionally inaccurate, it remains the best such work to date.] Rev. C. Broadbent, *Library Journal* 102 (1977): 944; P. Keating, *Times Literary Supplement,* 25 Feb. 1977, p. 217; L. Senelick, *Educational Theatre Journal,* June 1978; G.

Personalia

Speaight, *Theatre Notebook* 31 no. 3 (1977): 44–45.
1893. FELSTEAD, SIDNEY THEODORE. *Stars Who Made the Halls. A Hundred Years of English Humour, Harmony and Hilarity.* L: T. Werner Laurie, 1946.
1894. FERGUSSON, Sir LOUIS. *Old Time Music Hall Comedians.* Leicester: C. H. Gee, 1949. [Delightful and detailed essays on Herbert Campbell, Arthur Roberts, James Fawn, Chirgwin, Harry Randall, Marie Lloyd, Dan Leno, T. E. Dunville, Little Tich, R. G. Knowles, Eugene Stratton, Mark Sheridan, George Robey, Harry Lauder, *et al.*]
1895. FISHER, JOHN. *Funny Way to Be A Hero.* L: Frederick Muller, 1973. Paperback ed. L: Paladin, 1976. [Foreword by Chesney Allen. Afterword by Michael Parkinson. Lively and impressionistic critiques of twentieth-century comedians.]
1896. *The Green Room Book or Who's Who on the Stage.* L: Sealey Clark 1906–9. 4 vols. [1906 issue ed. Bampton Hunt; 1907 issue ed. F. Jerome Hart and John Parker; 1908 and 1909 issues ed. John Parker. Succeeded by *Who's Who in the Theatre.*]
1897. HALL, LILLIAN A. *Catalogue of Dramatic Portraits in the Theatre Collection of Harvard College Library.* 4 vols. Cambridge, Mass.: Harvard University Press, 1930. [Vol. 1: Arthur Albert; Fred Albert; Harry Anderson; Joe Archer; Henry C. Arnold; Wallis Arthur; Sam Bagnall; Wilkie Bard; Billie Barlow; Fred Barnes; Sidney Barnes; Leonard Barry; Edwin Barwick; Tom Bass; George Bastow; Harry Bawn; George Beauchamp; Harry Bedford; Bessie Bellwood; Charles Bignell; Bert Bijou; William Bint; Ada Blanche; Bessie Bonehill; Mrs J. F. Brian; Harry Brown; Lily Burnand; Jesse Burton; Herbert Campbell; Kate Carney; Morny Cash; Frank Cass; Ada Cerito; Harry Champion; Charles Chaplin; Kate Chard; Albert Chevalier; George H. Chirgwin; Harry Clifford; Harry Clifton; Charles Coborn; Lottie Collins; Marie Collins; Sam Collins; Arthur Corney; Tom Costello; Sam Cowell; Frank Coyne; Fred Coyne; Dan Crawley; Minnie Cunningham; Harry Dacre; George D'Albert; John Danvers; Daisy Dormer; Leo Dryden; T. E. Dunville; Fred Earle; Will Edwards; Gus Elen; Will Evans. Vol. 2: W. B. Fair; James Fawn; Harry Ford; Florrie Forde; George Formby; Louie Freear; Harry Freeman; Fred French; Gus Garrick; Alfred Gatty; Alfred Gibson; Bert Gilbirt; Charles Godfrey; Will Godwin; Tom Graham; Gracie Grahame; Edgar Granville; Yvette Guilbert; J. W. Hall; Edwin Hanford; Ted Hanley; Winifred Hare; Dolly Harmer; Fred Harvey; Lil, Lola and Nellie Hawthorne; Hettie Haywood; Ernest Heathcote; Will Hebden; Hedges Brothers;

168

J. C. Heffron; Fred Herbert; Jenny Hill; James Hillier; Annie Hindle; Billy Hobbs; Percy Honri; Lizzie Howard; Millie Hylton; F. Jongmans [sic]; Judic; Kearney & Moran; Marie Kendall; Harry Kent; Walter Kino; R. G. Knowles. Vol. 3: Walter Laburnum; George Lashwood; Sir Harry Lauder; Joe Lawrence; Katie Lawrence; Charles Lawrie; Leamor Sisters; Tom Leamore; Lily Lena; Arthur Lennard; Lottie Lennox; Dan Leno; Frank Leo; Georgina Leonard; Fannie Leslie; Levey Sisters; Edward Lewis; George Lewis; Henry Lewis; George Leybourne; George Leyton; Charles Lilburn; Letty Lind; Millie Lindon; Alice Lingard; Harry Linn; Harry Liston; Victor Liston; Arthur Lloyd; Marie Lloyd; Rosie Lloyd; Tom Lloyd; Cissie Loftus; Kitty Loftus; Marie Loftus; Frederic Maccabe; Barlett McCarthy; Charles McCarthy; G. H. Macdermott; E. W. Mackney; Lily Marney; Paul Martinetti; Edward Mason; Ernie Mayne; Harry Melville; J. H. Milburn; Horace Mills; Mark Milton; Alec Moore; Charles Morton; Edward Mosedale; Walter Munroe; Ella Murphy; Slade Murray; Will Musgrove; John Nash; Ben Nevis; Effie Newcombe; Will Newman; Harry Nicholls; G. W. Nicholson; W. H. Noel; Michael Patrick Nolan; James Norrie; Jack Norworth; Joe O'Gorman; Will Oliver; E. V. Page; William Parker; Paulus; Paul Pelham; Harry Pleon; Nelly Power; Pat Rafferty; Harry Randall; Henry Rands; Phil Ray; Kittie Rayburn; John Read; Sam Redfern; Charles Redmond; Arthur Reece; Ernest Rees; Ada Reeve; J. C. Rich; Nellie Richards; Sam Richards; Harry Rickards; Arthur Rigby; William Riley; George Ripon; Albert Rivers; Arthur Roberts; George Robey; Florrie Robina; Frederick Robson; W. G. Ross; Cliff Rylands. Vol. 4: F. V. St. Clair; Charles Seel; Frank Seeley; Burt Shepard; Mark Sheridan; Madge Shirley; Emily Soldene; Tom Squire; Charles Stanley; J. H. Stead; Fred W. Stephens; Eugene Stratton; Nellie Stratton; Harry Sydney; Joe Tennyson & W. H. Wallis; Th 5er 6esa; Vesta Tilley; Clara Torr; Sam Torr; E. J. Toussard; Nat Travers; Harry Turner; Lizzie Valrose; Lottie Venne; Harriet Vernon; Vesta Victoria; Alfred Walker; Bessie Wentworth; Florrie West; Marie Wilton; Thomas Woottwell.]

1898. HONRI, PETER. *Monarchs of the Music Hall.* L: Andre Deutsch/Chappell, 1980. [The Lions Comiques. Publication delayed.]

1899. LA BEAU, DENNIS, ed. *Theatre, Film and Television Biographies Master Index.* . . . Detroit, Mich.: Gale Research Co., 1979.

1900. LE ROY, GEORGE. *Music Hall Stars of the Nineties.* L: British

Technical and General Press, 1952. [Marie Lloyd, Dan Leno, The Lupinos, Charles Coborn, Harry Lauder, George Mozart, Albert Chevalier, Kate Carney, Arthur Roberts, Dr Walford Bodie, Jenny Hill, Harry Randall, Harry Houdini, Eugene Stratton, Harry Tate, Bessie Bellwood, Little Tich, Tom Costello, Joe Elvin, Chung Ling Soo, Vesta Tilley, G. H. Chirgwin, *et al.*]

1901. MACKIE, ALBERT D. *The Scotch Comedians from the Music Halls to Television.* Edinburgh: Ramsay Head Press, 1973.

1902. MIDWINTER, ERIC. *Make'em Laugh.* L: Allen & Unwin, 1979. Rev. P. Cotes, *What's On in London,* 27 Apr. 1979.

1903. "Monarchs of Mirth and Kings of Laughter." *New Penny Magazine* 163 (1902). [Dan Leno, Little George, Harry Payne.]

1904. "'My Most Amusing Experience.' A Symposium of Music-Hall Stars. Illustrated by N. Morrow." *Strand,* Dec. 1912, pp. 687-93. [Wilkie Bard, G. H. Chirgwin, T. E. Dunville, Joe Elvin, Geo. Leyton, Victoria Monks, R. A. Roberts, Geo. Robey, Mark Sheridan.]

1905. *Pantomime and Vaudeville Favorites.* [n.p.] A. W. Gamage, 1914.

1906. PARKER, JOHN, ed. *Who's Who in the Theatre.* 3rd ed. L: Pitman, 1916. [Contains special music-hall supplement.]

1907. RÉMY, TRISTAN. *Les Clowns.* Paris: Bernard Grasset, 1945. [Chapter 31, "Les Eccentriques solitaires: Bagessen, Little Tich, Joe Jackson," pp. 371-82.]

1908. SENELICK, LAURENCE. *A Cavalcade of Clowns. . . .* San Francisco, Cal.: Bellerophon Books, 1977. [Little Tich, Bagessen, Grock.]

1909. *Variety Stars.* L: The Variety Publishing Co. [1895]. [Preface signed A. J. Park, Charles Douglas Stuart. Repr. from *The Sun.* Contents: "How I became a 'Serio,'" by Marie Lloyd, pp. 5-8; "'Pantos' I have played in," by Dan Leno, pp. 9-11; "Coster ditties," by Gus Elen, pp. 12-15; "Descriptive Songs," by Charles Godfrey, pp. 16-18; "Character Vocalism," by Henry Randall, pp. 19-21; "Ventriloqual Vagaries," by Lieut. Cole, pp. 22-27; "Motley and Vermilion" by Harry Payne, pp. 28-30. "The Panto Art," by Paul Martinetti, pp. 31-35; "Music Hall Melodies," by George Le Brunn, pp. 36-38; "'Coon' Minstrelsy," by Nellie Richards, p. 39.]

1910. *Who Was Who in the Theatre: 1912-1976. A Biographical Dictionary of Actors, Actresses, Directors, Playwrights and Producers of the English-speaking Theatre. Compiled from Who's Who in the Theatre Volumes 1-15 (1912-1972).* 4 vols. Detroit, Mich.: Gale Research Co., 1978. [Includes Maud Allan, Wilkie

Bard, Walford Bodie, Kate Carney, Albert Chevalier, Paul Cinquevalli, Charles Coborn, G. H. Elliott, Joe Elvin, Will Evans, Sydney Fairbrother, Louie Freear, Gertie Gitana, Percy Honri, John Lawson, Alice Lloyd, Marie Lloyd, Rosie Lloyd, Marie Loftus, Cecilia Loftus, Clarice Mayne, Ernie Mayne, Billy Merson, George Mozart, J. W. Rickaby, Ella Retford, Arthur Roberts, George Robey, Clarkson Rose, Fred Russell, Harry Tate, Vesta Victoria, Bransby Williams, Nellie Wallace, Ray Wallace, Albert Whelan, Charles R. Whittle, Wee Georgie Wood, Tom Woottwell, *et al.*]

1911. *Who's Who in Variety: a Biographical Record of the Variety Stage.* L: The Performer, 1950. [Compiled and edited by Guy R. Bullar and Len Evans of 'The Performer.']

INDIVIDUALS

Cross-references

See also

Maud Allan **185, 1910.**

Wilkie Bard **320, 325, 1897, 1904, 1910, 3115, 3117, 3119, 3425, 3429, 3860.**

Bessie Bellwood **1890, 1897, 2109.**

Billy Bennett **174, 324, 1895, 3427, 3431, 3434.**

Walford Bodie **1910.**

Bessie Bonehill **1897.**

Herbert Campbell **1890, 1894, 1897, 3429, 3860.**

Kate Carney **178, 1897, 1910, 3217, 3429, 3431, 3860.**

Albert Chevalier **1, 180, 187, 200, 296, 318, 325, 339, 364, 1897, 1910, 2310, 3183, 3217, 3306, 3421, 3425–26, 3432.**

G. H. Chirgwin **355, 1894, 1897, 1904, 3425.**

Paul Cinquevalli **478, 1910.**

Harry Clifton **242, 1618, 1890, 1897, 3121.**

Charles Coborn **1494, 1897, 1910, 3423–26.**

C. B. Cochran **317–22, 324–25, 1910, 3199.**

Lottie Collins **325, 384, 1897, 3159, 3215.**

Tom Costello **325, 1897, 3429.**

Personalia

Sam Cowell **321, 1618, 1890, 1897, 2195, 3101, 3148, 3153-54, 3215, 3257.**

Maggie Duggan **3111-12.**

T. E. Dunville **325, 1894, 1897, 1904, 3111-12, 3115.**

Gus Elen **186, 318, 325, 364, 1897, 1909, 3120, 3217, 3421-22, 3424-25, 3429, 3431, 3435, 3861.**

G. H. Elliott **320, 1910, 3420, 3426.**

Joe Elvin **1904, 1910.**

Fred Emney **174, 321-22, 1910, 2195, 3417, 3426.**

Will Evans **1897, 1910, 3860.**

W. B. Fair **1897.**

Sydney Fairbrother **1910, 2186, 3426, 3429.**

James Fawn **1894, 1897, 3860.**

Sid Field **322-24, 1895, 1910, 3417.**

Happy Fanny Fields **3860.**

Gracie Fields **174, 186, 318, 320, 323, 364, 1895, 1910, 3306, 3414, 3428, 3436-40.**

Bud Flanagan **321-22, 325, 1895, 2109, 3417, 3428, 3441-42.**

Florrie Forde **1897, 3118-21, 3423-25, 3429, 3431-33.**

George Formby **321, 325, 1895, 3431, 3443.**

Harry Fragson **3426.**

Louie Freear **1897, 1910, 3417.**

Will Fyffe **174, 321, 325, 1895, 3306, 3414, 3444-45.**

Gertie Gitana **1910, 3424-25, 3429.**

Charles Godfrey **1897, 1909.**

Brothers Griffiths **174.**

Yvette Guilbert **180, 200, 281, 288, 1816, 1897, 3414, 3446-47, 3497, 3650-51.**

Will Hay **322, 1895, 3424, 3427.**

Jenny Hill **358, 1897, 2109.**

Stanley Holloway **3306, 3417, 3425, 3428, 3448, 3453.**

Percy Honri **1897, 1910.**

Alec Hurley **3118-19, 3439, 3860.**

Fred Karno **2109, 3404.**

Hetty King **3420, 3422, 3431, 3860.**

R. G. Knowles **186-87, 1894, 1897, 1910, 3112.**

Lupino Lane **321, 1619, 1910, 2529.**

George Lashwood **1817, 3117, 3414, 3425, 3429, 3860.**

Harry Lauder **174, 200, 320, 344, 1894, 1897, 3126, 3414, 3424-25, 3429, 3432, 3454, 3457.**

John Lawson **1910.**

Tom Leamore **1897.**

Dan Leno **88, 107, 180, 214, 325, 352, 364, 380, 478, 603, 762, 1889, 1894-95, 1897, 1903, 1909, 2109, 2547, 3104, 3421, 3424-25, 3429, 3432.**
Fanny Leslie **1897.**
George Leybourne **1890, 1897.**
Harry Liston **1897, 3127.**
Victor Liston **1897.**
Little Tich **187, 264, 319, 321, 325, 331, 339, 1894-95, 1907-8, 2109, 3421, 3424-25, 3429, 3432, 3557.**
Arthur Lloyd **374, 1322, 1618, 1897, 3093-94, 3207.**
Marie Lloyd **89, 174, 186-87, 200, 214, 317-18, 325, 329-30, 344, 355, 360, 363, 1889, 1894, 1897, 1909-10, 2109, 3110, 3372, 3421, 3424, 3426, 3429-30, 3432, 3860.**
Cissie Loftus **186-87, 1897, 1910, 3414.**
Marie Loftus **1897, 1910.**
Arthur Lucan **1895.**
Fred Maccabe **1816, 1897.**
G. H. Macdermott **358, 1897, 3135, 3218.**
E. W. Mackney **1897, 3103, 3136, 3148, 3262.**
Paul Martinetti **1897, 1909.**
Billy Merson **1889, 1910, 3417, 3423, 3425, 3431.**
Max Miller **1895, 3360, 3429, 3433, 3460-61.**
Charles Morton **358, 540, 551, 1816.**
George Mozart **1910.**
Jolly John Nash **1897.**
Jimmy Nervo **174, 1895, 3428.**
Harry Nicholls **1897.**
Renton Nicholson **336, 383, 447, 450, 3335.**
Harry Pleon **1897.**
Sandy Powell **1895, 3425.**
Nellie Power **1897.**
Harry Randall **325, 1894, 1897, 1909, 3860.**
Frank Randle **1895.**
Ada Reeve **200, 319, 1897, 3417, 3423, 3429, 3860.**
Ella Retford **1910, 3306, 3417, 3423, 3429.**
Harry Rickards **1816, 1897.**
Arthur Roberts **176, 318, 321, 1894, 1897, 1910, 3421.**
George Robey **174, 186, 264, 317-25, 1894-95, 1897, 1904, 1910, 3110, 3113-14, 3120, 3417, 3421, 3425-26, 3429, 3433.**
Frederick Robson **318, 358, 1897, 3257.**
Clarkson Rose **1910.**
Billy Russell **1895, 3431.**

Personalia

Henry Russell **1890, 3479.**
Eugen Sandow **1816.**
Ella Shields **3422, 3424–26.**
Charles Sloman **383, 3158.**
Emily Soldene **1816, 1910.**
J. H. Stead **1890, 1897, 3148.**
Oswald Stoll **123, 144, 705, 707, 711, 1007, 1816.**
Eugene Stratton **325, 1897, 3112, 3415, 3424, 3426, 3429, 3432.**
Harry Tate **264, 319–22, 325, 387, 712, 1895, 1910, 3305, 3417, 3424, 3427.**
Vesta Tilley **173–74, 317–21, 323, 325, 1897, 3112, 3114–20, 3414, 3425, 3429.**
A. G. Vance **1618, 3160–61.**
Vesta Victoria **200, 1897, 1910, 3414, 3421, 3423, 3429, 3860.**
Nellie Wallace **318, 1895, 1910, 3183, 3422, 3428.**
Harry Weldon **3860.**
Bransby Williams **363, 1889, 1910, 3305–6, 3860.**
Georgie Wood **1910, 2369.**
Tom Woottwell **1897, 1910.**
Zaeo **186.**
Zazel **359, 1671a, 1890.**

Maud Allan

Dancer; b. Toronto, Canada, 1879; d. Los Angeles, Cal., 7 Oct. 1956.
1912. "The Meaning of my Dancing." *London Magazine* 20 (1908): 400–404.
1913. *My Life and Dancing.* L: Everett, 1908.
Secondary Materials
EDS, 1:330–31 [Gino Tani].
1914. BEERBOHM, MAX. "At the Palace Theatre." *Saturday Review* 106 (4 July 1908): 11.
1915. KETTLE, MICHAEL. *Salome's Last Veil: The Libel Case of the Century.* L: Hart-Davis, Macgibbon, Granada, 1977. [MA's 1918 lawsuit against Pemberton-Billing.]
1916. SIMMONS, E. ROMAYNE and D. J. HOLLAND. "Salome and the King." *Dance Magazine* (N. Y.), Nov. 1967.
1917. VECHTEN, CARL VAN. "MA." N. Y. *Times*, 21 and 30 Jan. 1910. Repr. in *The Dance Writings of Carl van Vechten,* ed. Paul Padgette. N.Y.: Dance Horizons, 1974.

Wilkie Bard

Comedian; b. William Augustus Smith, Manchester, 19 Mar. 1874; d. 5 March 1944.

1918. "Ab initio." *Era Annual* (1905): 28–29. Repr. in *Music-hall Records* 6 (Apr. 1979): 118–19.
1919. "How to Lose a Fortune." *Era Annual* (1911): 98–99.

Secondary Materials

1920. "Mr WB (caricature by Kritikos)." *Stage*, 9 Dec. 1911.
1921. "Out o' th' Lunnon 'Alls." Boston *Transcript*, 2 Jan. 1924.
1922. "Stars as Seen from the Wings No. III—Mr. WB." *Stage*, 12 July 1910.
1923. [Tour begins] N.Y. *Times*, 9 Oct. 1919.
1924. "WB a fun maker." N.Y. *Tribune*, 22 Oct. 1919.
1925. "WB gets peculiar welcome on his debut here." N.Y. *Tribune*, Oct. 1921.
1926. "WB makes a hit." N.Y. *Times*, 21 Oct. 1913.

Bessie Bellwood

Serio-comic singer; b. Elizabeth Ann Catherine Nicholson Mahoney, Monkstone, Northern Ireland, 1857; d. West Kensington, London, 24 Sept. 1896.

Secondary Materials

Le Roy, chapter 16; OCT., p. 100.
1927. "Action against Miss BB." *Era*, 1 June 1889, p. 15; 24 Aug. 1889, p. 15; 31 Aug. 1889, p. 15.
1928. "Action against Miss BB." *Era*, 18 May 1895, p. 16.
1929. "Action by Miss BB." *Era*, 20 Apr. 1889, p. 15.
1930. "BB and the Duke [of Manchester]." *Era*, 25 June 1892, p. 14.
1931. "BB appeals." *Era*, 3 May 1890, p. 15; 17 May 1890, p. 15.
1932. "BB hissed." *Recorder*, 20 Aug. 1892.
1933. "Miss BB in America." *Era*, 11 Jan. 1896, p. 16; 18 Jan. 1896, p. 16.
1934. "An Original Artist." N.Y. *Mirror*, 7 Dec. 1895.
1935. ROSS, BERT. "The Lives of Three Bessies." *The Call Boy*, 4, no. 2 (June 1967).
1936. "Scene at a Concert Hall [in Birmingham]." *Era*, 19 July 1890, p. 16.
1937. WATSON, ROBERT PATRICK. *Memoirs of R. P. Watson; a Journalist's Experience of Mixed Society.* [L] Smith, Ainslie [1899].

1938. [Obit.: *Era*, 26 Sept. 1896, p. 18; 3 Oct. 1896, p. 19 (funeral); *Sketch*, 30 Sept. 1896, pp. 391–93; *Illustrated Sporting and Dramatic News*, 3 Oct. 1896.]

Billy Bennett

Comedian; b. Glasgow, 1887; d. Blackpool, 30 June 1942.

1939. *BB's First Budget of Burlesque Monologues.* L: Paxton, n.d. [T. W. Connor given as author.]

1940. *BB's Second Budget of Burlesque Monologues . . . as written, performed and broadcast by BB.* L: Paxton, n.d.

1941. *BB's Third Budget of Burlesque Monologues as written, performed and broadcast by BB.* L: Paxton, n.d.

1942. *BB's Fourth (Souvenir) Budget of Burlesque Monologues as written, performed and broadcast by BB.* L: Paxton, n.d.

Dr. Walford Bodie

Conjurer, ventriloquist, and faith healer; b. Samuel Murphy, Aberdeen, 11 June 1870; d. 19 Oct. 1939.

1942a. *The Bodie Book.* L: Caxton, 1905. [Anecdotes.]

1942b. *Harley the Hypnotist.* L: Pearson [c. 1910] [Novel.]

1943. "Music Hall Sketches." *Era*, 11 Mar. 1889, p. 19.

1944. *Stage Stories.* L: Simpkin, Marshall, Hamilton, Kent, 1908. Rev. *Era*, 10 Oct. 1908, p. 25.

Secondary Materials

1945. "A Chat with WB." *Era*, 30 Jan. 1897, p. 20.

1946. "Dr WB." *Era*, 23 May 1903.

1947. "Dr WB." *Era*, 3 Apr. 1909.

1948. "Dr WB at the Palace Theatre, Aberdeen." *Era*, 19 Aug. 1899, p. 16; 28 Aug. 1889, p. 19.

1949. "Dr WB at the Theatre Royal, Coatbridge." *Era,* 29 Sept. 1900, p. 19; 6 Oct. 1900, p. 19.

1950. "Dr WB in Bolton." *Era*, 31 Mar. 1900, p. 19.

1951. "Dr WB in Leicester and Falkirk." *Era*, 18 Nov. 1899, p. 21.

1952. "Dr WB in Wolverhampton." *Era*, 22 June 1895, p. 16.

1953. WILLIAMS, ELLIOT. "The Modern Miracle Worker." *Call Boy* 6, no. 2 (June 1969): 4–5.

1954. [Appears as the character McKyle in Peter Barnes, *The Ruling Class, a baroque comedy.* L: Heinemann; N.Y.: Grove Press, 1969.]

Bessie Bonehill

Male impersonator; b. West Bromwich, c. 1857; d. Portsea, 21 Aug. 1902.

Secondary Materials
1955. "BB." N.Y. *Clipper,* 11 Jan. 1890, p. 723. [Portrait and biography.]
1956. "BB." N.Y. *Dramatic Mirror,* 16 Oct. 1897.
1957. "BB at home." *Era,* 29 Nov. 1890, p. 17.
1958. "BB likes America." N.Y. *Dramatic Mirror,* 2 Aug. 1900.
1959. "BB's farewell." N.Y. *Clipper,* 14 Dec. 1889.
1960. "Bonnie BB." N.Y. *Dramatic Mirror,* 29 Feb. 1896.
1961. "Miss BB." *Era,* 18 Jan. 1890, p. 27.
1962. "Miss BB's pet dog." *Era,* 17 Oct. 1891, p. 17.
1963. ROSS, BERT. "The Lives of Three Bessies." *Call Boy* 4, no. 2 (June 1967).
1964. [Obit.: *Era,* 21 Aug. 1902; N.Y. *Dramatic Mirror,* 30 Aug. 1902, p. 20.]

Herbert Campbell

Comedian; b. Herbert Story, Lambeth, London, Dec. 1846; d. Highbury, 19 July 1904.

Secondary Materials
1965. "HC's start." *Era,* 22 Sept. 1888, p. 15.
1966. "Methodical HC." *M.A.P.*, 30 July 1904, pp. 129–30.

Kate Carney

Coster singer; b. Kate Raynard or Paterson, South London, 1870; d. London, 1 Jan. 1950.

Secondary Materials
EDS, 3:78 [Harold Scott].
1967. BARKER, TONY. "KC." *Music Hall Records* 4 (Dec. 1978): 64–71; 5 (Feb. 1979): 83. [Includes discography.]
1968. "KC at Bristol." *Era,* 1 Oct. 1898, p. 18.
1969. "KC at Cardiff." *Era,* 24 Sept. 1898, p. 18.

J[oseph] A[rnold] Cave

Manager and Ethiopian singer; b. Maida Hill, 21 Oct. 1823; d. London, 20 Nov. 1912.

Personalia

Secondary Materials
1970. "A Chat with JC." *Era*, 20 Jan. 1894, p. 10.
1971. "Mr JAC's benefit matinee." *Era*, 14 July 1894 , p. 16.
1972. "Mr JC's 89th Birthday." *Telegraph*, 22 Oct. 1912.
1973. SOUTAR, ROBERT, ed. *Jubilee of Dramatic Life and Incident of JAC.* L: T. Vernon [1894].

Albert Chevalier

Actor and comic singer; b. Albert Onesime Britannicus Gwathveoyd Louis Chevalier, Notting Hill, London, 21 March 1862; d. London, 11 June 1923.
1974. *AC, a Record by Himself.* L: John Macqueen, 1896. [Biographical and other chapters by Brian Daly.] Rev. *Era*, 30 Nov. 1895, p. 18; N.Y. *Daily News*, 30 Nov. 1895.
1975. "All Right at Night (a Theatrical Tradition)." *Entr'acte Annual* (1892): 12.
1976. *Before I Forget—the Autobiography of a Chevalier d'Industrie.* L: T. Fisher Unwin, 1902.
1977. "Character Studies." *Pall Mall Magazine* 49 (Apr. 1912): 478–88.
1978. "The Coster in Society." *Graphic*, 29 Nov. 1892.
1979. "Dramatic Criticism in Muddletown, a Page for the Local Critic's Diary." *Era Annual* (1909): 68–69.
1980. "Drinks in Music Halls." *Era*, 3 Mar. 1894, p. 17.
1981. "Experiences in Moving Pictures." *Strand* (N.Y.), 50 (Jan. 1916): 827–28.
1982. "The Late Charles Ross." *Era*, 10 Mar. 1894, p. 16.
1983. *Limelight Lays.* Bristol: J. W. Arrowsmith, 1903.
1984. "'My Old Dutch.'" *The Bioscope*, 8 July 1915, p. 169.
1985. "On Costers and the Music-halls." *English Illustrated Magazine* 10 (1893): 479–90. [Ills. H. G. Banks.]
1986. *Six Burlesque Lectures: Dissertations on Mediaeval Poetry.* L: Reynolds & Co., n.d. [Subjects considered: No. 1, Mary had a Little Lamb; No. 2, Taffy was a Welshman; No. 3, Old Mother Hubbard; No. 4, Humpty Dumpty; No. 5, Little Jack Horner; No. 6, Little Miss Muffit.]
1987. *The "Uninitiated," his Experiences and Impressions. A Fool's Philosophy. . . .* L: Sonnenschein, 1896. [Ills. Charles Pears, and a photograph of the author.]
Secondary Materials
DNB [J. Parker] 1922–30; EDS [Harold Scott, Rachael Low, Davide Turconi] 3:615; OCT, p. 169; Le Roy, chapter 7.

1988. "AC." Boston *Advertizer*, 3 Oct. 1896.

1889. [AC] *Theatre* (N.Y.) 6, (Oct. 1906): 274; 13 (Jan. 1911): 29.

1990. "AC in America." *Era*, 4 Apr. 1896; 11 Apr. 1896, p. 18; 20 June 1896, p. 16; 3 Oct. 1896, p. 19; 20 Mar. 1897, p. 10.

1991. "AC's American Debut." N.Y. *Clipper*, 28 Mar. 1896.

1992. "AC's Career." Boston *Herald*, 1 Oct. 1896.

1993. "A Chat with C." N.Y. *Mirror*, 28 Mar. 1896.

1994. "C a Success." N.Y. *Mail and Express*, 24 Mar. 1896.

1995. "C and his Songs." *Ages*, 22 Nov. 1896.

1996. "C and his Songs." N.Y. *Sun*, 29 Mar. 1896.

1997. "C and his Songs." N.Y. *Times*, 22 Mar. 1896.

1998. CHEVALIER, FLORENCE. *AC Comes Back . . . inspired by the Spirit of AC.* L: Rider & Co. [c. 1930]. [Account by AC's wife of her attempt to communicate with his spirit through mediums.]

1999. "C has a Grievance." Boston *Advertizer*, 3 July 1896.

2000. "C Makes a Hit." N.Y. *Commercial Advertizer*, 24 Mar. 1896.

2001. "C the Cockney Laureate." *Dominant*, 6 July 1893.

2002. "C's Great Hit." N.Y. *World*, 24 Mar. 1896.

2003. "The Coster's Laureate." *Era*, 7 Dec. 1901.

2004. "The 'Coster's' Poet." N.Y. *Commercial Advertizer*, 11 Jan. 1896.

2005. "The Critic's Saturday Night." Boston *Courier*, 18 Oct. 1896.

2006. DODGSON, CHARLES LUTWIDGE. *The Diaries of Lewis Carroll.* L: Cassell, 1953. [Ed. R. L. Greene. Pp. 460, 472, 500.]

2007. DOUGLAS, JAMES. *Adventures in London.* L: Herbert Jenkins, n.d. ["AC," pp. 165–71.]

2008. "Favourite Entertainers, No. 2: Mr AC." *Playgoer*, 15 Jan. 1902, pp. 235–40.

2009. "First Appearance Here of AC." Boston *Globe*, 13 Oct. 1896.

2010. "FRYERS, AUSTIN" [pseud.] "The Reminiscences of Mr AC, a Foretaste." *St. Paul's*, 29 Sept. 1894, p. 655.

2011. "A Genuine Chevalier d'Industrie." *Punch*, 28 June 1899, p. 310. [At the Queen's Hall.]

2012. "Hollis Street Theatre, AC." Boston *Transcript*, 3 Oct. 1896.

2013. "In the Land of Nod, a Talk with Mr AC." *Pall Mall Gazette*, 13 Sept. 1898.

2014. "Is Realism Possible in Music Hall Art?" Boston *Journal*, 18 Oct. 1896.

2015. JOHNSTON, WILL H. "'Old Dutch.'" *Picture-Play Magazine* (1915): 45–58.

2016. "Laureate of the Costermongers." N.Y. *Herald*, 12 Jan. 1896.

2017. LAWSON, MALCOLM. "C." *Playgoer*, 15 Jan. 1902, pp. 240–41.

2018. "Made a Great Hit." Boston *Herald*, 19 Oct. 1896.
2019. "A Man of Magnetism." N.Y. *Dramatic Mirror*, 3 Oct. 1896.
2020. "Mr AC in 'The Land of Nod.'" *Era*, 8 Oct. 1898, p. 19.
2021. "Mr AC. Liverpool, Manchester." *Era*, 3 July 1897, p. 18.
2022. "Mr AC's Recitals." *Era*, 16 Dec. 1899, p. 20.
2023. "Mr C. . . . says farewell to his old associates." *Punch*, 20 June 1906, 450. [Cartoon.]
2024. "Mr C's Recital." Boston *Post*, 20 Oct. 1899.
2025. "Mr C's Recitals." *Daily Chronicle*, 4 Dec. 1896.
2026. "A Nightly Chevalier." *Punch*, 10 Sept. 1892, p. 117. [At the Tivoli.]
2027. "On the River with AC." *Era*, 27 August 1892, p. 15.
2028. "The Queen's (Small) Hall." *Standard*, 1 Jan. 1900.
2029. "Some Music-hall Questions; talk with Mr AC." *Pall Mall Gazette*, 7 Nov. 1894, p. 8.
2030. SYMONS, ARTHUR. [On AC] *Black and White*, 18 June 1892.
2031. ———. [On AC] *Star*, 2 May 1891.
2032. "'Tis Merry in Hall." *Punch*, 2 Apr. 1892, p. 157. [AC at the London Pavilion.]
2033. "Worth the Price." Boston *Herald*, 14 Oct. 1896.
2034. [Obits.: *Daily Telegraph*, 12 July 1923; *Times*, 12 July 1923; N.Y. *Herald*, 19 July 1923.]

George H. Chirgwin

Comedian and minstrel; b. St. Pancras, London, 13 Dec. 1854; d. Streatham, 14 Nov. 1922.
2035. *C's Chirrup: being the Life and Reminiscences of GC, the 'White Eyed Musical Kaffir.'* L: J. & J. Bennett, 1912.
2036. "'Ma'—the Landlady." *Era Annual* (1904): 62–63.
2037. "Pro's Digs." *Entr'acte Annual* (1899): 30.
Secondary Materials
Le Roy, chapter 22; OCT, p. 176.
2038. BARKER, TONY. "GHC." *Music Hall Records* 2 (Aug. 1978): 3–7; 3 (Oct. 1978): 50; 5 (Feb. 1979): 83. [Includes discography.]
2039. [Caricature] *Era*, 7 Sept. 1911, p. 23.
2040. "A Chat with GC." *Era*, 10 Oct. 1896, p. 19.
2041. "C at Home." *Era*, 3 Feb. 1894, p. 16.
2042. "C in New York." *Era*, 19 Mar. 1898, p. 18.
2043. "The C Jubilee." *Era*, 13 May 1911, p. 26.
2044. "The C Jubilee." *Stage*, 11 May 1911.
2045. COBORN, CHARLES. "GHC." *Era*, 29 Apr. 1911, p. 26.
2046. "Donkeys at a Theatre." *Era*, 10 Apr. 1886, p. 10.

2047. "Mr GHC in Australia." *Table Talk*, 5 Dec. 1896. Repr. in *Music-Hall Records* 6 (Apr. 1979): 119-20.
2048. "Mr GHC's concert." *Era*, 17 Nov. 1883, p. 4.
2049. "The White-eyed Kaffir." *Era*, 3 July 1886, p. 10.
2050. "The White-eyed Kaffir at the Empire, Newcastle-on-Tyne." *Era*, 17 Mar. 1900, p. 18.
2051. "The White-eyed Musical Kaffir." *Era*, 14 Nov. 1880, p. 4. [GHC vs Sandler.]

Paul Cinquevalli

Juggler; b. Paul Kestner, Lissa, Poland, 30 June 1859; d. Brixton, 14 July 1918.
2052. "How to Succeed as a Juggler." *Cassell's Magazine*, Mar. 1909.
2053. "Lex Talionis!" *Era Annual* (1911): 76.
2054. "Twenty Years as a Juggler." *Royal Magazine*, May 1909.
Secondary Materials
EDS [Harold Scott] 3: 871; OCT, p. 178.
2055. "Chat with PC." *Era*, 5 May 1906.
2056. "C: an Illustrated Interview." *Playgoer*, Oct. 1901. Repr. *Theatre Quarterly* 9, no. 36 (winter 1980): 77-81.
2056a. "Cinquevalli to retire." N.Y. Dramatic Mirror, 19 May 1900, p. 20.
2057. DAUVEN, L.-R. "Un Grand Jongleur d'hier: C." *Le Cirque dans l'Univers* 94 (3e trimestre 1974) 9-10.
2058. "Early Days of a Great Juggler." *Chums*, 13 Nov. 1895.
2059. FITZGERALD, WILLIAM G. "The Greatest Juggler in the World." *Strand* 13, no. 13 (Jan. 1897): 92-100.
2060. GAUDREAN. "PC." *The White Tops* (Rochelle, Ill.), Apr.-May 1942.
2061. "How a Famous Juggler Works. PC's Career." *The Million*, 17 Mar. 1894.
2062. "A Juggler of Genius." *Pall Mall Budget*, 21 Mar. 1895.
2063. "M. PC." *Picture Magazine*, Sept. 1894.
2064. "PC." *Era*, 20 Feb. 1886, p. 10.
2065. "PC, an appreciation." *Era*, 19 Mar. 1910, p. 22.
2066. "PC and his Tricks." *Westminster Budget*, 24 Nov. 1893.
2067. "PC on Tour." *Era*, 11 May 1906.
2068. STEVENS, C. L. "The Father of Modern Juggling." *Everybody's Weekly*, June 1928.
2069. "A Talk with PC." *Sketch*, 27 Dec. 1893.
2070. WHITE, S. "The King of Jugglers." *Royal Magazine*, Feb. 1902.

2071. [Obit.: *Chronicle*, 15 July 1918.]

Harry Clifton

Comic singer; b. Henry Robert Clifton, Hoddesdon, Herts, 1832; d. Shepherd's Bush, London, 15 July 1872.

Secondary Materials

OCT, p. 183.

2072. "HC's Songs." *Era*, 10 June 1899, p. 19.
2073. [Obit.: *Era*, 21 July 1872, p. 12.]

Charles Coborn

Comic singer; b. Colin Whitton McCallum, Mile End, London, 4 August 1852; d. 23 Nov. 1945.

2074. "Arthur Young Fund." *Era*, 10 Nov. 1888, p. 18; 16 Feb. 1889, p. 17.
2075. "CC's Challenge," *Era*, 4 Apr. 1891, p. 16; 11 Apr. 1891, p. 16 [follow-up].
2076. "Copyright Songs." *Era*, 5 Feb. 1887, p. 10.
2077. "A Defence of the Music Halls." *Era*, 26 Feb. 1881, p. 5; 5 Mar. 1881, p. 5 [reply by S. Lanfre].
2078. "A Deserving Case." *Era*, 8 Sept. 1888, p. 10.
2079. "Dramatic Sketches at Music Halls." *Era*, 22 Oct. 1892, p. 17.
2080. *'The Man Who Broke the Bank': Memories of the Stage & Music Hall*. L: Hutchinson [1928].
2081. "Music Hall Agreements." *Era*, 5 July 1884, p. 15; 12 July 1884, p. 15.
2082. "Music Hall Benefit Society." *Era*, 12 Sept. 1885, p. 10.
2083. "A Music Hall Benevolent Fund." *Era*, 2 Dec. 1882, p. 4; 23 Dec. 1882, p. 4; 3 Feb. 1883, p. 4; 29 Feb. 1883, p. 4.
2084. "Music Hall Morals." *Era*, 25 Nov. 1877, p. 4. [On S. D. Headlam.]
2085. "Music Hall Protection." *Era*, 13 July 1889, p. 15.
2086. "Music Hall Saturdays." *Era*, 17 Apr. 1886, p. 10; 1 May 1886, p. 10. [Replies by G. W. Hunt and John Nash, 24 Apr. 1886, p. 10; and 8 May 1886, p. 10.]
2087. "Music Hall Songs." *Era*, 17 Oct. 1885, p. 10; 24 Oct. 1885, p. 10 [reply].
2088. "Music Hall Songs." *Era*, 5 Mar. 1887, p. 10. [Follow-ups in 12 Mar. 1887, p. 15; 19 Mar. 1887, p. 15; 25 Mar. 1887, p. 16; 9 Apr. 1887, p. 16; 23 Apr. 1887, p. 16.]
2089. "The Music Hall System." *Era*, 5 Nov. 1881, p. 4. [Reply by S.

Lanfre, 12 Nov. 1881, p. 4.]
2090. "Nonsensationesses." *Era Almanack* (1899): 69–70.
2091. "'Tagging the Tag' or 'How I Became a Sandwich Man.'" *Era*, 10 June 1911, p. 24.

Secondary Materials

EDS [Harold Scott], 3: 1001,; Le Roy, chapter 4; OCT, p. 186.
2091a. "Action by a Music Hall Performer." *Era*, 21 June 1884, p. 11.
2092. BARKER, TONY. "The Man Who Broke the Bank at Monte Carlo." *Music Hall Records*, Oct. 1978, pp. 58–60.
2093. "CC at 82. Memories of a Popular Star." *Observer*, 12 Aug. 1934.
2094. "CC in New York." *Era*, 27 Oct. 1900.
2095. "A Chat with CC." *Era*, 3 Dec. 1892, p. 16.
2096. "400 Miles Walk." *Times*, 29 May 1921.
2097. "Mr CC." *Era*, 11 Aug. 1900, p. 18.
2098. "Mr CC in Paris." *Era*, 5 July 1890, p. 15. [Interview.]
2099. "Mr CC on Art." *Era*, 23 Dec. 1899, p. 18. [Repr. from *Nottingham Football News*.]
2100. "Mr CC's Benefit." *Era*, 10 Dec. 1898, p. 20.
2101. "Mr CC's Entertainment." *Era*, 6 June 1891, p. 15.
2102. "Mr C and the Palace Theatre." *Era*, 8 Dec. 1894, p. 17.
2103. "Songs of Long Ago. Reminiscences of Mr CC. Music Halls in the 'Eighties." *Observer*, 12 Oct. 1919.
2104. [Obit.: N.Y. *Herald Tribune*, 24 Nov. 1945.]

Sir Charles Blake Cochran

Impresario and manager; b. Lindfield, Sussex, 25 Sept. 1872; d. London, 31 Jan. 1951.
2105. *Cock-a-Doodle-Doo.* L: J. M. Dent & Sons, 1941.
2106. *I Had Almost Forgotten.* L: Hutchinson, 1932.
2107. *Review of Revues, & Other Matters.* L: Jonathan Cape, 1930.
2108. *The Secrets of a Showman.* L: William Heinemann, 1925. [His first and best autobiography.]
2109. *A Showman Looks On.* L: J. M. Dent & Sons, 1945. [Chapter 4, "Famous Clowns," pp. 41–54 (GBS and music hall, Dan Leno and Charles Chaplin, Fred Karno, Stan Laurel, Bud Flanagan, Marie Lloyd, Jennie Hill, Bessie Bellwood, Little Tich, etc.); chapter 7, "Tout Paris" (French café-chantant), pp. 88–117; chapter 15, "Seventy Years of Song," pp. 235–51.]
2110. "Variety Theatre," *Encyclopedia Britannica.* 13th ed. L: Encyclopedia Britannica Co. [c. 1926]. [3:930–33.]

Personalia

Secondary Materials
DNB [Vivian Ellis], 1951–60; EDS [Ernest H. Short], 3: 1014; OCT [W. Macqueen-Pope], p. 186.
2111. "The Champion Showman. A Britisher who Designed to Make England One Vast Fun City." *World's Fair* (Oldham), 25 Jan. 1908.
2112. CLEUGH, JAMES. *CBC Lord Bountiful.* L: Pallas Pub. Co., 1938.
2113. GRAVES, CHARLES. *The Cochran Story: a Biography of Sir CBC, Kt.* L: Allen & Unwin [1951].
2114. HEPPNER, SAM. *Cockie.* L: Leslie Frewin, 1969.
2115. "Mr CBC in Big Booms." *World's Fair* (Oldham), 3 Aug. 1912.
2116. SAUNDERS, PETER. *Cockie (Memories from the Musical Career of CBC).* [A musical comedy, opened Vaudeville Theatre, L, 12 Dec. 1973.]

Lottie Collins

Singer and dancer; b. Charlotte Louise Tate, London, 1866; d. London, 2 May 1910.
Secondary Materials
OCT [W. Macqueen-Pope], p. 190.
2117. "Action by Miss LC." *Era*, 17 July 1897, p. 17; 20 Nov. 1897, p. 21.
2118. "A Chat with Miss LC." *Era*, 10 Aug. 1895, p. 14.
2119. "A Chat with Miss LC." *Era*, 29 June 1901.
2120. COLLINS, JOSE. *The Maid of the Mountains: her Story.* L: Hutchinson, 1932. [Autobiography of LC's daughter.]
2121. "The Dance." Boston *Saturday Evening Gazette*, 19 Nov. 1892.
2122. DAVID, JOHN. *A Black Trilogy: Folk Lore and Folk Music from St. Louis.* Ph.D. dissertation, University of Missouri, 1976. [On origins of "Ta-ra-ra-boom-de-ay."]
2123. GELLER, J. J. "The Story behind the Song." N.Y. *Herald Tribune*, 21 Mar. 1926.
2124. HALE, PHILIP. "When 'Ta-ra'ra' was Sung Here." Boston *Sunday Herald*, 15 May 1910.
2125. "Haymarket." Chicago *Interocean*, 11 Dec. 1894.
2126. JACKSON, HOLBROOK. *The Eighteen Nineties.* L: Grant Richards, 1913. [Relevance of LC to the '90s.]
2127. "LC." Chicago *Interocean*, 8 Nov. 1892.
2128. "LC." Boston *Journal*, 30 Dec. 1892.
2129. "LC and 'Ta ra ra.'" Boston *Herald*, 19 Sept. 1892.

8ht154t

2130. "LC attempts Suicide." Philadelphia *Times,* 13 Nov. 1898.
2131. "LC vs. Uncle Sam." Boston *Herald,* 12 Aug. 1893.
2132. "LC's Dance." N.Y. *Recorder,* 31 July 1892.
2133. "Miss LC has Returned from Australia." *Era,* 6 July 1901, p. 21.
2134. "Miss LC Stands Fire Well." N.Y. *Herald-Tribune,* 25 Sept. 1892, p. 36.
2135. "The Moan of the Music Hall Muse." *Punch,* 11 June 1892, p. 278. [Waning of "Ta-ra-ra."]
2136. "Singing of 'Ta-ra-ra.'" Haverhill [Mass.] *Gazette,* 12 July 1892.
2137. "Ta-ra-ra-boom-de-ay." *Era,* 8 Oct. 1892, p. 17. [Interview with LC.]
2138. "The 'Ta-ra-ra' Boom." *Punch,* 26 Mar. 1892, p. 149.
2139. [Obits.: *Era,* 7 May 1910, p. 23; Boston *Herald* and Boston *Journal,* 3 May 1910.]

Tom Costello

Comic singer; b. Thomas Costellow, Birmingham, 30 Apr. 1863; d. London, 8 Nov. 1943.
Secondary Materials
Le Roy, chapter 18; OCT, p. 209.
2140. BARKER, TONY. "TC." *Music-hall Records* 7, (June 1979): 4-17.
2141. BENSON, BRUCE. "The Famous TC." *Call Boy* 7, no. 2 (June 1970): 19-20.
2142. "A Chat with TC," *Era,* (23 June 1894) 16.
2143. "TC in Dublin." *Era,* 22 Dec. 1894, p. 16.

Sam Cowell

Comic singer; b. Samuel Houghton Cowell, London, 5 Apr. 1820; d. Blandford, 11 Mar. 1864.
Secondary Materials
DNB [John Ebsworth], 12: 377; EDS [Phyllis Hartnoll], 3: 1662; OCT, p. 218.
2144. BRISTOW, EUGENE K. "'Tapping the Pockets' in 1860: an Economic Portrait of SC's American Tour." *Theatre Annual* (State University of N.Y. at Albany) 22 (1965-66): 48-64.
2145. COWELL, EMILIE MARGUERITE, née EBSWORTH. *The Cowells in America, being the Diary of Mrs. SC during her Husband's Concert Tour in the Years 1860-1861.* Ed. M. Willson

Disher. L: Oxford University Press, Humphrey Milford, 1934.
2146. "Sketch of the Life of SC." Prefixed to *SC's Collection of Comic Songs*. Edinburgh: 1853.

Maggie Duggan

Singer and dancer; b. 1860, d. 5 Oct. 1919.
Secondary Materials
2147. "A Chat with MD." *Era*, 29 Dec. 1894, p. 11.
2148. "MD in Bradford." *Era*, 15 June 1895, p. 11.
2149. "MD in Bristol." *Era*, 25 May 1895, p. 16.
2150. "Miss MD." *Era*, 14 June 1888.
2151. "Miss MD. Her successful song at the London Pavilion." *Era*, 1 July 1899, p. 17.
2152. "Miss MD in Glasgow." *Era*, 4 June 1898, p. 19.

T. E. Dunville

Comedian; b. Thomas Edward Wallen, Coventry, 26 July 1868; d. Reading, 23 March 1924.
2153. *The Autobiography of an Eccentric Comedian*. L: Everitt [1912]. [First pub. in *Answers*, 1910.]
Secondary Materials
2154. BARKER, TONY. "TED." *Music Hall Records* 8 (Aug. 1979): 24–31. [Discography.]
2155. ———. "The Tragic Death of TED." *Music Hall Records* 4 (Dec. 1978): 72–74.
2156. TED [featured in the comic journal] *The Firefly*, 20 Feb. 1915–31 Mar. 1917. [Sample from 9 Dec. 1916 repr. in George Perry and Alan Aldridge, *The Penguin Book of Comics* (Harmondsworth: Penguin Books, 1967), p. 71.]

Gus Elen

Comic singer; b. Ernest Augustus Elen, Pimlico, London, 22 July 1862; d. Balham, 17 Feb. 1940.
2157. "GE on the Moors." *Era*, 20 Nov. 1897, p. 20.
2158. "Mr Harry Sanson." *Era*, 21 Dec. 1895, p. 16.
2159. "Music Hall Engagements." *Era*, 25 June 1887, p. 17.
2160. "Shooting." *Era Annual* (1909): 72–73.
2161. "Who's Pip?" *Era Annual* (1904): 64–65. [Autobiographical.]
Secondary Materials
OCT [Macqueen-Pope], p. 272.

2161a. "A Clever Coster Comedian." N.Y. *Dramatic Mirror*, 28 Jan. 1899, p. 18.

2162. BARKER, TONY. "GE." *Music Hall Records* 5 (Feb. 1979): 85-95. [With discography.]

2163. BEERBOHM, MAX. [Caricature in] *Pick-Me-Up*, 15 Sept. 1894.

2164. "Chat with Mr GE." *Era*, 23 Sept. 1905.

2165. "E v. the London Music Hall (Limited) & Another." *Times*, 31 May 1906, 1 June 1906.

2166. "GE at the Empire." *Era*, 16 Sept. 1899, p. 18. [Repr. from *Nottingham Daily Express*, 12 Sept. 1899.]

2167. "GE's Growth in Grace." *Era*, 8 Aug. 1896. p. 17.

2168. "GE's New Song ['The Cockney's Garden']." *Era*, 1 Dec. 1894, p. 16.

2169. "Heyday of the Cockney Comedian." *Times*, 9 Jan. 1958.

2170. "Mr GE." *Era*, 18 July 1896, p. 17. [Repr. from *Sporting Mirror*, 13 July 1896.]

2171. "Mr GE at the Trocadero." *Era*, 17 Mar. 1894, p. 16.

2172. "Mr GE [in Birmingham]." *Era*, 31 Aug. 1895, p. 16.

2173. "Mr GE in Edinburgh." *Era*, 28 Apr. 1894, p. 16.

2174. "Mr GE in town." *Era*, 2 June 1894, p. 16.

2175. "What They Think in Birmingham." *Era*, 12 May 1894, p. 16.

G[eorge] H[enry] Elliott

Coon singer; b. Rochdale, 3 Nov. 1884; d. Brighton, 1962.
Secondary Materials
OCT, p. 273.

2176. "GHE. A Chat about Advertising." *Era*, 7 Jan. 1911, p. 28.

2177. "GHE's Benefit." *Era*, 18 Mar. 1911, p. 30.

2178. "Music Hall Celebrities. Mr GHE." *Era*, 20 Mar. 1909.

Joe Elvin

Comic singer; b. Joseph Keegan, London, 29 Nov. 1862; d. 3 Mar. 1935.

2179. "It's Very Hard." *Era Annual* (1908): 45. [Poem.]

2180. "Life's a Sketch." *Era Annual* (1911): 83. [Poem.]
Secondary Materials
Le Roy, chapter 19; OCT, p. 274.

2181. "A Chat with Keegan and Elvin." *Era*, 6 Apr. 1895, p. 16.

2182. "JE and Co." *Era*, 11 Nov. 1899, p. 21.

2183. "JE's Complimentary Night." *Era*, 18 Mar. 1899, p. 19.

2184. "Mr JE as One of the Boys." *Era*, 23 Apr. 1898, p. 22; 30 Apr. 1898, p. 20.

2185. "Stars as Seen from the Wings No. VI—JE." *Stage*, 18 Aug. 1910, p. 13.

Fred Emney

Comedian; b. Islington, 5 Mar. 1865; d. London, 7 Jan. 1917.
Secondary Materials
OCT [W. Macqueen-Pope], p. 285.
2186. FAIRLIE, G. *The FE Story*. L: Hutchinson, 1960. [Biography of FE's son, FE, Jr., b. 1900.]
2187. "Mr FE." *Era*, 27 Sept. 1912.

Will Evans

Comedian; b. London, 29 May 1875; d. 11 Apr. 1931.
2188. "I interview myself." *Era Annual* (1907): 38–40.
2189. "I Must Get On It." *Era Annual* (1905).
Secondary Materials
OCT, p. 302.
2190. "WE, Poultry Farmer." *Era*, 17 Dec. 1910, p. 29.
2191. [Obit.: N.Y. *Times,* 12 Apr. 1931.]

W[illiam] B[urnham] Fair

Comic singer; b. Camden Town, London, 1850; d. London, 22 July 1909.
Secondary Materials
OCT, p. 307.
2192. "Mr WBF's Bankruptcy." *Era*, 14 Nov. 1885, p. 10.
2193. "Mr WBF's Concert." *Era*, 26 Jan. 1884, p. 10.
2194. [Obit.: *Era*, 24 June 1909.]

Sydney Fairbrother

Comic actress; b. Sydney Parselle, London, 31 July 1873; d. 10 Jan. 1941.
2195. *Through an Old Stage Door*. L: Frederick Muller, 1939. [With an appreciation by Sydney Carroll and an introduction by Stephen Gwynn. Chapter 8, "The Halls," pp. 133–39. Information on Fred Emney's "A Sister to Assist'er" and on Sam Cowell.] Rev. R. Prentis, *John O'London's Weekly*, 15 Dec. 1939, p. 346.
Secondary Materials
EDS [Phyllis Hartnoll], 3: 1663; OCT, p. 218.

2196. "An Able Actress." *Dramatic World,* June 1895, p. 3.
2197. " 'Modern Actresses Do Not Work.' Reminiscences by Miss SF."
      Lloyd's Sunday News, 5 Aug. 1923.
2198. "SF." *M. A. P.,* 8 Oct. 1898.

James Fawn

Comic singer; b. 1849; d. 19 Jan. 1923.
Secondary Materials
2199. "Ask a Pliceman." *Era,* 7 Dec. 1889, p. 17.

Sid Field

Comedian; b. Sidney Arthur Field, Edgbaston, Birmingham, 1 Apr.
1904; d. Wimbledon, 3 Feb. 1950.
2200. "Has Comedy a Future?" *News Chronicle,* 27 Jan. 1949.
2201. "Self-profile." *Tatler,* 4 Feb. 1948.
Secondary Materials
2202. CLAYTON, PETER. "Evergreen Fields." *Sunday Telegraph,* 24
      Aug. 1975, p. 12.
2203. "A Comedian visits his home town." *Picture Post,* 19 Oct. 1946,
      pp. 25–27.
2204. CONWAY, HAROLD. "Backyard Actor." *Evening Standard,* 3
      Feb. 1950, p. 3.
2205. FISHER, JOHN. *What a Performance. The Life of SF.* L:
      Seeley, Service, 1975.
2206. MANN, RODERICK. "He Never Saw His Name in Lights."
      Graphic, 4 Feb. 1950.
2207. NOBLE, PETER. "SF." In *Profiles and Personalities.* L:
      Brownlee, 1946. [Pp. 21–24. Ills. Vicky.]
2208. PRIESTLEY, J. B. "SF." *New Statesman,* 11 Feb. 1950.
2209. SF [featured in] *Film Fun.* L: Amalgamated Press, 1950. [Ills.
      Bertie Brown.]
2210. TYNAN, KENNETH. "SF." *Listener,* 24 Jan. 1974.
2211. [Obits.: *Evening News,* 3 Feb. 1950; *Evening Standard,* 3 Feb.
      1950; *Star,* 3 Feb. 1950; *Times,* 4 Feb. 1950.]

Happy Fanny Fields

Comic singer; b. New York City, 1881; d. America, 1961.
2212. "The Story of a Presentation." *Era Annual* (1913): 51–52.
Secondary Materials
2213. BARKER, TONY. "HFF." *Music Hall Records* 8 (Aug. 1979):

37–40. [Discography.]
2214. "A Chat with HFF." *Era*, Dec. 1908.
2214a. "Happy Fanny Fields." N.Y. *Dramatic Mirror*, 12 Sept. 1903, 1, 2; 10 Sept. 1904, 1, 13; 16 Dec. 1905, 1, 11.

Dame Gracie Fields

Comedienne and singer; b. Grace Stansfield, Rochdale, 9 Jan. 1898, d. Capri, 27 Sept. 1979.
2215. "From Factory to Stage, the Romance of a Lancashire Mill Girl." *T.P.'s Weekly,* 10 May 1928, p. 106.
2216. *Sing as We Go: the Autobiography of GF.* L: Frederick Muller, 1960.
2217. "What I Want from Life." In *What I Want from Life,* ed. Edmund George Cousins. L: Allen Unwin, 1934.
2218. "Witty GF Tells of British Tour." Boston *Globe*, 25 Aug. 1945.
Secondary Materials
EDS [Vittoria Ottolenghi and Davide Turconi], 6: 280–82; OCT, p. 316.
2219. AZA, BERT. *Our Gracie. The Story of Miss GF, C.B.E., M.A.* L: Pitkins [c. 1952]. [Primarily pictures.]
2220. BEAVAN, J. "The Secret of London's Most Popular Music Hall Artists." *World Review,* n.s. 5 (July 1949): 17–21. [Also discusses Danny Kaye and Maurice Chevalier.]
2221. BRAUN, ERIC. "GF Sings Again!" *Stage,* 27 Dec. 1974, p. 20.
2222. CLAYTON, PETER. "Rochdale Hunt." *Sunday Telegraph*, 4 Jan. 1976.
2223. DEAN, BASIL. "Is GF Worth £2—a—minute?" *Film Pictorial*, 30 Sept. 1933, p. 20.
2224. "Flashback." *Radio Times*, 26 Oct. 1972.
2225. "GF." *Current Biography Yearbook.* N.Y.: Current Biography, 1943.
2226. "GF." *Life* (N.Y.), 21 Dec. 1942.
2227. "GF." *Times*, 9 Apr. 1936; 18 Jan. 1937; 28 Oct. 1938; 1 Sept. 1943.
2228. "GF Once Again is Great Britain's Darling." Boston *Globe*, 16 July 1941.
2229. GF [featured in] *Radio Fun.* L: Amalgamated Press, 1948. [Ills. Bertie Brown.]
2230. HILL, DESMOND. "From my Scrapbook." *TV Times*, 19 Nov. 1970, pp. 10–12.
2231. ———. "Our Gracie." *TV Times*, 12 Nov. 1970, pp. 2–5.
2232. ———. "Our Gracie even Charmed the Ticket Collector with a Song." *TV Times*, 3 Nov. 1977, pp. 7–11.

2233. JONES, D. A. N. " Amazing Gracie." *Radio Times*, 24–30 Jan. 1976, pp. 54–57.
2234. MORROW, ANN. "Our Gracie Comes Home in Style." *Daily Telegraph*, 18 Sept. 1978, p. 15.
2235. ———. "Red Roses for Gracie as She Sings Her Heart Out." *Daily Telegraph*, 18 Sept. 1978, p. 19.
2236. ROCHDALE MUSEUM. *Our Gracie . . . September 9th–October 7th 1978 . . .* Rochdale: Rochdale Arts and Entertainments Service, 1978. [Text by Elizabeth Pollitt.]
2237. ROCHDALE OBSERVER. *Gracie Extra.* Rochdale: Rochdale Observer, 13 Sept. 1978.
2238. VAUNCE, SIDNEY. "Amazing Gracie." *Stage*, 21 Sept. 1978, pp. 20–23.
2239. WHITEHEAD, DON. "She Makes 'Em Weep or Laugh. GF Knows Soldiers." N.Y. *Times*, 7 June 1942.
2240. [Obits. and tributes: *Daily Telegraph*, 28 Sept. 1979, pp. 1, 3, 36; *Guardian*, 28 Sept. 1979, p. 11; *Sunday Telegraph*, 30 Sept. 1979; *Observer*, 30 Sept. 1979, p. 20; *Stage and Television Today*, 4 Oct. 1979, p. 9.]

Repertoire

2241. *GF's Album of Songs.* L: Francis, Day & Hunter, n.d. [Fred Fannakapan; Grannie's Little Old Skin Rug; Heaven Will Protect an Honest Girl; The Little Pudden Basin; The Lovely Aspidistra in the Old Art Pot; The Rochdale Hounds; Stop and Shop at the Co-op Shop; We've Got to Keep up with the Joneses; Will You Love Me When I'm Mutton.]

Bud Flanagan

Comedian; b. Chaim Reuben Weintrop, Whitechapel, London, 14 Oct. 1896; d. London, 20 Oct. 1968.
2242. "Knowing Your Audience." *20th Century* 170 (July 1961): 35–39.
2243. *My Crazy Life. The Autobiography of BF.* L: Muller, 1961. Repr. L: Four Square Books, 1962. Rev. C. MacInnes, *Spectator*, 20 Oct. 1961, p. 547.

Secondary Materials

2244. [Flanagan and Allen featured in] *Radio Fun.* L: Amalgamated Press, 1938. [Illus. Alex Akerbladh.]
2245. FORSTER, PETER. "How BF Cut the World Down to Size. . . . " *Evening Standard*, 21 Oct. 1968, p. 11.
2246. "The Halls Today: BF Talks to Charles Graves." *Sphere*, 12 Jan. 1935, pp. 52–53.

2247. [Obit.: *Times*, 21 Oct. 1968.]

Florrie Forde

Singer; b. Florence Flanagan, Fitzroy, Melbourne, Australia, 14 Aug. 1876; d. Aberdeen, Scotland, 18 Apr. 1940.
2248. "How I First Went On and Off." *Era Annual* (1905): 31–32.
Secondary Materials
2249. DEBUS, ALLEN. "FF." *Hobbies. The Magazine for Collectors,* July 1965, p. 36 [Her recordings.]
2250. "FF's Benefit."*Era*, 20 Mar. 1909.
2251. MACNEICE, LOUIS. "Death of an Actress." In *Eighty-Five Poems.* L: Faber, 1959. [P. 967, poem.]
2252. ROSS, BERT. "FF's Centenary." *Call Boy* 13, no. 3 (autumn 1976): 1–2.
2253. [Obit.: N.Y. *Herald Tribune*, 19 Apr. 1940.]

George Formby

Comedian; b. George Hoy Booth, Wigan, 26 May 1904; d. Penwortham, 6 Mar. 1961.
2254. *The GF Book.* L: Music Sales, n.d.
Secondary Materials
EDS [Rachael Low and Davide Turconi], 5: 538; OCT, p. 331.
2255. CLAYTON, PETER. "On F." *Sunday Telegraph*, 6 Jan. 1974, p. 1.
2256. COOPER, JOE. "F—Holy Fool." *New Society*, 8 Aug. 1974, p. 364.
2257. FISHER, JOHN. *GF.* L: Woburn-Futura, 1975. [Concentrates on film career.]
2258. [GF featured in] *Film Fun.* L: Amalgamated Press, 1938.
2259. "The Lancashire Buffoon." N.Y. *Times*, 18 Dec. 1940.
2260. LE JEUNE, C. A. "Recording a Royal Presentation." N.Y. *Times*, 6 July 1941.
2261. RANDALL, ALAN and RAY SEATON. *GF.* L: W. H. Allen, 1974.
2262. ROSIE, GEORGE. "It's Turned Out Nice Again for George." *Radio Times*, 8 Apr. 1971, p. 10.
2263. *The Vellum.* [Journal of the George Formby Society. "For Private Circulation Only." John Willey, Secretary, 105 Kidsgrove Road, Goldenhill, Stoke-on-Trent, Staffs.]
2264. [Obit.: *Times,* 7 Mar. 1961.]

Harry Fragson

Comedian; b. Leon Vince Philip Pott, Richmond, Surrey, 10 July 1866; d. Paris, 30 Dec. 1913.

EDS,S: 1570-71; OCT [W. Macqueen-Pope] p. 334.

2265. "In the Days of My Youth. Chapters of Autobiography." *M. A. P.*, 9 Dec. 1905, pp. 610–11.

2266. "Wanted—a School for Music Hall Artists." *Era Annual,* (1911): 82.

Secondary Materials

2267. HAMILTON, COSMO. *Unwritten History.* L: Hutchinson; Boston: Little, Brown, 1924. [pp. 90–96.]

2268. [Report of murder] *Times*, 31 Dec. 1913; *Morning Telegraph*, 31 Dec. 1913; N.Y. *Tribune*, 31 Dec. 1913; *Daily Telegraph*, 1 Jan. 1914.

2269. ROSS, BERT. "HF—his centenary."*Call Boy*, 6, no. 2 (June 1969): 6-7.

2270. ST. LAWRENCE, BERNARD. "'Monsieur' HF. An Interview with the new 'Star' at Drury Lane." *Pall Mall*, Nov. 1905: 650–51.

W[illiam] F. Frame

Comedian; b. Flint, Glasgow, 1848; d. 1919.

Secondary Materials

2271. "A Chat wi' WF." *Era*, 8 Aug. 1908.

2272. "A Singer of Scottish Songs." N.Y. *Dramatic Mirror,* 31 Dec. 1898, p. 17.

2272a. "W.F. Frame and his Company." N.Y. *Dramatic Mirror,* 14 Jan. 1899, p. 13.

Louie Freear

Comedienne; b. London, 26 Nov. 1873; d. London, 23 Mar. 1939.

2273. "Some Thoughts." *Era Annual* (1910): 82.

Secondary Materials

2274. "A Chat with LF." *Era*, 19 Sept. 1896, p. 13; 11 Mar. 1899, p. 13.

2275. "Miss LF as Liza Ellen in 'The Man in the Moon.'" *Era*, 27 May 1899, p. 9.

2275a. [Obits.: N.Y. *Herald Tribune,* 24 Mar. 1939; *Times* 24 Mar. 1939.]

Will Fyffe

Comedian; b. Dundee, Scotland, 16 Feb. 1885; d. St. Andrews, Scotland, Dec. 1947.

Secondary Materials

OCT [W. Macqueen-Pope], p. 358.

2276. CROWTHER, BOSLEY. "Bacchantic Notes from an Unmartial Fyffe." N.Y. *Times*, 23 Apr. 1937.

2277. "Scotch Comedian in Palace Debut." N.Y. *Times*, 5 Apr. 1927, p. 30.

2278. "Scotchman Turns Down a Three-year Contract." N.Y. *Herald Tribune*, 30 Apr. 1939.

2278a. "A Wise Chap is WF," Boston *Evening Transcript,* 2 Dec. 1939.

Repertoire

2279. *Francis & Day's Album of WF Songs*. L: Francis, Day & Hunter, 1953. [Daft Sandy; The Engineer; I Belong to Glasgow; I'm Ninety-four This Mornin'; Mrs McKie; Sailing up the Clyde; Sandy's Holiday; You Can Come and See the Baby.]

Gertie Gitana

Singer and dancer; b. Gertrude Mary Ross, Longport, 1888; d. 5 Jan. 1957.

Secondary Materials

OCT, p. 390.

2280. "There's an Old Mill by the Stream, Nellie Dean." *Stage*, 31 Dec. 1975.

Charles Godfrey

Singer; b. Paul Lacey, London, 26 Apr. 1851; d. Brierley Hill, Staffs, 28 Mar. 1900.

Secondary Materials

OCT, p. 393.

2281. "CG's Stage Clothes." *Era*, 29 Mar. 1890, p. 15.

2282. MOORE, H. "Music-hall Memories." *John O' London's Weekly*, 3 Nov. 1931.

2283. "Mr CG." *Era*, 9 Oct. 1897, p. 31.

2284. "Mr CG's Bankruptcy." *Era*, 10 July 1886, p. 10; 17 July 1886, p. 10.

2285. "Music Hall Litigation." *Era*, 21 Mar. 1885, p. 10. [Breach of contract.]

2286. "A Music Hall Suit." *Era*, 24 Jan. 1885, p. 10. [CG sued by agent.]
2287. "Re CG." *Era*, 18 June 1887, p. 17.
2288. [Obits.: *Era*, 31 Mar. 1900, p. 18; 7 Apr. 1900, p. 18.]

George Gray

Actor.
2289. *"The Fighting Parson." Vagaries of a Vagabond.* L: Heath Cranton, 1930. [With an introduction by Dame Madge Kendal.]
2290. "GG and the Babies." *Era Annual* (1911).
Secondary Materials
2291. "'The Fighting Parson' Case." *Era*, 23 July 1910, p. 16; 6 Aug. 1910, p. 22.
2292. "'Parson Gray, V.C.' at the Metropolitan." *Era*, 12 Nov. 1910, p. 29.

The Brothers Griffiths

Animal impersonators and acrobats: Frederick George Delaney, b. Corfu, 1856, d. 11 July 1940; Joseph Delaney, b. Oxford, 1852, d. London, 13 May 1901; Frederick Victor Griffiths.
Secondary Materials
2293. "The Blondin Donkey with a Few Sketches and an Interview." *Sketch*, 15 Jan. 1891.
2294. "The English Family Words Concern." N.Y. *Times*, 19 Jan. 1930.
2295. STONE, PERCY N. "The Tale of the Head of a Horse." N.Y. *Herald Tribune*, 2 Feb. 1930.
2295a. [Obit. of Joseph Griffiths. N.Y. *Dramatic Mirror*, 1 June 1901, p. 15.]

Yvette Guilbert

Diseuse and singer; b. Emma Laure Esther Guilbert, Paris, 20 Jan. 1865; d. Aix-en-Provence, 3 Feb. 1944.
2296. "The Actress of Tomorrow." *Theatre* (N.Y.) 24 (Dec. 1916): 366, 406.
2297. *L'Art de chanter une chanson.* Paris: Grasset, 1928.
2298. *Autres temps, autres chants.* Paris: Robert Laffont, 1946. [With a preface by Dussane. Reminiscences of café-chantant song repertoire.]
2299. *La Chanson de ma vie (Mes mémoires).* Paris: Bernard Grasset,

1927. English trans.: *The Song of My Life. My Memories.* L: Harrap, 1929. Rev. W. Steed, *Review of Reviews* 75 (Sept.-Oct. 1929): 236-38; *Theatre Arts Monthly* (N.Y.) 29 (Aug. 1945): 494.

2300. *Les Demi-vieilles.* Paris: Juven, 1902. [Novel.]

2301. *How to Sing a Song.* N.Y.: Macmillan, 1918.

2302. *Mes Lettres d'amour.* Paris: Denoël & Steele, 1933.

2303. *La Passante émerveillée.* Paris: Grasset, 1929.

2304. "Some Impressions of the American Stage." *Drama League Monthly* (N.Y.) 1 (Dec. 1916): 209-12.

2305. "Vaudeville Experiences in America." *American Mercury* (Baltimore) 69 (Apr. 1910): 840-43.

2306. *La Vedette.* Paris: Simonis Empis, 1902. [Novel.]

2307. "What My Art Means to Me." *Delineator* (N.Y.) 89 (Nov. 1916): 15.

2308. [with HAROLD SIMPSON]. *YG: Struggles and Victories.* L: Mills and Boon [1910]. Rev. *Era*, 8 Oct. 1910, p. 27.

Secondary Materials

EDS [Corrado Pavolini & Alessandro Cervellati], 6: 48-49; OCT, p. 420.

2309. BAB, JULIUS. *Schauspieler und Schauspielerkunst.* Berlin: Olsterheld, 1926. [Pp. 247-50.]

2310. BEERBOHM, MAX. "YG and Albert Chevalier." *Saturday Review*, 23 June 1892. Repr. in *Around Theatres*. L: Rupert Hart-Davies, 1953. [Pp. 436-39.]

2311. BYL, ARTHUR. *YG.* L: Bliss, Sands & Co., 1898. [Drawn by Toulouse-Lautrec. Described by Arthur Byl. Trans. A. Texeira de Mattos.]

2312. CASS, MARY CANFIELD. "YG." In *Grotesques and Other Reflections*. N.Y. and L.: Harper, 1927.

2313. FERRARI, GUSTAVE. *Selections from Collection YG.* L: Augener, 1912. [English trans. by Ezra Pound.]

2314. GEFFROY, GUSTAVE. *YG.* Paris: Marty, 1894. Repr. as *YG*. N.Y.: Walker in association with the Department of Printing and Graphic Arts, Harvard College Library, 1968. [Text by Gustave Geffroy; ills. Henri de Toulouse-Lautrec, introduction by Peter Wick.]

2315. HAMILTON, CLAYTON MEEKER. "YG." In *Theory of the Theatre and Other Principles of Dramatic Criticism. Consolidated Edition, including the Theory of the Theatre, Studies in Stagecraft, Problems with the Playwright seen on Stage.* N.Y.: Holt; Toronto: Oxford University Press, 1939. [With a Foreword by Burns Mantle.]

2316. HAMILTON, COSMO. "Sketch of YG." *Bookman* 96 (Jan. 1918): 537-38.

Individuals

2317. [Interview with YG] *Current Opinion* (N.Y.) 62 (Jan. 1917): 30.
2318. KNAPP, BETTINA and MYRA CHIPMAN. *That Was Yvette: The Biography of YG, the Great Diseuse.* N.Y.: Holt, Rinehart and Winston, 1964. Rev. S. Raven, *N.Y. Review of Books*, 22 Apr. 1965.
2319. MACFALL, HALDANE. "Appreciation of YG." *Mask* 1 (Sept. 1908): 130–33.
2320. ROGER-MARX, CLAUDE. *YG vue par Toulouse-Lautrec.* Paris: Au Pont des Arts, 1950.
2321. ROW, A. "Interview of YG." *Poet Lore* (N.Y.) 30 (spring 1919): 144–47.
2322. VALERIO, EDITH. "YG to Revisit America." *Theatre* (N.Y.) 22 (Oct. 1915): 187–88.
2323. VECHTEN, CARL VAN. "YG." In *Interpreters.* New revised ed. N.Y.: Alfred A. Knopf, 1920. Repr. N.Y.: Arno, 1976. [Pp. 135–47.]
2324. "YG as a Song Reformer." *Era*, 24 Sept. 1910, p. 27.
2325. [Obits.: *Musical Courier* 129 (20 Feb. 1944): 42; *Newsweek* (N.Y.), 14 Feb. 1944, p. 92.]

Will Hay

Comedian; b. William Thompson Hay, Stockton-on-Tees, 6 Dec. 1888; d. Chelsea, London, 18 Apr. 1949.
Secondary Materials
2326. SEATON, RAY and ROY MARTIN. *Good Morning Boys: WH Master of Comedy. . . .* L: Barrie & Jenkins, 1978. [Foreword by Eric Morecambe.]

Jenny Hill

Serio-comic; b. Jane Woodley, Paddington, London, 1848; d. Brixton, 28 June 1896.
2327. "JH's Brougham." *Era*, 16 Oct. 1886, p. 10.
2328. [Letter to editor] *Era*, 1 Sept. 1888, p. 10.
Secondary Materials
Le Roy, chapter 11; OCT, p. 444.
2329. "Action by Miss JH." *Era*, 10 Oct. 1884, p. 10.
2330. "Assault on JH." *Era*, 27 Oct. 1886, p. 10.
2331. "By the Death of JH." *Referee*, 5 July 1896.
2332. [Interview] *Sketch*, 15 Nov. 1893.
2333. "JH." N.Y. *Clipper*, 28 Feb. 1891, p. 801. [Portrait and biography.]

Personalia

2334. "JH at Home." *Era*, 26 May 1894, p. 16.
2335. "JH in South Africa." *Era*, 3 Feb. 1894, p. 18; 5 May 1894, p.16.
2336. "The JH Testimonial." *Era*, 20 Dec. 1890, p. 17.
2337. "JH's Farewell to England." *Era*, 24 Sept. 1892, p. 16.
2338. "JH's Garden Party." *Era*, 25 June 1887, p. 17.
2339. "JH's Water Party." *Era*, 23 July 1887, p. 14.
2340. "The Late JH." Boston *Evening Transcript*, 16 July 1896 [copied from *Pall Mall Gazette*].
2341. "Miss JH's Jewels." *Era*, 21 June 1884, p. 11.
2342. "Two Idols of the People." *Sphere*, 8 July 1896, p. 424.
2343. "The Vital Spark." *Era*, 12 Feb. 1887, p. 23; 31 Dec. 1887, p. 27; 14 Jan. 1888, p. 23; 23 Nov. 1889, p. 23.
2344. [Obit.: *Era*, 4 July 1896, p. 16.]

Stanley Holloway

Comedian; b. Manor Park, E. London, 1 Oct. 1890.
2345. *Wiv a Little Bit o' Luck. The Life Story of SH as Told to Dick Richards.* N.Y.: Stein & Day, 1967.
Repertoire
2346. EDGAR, MARRIOTT. *Albert, 'Arold and Others.* L: Francis, Day & Hunter, n.d. [Performed by SH and Marriott Edgar. With forty-six character ills. by John Hassall.
2347. ———. *Albert and Balbus and Samuel Small.* L: Francis, Day & Hunter, n.d. ["Sam's Medal," by Mabel Costanduros and Michael Hogan. With forty-two character ills. by John Hassall.]
2348. ———. *Normans and Saxons and Such: Some Ancient History.* L: Francis, Day & Hunter, n.d. [With forty-five character ills. by John Hassall.]
2349. MARSHALL, MICHAEL, ed. *The SH Monologues.* L: Elm Tree Books/EMI, 1979. [Ills. Bill Tidy.]

Percy Honri

Musical entertainer; b. Percy Henry Thompson, Thorpe Mandeville, 24 June 1874; d. 24 Sept. 1953.
Secondary Materials
2350. HONRI, PETER. *Working the Halls. The Honris in One Hundred Years of British Music Hall.* Farnborough, Hants: Saxon House, 1973. Repr. L: Cremonesi, 1975. Rev. M. Vicinus, *Victorian Studies* 18, no. 4 (June 1975): 473. [Overture by Spike

Milligan. Decor by Helen Grant Ferguson.] Includes 7" gramophone record, "Concert-in-a-turn," Peter & Mary Honri entertaining the BMHS, 3 July 1973, with excerpts from Regal 1117 and Columbia CEA 2130.]
2351. [Interview with PH] *Cambria Daily Leader*, 4 Aug. 1898.
2352. "PH in 'Bohemia.'" *Era*, 7 Sept. 1911, p. 22.
2353. "PH in Bristol." *Era*, 2 Sept. 1899, p. 18.

Alec Hurley

Comic singer; b. London, 24 Mar. 1871; d. Hampstead, London, 6 Dec. 1913.
Secondary Materials
OCT [W. Macqueen-Pope], p. 457.
2354. [Obit.: *Chronicle*, 8 Dec. 1913.]

Fred Karno

Manager and entrepreneur; b. Frederick Westcott, Exeter, 26 Mar. 1886; d. Lilliput, Dorset, 18 Sept. 1941.
2355. "FK's Story of a Tour that Failed." *World's Fair* (Oldham), 15 Feb. 1908.
Secondary Materials
OCT [W. Macqueen-Pope], p. 528.
2356. "Action by FK." *Era*, 22 Oct. 1910, p. 27.
2357. ADELER, EDWIN and CON WEST. *Remember FK? The Life of a Great Showman*. L: John Long, 1939.
2358. EAST, JOHN. "K's Folly, or How to Lose a Show-business Fortune." *Theatre Quarterly* 1, no. 3 (1971).
2359. GALLAGHER, J. P. *FK, Master of Mirth and Tears*. L: Robert Hale, 1972.
2360. "Zena Dare's Engagement." *Era*, 13 May 1911, p. 26. [FK sues Seymour Hicks.]
2361. [Obit.: *N.Y. Herald Tribune*, 20 Sept. 1941.]

Hetty King

Singer; b. New Brighton, 1883; d. 28 Sept. 1972.
Secondary Materials
2362. HOSIE, IAN. "The One and Only HK." Liverpool *Daily Post and Echo*. Repr. in *Call Boy* 6, no. 2a (June 1968): 5.
2363. KEMP, GERARD. "HK at 86, burning two matches at one

end." *Radio Times*, 25 Sept. 1969, p. 12.
2364. KYNASTON, JUNE. "HK." In *Stay Young and Enjoy It*. L: A. Thomas, 1967.
2365. LEWSEN, CHARLES. "The Art of HK." *Panto!*, no. 1 (Christmas 1972): 17–19.
2366. ROBINSON, DAVID. "The Last Star." *Financial Times*, 7 Oct. 1972.
2367. "Sixty Years of HK: Last of the Music-hall's Great Impersonators." *Times*, 8 Feb. 1957.
2368. WOOD, GEORGIE. "End of an Era." *Stage*, 5 Oct. 1972, p. 5.
2369. [Obits.: *Times*, 29 Sept. 1972; *Guardian*, 29 Sept. 1972; *Daily Telegraph*, 29 Sept. 1972, p. 17 (R. Hastings).]

R[ichard] G[eorge] Knowles

Comedian; b. Hamilton, Ont., Canada, 7 Oct. 1858; d. New York City, 1 Jan. 1919.
2370. *A Modern Columbus. His Voyages, His Travels, His Discoveries.* L: T. Werner Laurie, n.d.
2371. *Of Stories Just a Few*. L: Witmark & Sons [1904?]. [Written with Richard Morton.] Rev. *Entr'acte*, 11 June 1904, p. 14.
2372. *RGK Knowledge of the World and its Ways: being a Collection of Stories told by RGK . . . and chronicled by Richard Morton, together with a biographical sketch*. L: Francis & Day, 1894.
2373. "The Unrehearsed Effect." *Era Almanack* (1899): 48.
Secondary Materials
2374. BEERBOHM, MAX. [Caricature] *Pick-Me-Up*, 29 Sept. 1894.
2375. "A Chat with RGK." *Era*, 29 Sept. 1894, p. 10.
2376. "A Chat with RGK." *Era*, 8 Dec. 1900, p. 21.
2376a. "A Chat with RGK." N.Y. *Dramatic Mirror*, 17 Jan. 1903, p. 18.
2377. "A Chat with Winifred Johnson [Mrs RGK]." *Era*, 30 Mar. 1895, p. 16.
2378. "Dick K at Hippodrome." *Era*, 14 Sept. 1912, p. 21.
2378a. "Lecture by RGK." N.Y. *Dramatic Mirror*, 23 Feb. 1907, p. 18.
2379. MAR, HELEN. "In Old London Town." Toledo (Ohio) *Blade*, 18 Feb. 1899.
2380. "Mr RGK the Funny Man from America." *Tatler* 69 (1902): 151.
2381. "RGK." *M. A. P.*, 16 Feb. 1907.
2382. "RGK." N.Y. *Clipper*, 19 July 1890, p. 298. [Portrait and biography.]
2383. "RGK and Winifred Johnson." N. Y. *Dramatic Mirror*, 2 May 1896.
2384. [Obits.: *Daily Chronicle*, 4 Jan. 1919; *Stage*, 19 Jan. 1919.]

Lupino Lane

Comedian; b. Henry William George Lupino, London, 16 June 1892; d. London, 10 Nov. 1959.

Secondary Materials

DNB [W. A. Darlington], 1951-60; EDS [Giulio Cesare Castello], 4: 1742-47; Le Roy, chapter 3; OCT, p. 590.

2385. LL [featured in] *Film Fun*. L: Amalgamated Press, 1929 [Ills. W. Radford.] and 1930 [Ills. G. Wakefield.].
2386. WHITE, JAMES DILLON. *Born to Star: The LL Story*. L: Heinemann, 1957.
2387. [Obit.: *Times*, 11 Nov. 1959.]

George Lashwood

Singer; b. Birmingham, 25 Apr. 1863; d. Wychbold near Droitwich, 20 Jan. 1942.

Secondary Materials

2388. BARKER, TONY. "GL." *Music Hall Records* 3 (Oct. 1978): 44-50. [With discography.]

Sir Harry Lauder

Comedian; b. Portobello, Scotland, 4 Aug. 1870; d. Strathaven, 26 Feb. 1950.

2389. [Autobiography] *Green Book* (N.Y.) 9 (June 1913): 967-71.
2390. *Between You and Me*. N.Y.: J. A. McCann, 1919.
2391. *HL at Home and on Tour, by Ma' Sel'*. L: Greening, 1907.
2392. *HL at Home and on Tour*. New ed. with an epilogue in three chapters by Charles Wilmott. L: Greening, 1914.
2393. *HL's Logic*. L: Palmer & Hayward, 1917.
2394. *A Minstrel in France*. N.Y.: Hearst's International Library, 1918.
2395. *My American Travels*. L: Newnes, 1910.
2396. *My Best Scotch Stories*. Dundee & L: Valentine, 1929.
2397. "My Reminiscences." *Strand* (N.Y.) 37 (Feb. 1909): 19-30 *et seq.*
2398. *Roamin' in the Gloamin'*. L: Hutchinson; Philadelphia: J. B. Lippincott, 1928. [Autobiography. Also pub. in eight installments in *Saturday Evening Post*, concluding 3 Mar. 1928.] Repr. East Ardsley, Wakefield: EP Publishing, 1976.
2399. "Story of the War." *Hearst's Magazine* (N.Y.) 33 (Mar. 1918): 187-88, 230-31 *et seq.*
2400. *Ten Tales*. N.Y.: T. B. Harms and Francis, Day & Hunter, 1908. Toronto: McLeod & Allen, 1909.

Personalia

2401. *Ticklin' Talks.* L: D. C. Thomson, 1934.
2402. *Wee Drappies.* L: Hutchinson, 1931. [With 24 ills. by R. St. John Cooper.]

Secondary Materials

DNB [Ivor Brown], 1941-50; EDS [Dorotheen Allen & Davide Turconi], 6: 1276-77; Le Roy, chapter 5; OCT [W. Macqueen-Pope], p. 549.
2403. ADAM GEORGE. "The Heart of HL." *Congregationalist* (Boston), 9 Aug. 1917.
2404. "Among the Heather." Boston *Transcript*, 21 Dec. 1915.
2405. "Au Revoir to Sir HL." *Actor*, June 1922, pp. 13-14.
2406. "Aye, 'tis Sir H in print now a-roamin.'" Boston *Evening Transcript*, 27 Oct. 1928.
2407. CARRAGHER, P. CHARLES [known as Ray Garrick]. *Redlight Recollections representing the hitherto Unwritten Story of Forty Years of Fairport from the Footlights. . . .* Arbroath: T. Buncle, 1906. ["The Prince of the Music Halls," pp. 73-76; L's first appearances.]
2408. [Concert at Princess Theatre, London] *Saturday Review* 133 (6 May 1922): 460.
2409. DISHER, M. WILLSON. "Preface to Sir Harry's Final Tour." Boston *Transcript*, 21 Jan. 1928.
2410. E.F.S. "Mr HL and the Modern British Drama." *Westminster Gazette* (1909).
2411. "Farewell Visit of Jovial HL." Boston *Traveller*, 24 Nov. 1917.
2412. "Gave his Time and Purse for Allies' Cause." Boston *Traveller*, 15 Dec. 1915.
2413. [Goes to Church] *Daily Mail*, 24 Jan. 1913.
2414. HADDON, ARCHIBALD. *Green Room Gossip.* L: Stanley Paul, 1922. [Chapter 6, "On and Off the 'Halls'" (interview with HL).]
2415. HAMILTON, CLAYTON. "When Personality Plays Upon Public." *Vogue* (N.Y.), Dec. 1917.
2416. "HL." N.Y. *Globe*, 24 Nov. 1914.
2417. "HL." *P. T. O.*, 12 Jan. 1907.
2418. [HL] *Theatre Magazine* (N.Y.), 20 (Sept. 1914): 147; 26 (Dec. 1917): 363; 27 (Jan.1918): 17; 27 (Mar. 1918): 157; 27 (May 1918): 207; 43, (May 1926): 25; 52 (July 1930): 8.
2419. "HL Again." Boston *Evening Transcript*, 31 Dec. 1912.
2420. "HL at New York." N.Y. *Sun*, 24 Nov. 1914.
2421. "HL at Orpheum Theatre." Boston *Herald*, 12 Jan. 1909.
2422. "HL at the Shubert." Boston *Globe*, 31 Dec. 1912.
2423. "HL at the Tivoli." *Times*, 13 Mar. 1912.

2424. "HL Back." N.Y. *Dramatic Mirror*, 21 Dec. 1918.
2425. "HL Here." N.Y. *Tribune*, 24 Nov. 1914.
2426. "HL in New Role." N.Y. *Times*, 3 Oct. 1922.
2427. "HL in Old Songs and New Skills." Boston *Transcript*, 1 Dec. 1914.
2428. "HL is Back Once More." N.Y. *Morning Telegraph*, 24 Nov. 1914.
2429. "HL Preaches." N.Y. *Tribune*, 24 June 1913.
2430. "HL Returns." Boston *Transcript*, 12 Jan. 1909.
2431. "HL Returns in New Kilts and Songs." N.Y. *Herald*, 6 Jan. 1914.
2432. "HL Returns; Sings an Irish Song." N.Y. *Herald*, 24 Nov. 1914.
2433. "HL Sings New Rollicking Songs." N.Y. *Times*, 27 Oct. 1926.
2434. "HL to Appear at a Matinee in 'A Scrape o' the Pen.'" *P.M.G.*, 8 Oct. 1912.
2435. "HL to Have Edinburgh High Honor." N.Y. *Times,* 28 Aug. 1927.
2436. "HL to Play in Comedy." *Chronicle*, 8 Oct. 1912.
2437. "HL Welcomed." N.Y. *Times*, 24 Dec. 1912.
2438. "HL Welcomed by Shubert Crowd." Boston *Herald*, 1 Dec. 1914.
2439. "HL Wins Audience at Start." Boston *Herald*, 10 Nov. 1908.
2440. "HL Writes a Play." Boston *Herald*, 29 Dec. 1915.
2441. [In the film *Huntingtower*] *Graphic* 118 (17 Dec. 1927): 514–15.
2442. IRVING, GORDON. *Great Scot! The Life Story of Sir HL, Legendary Laird of the Music Hall*. L: Frewin, 1968.
2443. ———. "L Legend Not All Laughs." *Christian Science Monitor* (Boston), 19 Aug. 1970.
2444. ———. "Sir HL." *Call Boy* 7, no. 2 (Sept. 1970): 12–13.
2445. KENNEDY, J. B. "Interview with HL." *Collier's* (N.Y.) 79 (Feb. 1927): 14.
2446. "King of the Vaudeville Stage." *Current Literature* (N.Y.) 46 (Jan. 1909): 84–86.
2447. "L Analyzes 3 Nations' Fun." N.Y. *Telegraph*, 17 Oct. 1909.
2448. "L at the Opera House." Boston *Herald*, 10 Oct. 1922.
2449. "L Cheered at the Shubert." Boston *Globe*, 31 Dec. 1912.
2450. "L Depicts Scottish Types." Boston *Herald*, 4 Dec. 1917.
2451. "L Gives Counsel." N.Y. *Tribune*, 23 Oct. 1917.
2452. "L in Film Comes to Sing Farewell Again." N.Y. *Herald Tribune*, 5 May 1940.
2453. "L in Serious Role." N.Y. *Times*, 22 Oct. 1917.
2454. "The L Legend." Boston *Transcript*, 24 Oct. 1928.

2455. "L Lingers Longer. Scots and Scots' Humor." Boston *Transcript*, 10 Feb. 1920, p. 12.

2456. "L Warns America She Must Do Her Very Best." N.Y. *Herald*, 22 Oct. 1917.

2457. "L Welcomed Back." N.Y. *Times*, 23 Apr. 1918.

2458. "L's Son Wounded." N.Y. *Telegraph*, 9 July 1915.

2459. MALVERN, GLADYS. *Valiant Minstrel. The Story of Sir HL.* N.Y.: Julian Messner, 1943. [Ill. Corinne Malvern. Children's book.]

2460. "Minor Plays—and L." Boston *Evening Transcript*, 10 Nov. 1908.

2461. MORRIS, WILLIAM. "Needs Must When Delay Whips Hard." Boston *Transcript*, 6 Nov. 1926.

2462. "Mr HL on the Stage." *Telegraph*, 20 Oct. 1912.

2463. "The New Hamlet." *P. M. G.*, 18 Oct. 1912.

2464. "A New Sir H. Still in Prime. Generous Withal." Boston *Transcript*, 16 Nov. 1926.

2464a. "On Boston Boards." Boston *Transcript*, 7 Mar. 1931.

2465. "A Play by Mr HL." *Times*, 5 Aug. 1910.

2465a. [PAGE, WILL A.] "How HL composed his Famous Songs." *Theatre Magazine* (N.Y.) 8 (Dec. 1908): 322, 324.

2467. QUIGLEY, Private JOSEPH. *The Slogan. Sidelights on Recruiting with HL's Band.* . . . Ed. by T. S. Dickson, ill. George Whitelaw. L: Simpkin, Marshall, 1916.

2468. QUIMBY, HARRIET. "The Secret of HL's Success." *Leslie's Weekly* (N.Y.) 110 (8 Jan. 1910).

2469. S. R. L. "A Real Artist of the 'Halls.'" *Daily Chronicle*, 31 Mar. 1906, p. 7.

2470. "Shubert Crowds Greet HL." Boston *Globe*, 1 Dec. 1914.

2471. "Sir Harry Came a Rovin.'" N.Y. *Times*, 20 Mar. 1938.

2472. "Sir Harry Joins Red Cross." Boston *Transcript*, 17 Nov. 1926.

2473. "Sir HL Again Wins N.Y. Audience." N.Y. *Tribune*, 3 Oct. 1922.

2474. "Sir HL at the Colonial." Boston *Globe*, 13 Mar. 1928.

2475. "Sir HL Makes a Dime Tour of World." N.Y. *Herald Tribune*, 18 May 1937.

2476. "Sir HL's Farewell Philosophy." Glasgow *Sunday Post*, Nov. 1926.

2477. "Sir HL's Return." *Morning Post*, 1 Feb. 1921.

2478. "Sir HL's Returns." *Times*, 1 Feb. 1921.

2479. "Stars as Seen from the Wings: No. VIII—HL." *Stage*, 22 Sept. 1910.

2480. "Theatre Morality. Mr HL's Criticisms Provoke a Piquant Controversy. His Views on a Barrie Play." *Reynolds Newspaper* (1909).

2481. "'Tis Harry Himself Again, Unchanged." Boston *Transcript*, 11 Mar. 1930.

2482. "Ward's Island Greets L and the Elks." N.Y. *Times*, 27 Sept. 1922.

2483. WILSON, P. W. "Here's Looking at You, Sir Harry." N.Y. *Times Book Review*, 23 Sept. 1928.

2484. [Obits.: N.Y. *Herald*, 27 Feb. 1950; *Times*, 27 Feb. 1950.] HL SOCIETY. 11 Moray Place, Edinburgh. Chris Martin, Secretary.

Repertoire

2485. *Francis & Day's 1st Album of HL's Popular Songs.* L: Francis, Day & Hunter, n.d. [HL the Artist: an Appreciation; and HL the Man, a Biographical Sketch, by Charles Wilmott. I love a Lassie; She's Ma Daisy; The Saftest o' the Family; Stop Yer Tickling, Jock!; Wee Nelly McKie frae Skye; Early in the Morning; Bonnie Hielan' Mary; The Last of the Sandies; Tobermory; Killiecrankie; If I Were in the L.C.C.; Callegan—Call Again!; Jerry Co.; I'm the Man They Left Behind; Some Folks Do and Other People Don't; I Took Him Up to Take Him Down; That's the Reason Noo I Wear a Kilt.]

2486. *Francis & Day's 2nd Album of HL's Popular Songs.* L: Francis, Day & Hunter, n.d. [Queen Amang the Heather; The Wedding o' Sandy MacNab; When I Get Back Again to Bonnie Scotland; I've Loved Her Ever Since She Was a Baby; Bonnie Leezie Lindsay; Fou the Noo; Rob Roy Macintosh; We Parted on the Shore; Gilt-Edged Bertie; The South Pole or, The Bounding Bounder; Mr. John Mackie; Mrs. Jean Macfarlane; The Wedding o' Lauchie M'Graw; Inverary; Is That You, McAllister?; Piper Macfarlane; I Wish You a Happy New Year.]

2487. *Francis & Day's 3rd Album of HL's Popular Songs.* L: Francis, Day & Hunter, n.d. [Roamin' in the Gloamin'; The Same as His Faither did before Him; It's Nice When You Love a Wee Lassie; The Message Boy; Breakfast in My Bed on Sunday Morning; The Picnic, or Every Laddie Loves a Lassie; The Inverary Harriers; Sound Advice; Hey Donal!; Charlie MacNeil; At the Sign of "The Bluebell Inn"; I Love You, Jean McNeil; I Wish I Had Someone to Love Me!; He Was Very Kind to Me; Aye, Wakin' O!; The Auld Brig of Ayr.]

2488. *Francis & Day's 4th Album of HL's Popular Songs.* L: Francis,

Day & Hunter, n.d. [The Wee House 'mang the Heather; Ta-ta my Bonnie Maggie Darling!; The Laddies Who Fought and Won; The Waggle o' the Kilt; It's Nice to Get Up in the Mornin'; My Bonnie, Bonnie Jean; While the British Bull-dog's Watching at the Door; The Portobello Lassie; She's the Lass for Me; Bonnie Maggie Tamson; The Kilty Lads; Nanny; I'm Going to Marry-arry; She is My Rosie; Bonnie Wee Annie; Shouther to Shouther; The Blarney Stone.]

2489. *Francis & Day's 5th Album of HL's Popular Songs.* L: Francis, Day & Hunter, n.d. [The End of the Road; It's a Fine Thing to Sing; I Like My Old Home Town; Oh! How I Weary, Dearie; Boss o' the Hoose; Soosie MacLean; The Pirate; I'm Looking for a Bonnie Lass; Love Makes the World a Merry-Go-Round; O'er the Hill to Ardentinny; Sunshine o' a Bonnie Lass's Smile; When I Was Twenty-One; Bella McGraw; There is Somebody Waiting for Me; I'd Love to Be a Sailor; We a' Go Hame the Same Way.]

John Lawson

Sketch artist; b. Hollingwood, Manchester, 9 Jan. 1865; d. 25 Nov. 1920.

2490. "The Dark Seance." *Era Annual* (1906): 46–8.
2491. "A Hindoo's 'Humanity.'" *Era Annual* (1908): 47–9.
2492. "How I Was Barred." *Era Annual* (1907): 44–45.
2493. "'Humanity' under Difficulties." *Era Almanack* (1909): 61–2.
2494. "Something New." *Era Annua!* (1910): 95–96.
2495. "A Touring Grievance." *Era*, 13 June 1891, p. 7.
2496. "Wolves!" *Era Annual* (1909): 97–98.
2496a. "JL Chats to a Bristol journalist," *Era* (2 Sept. 1905).
Secondary Materials
2497. M'KEE, SAM. "JL, the Belasco of Vaudeville." N.Y. *Morning Telegraph*, 25 Oct. 1910.
2497a. "Music hall celebrities. JL," *Encore* (8 Oct. 1896) 8–9.

Tom Leamore

Comic singer; b. London, 1866; d. Lambeth, London, 6 Sept. 1939.
Secondary Materials
2498. BARKER, TONY. "TL." *Music Hall Records* 6 (Apr. 1979): 104–12. [With discography.]
2499. "A Chat with TL." *Era*, 29 Sept. 1894, p. 16.
2500. "Leamore vs. Macnaghten and Another." *Era*, 15 July 1911, p. 27.

2501. [Obit.: N.Y. *Herald Tribune*, 9 Sept. 1939.]

Dan Leno

Comedian, b. George Galvin, London, 20 Dec. 1860; d. Balham, 31 Oct. 1904.

2502. *DL Hys Booke written by himself. A Volume of Frivolities auto-biographical, historical, philosophical, anecdotal and nonsensical . . . with an appreciation of the Author by Clement Scott.* L: Greening, 1899. New and cheap ed., 1901. [5th ed. has new appendix. Each ed. has different selection of ills.] Repr. L: Hugh Evelyn, 1968. [Ed. by John Duncan with an introduction by Roy Hudd. Abridged. The actual author was T. C. Elder.]

[2503 omitted.]

2504. "I Remember." *Era Annual* (1904): 18.

2505. "Jack and the Beanstalk." *Era Almanack* (1900): 27.

2506. "The Late G. B. Prior." *Era*, 10 July 1897, p. 16.

2507. "My Autobiography in a Nut-shell." *Yule-tide Tales.* L: Geering [n.d.].

2508. *The Sun*, 1 Apr. 1902. [Edited special edition.]

2509. "When I Was a Widow." *Era Annual* (1902): 39.

Secondary Materials

DNB [E. V. Lucas], supp. 2; EDS [Mollie Sands], 6: 1382–83; Le Roy, chapter 2; OCT, p. 554.

2510. "Airy Alf and Bouncing Billy Interview DL." *Big Budget*, 29 Jan. 1898. Reproduced in Denis Gifford, *Victorian Comics.* L: George Allen & Unwin, 1976. [P. 86.]

2511. ASHTON, ELLIS. "Poor Dan." *Call Boy* 4, no. 2 (June 1967).

2512. BEERBOHM, MAX. "DL." *Saturday Review*, 5 Nov. 1904. Repr. in A.C. Ward, ed., *Specimens of English Dramatic Criticism XVII–XX Centuries*, L: Oxford University Press, 1945 (World's Classics); and in George Rowell, ed., *Victorian Dramatic Criticism*, L: Methuen, 1971 [pp. 339–42].

2513. "Best-loved Music-hall Comedian." *Times*, 19 Dec. 1960, p. 12.

2514. BRANDRETH, GYLES. *"The Funniest Man on Earth": The Story of DL.* L: Hamish Hamilton, 1977.

2515. "A Chat with DL." *Era*, 26 Oct. 1901.

2516. COLLIER, CONSTANCE. *Harlequinade: The Story of My Life.* L: John Lane, 1929. [Account of meeting DL.]

2517. "DL." *Morning Leader*, 12 Oct. 1905.

2517a. "DL at Warwick Castle." *Era*, 31 Aug. 1901.

2518. "DL Crazy." N.Y. *World*, 21 June 1903.

2519. "DL in America." *Era*, 27 Apr. 1897, p. 19.

2520. "DL the Second." *Era*, 6 Jan. 1912. [On his son's inheriting the comic mantle.]

2521. *DL's Comic Journal*. L: C. Arthur Pearson. 1898 (ills. Tom Browne); 1899 (ills. Frank Holland and Charles Genge). [26 Feb. 1898–2 Dec. 1899, ninety-three issues. Issue for 17 Dec. 1898, "Daniel on the Bust," repr. in Denis Gifford, *op. cit. supra*, p. 87. Other issues repr. in George Perry and Alan Aldridge, *The Penguin Book of Comics*, Harmondsworth: Penguin Books, 1967, pp. 56, 58.]

2522. "DL's Success." N.Y. *Herald*, 13 Apr. 1897.

2523. DUNCAN, JOHN. "A Ghost Comes to Life." *Radio Times*, 29 Feb. 1968, p. 19.

2524. FINDLATER, RICHARD. "The Star of Christmas." *Observer Magazine*, 21 Dec. 1975, pp. 1, 11–17.

2525. "The Garrick of the Halls." *John O'London's Weekly*, 6 Dec. 1924, p. 381.

2526. "A Hoax at Gravesend." *Era*, 8 Dec. 1900, p. 20.

2527. "JOHN O' LONDON" [Pseud. of Wilfred Whitten]. "DL." *T. P.'s Weekly*, 11 Nov. 1904, p. 638. Repr. in *The Joy of London and Other Essays*, ed. Frank Whitaker. L: George Newnes, 1943. p. 48–51.

2528. "Lancashire Clog-dancing Match." *Era*, 14 Nov. 1885, p. 10. [First mention of DL in professional press.]

2529. LUPINO, STANLEY. *From the Stocks to the Stars. An Unconventional Autobiography*. L: Hutchinson, 1934. [Tale of DL's ghost.]

2530. MacINNES, COLIN. "Out of the way: Dan." *New Society*, 23 Dec. 1965, p. 23.

2531. MELLOR, GEOFF. "Fun and Dames." *Stage*, 18 Dec. 1976.

2532. MONTGOMERY, JOHN. "King's Jester." *Guardian*, 29 Oct. 1974, p. 16.

2533. "Mr. DL as 'Mother Goose' at Drury Lane." *Tatler* 82 (1903): 107.

2534. [SYMONS, ARTHUR?] "At the Middlesex." *Star*, 10 Sept. 1892.

2535. WALKLEY, A. B. "Frame of Mind. DL." *Star*, 14 Jan. 1899.

2536. WILSON, A. E. "DL at Drury Lane." In *Pantomime Pageant*. L: Stanley Paul, 1946. [Chapter 12. See also chapter 13, "Drury Lane under Arthur Collins."]

2537. ———. "DL Nights." In *Christmas Pantomime*. L: E. P. Dutton, 1933. [Chapter 16.] Pub. in U.S. as: *King Panto*. N.Y.: E. P. Dutton, 1935.

2538. ———. "The Story of DL." In *The Story of Pantomime*. L:

Home & Van Thal, 1949. [Chapter 13.]
2539. WOOD, J. HICKORY [Pseud. of Owen Hall]. *DL, his infinite Variety.* L: Methuen, 1905, [Still the best biography.]
2540. [Obits.: *Times*, 1 Nov. 1904, p. 6; *Daily Telegraph*, 1 Nov. 1904, p. 7, 3 Nov. 1905; N.Y. *Dramatic Mirror*, 5 Nov. 1904, p. 18. *Stage*, 10 Nov. 1904 (on funeral). *Daily Chronicle*, 13 Dec. 1904 (on distribution of property).]

Fanny Leslie

Dancer; b. 1857; d. 1935.
Secondary Materials
2541. "Miss FL." *Era*, 30 Nov. 1895.

George Leybourne

Lion comique; b. Wolverhampton, 1842; d. Islington, 18 Sept. 1884.
Secondary Materials
OCT, P. 558.
2542. "Champagne Charlie Again," *John o'London's Weekly*, 3 Sept. 1912.
2543. [GL] *Entr'acte*, 2 Dec. 1876, p. 3.
2544. "GL and his Late Agent." *Era*, 3 Nov. 1878, p. 3; 10 Dec. 1878, p. 4; 17 Dec. 1878, p. 4.
2545. "GL's Coachman in Trouble." *Era*, 4 Feb. 1872, p. 13.
2546. "GL's Prize Song." *Era*, 14 Feb. 1875, p. 6; 21 Feb. 1875, p. 7; 8 Aug. 1875, p. 7.
2547. LENO, DAN. "The Late GL." *Era*, 5 Sept. 1891, p. 14. [Follow-up, 19 Dec. 1891, p. 17.]
2548. "Mr GL at St. James' Hall." *Era*, 26 July 1874, p. 4.
2549. "Mr GL's Benefit at the East London." *Era*, 1 Sept. 1872, p. 4.
2550. [Portrait of GL] *Illustrated Sporting News*, 21 Apr. 1866, pp. 227, 236.
2551. [Obits.: *Era*, 20 Sept. 1884, p. 9; *Entr'acte*, 20 Sept. 1884, p. 11.]

Harry Liston

Comic singer; b. Manchester, Sept. 1843; d. 8 Apr. 1929.
2552. "False Reports." *Era*, 27 Mar. 1886, p. 10.
Secondary Materials
2553. "Mr HL and the Little Sisters of the Poor." *Era*, 19 Mar. 1876, p. 5.
2554. "Theft from a Music Hall." *Era*, 19 Nov. 1891, p. 4.

Victor Liston

Comic singer; b. 1838; d. 11 July 1913.
Secondary Materials
OCT [W. Macqueen-Pope], p. 580.
2555. "Mr VL's Benefit." *Era*, 2 Apr. 1881, p. 4.

Little Tich

Comedian; b. Harry Relph, Cudham, Kent, 21 July 1867; d. Hendon, N.
London, 10 Feb. 1928.
2556. "Concerning Hats." *Era Annual* (1911): 78.
2557. "I Try Golf." *Era Annual* (1904): 67.
2558. *LT, a Book of Travels and Wanderings.* L: Greening, 1911. Rev.
Era, 22 July 1911, p. 23. [Ghostwritten by Sax Rohmer (pseud. of
A. H. Ward) and held in contempt by LT.]
2559. "A Theatrical Story." *Panto Annual* (1896): 2–8.
Secondary Materials
EDS [Alessandro Cervellati], 6: 1545–46; Le Roy, chapter 17; OCT,
p. 580.
2560. ANDRIEU, P. *Souvenir des Frères Isola.* Paris: 1943.
2561. ASHTON, ELLIS. "LT." *Stage*, 22 May 1959, p. 6.
2562. BARKER, TONY. "LT." *Music Hall Records* 1 (June 1978):
3–7; 2 (Aug. 1978): 7; 3 (Oct. 1978): 50; 5 (Feb. 1979): 83. [With
discography.]
2563. BEERBOHM, MAX. [Caricature.] "Plate 28. the Encaenia of
1908." In *Caricatures by Max. From the Collection in the
Ashmolean Museum.* [Oxford] Oxford University Press, 1958.
2564. CARDUS, NEVILLE. "LT." *Guardian*, 31 July 1967, p. 5.
2565. CERVELATTI, A. *Storie del Clown.* Firenze: 1946.
2566. "Chat with LT." *Era*, 9 Sept. 1905.
2567. GUITRY, SACHA. "LT." *Candide* (Paris), 17 Dec. 1925.
2568. HADDON, ARCHIBALD, "LT. Memories and Anecdotes."
Theatre World, 12 Feb. 1928.
2569. "'Hop-o'-my-Thumb' at Home. A Chat with 'LT.'" *Sketch*, 31
May 1898, p. 255.
2570. LECOY, J. "Les Souliers de LT." *Le Petit journal* (Paris), 13
fév. 1928.
2571. NASH, PAUL. *Outline: an Autobiography.* L: Faber & Faber,
1949.
2572. POWELL, MARY RELPH [*pseud.* MARY TICH] and RICH-
ARD FINDLATER. "LT." *Observer Magazine*, 8 Apr. 1979,
pp. 60–65.

2573. ———. *LT. Giant of the Music Hall.* L: Elm Tree, 1979. Rev. B. Green, *Spectator*, 12 May 1979, pp. 24-25; H. Spurling, *Observer*, 22 Apr. 1979, p. 37.
2574. PRIESTLEY, J. B. "LT." In *The Balconinny and Other Essays.* L: Methuen, 1929. Repr. in *Essays of Five Decades*, ed. Susan Cooper. Harmondsworth: Penguin Books, 1969. [Pp. 167-70.]
2575. ROSS, BERT. "LT—('his Centenary')." *Call Boy* 5, no. 2a (June 1968): 3-4.
2576. SHARPLEY, ANNE. "LT and the Memory that Lingers in Hendon, NW." *Evening Standard*, 13 July 1967, p. 7.
2577. "SPECTATOR, THE" [*Pseud.*] [Letter] *Star*, 9 Sept. 1893.
2578. [Obits.: N.Y. *Telegraph*, 11 Feb. 1928; *Comoedia* (Paris), 11 fév. 1928; *Le Journal* (Paris), 11 fév. 1928; *Candide* (Paris), 16 fév. 1928.]

Arthur Lloyd

Comedian; b. Edinburgh, 1840; d. Edinburgh, 20 July 1904.
2579. "AL's Songs." *Era*, 7 June 1890, p. 15.
Secondary Materials
2580. "AL in Edinburgh." *Era*, 27 July 1895, p. 14.
2581. "AL in New Sketch 'Kruger's Double.'" *Era*, 24 Mar. 1900, p. 18.
2582. "AL Interviewed." *Era*, 19 July 1890, p. 16.
2583. [AL "most deservedly popular of comic singers."] *Sketch*, 3 May 1879.
2584. "AL's Farewell Benefit." *Era*, 18 Aug. 1872, p. 13.
2585. "Death of Miss Katy King [Mrs AL]." *Era*, 9 May 1891, p. 16.
2586. "G. W. Hunt and AL." *Era*, 26 July 1890, p. 15.
2587. "Mr AL." *Era*, 24 Sept. 1871, p. 10. [Description of his show.]
2588. "Mr AL's Benefit." *Era*, 28 Mar. 1891, p. 14.
2589. "Mr AL's Benefit." *Era*, 15 Dec. 1900, p. 21.
2589a. "A Music-hall Missionary." *Tomahawk* 139 (1 Jan. 1870): 4.

Marie Lloyd

Comedienne and singer; b. Matilda Alice Victoria Wood, Hoxton, London, 12 Feb. 1870; d. Golders Green, London, 7 Oct. 1922.
2590. *ML's Blue Book.* L: 1896. Rev. *Era*, 1 Aug. 1896, p. 17. [Includes axioms, American stories, one-act comedy *The Broker's Man.*]
2591. "Miss ML Criticizes Her Own Risque Songs." N.Y. *Telegraph*, 14 Nov. 1897.
2592. "The Single Turn's Return." *Era Annual* (1918): 79-80.

Secondary Materials

DNB [H. H. Child], 1922-30; EDS [St. Vincent Troubridge], 6: 1578-79; Le Roy, chapter 1; OCT, p. 584.

2593. AGATE, JAMES. "ML." *Saturday Review* 134 (14 Oct. 1922): 536. Repr. in *At Half Past Eight: Essays of the Theatre 1921-1922,* L: Cape, 1923; in *The Post Victorians*, with an introduction by the Very Rev. W. R. Inge, L: Nicholson & Watson, 1933, pp. 343-60; and in A. C. Ward, ed. *Specimens of English Dramatic Criticism XVII-XX Centuries*, L: Oxford University Press, 1945 (World's Classics).

2594. ASHTON, ELLIS. "Queen of the Music Hall . . . ML." *Call Boy* 4, no. 3 (Sept. 1967): 6.

2595. BRENT, PETER. "ML." In *The Edwardians.* L: BBC, 1972. [Pp. 97-117.]

2596. BROWN, IVOR. "Legendary Lustre." *Drama*, spring 1968, pp. 28-29.

2597. "A Chat with ML." *Era*, 9 Feb. 1901.

2598. CROSS, JOHN E. "Our Marie—She Was a Goer!" *New Theatre*, Dec. 1946, pp. 2-3. [Listed in Contents as "Memories of ML."]

2599. "Early Struggles of ML." *Strand* (N.Y.) 43 (Mar. 1912): 266-68.

2600. "East and West with ML." *Sketch*, 25 Dec. 1895, p. 452.

2601. ELIOT, T[HOMAS] S[TEARNS] "London Letter." *Dial* (N.Y.) 62 (Dec. 1922); 659-63. Revised and repr. as "In Memoriam: ML," *Criterion*, Jan. 1923, pp. 192-93. Repr. "ML" in *Selected Essays*, enlarged ed. L: Faber & Faber, 1951, pp. 456-459.

2602. FARSON, DANIEL. "Bold M." *Observer Magazine*, 26 Nov. 1967, pp. 47-50.

2603. ———. *ML & Music Hall.* L: Tom Stacey, 1972.

2604. ——— and HENRY MOORE. *The ML Story.* [Original lyrics by Daniel Farson and music by Norman Kay. A Musical Comedy, opened at Joan Littlewood's Theatre Workshop, Stratford East, 22 Nov. 1967, with Avis Bunnage as ML.]

2605. FERGUSON, RACHEL. "ML." *Sunday Chronicle*, 3 Aug. 1919.

2606. "A Few Press Notices of ML in America." *Era*, 7 Dec. 1907, p. 27.

2607. GREEN, BENNY. "Marie." *Spectator,* 7 Oct. 1972.

2608. HONRI, PETER. "ML Verbatim." *Call Boy* 7, no. 2 (June 1970): 16.

2609. JACOB, NAOMI ELLINGTON. *"Our Marie" (ML) a Biography.* L: Hutchinson [1936]. Rev. R. Prentis, *John o'London's Weekly,* 18 Apr. 1936, 80; D. Gauette, *New Statesman*

(1936); St John Ervine, *Observer*, 28 June 1936; *Sunday Times*, 19 Apr. 1937.

2610. MACQUEEN-POPE, W. *Queen of the Music Halls being the Dramatized Story of ML.* [L] Oldbourne, n.d. (Close-up Biographies.) [On spine and title: *ML: Queen of the Music Halls.*]

2611. [ML] *Theatre* (N.Y.) 19 (17 Apr. 1914): 199.

2612. "ML." *Times*, 16 Nov. 1922, p. 15.

2613. "ML at the People's Palace [Bradford]." *Era*, 11 May 1895, p. 16.

2614. "ML in New York." *Era*, 23 Oct. 1897, p. 18.

2615. "ML . . . She was a Loner." *Radio Times*, 16 Nov. 1972, p. 91.

2616. "ML, singer, is sued for divorce." *Stage*, 1 Nov. 1906.

2617. "ML's Benefit." *Era*, 17 Feb. 1900, p. 18.

2618. "ML's Engagements." *Era*, 26 Nov. 1898, p. 18.

2619. "ML's Farewell." *Era*, 16 Feb. 1901.

2620. "ML's Husband [Percy Charles Courtenay]." *Era*, 16 June 1894, p. 16; 23 June 1894, p. 16.

2621. "ML's Trials." *Era*, 20 Oct. 1894, p. 16.

2622. "ML's Wedding." *Era*, 3 Nov. 1906.

2623. "Miss L Wears Costumes to Suit Songs." N.Y. *Herald*, 14 Oct. 1913.

2624. "Miss ML." *Era*, 11 Feb. 1899, p. 23.

2625. "Miss ML's Coachman." *Era*, 21 Mar. 1896 p. 18.

2626. "Miss ML's Matinee." *Era*, 7 Nov. 1891, p. 16.

2627. "Miss ML's Return." N.Y. *Herald*, 12 Oct. 1897.

2628. "Presentation to Miss ML." *Era*, 6 May 1899, p. 19.

2629. SENELICK, LAURENCE. "ML v. Mrs Grundy at Ellis Island." *Call Boy* 15, no. 2 (summer 1978): 3–4.

2630. SHERRIN, NED and CARYL BRAHMS. *Sing a Rude Song.* [Musical comedy with music by Ron Grainer, opened at the Greenwich Theatre, 1969, with Barbara Windsor as ML.]

2631. "SPECTATOR, THE." [pseud.] [Letter] *Star*, 14 Oct. 1893. [Unfavorable.]

2632. STONE, FRED and DENIS MARTIN. *The Story of ML, a Musical Play.* [Opened at Player's Theatre, London, Apr. 1979.]

2633. "To Marie, Riding My Bicycle." *Punch*, 27 Sept. 1899, p. 155.

2634. "The Unbeatable Lady from Peerless Street." *Radio Times*, 5 Feb. 1970, p. 7.

2635. WOOD, GEORGIE. "Our Marie—She was Everybody's." *Stage*, 12 Feb. 1970, p. 7.

2636. ———. "Will the Real ML Stand Up?" *Stage*, 26 Feb. 1970, p. 5.

2637. [Obits. and tributes: *News of the World*, 7 Oct. 1922; *Referee*, 8

Personalia

Oct. 1922 ("Carados"); *Observer,* 8 Oct. 1922 (H.G.); *Sunday Times,* 8 Oct. 1922 (Hannen Swaffer); *Daily Telegraph,* 9 Oct. 1922, p. 6 (H. G. Hibbert); N.Y. *Clipper* 70 (11 Oct. 1922): 30. (Reports of funeral) *Daily Telegraph,* 13 Oct. 1922, p. 11; N.Y. *Daily Telegraph,* 13 Oct. 1922, p. 7; N.Y. *Times,* 13 Oct. 1922; *Times,* 13 Oct. 1922, p. 9. "ML." *Nation* 32 (14 Oct. 1922): 52–53; "Players and Plays" (Hannen Swaffer) *Times,* 15 Oct. 1922. "Miss ML's Sale," *Times,* (20 Dec. 1922, p. 7.]

Repertoire

2638. *Feldman's ML Song Album.* L: B. Feldman [1954].
2639. *ML.* L: EMI Music Publishing, 1977. (The Music Makers.) [Anthology of songs with excellent succinct biography.]

Kitty Lofting

Actress.
2640. "A Dramatic Restoration: a Vision." *Era Alamack* (1899): 74–75.
2641. "The Price of a Christmas Dinner." *Era Annual* (1910): 86–87.

Secondary Materials

2642. "A Chat with KL." *Era,* 10 Feb. 1894, p. 11.
2643. "KL in Court." *Era,* 18 Jan. 1896, p. 17.
2644. MARE, E. "The Sarah Bernhardt of the Music Halls." *Era Almanack* (1896).

[Marie] Cecilia "Cissie" Loftus

Actress and mimic; b. Glasgow, Scotland, 22 Oct. 1876; d. U.S., 12 July 1943.
2645. "My Yesterdays." *Bohemia* (N.Y.), May 1907.

Secondary Materials

OCT [W. Macqueen-Pope.], p.585.
2646 BEERBOHM, MAX. "Lines suggested by Miss CL."*Sketch,* 9 May 1894.
Repr. with other caricatures of CL in *Letters to Reggie Turner,* ed. R. Hart-Davis. L: R. Hart-Davis, 1964. [Pp. 49, 66, 81. Poem.]
2647 [Biographical Sketch] *Illustrated London News* 163 (15 Aug. 1923) 492.
2647a. "CL." N.Y. *Dramatic Mirror,* 7 Dec. 1901, p. 15.
2647b. "CL chats." N.Y. *Dramatic Mirror,* 22 July 1899, p. 18.
2648. "CL in New York."*Era,* 21 Jan. 1899, p. 20.
2648a. FORNARO, C. DE. "CL." N.Y. *Dramatic Mirror,* 10 June

1899, p. 2. [Caricature and poem.]

2648b. LEVY, LEO. "CL Sinks her Personality into her Art." Oakland, Cal.*Tribune*, 27 Jan. 1912.

2649. "L, C." *Current Biography Yearbook I.* N.Y.: Current Biography, 1940. [Pp. 515-16.]

2650. "Marriage of CL."*Era*, 8 Sept. 1894, p. 16.

2651. "Miss CL." Boston *Evening Transcript*, 6 Apr. 1895.

2652. "Miss CL at the Alhambra." *Era*, 11 Apr. 1896, p. 18.

2653. "Miss CL in America." *Era*, 24 Mar. 1900, p. 9.

2654. "Miss CL in *Don Juan.*" *Era*, 27 Jan. 1894, p. 9; 3 Feb. 1894, p. 7.

2655. "Miss CL in her Imitations." *Era*, 28 May 1898, p. 18.

2656. "Miss CL in the Provinces." *Era*, 4 Jan. 1896, p. 8.

2657. "Miss CL in Town." *Era*, 19 Aug. 1911, p. 11.

2658. "Miss CL on Tour in Glasgow." *Era*, 16 Nov. 1895, p. 9.

2659. "Miss CL's Posters." *Era*, 21 Mar. 1896, p. 18.

2660. NEWMAN, ALEXANDER. "The Genius of CL." *Illustrated American* (N.Y.), 19 Jan. 1895.

Marie Loftus

Singer; b.Glasgow, Scotland, 24 Nov. 1857; d. 7 Dec. 1940.

Secondary Materials

2661. "ML." N.Y. *Clipper*, 18 Oct. 1890, p. 496 [portrait]; 15 Nov. 1890, p. 561 [biography].

2662. "ML at the Empire, Newport." *Era*, 18 Nov. 1899, p. 21.

2663. "ML in Bristol." *Era*, 12 Nov. 1898, p. 21.

2664. "ML in Glasgow." *Era*, 24 Nov. 1894, p. 16.

2665. "ML in Glasgow." *Era*, 25 Jan. 1896, p. 9.

2666. "ML in Liverpool." *Era*, 6 Mar. 1897, p. 14; 13 Mar. 1897, p. 19.

2667. "ML in Nottingham." *Era*, 18 Mar. 1899, p. 18.

2668. "ML in Scotland." *Era*, 18 Aug. 1900, p. 16.

2669. "ML Moss & Thornton Tour." *Era*, 7 May 1898, p. 19; 14 May 1898, p. 19.

2670. "ML on Tour." *Era*, 15 July 1899, p. 16.

2671. "Miss ML." *Era*, 30 Apr. 1887, p. 16. [Interview.]

2672. "Miss ML." *Sketch*, 26 Dec. 1894.

2673. "Miss ML Alhambra Theatre." *Era*, 1 July 1899, p. 16.

2674. "Miss ML in Liverpool." *Era*, 30 June 1900, p. 18.

2675. "Miss ML in Manchester." *Era*, 19 Jan. 1895, p. 16; 26 Jan. 1895, p. 19.

2676. "Miss ML in Manchester." *Era*, 12 Feb. 1898, p. 18; 19 Feb. 1898, p. 19.

Personalia

Arthur Lucan ["Old Mother Riley"]

Dame comedian; b. Arthur Towle, Boston, Lancashire, 1887; d. Hull, 17 May 1954.

Secondary Materials

2677. ASHTON, ELLIS. "In Me Bonnet and Shawl." *Call Boy,* Mar. 1966.
2678. "The Lucans Stepping Out." *Daily Mail,* 5 Dec. 1949.
2679. "'Mother Riley' in a Spot." *Daily Herald,* 19 Aug. 1955.
2680. "Mother Riley Paid 10d. a Week." *News Chronicle,* 25 May 1954.
2681. [Old Mother Riley featured in] *Film Fun.* L: Amalgamated Press, 1940. [Ills. Norman Ward.]
2682. "Variety Artist's Debts." *Times,* 10 Mar. 1954.
2683. [Obits.: *Daily Mirror,* 18 May 1954; *Daily Telegraph,* 18 May 1954; *News Chronicle,* 18 May 1954; *Times,* 18 May 1954; Manchester *Guardian,* 19 May 1954.]

Frederic Maccabe

Comedian and ventriloquist; b. Liverpool, 1831; d. Ormskirk, 23 Apr. 1904.

2684. *The Art of Ventriloquism, including full Directions to Learners to Acquire a Pleasing Vocalization; a Record of a Life's Experiences.* L: Warne [n.d.] (Warne's Useful Books). Repr. as *FM on Voice Production, the Arts of Speaking, Singing, Acting and Ventriloquism: a Record of a Life's Experiences.* Wolverhampton: Whitehead, 1893.
2685. *Maccabe's Ventriloquism and Vocal Illusions.* N.Y.: Henry J. Wehman, 1875.

Secondary Materials

2686. "Complimentary Dinner to Mr. M." *Era,* 19 Dec. 1880, p. 7.
2687. "The Great M in Court." *Era,* 10 Aug. 1873, p. 7.
2688. "M's Entertainment." *Era,* 28 June 1874, p. 12.
2689. "Mr. FM." *Era,* 28 June 1884, p. 7; 17 Dec. 1898, p. 20.
2690. "Mr. M at Bow." *Era,* 16 Sept. 1877.
2691. "Mr. M at Charing Cross." *Era,* 11 Feb. 1872, p. 12; 21 Apr. 1872, p. 12.
2692. "Mr. M's Entertainment." *Era,* 12 May 1872, p. 12.
2693. "Mr. M's New Entertainment." *Era,* 26 May 1872, p. 13.
2694. "The Narrow Escape of Mr. M." *Era,* 30 Jan. 1876, p. 4.

Repertoire

2695. *The Songs Sung by FM in his Musical, Dramatic and Ventrilo-*

quial Entertainment entitled "Begone, Dull Care." [L: 1875]

The Great Macdermott

Lion comique; b. Gilbert Hastings Farrell, 27 Feb. 1845; d. Clapham, 8 May 1901.
2696. "Mr. M's Age." *Era,* 27 Jan. 1894, p. 16.
2697. "Music Hall Disturbances." *Era,* 24 Dec. 1887, p. 16.
Secondary Materials
DNB supp. 2 [John Parker]; OCT, p. 595.
2698. [GHM] *Notes & Queries,* 20 July 1901.
2699. HONRI, PETER. "A Day in the Life of a Lion Comique." *Call Boy,* Spring 1978, p. 7.
2700. "Mr. GHM at Theatre Royal, Birmingham." *Era,* 22 Feb. 1874, p.7.
2701. "Mr. GHM's Bankruptcy." *Era,* 1 Aug. 1885, p. 10; 8 Aug. 1885, p. 10.
2702. " A Music Hall Agent's Commission." *Era,* 2 Apr. 1892, p. 17.
2703. [Obits.: *Era,* 11, and 18 May 1901; *Daily Telegraph,* 9 May 1901; *Times,* 10 May 1901.]

E[dmund] W[illiam] Mackney

Blackface minstrel; b. London, or Morpeth, Northumberland, Feb. 1825; d. 26 Mar. 1909.
2704. *The Life and Reminiscences of EWM, Ethiopian Entertainer.* L: 1897.
2705. "Negro Minstrelsy. My Life and Experiences." *Stage,* 13 Feb. 1896, p. 15; 27 Feb. 1896, p. 15; 5 Mar. 1896, p.14 *et seq.*
Secondary Materials
OCT [W. Macqueen-Pope], p. 600.
2706. "M in Bradford." *Era,* 10 Nov. 1872, p. 13.
2707. "M's Benefit." *Era,* 2 Feb. 1873, p. 7.
2708. [Obit.: *Era,* 3 Apr. 1909.]
Repertoire
2709. *M's Songs of Negro Life as Sung by Him at St. James Hall.* L: 1860.

Paul Martinetti

Mime; b. New York City, 22 Jan. 1851; d. Algiers, 26 Dec. 1924.
2710. "In the Days of My Youth. Chapters of Autobiography CCCXLIX—PM." *M. A. P.,* 18 Feb. 1905, pp.156-57.

Secondary Materials
2711. "A Chat with PM." *Era,* 13 Jan. 1900, p. 18.
2712. "A Chat with PM." *Era,* 15 June 1901.
2713. "Dinner to PM." *Era,* 14 June 1890, p. 15.
2714. "M the Pantomimist." N.Y. *Times,* 22 Dec. 1898.
2715. "PM." N.Y. *Clipper,* 29 Nov. 1890, p. 593. [Portrait.]
2716. "PM Back Again." *Era,* 1 Dec. 1900, p. 20.
2717. "PM's Farewell." *Era,* 24 Feb. 1900, p. 18.

Billy Merson

Comedian; b. William Henry Thompson, Nottingham, 29 Mar. 1881; d. 25 June 1947.
2718. *Fixing the Stoof Oop. Reminiscences of Variety and Musical Comedy.* L: Hutchinson, 1926.
Secondary Materials
OCT [W. Macqueen-Pope], p. 636.

Max Miller

Comedian; b. Thomas Henry Sargent, Brighton, Nov. 1895; d. 7 May 1963.
2719. Column in *The Leader,* 1939. [Ghostwritten.]
2720. Column in *Sunday Dispatch,* 1939-41. [Written by himself.]
2721. *The MM Blue Book,* comp. by Barry Took. Ills. Trog. L: Robson Books, 1975.
Secondary Materials
2722. COTES, PETER. "Memories of MM." *What's On in London,* 30 Sept. 1977, pp. 40-41.
2723. EAST, JOHN M. "The Cheeky Chappie — the Story of MM." *Listener,* 1 June 1978, pp. 685, 695-96.
2724. ———. "MM and the Smut in the Eye of the Beholder." *Listener,* 8 June 1978, pp. 733-34.
2725. ———. *MM: The Cheeky Chappie.* L: W. H. Allen, 1977.
2726. [MM featured in] *Film Fun.* L: Amalgamated Press, 1938. [Ills. G. Wakefield.]
2727. ORWELL, GEORGE. "A Note on MM." In *The Collected Essays, Journalism and Letters of George Orwell,* ed. Sonia Orwell and Ian Angus. L: Secker & Warburg, 1968. [Vol. 2, My Country Right or Left, 1940-43, pp. 161-62.]
2728. OSBORNE, JOHN. "MM." *Observer Magazine,* 19 Sept. 1965, pp. 26-29. [Ills. Barry Fantoni.]
2729. [Obit.: *Times,* 9 May 1963.]

Charles Morton

Manager and entrepreneur; b. Hackney, London, 15 Aug. 1819; d. London, 18 Oct. 1904.

2729a. "An after-the-war experience." N.Y. *Dramatic Mirror,* Christmas 1903, p. 66.
2730. "The Alhambra Exits." *Era,* 10 Sept. 1887, p. 10.
2731. "A Few Words from Mr. CM." *Entr'acte Annual,* (1893): 22-26.
2732. "A King for Half an Hour." *Era Annual,* (1904): 56-57.
Secondary Materials
2733. "Assault on Mr. CM." *Era,* 26 Sept. 1885, p. 10.
2734. "The CM Benefit." *Era,* 21 Mar. 1891, p. 16; 28 Mar. 1891, p. 14.
2735. "The CM Testimonial." *Era,* 23 Sept. 1899, p.19.
2736. "CM's Presentation." *Era,* 20 Aug. 1898, p. 16.
2737. MORTON, WILLIAM H. and HENRY CHANCE NEWTON. *Sixty Years' Stage Service, being a Record of the Life of CM, 'The Father of the Halls.'* L: Gale & Polden, 1905.
2738. "Mr. CM." *Era,* 7 Mar. 1891, p. 17.
2739. "Music Hall History. The Career of Mr. CM." *Era,* 18 Jan. 1894, p. 17. [Important article.]
2740. "Presentation to Mr. M." *Era,* 18 Aug. 1900, p. 17.
2741. "A Theatrical Libel Case." *Era,* 23 Feb. 1873, p. 7. [CM vs Charles Head.]
2741a. [Obit. N.Y. *Dramatic Mirror,* 29 Oct. 1904.]

George Mozart

Comedian; b. David John Gillings, Yarmouth, 1864; d. 9 Dec. 1947.
2742. "GM and Queen Alexandra." *Era Annual* (1904): 68-69.
2743. *July: a story* . . . . L: R. & T. Washbourne, 1919. [Novel.]
2744. *Limelight.* L: Hurst and Blackett, 1938. [Autobiography.]
2745. *Mary Ann.* L: T. Werner Laurie [1920]. [Novel.]
2746. "M's Busman's Holiday." *Era Annual* (1911): 79-80.
Secondary Materials
Le Roy, Chapter 6.

Jolly John Nash

Comic singer; b. Gloucestershire, 1830; d. Fulham, London, 13 Oct. 1901.
2747. *The Merriest Man Alive: Stories, Anecdotes, Adventures, etc.* L: General Publishing Co. [1891]. Rev. *Era,* 22 Aug. 1891, p. 11.

Secondary Materials

2747a. "A Chat with J N." N.Y. *Dramatic Mirror,* 17 Mar. 1900, p. 18.
2748. "A Chat with JJN." *Music Hall,* 23 Feb. 1889, p. 29.
2749. "A Chat with JJN." *Era,* 23 Feb. 1895, p. 16.
2750. "Farewell Dinner to JJN." *Era,* 4 Oct. 1874, p. 4.
2751. "The JJN Benefit." *Era,* 22 Apr. 1899, p. 19.
2752. "Mr. JJN." *Era,* 11 Mar. 1899, p. 19.
2753. [Obits.: *Era,* 19 Oct. 1901; *M. A. P.,* 20 Oct. 1901, p. 407.]

Jimmy Nervo

Comedian and juggler; b. James Holloway, 1897; d. 5 Dec. 1975.
Secondary Materials
2754. "When We Were Young." *Daily Telegraph,* 6 Dec. 1975, p. 14.
2755. [Obits.: *Evening Telegraph,* 5 Dec. 1975, p. 8; *Daily Telegraph,* 6 Dec. 1975, p. 10; *Stage,* 18 Dec. 1976, p. 6.]

Harry Nicholls

Comedian; b. London, 1 Mar. 1852; d. London, 30 Nov. 1926.
2756. "HN Tells Some Stories." *Era,* 30 Jan. 1892, p. 9. [Interview.]
2757. "Mr. HN on Acting." *Era,* 9 Nov. 1895, p. 17.
2758. "The 'Property' Room." *Era Almanack* (1900): 44-45.
2759. "Tuffy." *Era Annual* (1910): 68-70.

Renton Nicholson

"Bohemian" and showman; b. Islington, London, 4 Apr. 1809; d. London, 18 May 1861.
2760. *An Autobiography.* L: Vickers [c. 1860]. Repr. as *The Autobiography of a Fast Man,* L: 1863; and as *Rogue's Progress: The Autobiography of "Lord Chief Baron" N,* ed. John L. Bradley. L: Longmans; Boston: Houghton Mifflin, 1965; L: Longmans, 1966.
2761. *Nicholson's Sketches of Celebrated Characters, and Key to the Judge and Jury Society, Garrick's Head Hotel, Bow Street.* [L: 1844?] [Key to a picture by Archibald Henning.]
Secondary Materials
DNB [Geo. C. Boase], 41:25.
2762. " 'Baron N' at the Cider Cellars." *The John Johnson Collections Catalogue of an Exhibition.* Oxford; Bodleian Library, 1971. [Handbill, 56.]
2763. JAMES, LOUIS. *Fiction for the Workingman.* Harmondsworth:

Penguin books, 1974. [Pp. 35, 188-89 *ff.*]

2764. [Judge and Jury Society] *Bachelor's Guide to Life in London.* L: Ward's Readable Book Depot [c. 1850]. [P. 8.]

2765. [Judge and Jury Society] *Illustrated Sporting News,* 21 May 1864, pp. 129, 133.

2766. MILES, HENRY DOWNES. *Puglistica, being One Hundred and Forty-four Years of the History of British Boxing . . . from 1719 . . . to 1863.* 3 vols. L: Weldon & Co., 1880-81. [1: xii.]

2767. [RN] *Illustrated London Life,* 28 May 1843, p. 126; 11 June 1843, p. 161.

2768. [RN] *Notes & Queries,* 4th ser. (1870): vi, 477; (1871): vii, 18, 286, 327; 7 Jan. 1893, pp. 3-5.

2769. VIZETELLY, HENRY. *Glances Back Through Seventy Years: Autobiographical and Other Reminiscences.* 2 vols. L: Kegan Paul, 1893. [1: 168-70.]

Harry Pleon

Comedian; b. 1856; d. Mafeking, Transvaal, 23 Apr. 1911.

2770. "HP Protests." *Era,* 15 May 1897, p. 18.

2771. [Letter to Editors] *Era,* 2 July 1892, p. 14.

2772. "Nelson Off His Column." *Era,* 21 Apr. 1894, p. 16; 28 Apr. 1894, p. 17.

2773. *Recitations, Rhymes and Ridiculosities.* L: Howard, 1892.

2773a. "Mr HP," *Era,* 2 Dec. 1895.

Secondary Material

2774. [Obit.: *Era,* 29 Apr. 1911, p. 25.]

Sandy Powell

Comedian; b. Rotherham, Yorkshire, 30 Jan. 1900.

2775. *"Can You Hear Me, Mother?" SP's Lifetime of Music-hall. SP's Story Told to Henry Stanley.* L: Jupiter Books, 1975.

Secondary Materials

2775a. ASHTON, ELLIS. "SP, One of the 'Old Boys.' " *Call Boy* 16, no. 4 (winter 1979): 12.

2776. WALSH, MICHAEL. "After 35 Years, SP is Back in the Limelight." *Daily Express,* 6 Nov. 1970.

Nellie Power

Serio-comic; b. London, 10 Apr. 1854; d. Islington, London, 20 Jan. 1887.

Secondary Materials
2777. "The Late NP." *Era,* 19 Mar. 1887, p. 15; 26 Mar. 1887, p. 16;
     18 Feb. 1888, p. 15; 10 Mar. 1888, p. 15.
2778. "Miss NP and her Husband." *Era,* 21 Nov. 1875, p. 4. [Divorce.]
2779. "NP's Husband." *Era,* 8 Sept. 1888, p. 10; 15 Sept. 1888, p. 15.
2780. [Obits.: *Era,* 22 Jan. 1887; 29 Jan. 1887, p. 10.]

Billy Purvis

Showman and clown; b. Auchinderry near Edinburgh, 13 Jan. 1784;
d. 1853.

2781. [ARTHUR, THOMAS] *The Life of BP, the Extraordinary,
     Witty, and Comical Showman: with many facts not before
     published.* Newcastle-on-Tyne: 1875. ["A very inferior piece of
     work," David Mayer.]
2782. "BP the Pitman's Jester." *Era,* 14 Nov. 1880, p. 4.
2783. [BOWMAN, DANIEL?] *The Life and Adventures of BP, con-
     taining Many Humorous Incidents and Anecdotes, not hitherto
     published.* Newcastle-on-Tyne: 1875. ["Excellent account,"
     David Mayer.]
2784. MAYER, DAVID. "BP: Travelling Showman." *Theatre
     Quarterly,* 1, no. 4 (Oct.-Dec. 1971): 27-34.
2785. ROBSON, JOSEPH P. *The Life and Adventures of Far-famed
     BP.* Newcastle-on-Tyne: 1849. ["Subsequent biographies are
     largely based on this account," David Mayer.]
2786. STEVENSON, CHARLES H. " BP the Clown." N.Y. *Clipper,*
     30 Jan. 1875, p. 348.

Harry Randall

Comedian; b. High Holborn, London, 22 Mar. 1860; d. 18 May 1932.

2787. *HR Old Time Comedian by Himself, with a foreword by Charles
     B. Cochran.* L: Sampson Low, Marston [1930]. [Autobiography.]
2788. "My Letter Box." *Era Annual* (1904): 49. Repr. in *Music Hall
     Records* 4 (Dec. 1978): 78.
2789. "My Trip to Morocco." *Era Almanack* (1898): 49-51.
Secondary Materials
Le Roy, Chapter 12; OCT, p. 788.
2790. "Claim against a comic singer." *Era,* 4 Apr. 1885, p. 10. [For
     breach of contract.]
2791. "HR Story." *M. A. P.,* 1 Apr. 1905.
2792. "'Let 'em All Come.'" Boston *Herald,* 17 Jan. 1899.
2793. "Mr. HR." *Era,* 21 Dec. 1895.
2794. "Mr. HR." *Era,* 3 Dec. 1904.

2795. "R Up to Date." *Era,* 9 Mar. 1889, p. 17. [Lyrics of his Pigott song, sung only once.]

Frank Randle

Comedian; b. Arthur McEvoy, Wigan, 1902; d. Blackpool, 7 July 1957.
Secondary Material
2796. NUTTALL, JEFF. *King Twist, a Portrait of FR.* L: Routledge & Paul, 1979.

Ada Reeve

Comic actress and singer; b. Adelaide Mary Isaacs, Mile End, London, 3 Mar. 1874; d. 25 Sept. 1966.
2797. "A Comparison." *Era Annual* (1911): 60. [Poem.]
2798. *Take It for a Fact, (A Record of My Seventy-five Years on the Stage).* L: William Heinemann, 1954. [With a foreword by Sir Compton Mackenzie. Ills. from the Raymond Mander and Joe Mitchenson Theatre Collection.]
Secondary Materials
2799. BEERBOHM, MAX. [Caricature] *Pick-Me-Up,* 24 Nov. 1894. Repr. in *Max's Nineties,* L: Hart-Davis, 1958 pl. 6.
2800. "A Chat with Miss AR." *Era,* 10 Aug. 1901.
2801. FRYE, ANNE CUMMINGS. "Success in Vaudeville Work only Won by Closest Application, says AR." Boston *Advertizer,* 27 Nov. 1912.
2802. "In the Days of My Youth CCXIV—Miss AR." *M. A. P.,* 19 July 1902.
2803. "Marriage of Miss AR." *Era,* 19 July 1902.
2804. "Miss AR." *Era,* 30 Dec. 1911.
2805. "Miss AR's Marriage." *Era,* 26 July 1902.
2806. "A Welcome Rumour." *M. A. P.,* 4 Aug. 1906.
2807. [Obit.: *Times,* 26 Sept. 1966.]

Ella Retford

Serio-comic; b. Sunderland, 1886; d. 29 June 1962.
Secondary Materials
2808. "Marriage of ER." *Era,* 3 June 1911, p. 26.
2809. "Miss ER." *Era,* 17 May 1913.

Harry Rickards

Comic singer and manager; b. Henry Leete, London, 1841; d. London, 13 Oct. 1911.

2810. "HR's Salaries." *Era,* 24 Nov. 1900, p. 18.
Secondary Materials
2811. "A Chat with HR." *Era,* 12 Oct. 1895, p. 16.
2812. "A Chat with HR." *Era,* 10 Apr. 1896, p. 13.
2813. "A Chat with HR." *Era,* 16 July 1910, p. 21.
2814. "A Comic Singer and the Excise." *Era,* 13 Dec. 1883, p. 4.
2815. "Mr HR." *Era,* 30 Sept. 1899, p. 19.
2816. "Mr HR's Benefit." *Era,* 19 Nov. 1881, p. 5.
2817. "A Tribute to HR." *Era,* 13 Jan. 1912.

Arthur Roberts

Comedian; b. Westbourne Grove, London, 1852; d. 27 Feb. 1933.
2818. *The Adventures of AR by Rail, Road and River.* Bristol Library Series, vol. 65. Bristol: J. W. Arrowsmith [1895]. [Told by himself and chronicled by Richard Morton. Anecdotes about music-hall.]
2819. *Fifty Years of Spoof.* L: John Lane, The Bodley Head, 1927. [Autobiography.]
Secondary Materials
EDS [E. H. Short], 8: 1045; Le Roy, Chapter 9; OCT [W. Macqueen-Pope], p. 802.
2820. "Accident to Mr AR." *Era,* 7 Sept. 1889, p. 8.
2821. AGATE, JAMES. "Jubilee of AR." *Saturday Review,* 16 Nov. 1924.
2822. "AR in Rotten Row." *M. A. P.,* 27 Aug. 1904.
2823. "Beau AR." *M. A. P.,* 20 May 1905.
2824. BEERBOHM, MAX. [Caricature] in *The Savoy* (1896). Repr. in *Max's Nineties,* L: Hart-Davis, 1958, pl. 11.
2825. ———. [Caricature] in *Pall Mall Budget,* 4 Oct. 1894.
2826. "A Great Comedian." *Daily Telegraph,* 15 Nov. 1924.
2827. "The Great Trickoli." *Globe,* 22 Apr. 1897.
2828. "How 'Randy Pandy' became 'Jack the Dandy.' " *Pall Mall Budget,* 15 Oct. 1891.
2829. "Mr AR." *Era,* 22 Aug. 1891, p. 9. [Interview.]
2830. "Mr AR's Knife." *Era,* 30 Jan. 1892, p. 9.
2831. "Mr AR's Matinee." *Era,* 25 Apr. 1885, p. 13; 26 June 1886, p. 16.
2832. "Of Comic Actors . . . ." Glasgow *Evening News,* 26 Aug. 1895.
2833. [Obit.: N.Y. *Times,* 28 Feb. 1933.]

Sir George Robey

Comedian; b. George Wade, Herne Hill, London, 20 Sept. 1869; d. London, 29 Nov. 1954.

2834. *After Dinner Stories.* L: Grant Richards, 1920. [With ten ills. by H. M. Bateman.]

2835. *Bits and Pieces: Humorous Stories.* L: Jarrolds [1928].

2836. *Don'ts.* L: John Long, 1926.

2837. *Family Affairs.* Ills. E. P. Kinsella and GR. L: John Long, 1924.

2838. *An Honest Living.* L: Cassell, 1922.

2839. *In Other Words. Humorous Stories.* L: Jarrolds, n. d.

2840. *Jokes, Jibes and Jingles: Jugged by GR.* L: Price & Reynolds, 1911. [Another ed.: Paxton's Edition 15053. L: W. Paxton (c. 1917).]

2841. *The Lady in Question and Other Stories.* L: Eveleigh Nash & Grayson, 1922.

2842. *Looking Back on Life.* L: Constable, 1933. [With an introduction "Mr R, auctioneer," by Sir James Barrie, Bart. Autobiography.]

2843. *Mental Fireworks.* Ills. E. P. Kinsella. L: Long, 1925.

2844. "A Muddled Melody." *Era Annual* (1904): 44.

2845. *My Life Up to Now. A Naughtibiography.* L: Greening, 1909.

2846. *My Rest Cure.* Ills. John Hassall. L: Grant Richards, 1919.

2847. *Old Bore's Almanac.* L: 1929.

2848. *Pause.* L: Greening, 1910.

2849. *Thereby Hangs a Tale.* L: Grant Richards, 1921. [Comic novel.]

2850. "What is Wrong with Variety?" *Nineteenth Century* 109 (Mar. 1931): 350-59. [Historical survey. Falling number of effective artists. Influence of cinema. No more top of bill or original songs.]

Secondary Materials

DNB [Ivor Brown], 1951-60; EDS [A. E. Wilson], 8: 1049-50; OCT, p. 803.

2851. BEERBOHM, MAX. "Manners." In *A Survey.* L: Wm. Heinemann, 1921. [Plate 48 shows GR with Asquith and Bonar Law.]

2852. CECCHI, E. "GR." In *Pesci rosse.* Firenze: Vallacchi [1920]. [Pp. 131-41.]

2853. COTES, PETER. *GR "The Darling of the Halls."* L: Cassell, 1959. [With a foreword by Neville Cardus.] Rev. P. Honri, *Call Boy* 9, no.1 (Mar. 1972): 9.

2854. ERVINE, ST. JOHN. "Mr R. looks back." *Observer,* 22 Oct. 1933.

2855. F.L.M. "GR 1869-1954." *Punch,* 8 Dec. 1954.

2856. "Forty Years on the Stage." *Observer,* 4 Mar. 1934.

2857. "GR and the Oxford Ltd." *Era,* 5 Mar. 1910, p. 18.

2858. *GR's Christmas Almanack.* L: 1920-?

2859. GREIN, J. T. "GR." *Christian Science Monitor,* 18 Mar. 1924.

2860. "Homage to Mr GR." *Observer,* 25 Oct. 1936.
2861. MACKENZIE, COMPTON. "Sidelight." *Spectator,* 10 Dec. 1954.
2862. MORGAN, CHARLES. "The R Falstaff." *Times,* 24 Mar. 1935.
2863. "Mr GR as Animal Trainer." *World's Fair* (Oldham), 27 June 1914. ["I suspect GR stole this story from Whimsical Walker!" Toole-Stott.]
2864. "Mr. GR as the 'Last of the Dandies,' at the Pavilion and the Tivoli." *Sketch,* 4 Dec. 1901, p. 253.
2865. "Mr. R and the Landladies." *T. P.'s Weekly,* 11 Aug. 1928, p. 484.
2866. "Mr. R's Press Fund Address." *Times,* 30 Mar. 1921.
2867. "Music Hall Artist's Contracts." *Era,* 12 Feb. 1898, p. 18. [GR vs. H. J. Didcott.]
2868. "A Music-hall Celebrity." *Sketch,* 26 Aug. 1896, p. 207. Repr. in *Music Hall Records* 1 (June 1978): 17-20.
2869. NORGATE, MATTHEW. "GR." *Programme by Theatre Print* 24 (Sept. 1977).
2870. PRENTIS, RICHARD. "R's Infinite Buffoonery." *John o' London's Weekly,* 14 July 1934, p. 532.
2871. PRESTON, Sir HARRY JOHN. *Letters from My Unwritten Diary.* L: Hutchinson, 1936.
2872. "R. Britain's Funniest Man." *Sun,* 15 June 1925.
2873. ROBEY, EDWARD. *The Jester and His Court.* L: Kimber, 1976. [Autobiography of GR's son.]
2874. "R's Falstaff Scores in London." N.Y. *Times,* 1 Mar. 1935.
2875. STUART-YOUNG, J. M. "The Perennial R." *John O'London's Weekly,* 13 Sept. 1934.
2876. WILSON, ALBERT EDWARD. *Prime Minister of Mirth: The Biography of GR, CBE.* L: Oldham Press, 1959.

Frederick Robson

Actor and comic singer; b. Thomas Robson Brownbill, Margate, 22 Feb. 1821; d. London, 12 Aug. 1864.

Secondary Materials

DNB [J. Knight], 17: 63-64; EDS [J. O. Bartley], 8: 1061-62; OCT, p. 804.
2877. COOKE, DUTTON. "FR." *Gentleman's Magazine,* n. s. 28 (June 1882): 715.
2878. "FR." *Era,* 17 June 1882, p. 5.
2879. HOTTEN, J[OHN] C[AMDEN]. "The Late FR." *Atlantic Monthly* (Boston, Mass.), June 1864. Repr. in SALA, *infra.*

2880. MACKIE, CRAVEN. "FR and the Evolution of Realistic Acting." *Educational Theatre Journal* (Washington, D.C.) 23, no. 2 (May 1971): 160-170.
2881. "Managers and Actors: Mr. FR." *Peeping Tom,* 1 (27 June 1859): 2.
2881a. MARSTON, [JOHN] WESTLAND. *Our Recent Actors: Being Recollections Critical, and, in Many Cases, Personal, of Late Distinguished Performers of Both Sexes. With some Incidental Notices of Living Actors.* L: Sampson Low, Marston, Searle & Rivington; N.Y.: Roberts Brothers, 1888. 2 vols. [Vol. 2, Ch. xiv, "Mr. Alfred Wigan and FR," pp.251-78.]
2882. MATTHEWS, J. B. and LAURENCE HUTTON. *Actors and Actresses of Great Britain and the United States.* N.Y.: Cassell, 1886.
2883. SALA, GEORGE AUGUSTUS. *R: a Sketch.* L: John Camden Hotten, 1864. [Includes "The Late FR," by J. C. Hotten, pp. (3)-28.]
2883a. SANDS, MOLLIE. *Robson of the Olympic.* L: Society for Theatre Research, 1979. [Excellent biography which conflates and supersedes all earlier accounts. Part 1, pp. 15-39 concentrates on FR's career as a comic singer. Appendix 3 discusses the song "Villikens and his Dinah."]
2884. SCOTT, CLEMENT. *The Drama of Yesterday & Today.* L: Macmillan, 1899. [1: 37-44, 2: 206-14.]
2885. [Obit.: *Sunday Times,* 21 Aug. 1864.]

Clarkson Rose

Comedian; b. Arthur Rose, Dudley, Worcestershire, 8 Dec. 1890; d. 23 Apr. 1968.
2886. *Beside the Seaside.* L: Museum Press, 1960. [History of pier entertainments.]
2887. *Red Plush and Greasepaint: a Memory of the Music-hall and Life and Times from the Nineties to the Sixties.* L: Museum Press, 1964.
2888. *With a Twinkle in My Eye.* L: Museum Press, 1951. [Foreword by Sir Barry Jackson. Preface by Collie Knox. Introduction by George F. Reynolds. Autobiography.]
Secondary Materials
OCT, p. 810.

Billy Russell

Comedian; b. Adam George Brown, Birmingham, 16 July 1893; d. London, 25 Nov. 1971.

Secondary Materials

2889. [Obits.: *Daily Telegraph,* 27 Nov. 1971, p. 15; *Stage,* 2 Dec. 1971, p. 3.]

Henry Russell

Songwriter and entertainer; b. Sheerness, Kent, 24 Dec. 1812; d. Maida Vale, 1 Dec. 1900.

2890. *Cheer! Boys, Cheer! Memories of Men and Music.* L: J. Macqueen, 1895. [Autobiography.]

2891. *HR's Dramatic Scenes and Cantatas with a Memoir.* L: 1846.

2892. "In the Days of My Youth, Chapters of Autobiography CCCLXXIII. HR." *M. A. P.,* 5 Aug. 1905, pp. 132-33.

2893. *Musical Bouquet Edition. Copyright Collection of the Songs, Scenas & & of HR . . . to which is Added a Variety of the Most Popular Songs of the Day.* L: Musical Bouquet Office [1855?].

Secondary Materials

DNB [F.G Edwards], 17: 1204-5.

2894. "Career of HR." Boston *Herald,* 9 Feb. 1896.

2895. FITZGERALD, S. J. ADAIR. *Stories of Famous Songs.* L: John C. Nimmo, 1898. [Chapter 13, "HR's Songs," pp. 179-92.]

2896. "HR." Boston *Herald,* 13 Sept. 1886.

2897. "HR." *Strand,* Sept. 1891, p. 280.

2898. "HR Who Composed 800 Songs." Chicago *Tribune,* 9 Dec. 1900.

2899. [HR's Career] *Biograph,* Oct. 1881, pp. 408-13.

2900. [HR's Performance] *Illustrated London News,* 9 Sept. 1854, p. 232.

2901. [Obits.: *Era,* 8 Dec. 1900, p. 22; *Illustrated London News,* 15 Dec. 1900, p. 906.]

Eugen Sandow

Strongman and physical culturist; b. Konigsberg, Germany, 10 Apr. 1867; d. London, 13 Oct. 1925.

2902. *Body-building, or Man in the Making.* L: Gale & Polden, 1905. Repr. 1919.

2903. *The Construction and Reconstruction of the Human Body: a Manual of the Therapeutics of Exercise . . . .* L: John Dale & Sons, 1907. [With a foreword by Sir A. C. D. Linden.]

2904. *Life is Movement: the Physical Reconstruction and Regeneration of the People.* L: Hedford, Simson, 1919.

2905. *Physical Culture Magazine.* [ed., Apr. 1898-Mar. 1899.]
2906. *The Power of Evidence, being a Series . . . of Reports . . . of Patients treated by the S Method.* L: Sandow Creative Institute, 1919.
2907. *Sandow's Magazine of Physical Culture.* [ed., Apr. 1899-July 1907.]
2908. *Strength and How to Obtain It.* L: Gale & Polden, 1897. (Revised ed. 1900; 3rd ed. 1905; new and revised ed. 1911.)

Secondary Materials

2909. ADAM, G. M. ed. *S on Physical Training: a Study . . . preceded by a Biography comp. and ed. under Mr. S's Direction by G. Mercer Allen.* L: Gale & Polden, 1894.
2910. "Advice of the Strong Men." Boston *Sunday Herald,* 1 Feb. 1894.
2911. "Distinguished People interviewed by A. Sloper: Sandow." *Ally Sloper's Half Holiday,* 21 Nov. 1891.
2912. LANE, FRANK W. " S the Strong Man." *Saturday Book 24* (1966): 140-47.
2913. LUCAS, C. D. "Another Talk with S." *Chums,* 3 Feb. 1896.
2914. "A Perfect Man." Chicago *Interocean,* 2 Aug. 1893.
2915. POPE, W. R. *The Science and Art of Physical Development: Hints on the S System.* L: Greening, 1902.
2916. "S and his Common Feat." *Era,* 8 Oct. 1892, p. 16.
2917. "S at Practice." *Era,* 15 Nov. 1890, p. 17.
2918. "S v. Hercules." *Era,* 13 Dec. 1890, p. 16.
2919. "S v. Samson." *Era,* 9 Nov. 1889, p. 15; "The Rival Samsons." p. 17.
2920. TREVOR, CHARLES T. *S the Magnificent.* L: Mitre Press, 1946.
2921. [Obits.: Boston *Transcript,* 14 Oct. 1925; Boston *Herald,* 18 Oct. 1925.]

Ella Shields

Singer and male impersonator; b. Baltimore, Maryland, 26 Sept. 1879; d. Morecambe, 3 Aug. 1952.

Secondary Materials

2922. DIXON, STEPHEN. "I'm All Airs and Graces, Correct Easy Paces, so Long without Food I Forgot Where My Face Is . . . ." *Guardian,* 28 Sept. 1979, p. 12.
2923. "ES Has Respect for the Number Thirteen." Boston *Globe,* 9 Jan. 1927.
2924. JOHNS, ERIC. "ES Off-stage or Burlington Bertie Goes to the

Opera." *Stage,* 17 Dec. 1970, p. 38.
2925. "Nautical Nonsense." Boston *Transcript,* 11 Jan. 1927.
2925a. ROBINSON, DAVID. "Burlington Bertie from Baltimore." *Times Saturday Review,* 29 Dec. 1979.
2926. [Obit.: N.Y. *Times,* 6 Aug. 1952.]

Charles Sloman

Improvisatore; b. 1808; d. London, 22 July 1870.
2927. *The Fitful Fancies of an Improvisatore.* L [1860]. [In verse.]
Secondary Materials
OCT, p. 888.

Emily Soldene

Singer and comic actress; b. Islington, London, 1844; d. London, 9 Apr. 1912.
2928. *My Theatrical and Musical Recollections.* L: Downey, 1897. New ed. 1898. Rev. *Era,* 30 Jan. 1897, p. 11. [Recollections of early Canterbury Hall.]
2929. *Young Mrs. Staples.* L: Downey, 1896. [Novel.]
Secondary Materials
OCT, p. 891.
2930. "Chat with ES." *Era,* 17 Nov. 1906.
2931. "ES." Boston *News,* 17 Oct. 1895.
2932. "ES." N.Y. *Clipper,* 17 June 1879, p. 81. [Portrait and biography.]
2933. "Favorite of Old Days." San Francisco *Bulletin,* 24 Oct. 1895.
2934. MARKS, EDWARD B. *They All Had Glamour from the Swedish Nightingale to the Naked Lady.* N.Y.: Julian Messner, 1944. [Chapter 4, "ES: Taking Harvard University by Charm," pp. 49-55.]
2935. "Recent London 'Farewell' Benefit to Miss ES a Reminder of Joyous and Unforgettable Days and Nights." Boston *Herald,* 2 Dec. 1906, p. 3.

Mel[ancthon] B[urton] Spurr

Monologuist; b. Selby, Yorkshire; d. 25 Sept. 1904.
2936. [with H. A. Spurr] *If We Only Knew & Other Poems.* Hull: Andrew, 1893.
2937. *MBS's Recitals and Monologues in Prose and Verse.* L: Samuel French, 1899.

2938. [with W. M. MAYNE] *Nursery Rhymes Parodied.* L: Samuel French, 1902.
2939. *"Snorkin."* L: Reynolds, 1928. [Monologue.]
Secondary Materials
2940. "A Comic Interview." *Era,* 18 Feb. 1911, p. 24.
2941. "Mr. MBS." *Era,* 13 Dec. 1902.
2942. SPURR, HARRY A. *MBS: His Life, Work, Writings and Recitations.* L: A. Brown [1905].

J[ames] H[urst] Stead

Eccentric singer and dancer; b. Hull, 1827; d. London, 25 Jan. 1886.
Secondary Materials
2943. BLANCHARD, EDWARD LEMAN. *The Life and Reminiscences of E. L. Blanchard.* . . . L: Hutchin, 1891. [Ed. Clement Scott and Cecil Howard. 1: 585.]
2944. DYER, JAMES SOMERS. "The 'Cure.' " *Era,* 20 Feb. 1886, p. 10.
2945. [JHS] *Players* 3 (1860): 335.
2946. "The JHS Benefits." *Era,* 5 Dec. 1885, p. 10; 12 Dec. 1885, p. 10; 16 Jan. 1886, p. 10.
2947. MURRAY, CHARLES. "JHS, the Cure." *Era,* 14 Mar. 1885, p. 9.
Repertoire
2948. *Fifty five of the Perfect Cure's Comic Songs.* L: C. Sheard, n.d. [Popular Comic Songs, in Sixpenny Books.]

Sir Oswald Stoll

Manager and entrepreneur; b. Oswald Gray, Melbourne, Australia, 20 Jan. 1866; d. London, 9 Jan. 1942.
2949. *Broadsheets on National Finance.* L: Roberts, 1921.
2950. *Freedom in Finance.* L: Fisher Unwin, 1918.
2951. "The Future of Music Halls." *Era,* 20 July 1895, p. 14.
2952. *The Grand Survival: a Theory of Immortality by Natural Law founded on a Variation of Herbert Spencer's Definition of Evolution.* L: Simpkin, Marshall, 1904.
2953. *Means to Pay: being an Address to Members of the National Liberal Club.* L: Roberts, 1923.
2954. *More "Broadsheets" on National Finance.* L: Roberts, 1922.
2955. [with C. GRAHAM HARDY] *National Credit and the Crisis.* L: Heinemann, 1924.
2956. *National Productive Credit.* L: Allen & Unwin, 1933.

2957. *People's Credit.* L: Everleigh Nash, 1916.
2958. *The Right to Create Credit.* L: Langley, 1916. [Another ed. pub. Eveleigh Nash, 1916.]
Secondary Materials
DNB [Herbert Grimsditch], 1941-50; OCT [W. Macqueen Pope], p. 919.
2959. "Mr. S and Mr. Moss." *Era,* 3 Sept. 1898, p.19. [OS's speech.]
2960. [OS] *Stage, 2 Apr. 1931.*
2960a. "Oswald Stoll in New York." N.Y. *Dramatic Mirror,* 29 Sept. 1906, p. 18.
2961. "OS's Manifesto." *Era,* 1 Oct. 1910, p. 22.
2962. OWL [Pseud.] "Sir OS, 'The Coliseum.' " *Vanity Fair,* 8 Oct. 1913. [Letterpress to accompany caricature by "Ape Junior."]
2963. "The Stoll-Gibbons Combine." *Era,* 19 Aug. 1911, p. 21.
2964. [Obits.: *Times,* 10 Jan. 1942; *Stage,* 15 Jan. 1942.]

Eugene Stratton

Blackface performer; b. Eugene Augustus Ruhlmann, Buffalo, N.Y., 8 May 1861; d. Christchurch, 15 Sept. 1918.
2965. "In the Days of My Youth, Chapters of Autobiography CLXIII, ES." *M. A. P.,* 27 July 1901, pp. 92-93.
Secondary Materials
Le Roy, chapter 14; OCT, p. 922.
2965a. BARKER, TONY. "ES." *Music Hall* 12 (Apr. 1980): 106-17. [Includes discography.]
2965b. "A Chat with ES." *Era,* 4 Mar. 1893.
2965c. [Interview with ES] *Evening News,* 20 Dec. 1913.
2966. "Stars as seen from the Wings, No. V, ES." *Stage,* 4 Aug. 1910.
2966a. "Still Popular in London." N.Y. *Dramatic Mirror,* 14 Oct. 1899, p. 18.
2967. [Obits.: Manchester *Guardian,* 16 Sept. 1918; *Stage,* 19 Sept. 1918, p. 11.]

Harry Tate

Comedian; b. Ronald Macdonald Hutchinson, Scotland, 4 July 1872; d. Dundee, Scotland, 14 Feb. 1940.
Secondary Materials
EDS [A. E. Wilson and Mollie Sands], 9: 702; OCT, p. 934.
2968. "HT Centenary." *Stage,* 14 Sept. 1972, p. 6.
2969. "HT, whose death . . . ." *John O'London's Weekly,* 23 Feb. 1940.
2970. HESTER, WALLACE. "HT, the King's Jester." *Vanity Fair,*

10 Sept. 1912. [Men of the Day No. 2291: caricature with letter press by "Jehu Junior".]
2971. "A Male Mimic." *Era,* 10 Aug. 1895, p. 14.
2972. "Motoring." *Stage,* 7 Sept. 1972, p. 6.
2973. [Obit.: Liverpool *Echo,* 14 Feb. 1940.]

Vesta Tilley

Male impersonator; b. Matilda Alice Powles, Worcester, 13 May 1864; d. Monte Carlo, France, 16 Sept. 1952. [Also known as Tilly Ball. Later, Lady de Frece.]
2974. "Concerning Audiences." *Era Almanack,* (1899): 66-67.
2975. "In the Days of My Youth." *M. A. P.,* 17 Mar. 1906.
2976. "Jolly Jack Tar!" *Era Annual* (1910): 91-92.
2977. "My Favourite Part." *Era Annual* (1906): 45-46.
2978. *Recollections by Lady de Frece.* L: Hutchinson, 1934. [With a foreword by Sir Oswald Stoll and an appreciation by Sir Alfred Butt.] Rev. St. John Ervine, *Observer,* 22 Apr. 1934.
2979. "The Story of a Song." *Era Annual* (1902): 27.
2980. "The Tale of a Wig." *Pelican Christmas Annual* (1906-7). Repr. in *Music Hall Records* 2 (Aug. 1978): 19-20.
Secondary Materials
DNB [W. Macqueen-Pope], 1951-60; EDS [Vittoria Ottolenghi and Mollie Sands], 9: 702; Le Roy, chapter 21; OCT, p. 947.
2981. ALLEN, TREVOR. "The Great Little T." *John O'London's Weekly,* 21 Aug. 1934.
2982. "A BOHEMIAN JOURNALIST." *The World's Idol. Queen of Varietyland. Illustrated Souvenir of VT: an Impression of a Great Artiste.* [n.p., n.d.]
2983. *Catalogue of Porcelain & Objects of Art, Decorative Furniture, Tapestries & Rugs sold by Order of the Executors at Christies in 1953 and including Items belonging to Lady de Frece (VT).* L: Christies, 1953.
2984. "Chat with Miss VT." *Era,* 7 July 1906.
2985. "A Chat with the London Idol." *Era,* 28 Mar. 1892, p. 17.
2986. "A Chat with VT." *Era,* 12 Oct. 1901.
2987. "Chicago Opera House." Chicago *Interocean,* 4 June 1895.
2988. ELLERY, CHANNING. "The Irving of the Halls." *Concertgoer* (Boston), Feb. 1898, pp. 3-5.
2989. "General Mention." Chicago *Interocean,* 16 June 1895.
2990. GREIN, J. T. "VT." In *World of the Theatre. Impressions and Memoirs March 1920-21.* L: Heinemann, 1921.
2991. HANNON, Sir PATRICK. "Miss VT." *Times,* 10 Oct. 1952.

Personalia

2992. "How VT is 'watched.'" N.Y. *Dramatic Mirror,* 12 May 1906, p. 18.
2993. "Illness of Miss VT." *Era,* 19 Dec. 1891, p. 16.
2994. "London's Idol Arrives." N.Y. *Mirror,* 2 Oct. 1897.
2995. "Miss VT." *Era,* 9 Mar. 1889.
2996. "Miss VT." *Era,* 18 Jan. 1890.
2997. "Miss VT." *Era,* 5 Oct. 1895, p. 27.
2998. "Miss VT." *Era,* 6 Nov. 1897.
2999. "Miss VT and the Waifs." *Era,* 5 June 1895, p. 19.
3000. "Miss VT as 'Dick Whittington.'" *Era,* 16 Mar. 1901, p. 23.
3001. "Miss VT in Chicago." *Era,* 22 June 1895, p. 17.
3002. "Miss VT, who plays Robinson Crusoe. . . ." *Era,* 4 Dec. 1895.
3003. "Miss VT's Benefit." *Era,* 3 Mar. 1894, p. 12.
3004. "Miss VT's Farewell." *Times,* 7 June 1920, p. 10.
3005. "Park Theatre." Boston *Advertiser,* 11 Jan. 1898.
3006. PRENTIS, RICHARD. "(VT)." *John O'London's Weekly,* 5 May 1934.
3007. "Queen Mary Frowns on VT."N.Y. *Times,* 2 July 1912.
3008. "To VT." Birmingham *Mail,* 4 Jan. 1920.
3009. [VT] *Theatre* (N.Y.) 3 (Aug. 1903): 192; 26 (Aug. 1917): 131.
3010. "VT at Liverpool." *Era,* 25 Mar. 1899, p. 19.
3011. "VT at New York." *Era,* 16 Oct. 1897, p. 23.
3012. "VT at the Park." Boston *Globe,* 11 Jan. 1898.
3013. "VT, Idol of the 'alls." N.Y. *Sun,* 29 Nov. 1903.
3014. "VT in town." Boston *Herald,* 10 Jan. 1898, p. 2.
3015. "VT is a more artistic performer. . . ." N.Y. *Sun,* 8 Oct. 1897.
3016. "VT is now Lady de Frece." N.Y. *Evening Sun,* 12 July 1919.
3017. "VT's American Triumphs." *Era,* 15 Jan. 1898, p. 19; 5 Feb. 1898, p. 19; 26 Feb. 1898, p. 19; 2 Apr. 1898, p. 22; 9 Apr. 1898, p. 18; 20 Apr. 1898, p. 18.
3018. "VT's Farewell." *Daily Telegraph,* 7 June 1920, p. 9.
3019. [Obits.: *Evening Standard,* 16 Sept. 1952; Manchester *Guardian,* 17 Sept. 1952; *Times,* 17 Sept. 1952; *Daily Telegraph,* 17 Sept. 1952. Disposition of fortune: *Evening Standard,* 11 Dec. 1952; *Daily Telegraph,* 12 Dec. 1952; *Times,* 31 Dec. 1952.]

Repertoire

3020. *Francis & Day's Album of VT's Popular Songs.* L: Francis, Day & Hunter, n.d. [Biographical sketch by Charles Wilmott. Jolly Good Luck to the Girl Who Loves a Soldier; I Know My Business (The Messenger Boy); By the Sad Sea Waves; I'm the Idol of the Girls; That's the Time a Fellow Wants His Ma; When a Fellah Has Turned Sixteen; It's Part of a P'liceman's Duty; Following a Fellah with a Face Like Me; S-U-N-D-A-Y; The Pretty Little

Maidie's Sea-Trip; Who said 'Girls'?; Give it to Father; Some Danced the Lancers; After the Ball; Algy, the Piccadilly Johnny; The Midnight Son; Following in Father's Footsteps.]

Alfred Granville "The Great" Vance

Lion comique; b. Alfred Peck Stevens, London, 1839; d. Knightsbridge, London, 26 Dec. 1888.

Secondary Materials

DNB [Joseph Knight], 8: 94; OCT, p. 982.

3021. "Assault on the Great V." *Era,* 12 Dec. 1885, p. 10.

3022. [AV] *Illustrated Sporting News* 3 (1864): 484.

3023. "The Great V." *Era,* 10 Apr. 1886, p. 10.

3024. "The Great V and his Wife." *Era,* 28 Nov. 1885, p. 10.

3025. "An Imitator of V." *Era,* 30 Sept. 1877, p. 4.

3026. "Mr. AGV [in Dublin]." *Era,* 5 Apr. 1874, p. 7.

3027. "Mr. AGV's Entertainment." *Era,* 29 Dec. 1872, p. 14.

3028. "Mr. V at Westbourne Hall." *Era,* 9 Feb. 1873, p. 12.

3029. "'V' at St. James' Hall." *Era,* 11 May 1873, p. 7; 17 May 1874, p. 12.

3030. "V at the Egyptian Hall." *Era,* 21 Nov. 1875, p. 10.

3031. "V in the County Court." *Era,* 9 Aug. 1874, p. 4.

3032. "V's Varieties." *Era,* 6 Jan. 1878, p. 7.

3033. "'V's Varieties' at St. James' Hall." *Era,* 12 Jan. 1873.

3034. [Obits.: *Era,* 29 Dec. 1888; 5 Jan. 1889, p. 16; 9 Feb. 1889, p. 17; *Times,* 28 Dec. 1888.]

Ada Victoria

Serio-comic; b. 1870.

Secondary Materials

3035. "Music Hall Centenarian." *Stage,* 31 Jan. 1970, p. 14.

Vesta Victoria

Serio-comic; b. Victoria Lawrence, Leeds, 26 Nov. 1874; d. London, 7 Apr. 1951.

Secondary Materials

3036. "Chat with Miss VV." *Era,* 16 June 1906.

3037. "Dream Music." *Punch,* 1 Oct. 1898, p. 142. ["Our Lodger's Such a Nice Young Man."]

3038. GREEN, BENNY. "It Wasn't the Girl I Saw You with at Brighton." *What's On in London,* 15 Sept. 1978, p. 36.

3039. "Keith's Has a Big Pie full of Plums, with VV as Choicest Plum in Dish." Boston *Herald,* 2 Apr. 1907.
3040. "Miss VV." *Era,* 20 Mar. 1909, p. 23.
3041. "Miss VV in Brighton." *Era,* 7 Mar. 1896, p. 18.
3042. "Miss VV [in Ireland]." *Era,* 8 June 1895, p. 16.
3043. "Miss VV Robbed." *Observer,* 18 Mar. 1934.
3043a. "VV" N.Y. *Dramatic Mirror,* 2 Mar. 1907, p. 17.
3044. "VV Married." N.Y. *Mirror,* 25 Sept. 1897.
3045. "'Way Out West': a Chat with VV." *Era,* 24 Sept. 1910, p. 27.

Repertoire

3046. *Francis, Day and Hunter's Song Hits that are Sweeping the Country: Waiting at the Church, The Next Horse I Ride on, It's All Right in the Summer Time, He Calls Me His Own Grace Darling, Coming through the Rye, Jenny Mine.* Philadelphia, Pa.: London Publishing Co. [1902]. [Sung by VV with her other successful songs.]

Nellie Wallace

Comedienne; b. Glasgow, Scotland, 18 Mar. 1870; d. London, 24 Nov. 1948.

Secondary Materials

OCT, p. 995.
3047. DOWDALL, JAMES. [On NW] *Vogue* (N.Y.), Dec. 1947. [With two photographs by Cecil Beaton.]
3048. GREIN, J. T. "NW." *Illustrated London News,* 23 Sept. 1924.
3049. MARRIOTT, R. B. "A Comic Genius of the Halls." *Stage,* 12 Mar. 1970.
3050. REDFERN, JOHN. "NW's Secret. She was 78." *Daily Express,* 25 Nov. 1948.
3051. ROBINSON, DAVID. "Essence of Eccentricity." *Financial Times,* 21 Aug. 1971, p. 8.
3052. ROSS, DON. "NW." *Call Boy* 7, no. 1 (Mar. 1970): 3-5.

Harry Weldon

Comedian; b. Liverpool, 1 Feb. 1881; d. 10 Mar. 1930.

Secondary Materials

3053. "Mr. HW." *Era,* 24 June 1911, p. 23.
3054. NORGATE, MATTHEW. "HW." *Programme by Theatre Print* 32 (May 1978): [19].

Bransby Williams

Actor and impersonator; b. Bransby William Pharez, London, 14 Aug. 1870; d. 3 Dec. 1961.

3055. *An Actor's Story.* L: Chapman & Hall, 1909. Rev. J. W. T. Ley, *Dickensian,* 5, no. 5 (May 1909): 117-21; *Era,* 3 Apr. 1909.

3056. *BW by Himself.* L: Hutchinson, 1954. [With a foreword by Naomi Jacob.]

3057. "Dog trainer and Actor." *Era Annual* (1911): 80-81.

3057a. *The Old Actor and Penny Showman.* N.Y. and L: Samuel French [1913]. [Recitation.]

Secondary Materials

OCT, p. 1010.

3058. "Dickens to Dooleyisms." Boston *Transcript,* 1 Dec. 1925.

3059. "The 'Era' Award Testimonial to Mr. BW." *Era,* 26 Aug. 1911, p. 24.

3060. HALE, PHILIP. "As the World Wags." Boston *Herald,* 12 Feb. 1923.

3061. "Mr. BW." *Era,* 5 May 1900, p. 19.

3062. "Mr. BW and the Raven." *Dickensian* 5, no. 6 (June 1909): 152-53.

3063. "Mr BW in Dickensland." *Era,* 14 May 1910, p. 20.

3064. ROBERTS, J. E. "BW." *Dickensian* 58, no. 1 (Jan. 1962): 59. [Obit.]

3065. "Two August Show biz Giants." *Stage,* 13 Aug. 1970, p. 10.

Wee Georgie Wood

Comedian; b. George Balmer, Jarrow, 17 Dec. 1897; d. London, 19 Feb. 1979.

3066. *I Had to be "Wee."* L: Hutchinson [1947]. [Foreword by Naomi Jacob. Autobiography.]

3067. *Royalty, Religion and Rats! An Autobiographical Scrapbook Miscellany.* Burnley, Lancs: Central Printing Co. (Chas. Sowden) Ltd. [n.d.]. [Limited to two thousand copies.]

3068. "Stage Man's Diary." *Stage.* [Weekly column.]

Secondary Materials

3069. BRIEN, ALAN. "'Metropolis,' Alan Brien's London." *Punch,* 7 Mar. 1979, pp. 380-81.

3070. COTES, PETER. "GW O.B.E.: An Appreciation." *Stage,* 22 Feb. 1979, p. 7.

3071. MacINNES, COLIN. "Seaham Harbour to the Savage Club."

Spectator, 10 Apr. 1971, pp. 486-87. [Ills. Richard Wilson.]

3072. TAPPENDEN, ARCHIE. "Reminiscences of GW in Birmingham." *Call Boy* 10, no. 3 (autumn 1973): 14-16.

Tom Woottwell

Comic singer; b. Highbury, 25 Mar. 1865.
Secondary Materials

3073. "A Chat with TW." *Era,* 9 Feb. 1895, p. 17.

3073a. FITZGERALD, WILLIAM G. "Side Shows V." *Strand,* Aug. 1897, pp. 91-97. [TW as mock strongman.]

3074. "TW in Africa." *Era,* 22 Apr. 1911, p. 25.

Zaeo

Acrobat and aerialist; (Mrs. Adelaide Wieland) b. Norwood, London, 31 Jan. 1866; d. London, 2 Apr. 1906.

3075. "The Making of Acrobats: an interview with Z." *Daily Graphic,* 13 Feb. 1892.

3076. S. R. *The Life of Z-Diva Dell, Aria: The Story of the Vigilance Persecution.* L: Universal Press Agency, 1891.

3077. "Shocking Accident to Z." *Illustrated Police News,* 8 Nov. 1879. [At Alexandra Palace.]

3078. "The Z Advertisement." *Era,* 24 May 1890, p. 15.

3079. "Z and her Major-domo." *Era,* 9 July 1892, p. 14; 16 July 1892, p.15; 30 July 1892, p. 15.

3080. "'Z' and 'The Era.'" *Era,* 25 Apr. 1891, p. 16; 29 Oct. 1892, p. 16.

3081. "Z at the Alexandra Palace." *Era,* 22 Dec. 1878, p. 5.

3082. "Z at the Aquarium." *Era,* 18 Jan. 1880, p. 4.

3083. "Z at the Canterbury." *Era,* 2 Feb. 1879, p. 7.

3084. "The Z Incident." *Era,* 14 Mar. 1891, p. 17; 28 Mar. 1891, p. 15. [About the advertisement.]

3084a. [Obit.: N.Y. *Dramatic Mirror,* 12 May 1906, p. 11.]

Zazel

Human cannonball; b. Rossa Matilda Richter, London, 14 Apr. 1862.
Secondary Materials

3085. "The Human Cannon Ball: Z." *Penny Illustrated Paper,* 7 Apr. 1877.

3086. O'CONNOR, T. P. "'Lulu' and 'Z'." *Sunday Times,* 12 Mar. 1922.

3087. "A Volley for Z." *Punch,* 12 May 1877, p. 216.

3088. "Z at the Aquarium." *Era,* 29 Apr. 1877, p. 4.

3089. "Z in a New Character." *Era,* 5 June 1879, p. 4. [Summonsed.]

3090. "Z in Court." *Era,* 20 Aug. 1881, p. 4; 2 Sept. 1881, p. 4.

3091. [Z's act] *Illustrated Sporting and Dramatic News* 7 (1877): 224.

3092. [Z's Career] *Truth* 5 (1879): 635.

X. PERFORMANCE MATERIAL

"At the Oxford later I collected two typical examples of music-hall ditties sung by Dan Crawley. The first had an idiotic but catching refrain of
   Ty-ump, ty-ump, ty-iddley-ump. Ty-um, ty-iddley-ay, and one verse ran thus:
   'E fired 'is bullet on the range,
   The bullet went astray,
   And shot the Sergeant-Major in
   'Is umpty-iddley-ay! (after which the refrain).
The second was sung in the character of an elderly female exulting hysterically in the prospect of her approaching wedding—
   I'm a-goin' to be married on Sunday!
(she informed us), and proceeded with a profusion of metaphor:
   As sure as I was born!
   There's another little bird a-going' to be caged,
   Another lot o'meat a-goin' to the butcher's,
   Another bit o'pickled pork a-goin' to be tied up,
   Next Sunday morn!
It was far from refined, but it was sung and danced with a delirious rapture that made it irresistibly funny."

F. Anstey (T. Anstey Guthrie) [writing in July 1907] *A Long Retrospect* (London and N.Y.: Oxford Unversity Press, 1936).

241

Anstey indicates the dilemma in examining music-hall material in cold print. On the page, lyrics and jokes usually seem flat, if not downright idiotic, unenlivened by the performer's skill and the jovial ambience that made them work on the stage. But examined with an eye to theme and structure, the songs can yield a good deal of information on the preoccupations and expectations of music-hall audiences. So far, however, Peter Davison's *Songs of the British Music Hall* has been the only book to analyze the songs in that regard, although there are many historical studies and collections.

The following section provides a sampling of the hundreds of song collections issued in the late nineteenth century; we have included those that are most obviously of relevance to the music-hall. In addition, there are enumerated the more accessible recent reissues of words-and-music, collections of prose material, and studies of British popular music. With this last, we have deemed it useful to include works dealing with composers, music-hall orchestras, and the illustrated sheet music covers which are frequently a prime source of portraiture of performers in costume.

CONTEMPORARY SONG COLLECTIONS

Cross-references

See also **631, 2146, 2241, 2279, 2313, 2485–89, 2638, 2695, 2709, 2891, 2893, 2948, 3020, 3046, 3515, 3560, 3618.**

[N.B. The songsters bearing names of performers include songs from other repertoires as well.]

3092a. *Allan's Illustrated Edition of Tyneside Songs and Readings.* Rev. ed. Newcastle: T & G. Allan, 1891.

3093. *Arthur Lloyd's Popular Comic Song Book containing Forty*

Comic Songs Sung by Himself and the Best Comic Singers. L: C. Sheard [n.d.].

3094. *Arthur Lloyd's Thirty New Comic Songs.* L: Charles Sheard [n.d.].

3095. *Beresford's Album of Popular Comic Songs.* L: [Beresford] 1891.

3096. *Bowerman's Sixpenny Pops in Progress.* L: Bowerman, 1908-18.

3097. *The Canterbury Mogul Songster: A Collection of Favourite Songs.* L [1892].

3098. *The Coal-hole Companion. A Collection of the Most Rummy Songs and Funny Staves Now Singing with Great Applause at the Coal-hole, Cider Cellars, Garrick, etc.* [L] H. Smith [n.d.].

3099. *The Comic and Sentimental Music Hall Song Book.* [L: 1862.]

3100. [*Comic Songs, 1879-90.* Collection at the British Library.]

3101. *The Comic Songster Illustrated, containing the Most Popular Songs of the Day Sung by Cowell, Mackney and Others at the Principal Music Halls, etc. in London.* Glasgow: Printed for the Book-sellers [c. 1860].

3102. *The Concert-Room Songbook.* L: T. Good [n.d.].

3103. D'ALCORN, H. *New Popular and Standard Comic Songs.* L: D'Alcorn, 1865.

3104. *Dan Leno's Songster.* L: W. S. Fortey, 1897.

3105. DIPROSE, JOHN. *The Best Songs Out: Diprose's New Music-Hall Song Book.* L: Diprose, 1865.

3106. *Diprose's Music-hall Song Book.* L: J. Diprose, 1862.

3107. *Diprose's New Music-hall Song Book.* L: J. Diprose, 1865.

3108. *Diprose's New Standard Song Book.* L: J. Diprose, 1877.

3109. *Evans's Music and Supper Rooms, Covent Garden. Selections and words of Madrigals, Glees, Choruses, Songs, &c. Sung Every Evening in the above Supper Rooms, Commencing at Eight o'Clock Precisely. . . .* [L] Barth [1867?].

3110. *Evans's Supper & Music Rooms. Vocalists . . . and All the Best Available Comic Talent. (Odds and Ends about Covent Garden. Glees, Madrigals, Choruses, Part Songs, &c. Sung Nightly in Evan's Supper and Music Rooms.)* [L: J. Green, 1866.]

3111. *Feldman's First Comic Annual, with tonic sol-fa setting.* L: B. Feldman, 1895. [*Charles Deane:* All in a row; K-N-O-W-I-N-G; We Sang a Song; Four Englishmen in Paree; To Your Girl, My Girl; *Walter Kino:* Down Rotten Row; Um-ta-ra-ra; *Maggie Duggan:* Give it a Wink; *Jenny Valmore:* He's Single, He's Married; *George Robey:* Kindly Note the Change in his Address; *Martin Adeson:* I Never Enjoyed Myself So Much Before; *T. E. Dun-*

ville: Remedies; *Arthur Lennard:* After the Show; *Rose Hamilton:* Nod Your Head; *Harry Anderson:* Lap, Lap, Lap; *Everybody:* Rose Marie.]

3112. *Feldman's Second Comic Annual.* . . . L: B. Feldman, 1896. [*Julie Mackay:* Say Au-revoir, but Not Good-bye; *Harry Champion:* We've Been Having a Go at It; *George Beauchamp:* They're All Getting It Up for Me; *Fred Earle:* His Room's to Let; *Maggie Duggan:* All Together; Making the Time Fly; *T. E. Dunville:* Babies; *Vesta Tilley:* Love's Language; *Harry Freeman:* That's All-Rum-fum-foozle-um; *R. G. Knowles:* Not Me; *Charles Deane:* All the Way; Now We Shan't Be Long; *Fred J. Little:* Bekase I'se Always Laffin'; *Rose Dearing and Ada Willoughby:* I've Only Just Come Up to London; *Walter Kino:* Oh! Jemima Mary Jane!; *Arthur Lennard:* Little Rosie Dean; *Eugene Stratton:* Thousand Yards in Rear; *Ted Cowan:* Lost, Stolen or Strayed; *Sadie Jerome:* Mammy's Baby Coon.]

3113. *Feldman's Third Comic Annual.* . . . L: B. Feldman, 1897. [*George Beauchamp:* I'm the Little Bit of Sweetstuff; *Clifford Essex and Ethel Sidney:* De Same Ole Moon am Shinin'; *Frank Seeley:* Father's Got 'em; *George Robey:* They Haven't Spoken Since; *Harry Champion:* We've All Been Having a Go at It; *Will Edwards and Edward Kent:* My Stars!; *Daisy Wood and Marie Lloyd:* Not for the Best Man Breathing; *Julie Mackay:* Her Memory Brings Me No Regret; *Harry Bedford:* On the March; *Charles Deane:* The Elephant and the Castle; Then We Went; *Harriet Vernon:* Tick Tock or Lady Telegraph Clerk; *Jenny Valmore:* Wrapped in the Evening News; *Will Johnson:* Don't Come Near Me; *Walter Kino:* Give It a Miss in Baulk; *Ada Willoughby:* To Improve Her Education; *Harry Jackson:* I'm Painting 'em; *F. V. St. Clair:* Busy; *Marie Montrose:* When De Lights Am All Turned Down; *Arthur Pearl:* They're All Coming Round.]

3114. *Feldman's Fourth Comic Annual.* . . . L: B. Feldman, 1898. [*Vesta Tilley:* For the Week End; *Harry Hampton;* The Oofless Duke; Love's Language; *Harry Bedford:* Cooking the Cock of the North; Jemima at Waterloo; *Clifford Essex and Ethel Sidney:* De Same Ole Moon Am Shinin'; *George Beauchamp:* Trying It On; *Charles Deane:* All Along the Rails; — *and Katie Lawrence:* The All-night Tram; *George Robey:* A Worm's Eye View; Draw Your Own Conclusions; There's Never Any Holding Me; *Frank Seeley:* It Will Save Cooking the Canary; *The Sisters Lloyd;* Come Down and Open the Door; *Lawrence Barclay:* Look What She's Done for Willie!; *Julie Mackay:* Stories Mother Told Me;

Honey, Spend Your Honeymoon with Me; *Fred Sinclair:* Found
Out the Difference Then; *Joe Archer:* Let 'em All Come.]

3115. *Feldman's Fifth Comic Annual. . . .* L: B. Feldman, 1899.
[*Bessie Wentworth, Herbert Shelley & others:* Smoke, Smoke; or,
Framed in Oak; Rudyard Kipling's the Absent Minded Beggar;
Ernest Shand: The Wide World; *The Japs:* Sweeter dan de Sugar
from de Cane; *Charles Deane:* All along the Rails; *Frank Coyne:*
You'd Better Come Down at Once; *Vesta Tilley:* Moonlight
Blossom; *Wilkie Bard:* Can't You Go Further than That?;
George Beauchamp: Here We Are Again; *Katie Lawrence:*
Humpy-umpy-ay; *Herbert Shelley:* Why, Boys, Why?;
Anonymous: Our Brave Soldier Lads; *T. E. Dunville:* There Must
Be Another One Somewhere; *The Two Bees, Harry & Flora
Blake, &c.:* Who Dares to Say?; *George Beauchamp:* All on the
Fidgety Fudge; *Victoria Monk:* As Big Ben Strikes; *Harry Champion:* Right on my Doo-dah; *Reddick Anderson:* In the Navy;
Edward Kent: The Stuttering Man and the Cuckoo Clock; *F. V.
St. Clair:* What Ho, She Bumps.]

3116. *Feldman's Sixth Comic Annual. . . .* L: B. Feldman, 1900. [*Vesta
Tilley:* Love or Gold; Scotch and Polly; That's Pa; *Julie Mackay:*
You'll Be with Me All the While; There's Only Two People on
Earth; *Albert Christian:* Commissionaire; *Herbert Shelley,
Arthur Lennard & Others:* Smoke, Smoke, Smoke; or, Framed in
Oak; *Lelia Roze:* Away in Ohio; *Frank Coyne:* Tonight's the
Night; *George Beauchamp:* I'd Do the Same for You; There's
Hair!; *Venie Belfry:* Sweet Maggie McGee; *Arthur Lennard:*
While I Am with You; *Ernest Shand:* Very Much Attached to Me;
Often Heard the Tale Before; *Carrie Scott:* I Wouldn't Leave Ma
Happy Home; *Edward Kent:* I'll Be with You Presently; The
Wireless Telegraphy; *Herbert Shelley:* Boys of the Fleet; *Gwennie
Hasto:* The March I Love.]

3117. *Feldman's Seventh Comic Annual. . . .* L: B. Feldman, 1901.
[*Julie Mackay:* Juliana; Her Name is Rose; Why Can't It Be
Always Christmas?; *James Norris, Florrie Forde & Others:* A
Bird in a Gilded Cage; *Frank Coyne:* Let's Go Round There
Now; Oh! That Top Hat; *Vesta Tilley:* The Naval Bazaar; *Wilkie
Bard:* You Have Been Busy; *Maude Mortimer:* You Can't Buy
Love; *Harry Anderson:* Top of the Class; *Ada Blanche:* My Little
Picture Book; *Ernest Heathcote:* Wall Flowers; *Lottie Collins:*
Coronation Song; *Ernest D'Almaine:* Soldiers of the King; *Millie
Hylton:* Sister Martha's Birthday; *Annette Fengler:* Love's
Sweetest Question; *Julie Mackay & Evie Greene:* She's Only a
Poor Little Factory Girl; *George Lashwood:* It's a Fing I Never

Interfere Wiv; *Jessie Preston:* Boom with a Ra-ta-ta.]
3118. *Feldman's Eighth Comic Annual.* . . . L: B. Feldman, 1902.
[*Vesta Tilley:* Sweethearts Still; *Frederic Norton & Others:* Oh!
Mr. Moon; *Herbert Shelley:* As I Dream; *Alec Hurley:* All Pals
Together; Thick-ear'd Jim; *Florrie Forde & Julie Mackay:* On a
Sunday Afternoon; *Julie Mackay:* Why Won't Yer Let Me Kiss
Yer?; *Florrie Forde:* Day by Day; *Sam Mayo:* Oh! Oh! Oh! Oh!
Oh! We All Jumped Out of Bed: *F. V. St. Clair & Others:* John
Bull's Telephone; *Richard Temple:* Rose! Rose! Rose!; *Herbert
Betts:* All of a Dither'em; *John F. McArdle & Others:* Jane!;
George Bastow: She's a Dear Old Girl; *T. C. Callaghan:*
1,2,3,4,5,6,7,8 Funny Little Kids; *Ernest Shand:* He Put the Idea
in My Head; *Arthur Rigby:* Eighteen; *Harry Champion;* It Makes
Me Go All Goosey.]
3119. *Feldman's Ninth Comic Annual.* . . . L: B. Feldman, 1903. [*The
Two Bees (Harry and Flora Blake):* Hiawatha; *Vesta Tilley:* The
Anglo Saxon Language; Midnight Son's Farewell; *Wilkie Bard:*
O! O! Capital O!; They've All Got Sticky Backs; *Victoria Monks:*
You'll Have to Read Your Answer in the Stars; *Alec Hurley:* All
Pals Together (New Version); *Florrie Forde:* The Mansion of
Aching Hearts; A Picture No Artist Can Paint; *Julie Mackay:* In
the Sweet Bye-and-bye; Ma Little Honey Blossom; *Minnie Cunn-
ingham:* The Little Bit of Cloth We Love; *Hal Chapter:* Oh! Turn
Your Eyes Away; *Lily Morris:* That's Why I Love You; *Fifi Gor-
don:* Creole Belles; *Harry Mansfield:* She Need Not Have a Pretty
Face; *Maude Mortimer:* English Nell; *Queenie Leighton:* Col-
oured Angels.]
3120. *Feldman's Tenth Comic Annual.* . . . L: B. Feldman, 1904.
[*Florrie Forde:* Down at the Old Bull and Bush; Don't Fly Away,
Robin; England is England Still; *Winifred Hare and Florrie
Forde:* Anona; *Victoria Monks:* Brown Eyes, or Eyes of Blue;
Everybody: The Gondolier; *Harry Champion:* I was Out in Half
a Tick, or T.I.E.I.A.; Ping Pong; *Lawrence Barclay:* Pull and
Push; *Frank Seeley:* I Took It Home to Maria; *Mrs. Paul Knox:*
My East End Girl; *Bessie Featherstone:* The Latest London Bet-
ting; *Florrie Cooper:* Right at the Top; *Vesta Tilley:* When the
Early Morning Sun Comes in; *Julie Mackay:* While You're in
Love With Me; *Arthur Lennard:* The Chirp of the London Spar-
row; *George Robey:* Solid, Substantial and Thick; *Gus Elen:* The
Cabby: *Tom Leamore:* Gallant Deeds, or Heroes; *Ernest Shand;*
The Waiter.] [At least thirty-nine of these annuals can be traced.]
3121. *Forty of Harry Clifton's Comic Songs.* L: Charles Sheard [n.d.].

3122. *Forty of W. Randall's Gems of Comic Songs.* L: Charles Sheard [n.d.].

3123. *Francis and Day's British War Songs.* L: Francis, Day & Hunter, 1900.

3124. *Francis and Day's Comic Song Annual.* L: Francis, Day & Hunter, 1880. [At least forty-six of these annuals, 1880-1927, can be traced.]

3125. *Francis & Day's 1st Banjo Comic Annual with Tonic Sol-fa Setting.* L: Francis Day & Hunter [1891]. [Ten of these annuals in all, 1891-1901.]

3126. *Harry Lauder's Song Selection.* L: Francis, Day & Hunter [n.d.].

3127. *Harry Liston's Comic Song Book, containing Forty New and Popular Comic Songs, with All the Music and Words.* L: Charles Sheard [n.d.].

3128. HATTON, J. L. *A Collection of Humorous Songs.* L: 1875.

3129. *Hopwood & Crew's Comic Album.* L: Hopwood & Crew [n.d.]. [Twelve in all.]

3130. *Howard & Co's First Comic Annual.* L: Howard & Co., 1892. [Thirteen in all, 1892-1903.]

3131. HUNT, G. W. [Songs 1875-89. Collection at the British Library.]

3132. *The Imperial Comic Song Book.* L: 1877.

3133. *Leslie Stuart's Most Famous Songs.* L: Francis, Day & Hunter, 1898, 1914. [Lily of Laguna; My Little Octoroon; Little Dolly Daydream (Pride of Idaho); Tell Me, Pretty Maiden; "Is Yer Mammie Always with Ye?"; The Shade of the Palm; Sweetheart May; I May Be Crazy, but I Love You; The Soldiers of the King.]

3134. *Leslie Stuart's Song Album.* L: Francis, Day & Hunter, n.d.

3135. *Macdermott's Comic Song Album.* L: 1891-92.

3136. *Mackney's New Comic Song Book.* L: Charles Sheard [n.d.].

3137. McGLENNON, FELIX. *The Home Songster.* L: McGlennon [n.d.].

3138. ———. *McGlennon's Song Book No. 105.* L: McGlennon, 1896-97.

3139. ———. *McGlennon's Star Song Book.* Manchester: McGlennon, 1888. [Ten of these in all, 1888-1909.]

3140. ———. *The Modern Ballad Songster.* L: McGlennon [n.d.].

3141. *Metzler and Co's First Comic Song Book.* L: Metzler and Co., 1876.

3142. *Metzler and Co's Second Comic Song Book.* L: Metzler and Co., 1877.

3143. *The Music Hall Comic Song Book.* L: 1862. [Another issuing of pp. 37-72 of *Popular and Modern Songs. The Prince of Wales'*

Own Song Book.]

3144. *Music Hall Song Book. The Comic and Sentimental Music Hall Song Book.* L: 1862.

3145. *The Music Hall Songster, containing a Selection of the Latest Songs Now being Sung.* L: W. S. Fortey, 1893.

3146. *One Hundred Popular Comic Songs.* L: Charles Sheard [n.d.].

3147. *The Peg-top Trousers' Popular Songster.* L: R. Macdonald [n.d.].

3148. *The Perfect Cure's Comic Songs. Containing Forty-one of Mackney's, Stead's, Sam Collins' & Sam Cowell's Best Songs with Symphonies and Accompaniments for the Pianoforte.* L: Charles Sheard [c. 1860.].

3149. *Popular Comic Songs in Sixpenny Books.* L: C. Sheard, n.d. [60 of Sam Cowell's Selected Comic Songs; 55 of the Perfect Cure's Comic Songs; 30 of George Ford's Dialogue and Patter Songs; 40 of W. Randall's Gems of Comic Songs; 40 of Vance's Comic Songs; 40 of Arthur Lloyd's Comic Songs; 40 of Albert Steel's Comic Songs; 40 of Harry Clifton's Comic Songs; 40 of Lingard's Comic Songs; 40 of Leybourne's Comic Songs; 40 of Harry Liston's Comic Songs; 40 of Fred French's Comic Songs; 40 of Sam Collin's Irish Comic Songs; 40 of the Jolly Nash's Comic Songs; Champagne Charlie's 43 New Copyright Comic Songs; "Not for Joseph" Copyright Comic Song Book, containing 43 of the newest and best, several Ladies' serio-comic songs and motto songs.]

3150. PREST, THOMAS PECKETT, ed. *The Singer's Penny Magazine, and Reciter's Album: A Superior Collection of All the Most New and Popular Songs, Duets, Glees, Trios, Catches and Recitations, Comic, Sentimental, Bacchanalian, Sporting, Amatory, English, Irish and Scotch: with Many Excellent Original Productions.* 2 vols. L: G. Drake, 1835.

3151. *The Prize Comic Songster.* L: 1879.

3152. *Reeder and Walsh's Comic Annual.* L: Reeder & Walsh, 1897. [Twelve in all, 1897-1908.]

3153. *Sam Cowell's Comic Songster.* L: Charles Sheard [c. 1860].

3154. *Sam Cowell's New Universal Illustrated Pocket Songster. Containing All the Popular Songs.* 6 vols. L: W. Barker [c. 1860].

3155. *The Sam Hall Songster. The Most Unique Collection of Laughter, Moving, Soul-stirring Songs Ever Presented to the Human Eye.* L: E. Hewitt [c. 1855] [Fifteen series announced.]

3156. *Sheard's Comic Annual.* L: Charles Sheard, 1877. [Three in all, 1877-79.]

3157. *Sheard's First Banjo Album.* L: Charles Sheard, 1892. [Ten in all, 1892-1902.]

3158. SLOMAN, CHARLES, ed. *The Social Vocalist, containing upwards of Five Hundred Songs.* L: J. Diprose, 1842. [Without music.]

3159. *Ta-Ra-Ra-Boom-De-E Songster.* L: W. S. Fortey [1893].

3160. *Vance's Comic Song Book. Containing Forty Popular Songs, Music and Words, sung by all the Best Comic Singers.* L: C. Sheard [n.d.].

3161. *Vance's Thirty New Comic Songs.* L: Charles Sheard [n.d.].

3162. WILSON, JOE. *Tyneside Songs and Drolleries, Readings and Temperance Songs.* Newcastle: T. and G. Allen [1890?]. [With "Life of Joe Wilson," by W. H. Dawson.]

SONG-BOOKS AND COLLECTIONS ISSUED LATER THAN THE ORIGINAL PERFORMANCES

Cross-references

See also **2639, 3375, 3509.**

3167. ANSTEY, F. [pseud. of Thomas Anstey Guthrie]. *Mr Punch's Model Music-hall Songs & Dramas, Collected, Improved and Rearranged from "Punch."* L: Bradbury, Agnew, 1892. [Ills. Bernard Partridge]. Repr. as *The Young Reciter and Model Music Hall,* new and revised ed. L: Methuen, 1931. [Parodies.] [Letter claiming plagiarism by Richard Morton, *Era,* 18 July 1892, p. 15. First appeared in *Punch* under various rubrics: "Mr Punch's Moral Music-Hall Dramas, " "Mr Punch's Model Music-Hall Songs," and "Music-hall Inanities," 3 Aug. 1889, p. 49; 17 Aug. 1889, p. 84; 14 Dec. 1889, p. 281; 21 Dec. 1889, p. 292; 4 Jan. 1899, p. 6; 8 Feb. 1899, p. 66, etc.]

3164. DAVISON, PETER. *Songs of the British Music Hall.* L: Music

Sales; N.Y.: Oak pub., 1971. [Compiled and ed. Peter Davison with a critical history of the songs and their times. A Little Bit of Cucumber; A Motto for Every Man; A Thing He Had Never Done Before; And Her Golden Hair Was Hanging Down Her Back; Are We to Part Like This Bill?; 'Arf a Pint of Ale; At My Time of Life; Bang Went the Chance of a Lifetime; Champagne Charlie; Cushie Butterfield; Don't Go Out To-night, Dear Father; Every Little Movement; Following in Father's Footsteps; Half-past Nine or My Wedding Day; Have You Paid the Rent?; Heaven will Protect an Honest Girl; He's Going to Marry Mary Ann; His Lordship Winked at the Counsel; I Live in Trafalgar Square; If It Wasn't for the 'ouses in Between; It's Alright in the Summertime; I've Got Rings on My Fingers; I've Never Lost My Last Train Yet; "Jeerusalem's" Dead!; Keep Your Feet Still, Geordie Hinney; Lily of Laguna; My Fiddle Is My Sweetheart; My Fiddle Was My Sweetheart; Nanny; One of the Deathless Army; Penny Whistler; Prehistoric Man; Sam Hall; Seaweed; That's the Reason Noo I Wear a Kilt; The Fire Was Burning Hot; The Future Mrs. 'Awkins; The Huntsman; The Man Was a Stranger to Me; The Music-hall Shakespeare; The Swimming Master; Villikins and his Dinah; Waiting at the Church; We All to go to work but Father; We All Went Home in a Cab; When I Take My Morning Promenade; Wor Nanny's a mazer; Wotcher 'Ria; Young Men Taken in and Done for; You've Got a Long Way to Go.]

3165. *Feldman's Album of Song Memories.* L: B. Feldman, 1957. [Nos. 1-16.]

3166. *Feldman's Old Time Variety Song Album.* L: B. Feldman, 1954. [No.1.]

3167. *Feldman's Old Time Variety Song Album. N. 2.* L: B. Feldman, 1954. [Horsey, Keep Your Tail Up; If the Managers only thought the same as Mother; Dance with your Uncle Joseph; My Wife's Gone to the Country; From Poverty Street to Golden Square; I Don't Care What Becomes of Me; Watching the Trains Come in.]

3168. *Feldman's Old Time Variety Song Album No. 3.* L: B. Feldman, 1954. [All the Girls are Lovely by the Seaside; Hold Your Hand out!; Come over the Garden Wall; I Put on My Coat and Went Home; Somebody Else; Shufflin' Along; The Ship I Love; Sing Us a Song of Bonnie Scotland.]

3169. *Feldman's Old Time Variety Song Album No. 4.* L: B. Feldman, 1955. [The Pretty Little Girl from 'Nowhere'; She Told Me to Meet Her at the Gate; Wonder if the Girl I'm Thinking of Is Thinking of Me; Come in and Cut Yourself a Piece of Cake; Liza

Had Hold of My Hand; When Life's Sun is Setting; What a
Game It Is! Wow! Wow!; I Like Your Old French Bonnet.]
3170. *Francis & Day's Album of Famous Old Songs No. 1.* L: Francis,
Day & Hunter [n.d.]. [Across the Bridge; Father's Whiskers; The
Hobnailed Boots that Farver wore; Hold Your Hand Out,
Naughty Boy! I like your Toon; I Live in Trafalgar Square; The
Seventh Royal Fusiliers; Viewing the Baby.]
3171. *Francis & Day's Album of Famous Old Songs N. 2.* L: Francis,
Day & Hunter [n.d.]. [The Baby's Name; The Coon Drum-
Major; He's Been a Long Time Gorn; If the Missis Wants to Go
or Let her Drown; Kitty the Telephone Girl; Sister Susie's Sewing
Shirts for Soldiers; Somebody Would Shout out "Shop!"; That's
What God Made Mothers for.]
3172. *Francis & Day's Album of Famous Old Songs No. 3.* L: Francis,
Day & Hunter [n.d.]. [Nursie-Nursie; It's Nice to Have a Home
of Your Own; I Do Like an Egg for My Tea; It's All Right in the
Summer-time; Oh! Jack You are a Handy Man; On a Sunday
Afternoon; She Pushed Me into the Parlour; I Want to be a
Military Man.]
3173. *Francis & Day's Album of Famous Old Songs. No. 4.* L: Francis,
Day & Hunter [n.d.] [Gilbert the Filbert; What I want Is a Proper
Cup o'Coffee; Boys of the Chelsea school; Seaside Posters
Round the Home; He's Going There Every Night; A Boy's Best
Friend Is his Mother; Good Morning, Mr. Postman; Every Thing
in the Garden's Lovely.]
3174. *Francis & Day's Album of Famous Old Songs. No. 5.* L: Francis,
Day & Hunter [n.d.]. [Ta-ra-ra Boom-de-ay; Where did you get
that Hat; A Little Bit off the Top; If it Wasn't for the 'ouses In
Between; In the Twi-twi-twilight; Glorious Beer; If Those Lips
Could Only Speak; We All Go the Same Way Home.]
3175. *Francis & Day's Album of Famous Old Songs. No. 6.* L: Francis,
Day & Hunter [n.d.]. [Daddy Wouldn't Buy Me a Bow-wow!;
Following in Father's Footsteps; The Galloping Major; In the
Shade of the Old Apple Tree; I Wouldn't Leave my Little
Wooden Hut for You!; She was One of the Early Birds; Skylark!
Skylark!; Waiting at the Church.]
3176. *Francis & Day's Album of Famous Old Songs. No. 7.* L: Francis,
Day & Hunter [n.d.]. [Our Lodger's Such a Nice Young Man;
Young Men Taken in and Done for; Twiggy Vous; At My Time
o'Life; Why Did I Leave My Little Back Room?; Her Golden
Hair was Hanging Down Her Back; I Used to Sigh for the Silvery
Moon; Has Anybody Here Seen Kelly?]
3177. *Francis & Day's Album of Famous Old Songs. No. 8.* L: Francis,

Day & Hunter [n.d.]. [Put on Your Ta-ta, Little Girlie; I'm Henery the Eighth, I am!; Joshu-ah!; I'm Shy, Mary Ellen, I'm Shy; Every Little While; When Father Papered the Parlour; I Want to Sing in Opera; My Girl's a Yorkshire Girl.]

3178. *Francis & Day's Album of Famous Old Songs. No. 9.* L: Francis, Day & Hunter [n.d.]. [Oh! oh! Antonio; Darling Mabel; Golden Wedding; I Was a Good Little Girl Till I Met You; Here We Are, Here We Are, Here We Are Again; A Little of What You Fancy Does You Good; Billy Muggins; Down the Road.]

3179. *Francis & Day's Album of Famous Old Songs. No. 10.* L: Francis, Day & Hunter [n.d.]. [Now I Have to Call him Father; Ginger, You're Balmy; Poor John; Flanagan; He'd Have to Get Under, Get out and Get under; She Sells Sea Shells; I've Got Rings on My fingers; Waiting for the Robert E. Lee.]

3180. *Francis & Day's Album of Famous Old Songs. No. 11.* L: Francis, Day & Hunter [n.d.]. [Archibald, Certainly Not; The Gipsy Warned Me; I Parted My Hair in the Middle; It's a Different Girl Again; Jolly Good Luck to the Girl Who Loves a Soldier; On the Good Ship Yacki-Hicki-Doo-la; On the Road to Anywhere; She Cost me Seven and Sixpence.]

3181. *Francis & Day's Album of Famous Old Songs. No. 12.* L: Francis, Day & Hunter [n.d.]. [K-K-Katy; Seaweed; Captain Ginjah, O.T.; John Willie, Come on; The Army of Today's All Right; Hello! Suzy Green; Vot a game! Oi! oi!; Varmer Giles; Pansy Faces.]

3182. FREMONT, ROBERT A., ed. *Favorite Songs of the Nineties.* N.Y.: Dover books 1973.

3183. GAMMOND, PETER, ed. *Best Music Hall and Variety Songs.* L: Wolfe, 1972. [Songs written or sung by Arthur Askey, H. M. Burnaby, Albert Chevalier, George Grossmith, Tommy Handley, Leslie Henson, A. P. Herbert, Norman Long, Ernest Longstaffe, Greatrex Newman, Ralph Reader, Fred Rome, Nellie Wallace, The Western brothers, and many others.]
Rev. L. Senelick, *Educational Theatre Journal,* Oct. 1975, pp. 433-34.

3184. ———, ed. *Music hall Song Book: a Collection of 45 of the Best Songs from 1890-1920.* Newton Abbot: David & Charles; L: EMI Music pub., 1975. [Ask a P'liceman; Where Did You Get That Hat?; Wot Cher!; The Man Who Broke the Bank at Monte Carlo; Daddy Wouldn't Buy Me a Bow-wow; Daisy Bell; Ta-ra-ra-boom-de-ay!; My old Dutch; After the Ball; If it Wasn't for the 'ouses in Between; Her Golden Hair Was Hanging down her Back; It's A Great Big Shame; My Fiddle is my Sweetheart; At

My Time of Life; Lucky Jim; A Bird in a Gilded Cage; Goodbye, Dolly Gray; Following in Father's Footsteps; I Live in Trafalgar Square; Down at the Old Bull & Bush; I Love a Lassie; The Galloping Major; Waiting at the Church; Poor John; Jolly Good Luck to the Girl Who Loves a Soldier; Swing Me Higher, Obadiah; She Sells Seashells; When Father Papered the Parlour; If I Should Plant a Tiny Seed of Love; I Do Like to Be Beside the Seaside; Ship Ahoy!; I'm Henery the Eighth; Put on Your Ta-ta, Little Girlie; I'm Shy, Mary Ellen, I'm Shy; Come, Josephine, in My Flying Machine; Roamin' in the Gloamin'; The Spaniard that Blighted My Life; Oh, You Beautiful Doll; It's a Long Way to Tipperary; Hello! Hello! Who's your Lady Friend?; A Little of What You Fancy Does You Good; Joshuah; If You Were the Only Girl in the World; On the Good Ship Yacki-Hicki-Doo-la; Don't Dilly Dally on the Way.]

3185. GARRETT, JOHN M. *Sixty Years of British Music Hall.* L: Chappell, 1976. Rev. Peter Keating, *TLS*, 25 Feb. 1977, p. 217. [Bacon and Greens; Hop Light Loo; Polly Perkins of Paddington Green; Ticket of Leave Man; Slap bang, Here We Are Again; Up in a Balloon; Fashionable Fred; Brown the Tragedian; The Rustic Damsel; Captain Cuff; Dear Old Pals; Little Miss Muffet Sat on a Tuffett; Tuner's Oppor-tuner-ty; The Bulls Won't Bellow; In My Fust 'usband's Time; Up Went the Price; Baa Baa Baa; She Does the Fandango All Over the Place; The House that Jerry Built; What Cheer Ria; The Boy in the Gallery; The Funny Things They Do upon the Sly; Angels without Wings; Ti! Hi! Tiddelly Hi!; Buy Me Some Almond Rock; Oh! Mr. Porter; So Her Sister Says; Catch 'em Alive oh!; That Gorgonzola Cheese; Slight Mistake on the Part of my Valet; The Bobbies of the Queen; On the Day King Edward Gets His Crown on; An Old Man's Darling; Beautiful Dora; She's So Sweet (Sweet, Sweet, Sweet).]

3186. GRAHAM, FRANK, ed. *Joe Wilson Sings.* Newcastle: Graham, 1971.

3187. KEEPING, CHARLES. *Cockney Ding Dong.* Harmondsworth: Kestrel books; L: EMI Music pub, 1975. [The Hobnailed Boots that Farver Wore; What a Mouth!; The Golden Dustman; 'Alf a Pint of Ale; Down the Road; My London Country Lane; It's a Great Big Shame; Wot's the Good of Hanyfink! Why! Nuffink!; When the Old Dun Cow Caught Fire; The D.C.M.; If it Wasn't for the 'ouses in Between; In the Shade of the Old Apple Tree; They're Moving Father's Grave to Build a Sewer; Wot Cher!; Where Did You Get that Hat?; They're All Very Fine and Large;

On Monday I Never Go to Work; I'm Henery the Eighth I am!; Sing me to Sleep; Boiled Beef and Carrots; A Comical Cock; The Moon Shines Tonight on Charlie Chaplin; The Amateur White-washer; I'm a Navvy; Feeding the Ducks on the Pond; When I Went for a Soldier; Liza, you are a Lady; Liza, It's a Beautiful Starry Night; Liza Johnston; If Those Lips Could Only Speak; That's Where My Love Lies Dreaming; The Sunshine of Your Smile; Sons of the Sea; Granny; When the Summer Comes Again; Whilst the Dance Goes on; Jeerusalem's Dead!; Silver Bells; The Coster's Linnet; My old Dutch; I Speak the Truth; The Song of the Thrush; A Sailor's Song; The Blind Boy; The Blind Irish Girl; Pal of My Cradle Days; For I'm Not Coming Home; That's What God Made Mothers for; As Your Hair Grows Whiter; Knees up Mother Brown!; Any Old Iron?; Don't Dilly Dally on the Way; The Cokey Cokey; I've Got a Lovely Bunch of Coconuts; When There Isn't a Girl about; I Do Like to Be Beside the Seaside; Green Gravel; Chase Me Charley; The Naughty Sparrow; Pack Up Your Troubles in Your Old Kit-bag; Little Town in My Ould County Down; It's a Long Long Way to Tip-perary; Mademoiselle from Armentieres; Two Lovely Black Eyes; Maybe It's Because I'm a Londoner; Glorious beer; Come Inside, Yer Silly Bugger; We All Came in the World with Nothing; We All Go the Same Way Home; Fall in and Follow me; Memories.]

3188. *Music Hall Memories. (The Masterpieces of Variety.)* 2 vols. L: Amalgamated press, 1935. [Vol. 1: A Little Bit Off the Top; Ask a P'liceman; At Trinity Church I Met My Doom; Blind Boy; Coal-black Mammy; Comrades; The Corsican Maid; Daddy Wouldn't Buy Me a Bow-wow; Down the Road; Follow the Foot-prints in the Snow; Following in Father's Footsteps; For Old Time's Sake; Gilbert the Filbert; Ginger, You're Balmy!; The Good Old Annual; Has Anybody Here Seen Kelly?; Here We are! Here We are! Here We are Again!!; Hi-Tiddley-Hi-Ti; Hitchy Koo; Hold Your Hand Out, Naughty Boy; The Honeysuckle and the Bee; I May Be Crazy, But I Love You; If Winter Comes; I'm Afraid to Come Home in the Dark; I'm Henery the Eighth, I Am; I'm the Plumber; I'm Tickled to Death, I'm Single; I'se A-waiting for Yer, Josie; I Shall Get in Such a Row When Martha Knows; It's Nice To Get up in the Morning; I've Got My Eye on You; I've Got Rings on My Fingers; I want to Go to Idaho; I Want to Sing in Opera; I Was A Good Little Girl till I Met You; John Willie, Come on; Jolly Good Luck to the Girl Who Loves a Soldier; Just Like the Ivy I'll Cling to You; The Lambeth Walk; Let Her Drown; Let's All Go down the Strand; The Lily of

Laguna; Looking for a Coon like Me; Memories; My Fiddle is My Sweetheart; My Little Octoroon; Now We Are *All* Here? Yes!; On the Road to Anywhere; One Hour of Love with You; Our Lodger's Such a Nice Young Man; Pack up your Troubles; The Roses Have Made me Remember; The Shade of the Palm; Shadowland; Somebody would Shout out 'Shop!'; The Spaniard That Blighted My Life; Ta-ra-ra-Boom-de-ay; That's What God Made Mothers For; There They Are—The Two of 'Em, on Their Own; There's a Friend in Every Milestone; There's a Little Black Cupid in the Moon; They're All Very Fine and Large; Ting, Ting, That's How the Bell Goes; Two Little Girls in Blue; Two Lovely Black Eyes; We All Go the Same Way Home; What Ho! She Bumps!; When Father Papered the Parlour; Where Did You Get that Hat?; Young Men Taken In and Done For. Vol. 2: After You with That; All over the Shop; And the Parrot said—; Archibald, Certainly Not!; Awake!; Be a Man!; Bluebell; Boys of the Chelsea School; Brighton; Casey Jones; Cigarette; Daisy Bell; Flanagan; For Months and Months and Months; The Ghost of Benjamin Binns; He's Going to Marry Mary Ann; Hi Diddle Diddle Um; How's Your Father?; I Belong to Glasgow; I Can't Change It; I Do Love Myself Don't I; I Shall Sleep Well To-night; I Used to Sigh for the Silvery Moon; If It Wasn't for the 'Ouses in between; I'll Make a Man of You; I'm a Little Too Young to Know; I'm Setting the Village on Fire; I'm Shy, Mary Ellen, I'm Shy; In the Shade of the Old Apple Tree; Is Your Mother in, Molly Malone?; It's a Great Big Shame; It's Nice to Have a Home of Your Own; I've Got the Ooperzootic; Leettle Mister Baggy Breeches; Let Go, Eliza; Little Annie Rooney; Little Dolly Daydream; Make Me the King of Your Heart; The Man Who Broke the Bank at Monte Carlo; The Miner's Dream of Home; Molly Molyneux; Never Mind; Now We Shan't Be Long; Oh, Jack! You Are a Handy Man; Old Chap; On Mother Kelly's Doorstep; Our Threepenny Hop; Pansy Faces; The Preacher and the Bear; The Rest of the Day's Your Own; The Scientific Man; The Seventh Royal Fusiliers; Skylark; The Soldiers of the King; The Story of a Tin-tack; Tell Me, Pretty Maiden; That was the End of My Dream; Then We Had Another One; There's a Girl Wanted There; Too-ral-i-oo-rall-i-ay; Topsy-Turvy; Twiggy Voo?; Waiting for the Robert E. Lee; What Is the Use of Loving a Girl; When the Summer Comes Again; When They Ask You What Your Name Is; When You Are Near; Where There's a Girl There's a Boy; Why Did I Leave My Little Back Room?; You Made Me Love You.

255

3189. "O Did You Twig her Ancle?" *Punch's Almanack for 1864.* L: Bradbury & Evans, 1864. [Parody of typical music-hall chorus song.]

3190. PRENTIS, TERENCE, ed. *Music-hall Memories.* L: Selwyn & Blount [1927]. [Ills. Elizabeth Pyke. Foreword by Sir Harry Lauder. No music included; lyrics often incomplete. Mr. Spriggs, the Grocer; Her Mother's at the Bottom of It All; They Ain't No Class; It's the Seasoning Wot Does It; Leaning on a Balcony; How d'ye Do, Dear Boy?; Signor MacStinger—the Baritone Singer; In the Twi-twi-twilight; What Cheer, 'Ria?; At Trinity Church I Met My Doom; The Bond Street Tea-walk; Hi-Tiddley-Hi-Ti!; Such a Don, Don't you Know!; Daisy; Knock'd 'em in the Old Kent Road; The Future Mrs. 'Awkins; Daddy Wouldn't Buy Me a Bow-wow; Angels are Hovering Round; By the Sad Sea Waves: S-u-n-d-a-y; I'm a Little Too Young to Know; So Her Sister Says; Never Introduce Your Donah to a Pal; He Calls Me His Own Grace Darling; So Did Eve!; The Stormy Winds Did Blow; My Pal Jim; Fou the Noo; Is That You, MacAllister?; I Love a Lassie; Percy from Pimlico; I 'aven't Told 'Im—Not up to Now; I Ain't A Going to Tell; What Ho! She Bumps!; The Pretty Maid Was Young and Fair; Molly Molyneux; The Man Who Broke the Bank at Monte Carlo.]

3184. ———, ed. *Music hall Song Book: a Collection of 45 of the Best Songs from 1890-1920.* Newton Abbot: David & Charles; L: EMI Music pub., 1975. [Ask a P'liceman; Where Did You Get That Hat?; Wot Cher!; The Man Who Broke the Bank at Monte Carlo; Daddy Wouldn't Buy Me a Bow-wow; Daisy Bell; Ta-ra-ra-boom-de-ay!; My old Dutch; After the Ball; If it Wasn't for the 'ouses in Between; Her Golden Hair Was Hanging down her Back; It's A Great Big Shame; My Fiddle is my Sweetheart; At My Time of Life; Lucky Jim; A Bird in a Gilded Cage; Goodbye, Dolly Gray; Following in Father's Footsteps; I Live in Trafalgar Square; Down at the Old Bull & Bush; I Love a Lassie; The Galloping Major; Waiting at the Church; Poor John; Jolly Good Luck to the Girl Who Loves a Soldier; Swing Me Higher, Obadiah; She Sells Seashells; When Father Papered the Parlour; If I Should Plant a Tiny Seed of Love; I Do Like to Be Beside the Seaside; Ship Ahoy!; I'm Henery the Eighth; Put on Your Ta-ta, Little Girlie; I'm Shy, Mary Ellen, I'm Shy; Come, Josephine, in My Flying Machine; Roamin' in the Gloamin'; The Spaniard that Blighted My Life; Oh, You Beautiful Doll; It's a Long Way to Tipperary; Hello! Hello! Who's your Lady Friend?; A Little of What You Fancy Does You Good; Joshuah; If You Were the

Only Girl in the World; On the Good Ship Yacki-Hicki-Doo-la; Don't Dilly Dally on the Way.]

3185. GARRETT, JOHN M. *Sixty Years of British Music Hall.* L: Chappell, 1976. Rev. Peter Keating, *TLS*, 25 Feb. 1977, p. 217. [Bacon and Greens; Hop Light Loo; Polly Perkins of Paddington Green; Ticket of Leave Man; Slap bang, Here We Are Again; Up in a Balloon; Fashionable Fred; Brown the Tragedian; The Rustic Damsel; Captain Cuff; Dear Old Pals; Little Miss Muffet Sat on a Tuffett; Tuner's Oppor-tuner-ty; The Bulls Won't Bellow; In My Fust 'usband's Time; Up Went the Price; Baa Baa Baa; She Does the Fandango All Over the Place; The House that Jerry Built; What Cheer Ria; The Boy in the Gallery; The Funny Things They Do upon the Sly; Angels without Wings; Ti! Hi! Tiddelly Hi!; Buy Me Some Almond Rock; Oh! Mr. Porter; So Her Sister Says; Catch 'em Alive oh!; That Gorgonzola Cheese; Slight Mistake on the Part of my Valet; The Bobbies of the Queen; On the Day King Edward Gets His Crown on; An Old Man's Darling; Beautiful Dora; She's So Sweet (Sweet, Sweet, Sweet).]

3186. GRAHAM, FRANK, ed. *Joe Wilson Sings.* Newcastle: Graham, 1971.

3187. KEEPING, CHARLES. *Cockney Ding Dong.* Harmondsworth: Kestrel books; L: EMI Music pub, 1975. [The Hobnailed Boots that Farver Wore; What a Mouth!; The Golden Dustman; 'Alf a Pint of Ale; Down the Road; My London Country Lane; It's a Great Big Shame; Wot's the Good of Hanyfink! Why! Nuffink!; When the Old Dun Cow Caught Fire; The D.C.M.; If it Wasn't for the 'ouses in Between; In the Shade of the Old Apple Tree; They're Moving Father's Grave to Build a Sewer; Wot Cher!; Where Did You Get that Hat?; They're All Very Fine and Large; On Monday I Never Go to Work; I'm Henery the Eighth I am!; Sing me to Sleep; Boiled Beef and Carrots; A Comical Cock; The Moon Shines Tonight on Charlie Chaplin; The Amateur White-washer; I'm a Navvy; Feeding the Ducks on the Pond; When I Went for a Soldier; Liza, you are a Lady; Liza, It's a Beautiful Starry Night; Liza Johnston; If Those Lips Could Only Speak; That's Where My Love Lies Dreaming; The Sunshine of Your Smile; Sons of the Sea; Granny; When the Summer Comes Again; Whilst the Dance Goes on; Jeerusalem's Dead!; Silver Bells; The Coster's Linnet; My old Dutch; I Speak the Truth; The Song of the Thrush; A Sailor's Song; The Blind Boy; The Blind Irish Girl; Pal of My Cradle Days; For I'm Not Coming Home; That's What God Made Mothers for; As Your Hair Grows

Whiter; Knees up Mother Brown!; Any Old Iron?; Don't Dilly Dally on the Way; The Cokey Cokey; I've Got a Lovely Bunch of Coconuts; When There Isn't a Girl about; I Do Like to Be Beside the Seaside; Green Gravel; Chase Me Charley; The Naughty Sparrow; Pack Up Your Troubles in Your Old Kit-bag; Little Town in My Ould County Down; It's a Long Long Way to Tipperary; Mademoiselle from Armentieres; Two Lovely Black Eyes; Maybe It's Because I'm a Londoner; Glorious beer; Come Inside, Yer Silly Bugger; We All Came in the World with Nothing; We All Go the Same Way Home; Fall in and Follow me; Memories.]

3188. *Music Hall Memories. (The Masterpieces of Variety.)* 2 vols. L: Amalgamated press, 1935. [Vol. 1: A Little Bit Off the Top; Ask a P'liceman; At Trinity Church I Met My Doom; Blind Boy; Coal-black Mammy; Comrades; The Corsican Maid; Daddy Wouldn't Buy Me a Bow-wow; Down the Road; Follow the Footprints in the Snow; Following in Father's Footsteps; For Old Time's Sake; Gilbert the Filbert; Ginger, You're Balmy!; The Good Old Annual; Has Anybody Here Seen Kelly?; Here We are! Here We are! Here We are Again!!; Hi-Tiddley-Hi-Ti; Hitchy Koo; Hold Your Hand Out, Naughty Boy; The Honeysuckle and the Bee; I May Be Crazy, But I Love You; If Winter Comes; I'm Afraid to Come Home in the Dark; I'm Henery the Eighth, I Am; I'm the Plumber; I'm Tickled to Death, I'm Single; I'se A-waiting for Yer, Josie; I Shall Get in Such a Row When Martha Knows; It's Nice To Get up in the Morning; I've Got My Eye on You; I've Got Rings on My Fingers; I want to Go to Idaho; I Want to Sing in Opera; I Was A Good Little Girl till I Met You; John Willie, Come on; Jolly Good Luck to the Girl Who Loves a Soldier; Just Like the Ivy I'll Cling to You; The Lambeth Walk; Let Her Drown; Let's All Go down the Strand; The Lily of Laguna; Looking for a Coon like Me; Memories; My Fiddle is My Sweetheart; My Little Octoroon; Now We Are *All* Here? Yes!; On the Road to Anywhere; One Hour of Love with You; Our Lodger's Such a Nice Young Man; Pack up your Troubles; The Roses Have Made me Remember; The Shade of the Palm; Shadowland; Somebody would Shout out 'Shop!'; The Spaniard That Blighted My Life; Ta-ra-ra-Boom-de-ay; That's What God Made Mothers For; There They Are—The Two of 'Em, on Their Own; There's a Friend in Every Milestone; There's a Little Black Cupid in the Moon; They're All Very Fine and Large; Ting, Ting, That's How the Bell Goes; Two Little Girls in Blue; Two Lovely Black Eyes; We All Go the Same Way Home; What Ho! She

Bumps!; When Father Papered the Parlour; Where Did You Get
that Hat?; Young Men Taken In and Done For. Vol. 2: After
You with That; All over the Shop; And the Parrot said—; Archi-
bald, Certainly Not!; Awake!; Be a Man!; Bluebell; Boys of the
Chelsea School; Brighton; Casey Jones; Cigarette; Daisy Bell;
Flanagan; For Months and Months and Months; The Ghost of
Benjamin Binns; He's Going to Marry Mary Ann; Hi Diddle Did-
dle Um; How's Your Father?; I Belong to Glasgow; I Can't
Change It; I Do Love Myself Don't I; I Shall Sleep Well To-night;
I Used to Sigh for the Silvery Moon; If It Wasn't for the 'Ouses in
between; I'll Make a Man of You; I'm a Little Too Young to
Know; I'm Setting the Village on Fire; I'm Shy, Mary Ellen, I'm
Shy; In the Shade of the Old Apple Tree; Is Your Mother in,
Molly Malone?; It's a Great Big Shame; It's Nice to Have a
Home of Your Own; I've Got the Ooperzootic; Leettle Mister
Baggy Breeches; Let Go, Eliza; Little Annie Rooney; Little Dolly
Daydream; Make Me the King of Your Heart; The Man Who
Broke the Bank at Monte Carlo; The Miner's Dream of Home;
Molly Molyneux; Never Mind; Now We Shan't Be Long; Oh,
Jack! You Are a Handy Man; Old Chap; On Mother Kelly's
Doorstep; Our Threepenny Hop; Pansy Faces; The Preacher and
the Bear; The Rest of the Day's Your Own; The Scientific Man;
The Seventh Royal Fusiliers; Skylark; The Soldiers of the King;
The Story of a Tin-tack; Tell Me, Pretty Maiden; That was the
End of My Dream; Then We Had Another One; There's a Girl
Wanted There; Too-ral-i-oo-rall-i-ay; Topsy-Turvy; Twiggy
Voo?; Waiting for the Robert E. Lee; What Is the Use of Loving
a Girl; When the Summer Comes Again; When They Ask You
What Your Name Is; When You Are Near; Where There's a Girl
There's a Boy; Why Did I Leave My Little Back Room?; You
Made Me Love You.

3189. "O Did You Twig her Ancle?" *Punch's Almanack for 1864.* L:
Bradbury & Evans, 1864. [Parody of typical music-hall chorus
song.]

3190. PRENTIS, TERENCE, ed. *Music-hall Memories.* L: Selwyn &
Blount [1927]. [Ills. Elizabeth Pyke. Foreword by Sir Harry
Lauder. No music included; lyrics often incomplete. Mr. Spriggs,
the Grocer; Her Mother's at the Bottom of It All; They Ain't No
Class; It's the Seasoning Wot Does It; Leaning on a Balcony;
How d'ye Do, Dear Boy?; Signor MacStinger—the Baritone
Singer; In the Twi-twi-twilight; What Cheer, 'Ria?; At Trinity
Church I Met My Doom; The Bond Street Tea-walk; Hi-Tiddley-

Hi-Ti!; Such a Don, Don't you Know!; Daisy; Knock'd 'em in the Old Kent Road; The Future Mrs. 'Awkins; Daddy Wouldn't Buy Me a Bow-wow; Angels are Hovering Round; By the Sad Sea Waves: S-u-n-d-a-y; I'm a Little Too Young to Know; So Her Sister Says; Never Introduce Your Donah to a Pal; He Calls Me His Own Grace Darling; So Did Eve!; The Stormy Winds Did Blow; My Pal Jim; Fou the Noo; Is That You, MacAllister?; I Love a Lassie; Percy from Pimlico; I 'aven't Told 'Im—Not up to Now; I Ain't A Going to Tell; What Ho! She Bumps!; The Pretty Maid Was Young and Fair; Molly Molyneux; The Man Who Broke the Bank at Monte Carlo.]

3191. SCOTT, HAROLD, ed. *English Song Book collected and ed. with an introduction by Harold Scott.* N.Y.: Robert M. McBridge, 1926. [Lyrics often incomplete.] [Nineteenth-century songs, pp. 50–148. Includes, among others: Keemo Kimo, The Ballad of Sam Hall; Cheer! boys, Cheer!; Woodman, Spare That Tree; The Old Armchair; There's a Good Time Coming; We Met; Not for Joseph; I Wish We Would Decide; Dissolving Views, or Going, Going, Gone; Slap Bang, Here We Are Again; Bacon and Greens; Dark Times Cease for Evermore; Bobby Brush, the Bill Poster; Contrarieties; Little Billie; My Heart Is Like a Silent Lute; The Two Obadiahs; Champagne Charlie; The Gay Masquerade; I'll Strike You with a Feather; Covent Garden in the Morning; My Grandfather's Clock; My Angel Mother Dear; The Time is Coming; Nix, my Dolly Pals; Kissing on the Sly; The Grecian Bend; Oh, What a Forward Young Man You Are; Don't Go out To-night, Dear Father; Please Sell No More Drink to my Father; True Friends of the Poor; Tommy, Make Room for Your Uncle; The City Toff, or The Crutch and Toothpick; She Does the Fandango All over the Place; The New Electric Light; Dear Old Pals.]

3192. *Sixty Old Time Variety Songs.* L: Francis, Day & Hunter [n.d.]. [After the Ball; Ask a Policeman; At my Time o'Life; At Trinity Church; Banshee; Blind Boy; Broken Doll; Coal Black Mammy; Comrades; Daddy Wouldn't Buy Me a Bow-wow; Daisy Bell; Down the Road; Flanagan; Following in Father's Footsteps; Fol the Rol-lol; For Old Time's Sake; Galloping Major; Honeysuckle and the Bee; I Love a Lassie; I Married a Wife; If It Wasn't for the 'ouses in Between; If Those Lips Could Only Speak; I'll Take You Home Again, Kathleen; I'm Henery the Eighth; In the Shade of the Old Apple Tree; In the Twi-twi-twilight; In These Hard

Times; It's a Great Big Shame; It's Nice to Get Up in the Morning; Joshua; Just Like the Ivy; Let's All Go Down the Strand; Lily of Laguna; Little Bit off the Top; Little Dolly Daydream; Man Who Broke the Bank at Monte Carlo; Miner's Dream of Home; My Fiddle is My Sweetheart; Mystery of a Hansom Cab; Old Rustic Bridge by the Mill; Piccadilly Johnny; Put on your Ta-ta, Little Girlie; Shade of the Palm; She Was one of the Early Birds; Silver Threads Among the Gold; Sister Mary Walked Like That; Sky Lark; Soldiers of the King; Swanee; Ting, ting, that's How the Bell Goes; Twiggy Voo; Two Little Girls in Blue; Two Lovely Black Eyes; Waiting for the Robert E. Lee; What Ho, She Bumps; When You're All Dressed Up; Where Did You Get that Hat?; You Made Me Love You.]

3193. *Songs of Yesterday and Before*. L: Ascherberg, Hopwood & Crew [n.d.]. [The Amateur Whitewasher; Don't Make a Noise or Else You'll Wake the Baby; 'E Dunno Where 'e Are; My Old Kentucky Home; Never Desert a Friend; Oh! Mr. Porter; Our Hands Have Met but Not Our Hearts; Paddle Your Own Canoe; Percy from Pimlico; Polly Perkins of Paddington Green; The Ratcatcher's Daughter; Sweethearts and Wives; Tommy, Make Room for Your Uncle; The Two Obadiahs; Villikins and his Dinah.]

3194. SPEAIGHT, GEORGE, ed. *Bawdy Songs of the Early Music Hall*. Newton Abbot: David & Charles, 1975. Repr. L: Pan books, 1977. Rev. J. W. Robinson, *Theatre Notebook* 31, no. 1 (1977): 47; J. S. Bratton, *19th Century Theatre Research*, 5, no. 1 (spring 1977): 55-56. [The Drummer's Stick; The Maid and the Fishmonger; There's Somebody Coming; Johnny's Lump; The Flea Shooter; Cat's Meat Nell; He'll No More Grind Again; Mrs. Bond; Come Sleep with Me; The Blue Bells of Ireland; O What a Queer Sensation; He Did It Before My Face; The Magic Crabtree; The Friar's Candle; Colin and Susan; The Bower that Stands in Thigh Lane; The New Rolling Pin; The Copper Stick; The Ladies and the Candle; There is No Shove like the First Shove; The Way to Come over a Maid; The Amorous Parson and the Farmer's Wife; The Wonderful Belly Physic; Sally's Thatched Cottage; The Hedger and Ditcher and His Nothing at all; The Nipple; The Female Workwoman; Red Nosed Jemmy and Bandy Bet; I will be a Mot; Man's Yard of Stuff; The Blowen's Ball; Rural Felicity; Eyes Behind; The W-hole of the Ladies; The Bride.]

Performance Material

SONG AND MUSIC STUDIES AND SECONDARY MATERIALS

Cross-references

See also General **90, 123, 168, 351, 381, 414, 417, 1325, 1424, 1439, 1447, 1482, 1602–11, 1624, 1909, 2076, 2087–88, 2109, 2122–23, 2129, 2136–37, 2168, 2465a, 2546, 2795, 2883a, 2890, 2894, 2901.**
Composers **274, 339, 1611, 1860, 1880–81, 2586, 3336.**
Music Publishers **339.**
Orchestration **524, 771, 786.**
Sheet Music Covers **351.**

General

3195. ABRAHAMSEN, PER BRINK. *Dramaturgisk analyse af centrale typer music hall sange.* Ph.D. dissertation, Institut for Dramaturgi (Aarhus, Denmark), 1976.

3196. ANSTEY, F. [Thomas Anstey Guthrie]. *A Long Retrospect.* L: Oxford University Press, 1936. [Songs at the Oxford music hall, pp. 281–82, 288–89.]

3197. "'Arry on Politics." *Punch*, 11 May 1878, p. 205. ["Patriot-war-songs."]

3198. B., W. N. "Music Hall Songs." Manchester Central Reference Library. [Undated clipping, quoted in M. Vicinus, *The Industrial Muse.*]

3199. BOOTH, JOHN BENNION, ed. *Seventy Years of Song.* L: Hutchinson, 1943. [Essays commissioned by C. B. Cochran to coincide with a Toc H War Services Fund. Max Beerbohm, "Foreword"; D. L. Murray, "Our Back Street"; Noel Coward, "Songs I Remember?"; C. B. Cochran, "Melodies and Memories"; J. B. Booth, "Vox populi"; James Agate, "Some Pantomime Songs"; Stephen Williams, "Light Opera and Revue"; J. M. Bullock, "The Miracle of Gilbert & Sullivan"; Walter Elliott, "War Songs"; W. Macqueen Pope, "The Man Who Wrote the Songs"; M. Willson Disher, "The Ballad of Our

Day"; Philip Page, "Grand Opera"; W. Macqueen Pope, "Where Did You Get that Hat?"]

3200. BRATTON, JACQUELINE S. *The Victorian Popular Ballad.* L: Macmillan, 1975 [Chapter 6, "Comic Ballads in the Music Hall," pp. 155–202. Excellent scholarly analysis of lesser-known songs.]

3201. BROADWOOD, A. "Popular Songs." *Cornhill Magazine*, Apr. 1896, pp. 405–11.

3202. BROPHY, JOHN, and ERIC PARTRIDGE. *The Long Trail: What the British Soldier Sang and Said in the Great War of 1914–18.* L: Deutsch, 1965. [J. Brophy, "Music Hall Songs."]

3203. ———. Repr. L: Sphere books, 1969. [Appendix 1: J. Brophy, "From the Music-hall," pp. 169–75. Both of the above are revised eds. of *Songs and Slang of the British Soldier.*]

3204. BROWN, IVOR. "Songs after Sunset." *Drama* 80 (spring 1966): 28–30. [In part rev. of Mander and Mitchenson, *British Music Hall.*]

3205. "The Comedian and his Music." *Era*, 29 Oct. 1887, p. 10. [J. M. Gale v. Alderman Weighell.]

3206. "Comic Songs." *Era*, 23 Apr. 1876, p. 3.

3207. "Comic Songs and Comic Singers." *Era*, 16 Sept. 1877, p. 4; 23 Sept. 1877, p. 5; 30 Sept. 1877, p. 4 [letter by Arthur Lloyd]; 7 Oct. 1877, p. 4.

3208. DAVISON, PETER. "A Briton True? A Short Account of Patriotic Songs and Verse as Popular Entertainment." *Alta: University of Birmingham Review* (Birmingham), Spring 1970. Repr. in "Theatre and Song," vol. 8 of *Literary Taste, Culture & Mass Communication*, ed. P. Davison, R. Meyersoh, E. Shils. Teaneck, N.J.: Somerset House; Cambridge: Chadwick-Healey, 1978.

3209. DISHER, MAURICE WILLSON. *Victorian Song from Dive to Drawing Room.* L: Phoenix House, 1955. [Decorated with "fronts" from ballads and piano pieces.]

3210. DU MAURIER, GEORGE. "Unhappy Influence of Modern Music-Hall Melodies." *Punch*, 20 Sept. 1893, p. 50. [Cartoon concerning effigy on medieval tomb and "Daddy wouldn't buy me a bow-wow."]

3211. E[DWARDS], G. "Music Hall Songs, and Music Hall Singers." *Era Almanack* (1872): 38–41.

3212. ———. "Pimpleton's Plight, a Music-Hall Reminiscence." *Era Almanack* (1873). [On improvised political songs.]

3213. "Election Songs." *Era*, 18 June 1910, p. 24.

3214. "Figaro à Londres." *Punch*, 12 Jan. 1878, p. 9. [Hunt's "We Don't Want to Fight."]

3215. HAVERLY, C. E. "Ta-ra-ra-Boom-de-ay." *Era*, 5 Mar. 1892, p. 18. [Claims to have met it as a *danse de ventre*, Paris, 1873, and at Danzer's Orpheum, Vienna.]
3216. HAYWARD, ARTHUR L. *The Days of Dickens: a Glance at Some Aspects of Early Victorian Life in London.* N.Y.: E. P. Dutton; L: George Routledge & Sons, 1926. [Chapter 7, "Making a Night of It," pp. 112–28 (includes a version of 'Sam Hall'); chapter 12, "The Songs They Sang," pp. 202–18.]
3217. "Heyday of the Cockney comedian." *Times*, 9 Jan. 1958. [Elen, Chevalier, Carney.]
3218. HUNT, G. W. "Jingo." *Era*, 16 June 1878, p. 4; 23 June 1878, p. 4 [follow-up letters]; 30 June 1878, p. 4. [On authorship of "We Don't Want to Fight."]
3219. "Improper Songs in Music Halls." *Era*, 19 Sept. 1880, p. 4.
3220. JEVONS, WILLIAM STANLEY. "Amusements of the People." In *Methods of Social Reform*. L: Macmillan, 1883. [Pp. 1–27, argues for popular music as a panacea.]
3220a. KEIGWIN, R. P. "The Tip-topical Song." *Punch*, 6 May 1907, p. 163.
3221. KOVEN, REGINALD DE. "Music-halls and Popular Songs." *Cosmopolitan* (N.Y.) 23 (1897): 531–40. [Influence of contagious melodies on popular opinions and imaginations.]
3222. LANFRE, S. "Music Hall Politics." *Era*, 26 Mar. 1881, p. 4; 2 Apr. 1881, p. 4 [reply by G. W. Hunt]; 9 April 1881, p. 8. [On topical songs.]
3223. LEE, EDWARD. *Music of the People: a Study of Popular Music in Great Britain.* L: Barrie and Jenkins, 1970. [Chapter 5, "The Age of Victoria (1825–1911)," pp. 78–115.]
3224. MacINNES, COLIN. "The Old English Music Hall Songs." N.Y. *Times Magazine*, 28 Nov. 1965, pp. 62–63, 95, 98, 100, 103. [Popularized account.]
3225. ———. *Sweet Saturday Night.* L: MacGibbon & Kee, 1967. Revised ed. L: Panther books, 1969. Rev. C. Pulling, *Call Boy* 7, no. 2 (June 1970): 18. [Impressionistic but stimulating analysis of major songs and genres.]
3226. MACKERNESS, E. D. *A Social History of English Music.* L: Routledge & Kegan Paul, 1964.
3227. MERRITT, PAUL. "Amateur Comic Song Contest at Crocky's." *Entr'acte Almanack* (1876): 46–48.
3228. "Music and the war." *Spectator*, 16 Jan. 1915, pp. 73–74.
3229. "Music hall lyrics." *Saturday Review*, 20 Sept. 1862.
3230. "Music hall Songs." *Era*, 15 Nov. 1890, p. 16. [Suit against Duchess of Kent public house.]

Song and Music Studies and Secondary Materials

3231. "Music hall Songs." *Era*, 26 Dec. 1896, p. 17.
3232. "Music-hall Songs." *Musical News*, 8 Dec. 1917, p. 361.
3233. "Music-hall Songs and Music-hall Singers." *Era Almanack* (1872): 38–41.
3234. "Music in the Music-halls." *Musical News*, 2 Sept. 1916, p. 153.
3235. NETTEL, REGINALD. *Seven Centuries of Popular Songs: a Social History of Urban Ditties.* L: Phoenix house, 1956. [Chapter 13, "The Music-halls," pp. 203–16.]
3236. NIELSEN, JENS RØGIND HAUGE. *Musikken i den engelske music hall.* Ph.D. dissertation, University of Aarhus (Denmark) Department of Music, 1978.
3237. "Objectionable Titles [of comic songs]." *Era*, 8 Jan. 1881, p. 14.
3238. "Old Songs of Vauxhall." *Era*, 20 Nov. 1897, p. 22.
3239. PALMER, TONY. *All You Need is Love: the Story of Popular Music.* Ed. Paul Medlicott. L: Weidenfeld & Nicholson/Chappell, 1976. Paperback repr. L: Futura, 1977. [Chapter 5, "Rude Songs—Vaudeville and Music Hall," pp. 75-95.]
3240. PEARSALL, RONALD. *Edwardian Popular Music.* L: Rutherford; Fairleigh Dickinson University press, 1975. [Chapter 2, "Music Hall," pp. 46–73.]
3241. ———. *Popular Music of the Twenties.* Newton Abbot: David & Charles; Totowa, N.J.: Rowman & Littlefield, 1976. [Chapter 1, "The Changing Face of Variety," pp. 7–19.]
3242. ———. *Victorian Popular Music.* Newton Abbot: David & Charles, 1973. [Chapters 1–4.]
3243. "Political Songs." *Era*, 23 Mar. 1889, p. 17; 6 April 1889, p. 15 [edit.: Politics on the stage]; 13 Apr. 1889, p. 18.
3244. PUGH, EDWIN. "Songs the Pierrots Sang." *T.P.'s & Cassell's Weekly*, 26 June 1926, p. 29.
3245. PULLING, CHRISTOPHER. *They Were Singing and What They Were Singing About.* L: George G. Harrap, 1952. [With many line decorations by Muriel Bax. Important survey, well researched, with appendices on composers and publishers.]
3246. "The Queen and the Music-Hall Song." *Era*, 2 June 1878, p. 4. [Condemning Victoria's endorsement of a Jingoistic song.]
3246a. SCOTT, CHRISTOPHER and AMORET SCOTT. "The Music of the Halls." In *Saturday Book 20.* L: Hutchinson, 1960, Pp. 122-35.
3247. "Sea-side Music." *Era*, 20 Aug. 1876, p. 11.
3248. SENELICK, LAURENCE. "Politics as Entertainment: Victorian Music-hall Songs." *Victorian Studies* (Bloomington, Ind.) 19, no. 2 (Dec. 1975): 149–80. [Scholarly study of influence of music-hall on politics and vice versa.]

3249. "Shivery Shakey." *Era*, 24 Feb. 1894, p. 17.
3250. "Songs in Season." *Punch*, 3 June 1908, p. 398. ["Exhibition" songs.]
3251. "Songs of the Old Music Hall." *Times*, 4 June 1952; 6 June 1952 [reply]. [On topical songs.]
3252. "Strictly in Tune." *Punch*, 27 Apr. 1878, p. 191. [Disraeli's "music hall policy."]
3253. "Ta-ra-ra-Boom-de-ay." *Era*, 9 Apr. 1896, p. 16; 14 May 1892, p. 16. [Chas. Sheard v. D'Alcorn.]
3254. THOMAS, DYLAN. *Quite Early One Morning.* N.Y.: New Directions, 1954. ["On Poetry," pp. 191–92, music-hall song as poetry.]
3255. "Titles of Music Hall Songs." *Era*, 6 Jan. 1894, p. 18; 13 Jan. 1894, p. 17; 20 Jan. 1894, p. 17; 27 Jan. 1894, p. 17; 3 Feb. 1894, p. 18; 10 Feb. 1894, p. 17.
3256. "The Value of a Comic Song." *Era*, 28 Mar. 1891, p. 15. [Kennedy v. Majilton over "The Football Match."]
3257. "Villikens and his Dinah." *Era*, 8 Feb. 1896, p. 18. [Circumstantial history of the song.]
3258. VOIGT, EBERHARD. *Die Music-hall Songs und das öffentliche Leben Englands.* Greifswald, Germany: Emil Hartmann, 1929. [Thorough survey of songs as reflections of politics.]
3259. "Vox populi." *Punch*, 2 Feb. 1878, p. 45.
3260. WALSH, COLIN, èd. *There Goes that Song Again: One Hundred Years of Popular Song.* L: Elm Tree books/EMI music pub., 1977. [Section 1, "Playing the Halls."]
3261. "We Don't Want to Fight (Classically put . . . by an Etonian)." *Punch*, 25 May 1878, p. 238.
3262. *Which Song and When (1880 to 1974).* Edinburgh: Bandparts music store, 1976. [Dated listing of major popular songs.]
3262a. "The Whole Hog or None." *Era*, 27 Jan. 1894, p. 16. [The song's provenance.]

Composers and Song-writers

3263. "A Busy Song and Sketch Writer. Charles D. Hickman." *Era*, 23 Apr. 1910, p. 23.
3264. "A Celebrated Song and its Author." *Era*, 20 Aug. 1910, p. 16. [T. S. Lonsdale and "Tommy, Make Room for Your Uncle."]
3265. "A Chat with Felix M'Glennon." *Era*, 10 Mar. 1894, p. 16.
3266. "A Chat with G. W. Hunt." *Era*, 17 Mar. 1894, p. 16; 24 Mar. 1894, p. 16.

3267. "A Chat with Harry Dacre." *Era*, 25 Mar. 1911, p. 24.
3268. "A Chat with Joseph Tabrar." *Era*, 10 Feb. 1894, p. 16; 17 Feb. 1894, p. 16.
3269. "A Chat with Morris Abrahams." *Era*, 18 Aug. 1894, p. 8.
3270. "A Chat with Warwick Williams." *Era*, 18 May 1895, p. 16.
3271. FINCK, HERMAN. *My Melodious Memories*. L: Hutchinson, 1937.
3272. "How Popular Songs are Made. A Chat with Harry Dacre." *Era,* 19 Oct. 1901.
3272a. HUDD, ROY and GRAHAM WEBB. "Weston & Lee, a Biography." *Call Boy* 17, no. 1 (spring 1980): 6–7. [Lives of Robert P. Weston (1878–1936) and Bert Lee (1880–1946.]
3273. MORTON, RICHARD. "A Song-writer's Nightmare." *Era*, 18 Apr. 1891, p. 12.
3274. "Mr Joe Tabrar's Benefit." *Era*, 13 May 1899, p. 19.
3275. "Music Hall Songs and Song Writers." *Era*, 6 Jan. 1894, p. 17; 20 Jan. 1894, p. 17; 3 Feb. 1894, p. 17, 18; 17 Feb. 1894, p. 18; 24 Feb. 1894, p. 16; 10 Mar. 1894, p. 16; 17 Mar. 1894, p. 16; 24 Mar. 1894, p. 16.
3276. PRATT, A. T. CAMDEN. "Poverty Corner." In *Unknown London: Its Romance and Tragedy*. L: Neville Beeman [1900?]. Repr. L: B. T. Batsford, 1938. [Pp. 59–60. On indigent music-hall composers.]
3277. "Price of Music-hall Songs." *Sala's Journal* 2, no. 42 (11 Feb. 1893): 121. [Action of Slaughter v. Moore of Moore & Burgess Minstrels.]
3278. SABENE, ED. "How Songwriters are Treated." *Era*, 4 Feb. 1882, p. 4; 11 Feb. 1882, p. 4 [reply].
3279. STEPHEN, PHILIP. "Song-writers and Singers." *Era*, 13 Nov. 1886, p. 10; [replies] 27 Nov. 1886, p. 10; 4 Dec. 1886, p. 16.
3280. "Then and Now." *Era*, 7 May 1910, p. 26. [Fred Bowyer's memoirs.]

Music Publishers

3281. ABBOTT, JOHN. *The Story of Francis, Day & Hunter*. L: Francis, Day & Hunter, 1952.
3282. "Chas. Sheard and Co. Publications." *Era*, 2 Feb. 1889, p. 12.
3283. "A Chat with David Day." *Era*, 25 Sept. 1897, p. 18. [Of Francis, Day & Hunter.]
3284. "Mr. Charles Day's Farewell Party." *Era*, 29 Oct. 1898, p. 22.

Orchestration

3285. "Death of Herr Schalkenbach." *Era*, 16 Apr. 1910, p. 23 [Conductor of L'Orchestre du Diable.]
3286. HOLLINGSHEAD, JOHN. *According to My Lights*. L: Chatto & Windus, 1900. ["Soothing the Savage Breast." pp. 228–33: park band music as competition for music-hall.]
3287. "Music Hall and Special Concerts." *Era*, 12 Sept. 1880, p. 4.
3288. "Music Hall Bands." *Era*, 4 Mar. 1889, p. 20.
3289. "Music Hall Orchestras." *Era*, 5 Oct. 1879, p. 4; 12 Oct. 1879, p. 4; 19 Oct. 1879, p. 4; 28 Oct. 1879, p. 4; 2 Nov. 1879, p. 4.
3290. "A Music Hall Piano." *Era*, 22 June 1879, p. 4.

Sheet Music Covers

3290a. *The Art of Alfred Concanen. An Exhibition of Victorian Lithograph Song Covers April-June 1962*. L: Museum Street Galleries, 1962.
3291. IMESON, W. E. *Illustrated Music Titles and Their Delineators*. [N.p.] Printed for the Author [1912].
3292. KING, ALEC HYATT. "English Pictorial Music Pages 1820–1885: Their Style, Evolution and Importance," *Library*, 5th ser. 4, pp. 262–72.
3293. PEARSALL, RONALD. *Victorian Sheet Music Covers*. Newton Abbot: David & Charles, 1972.
3294. SITWELL, SACHEVERELL. *Morning, Noon and Night in London*. L: Macmillan, 1948. [Discursive essays on Alfred Concanen and his song covers.]
3295. SPELLMAN, DOROTHY and SIDNEY. *Victorian Music Covers*. L: Evelyn, Adams & Mackay, 1969.

JOKES, MONOLOGUES, AND SKETCHES

Cross-references

See also **242, 381, 1939, 1942–43, 1986, 2195, 2289, 2292, 2346–49,**

2371-72, 2390, 2396, 2401-2, 2581, 2721, 2747, 2773, 2818, 2835, 2839-40, 2849, 2936-39, 3057a, 3162, 3515-16, 3564-66.

3296. CLEWES, CHARLES. *Comic Sketches*. [N.p., 1884?]
3297. CRAVEN, TOM. *Tom Craven's Mixture of Recitation and Monologues*. L: Samuel French [1910].
3298. "CUE." *"Extra Turns" or Footlight Flashes from a Music Hall Matinee as Heard in the Stalls*. L: Joseph Williams [1922]. [By "Cue," the Comedians' "Cue."]
3299. HAYMAN, JOE. *Twenty Different Adventures of Cohen on the Telephone and Other Examples of Hebrew Humour*. Ills. Charles O'Neill. L: Austin Rogers, 1929.
3300. IRVING, GORDON, comp. *The Wit of the Scots*. L: Frewin [1969]. ["At the Music Hall," pp. 42-49.]
3301. KILGARIFF, MICHAEL. *It Gives Me Great Pleasure. The Complete Vade Mecum for the Old Time Music Hall Chairman*. L: Samuel French, 1972.
3302. LEYCESTER, LAURA. "It's a Way They Have in the Music Halls." *Era*, 3 Dec. 1910, p. 25. [Parody of typical sketch.]
3303. LORNE, TOMMY. *Tommy Lorne's Book of Scottish Humour*. Ills. Fred Bennett. Dundee & L: Valentine, 1930.
3304. *The Mohawk Minstrels' 'Nigger' Dramas, Dialogues and Drolleries*. No. 1, 1888. [Continued as *The Mohawk Minstrels' Annual*, nos. 2-10, continued as *Francis & Day's 11th/12th Book of Dialogues* (No. 12, 1910). Ed. C. Townley (?), no. 1; T. Little, nos. 2-10.]
3305. *The Old Time Stars' Book of Comedy Sketches. A Humorous Playbill featuring Harry Tate, Bransby Williams, Biddy and Fanny, Scott and Whaley, Ernest Longstaffe and many others*. L: Wolfe, 1971.
3306. *The Old Time Stars' Book of Monologues*. L: Wolfe, 1972. [300 Monologues written or performed by Chesney Allen, Arthur Askey, H. M. Burnaby, Albert Chevalier, Gracie Fields, Cyril Fletcher, Will Fyffe, George Grossmith, Milton Hayes, Harry Hemsley, Stanley Holloway, Nosmo King, Norman Long, Ernest Longstaffe, Ella Retford, Sax Rohmer, Suzette Tarri, Jack Watson, Albert Whelan, Bransby Williams, and others. Introduction by Cliff Parker.]
3307. *PAD: Patter and Dialogue for Ventriloquists, Conjurors, Raconteurs, Minstrels, Pierrots, Single-handed Comedians, Cross-talkers, and Burlesque-double Turns*. No. 1 [1902]. [Incorporated in *The Playlet and Monologue Magazine*, conducted by

C. D. Hickman (Nos. 1–5, 1901-2.) Monthly.]

3308. *"Pouf-La."* *A String of Wheezes by Thirty-nine Music-hall Artistes*. L: Gilbert Dalziel, "Judy" Office, 1892. [Ills. Alfred Bryan, Hal Ludlow, and Geo. Gatcombe. Forty-one ills. of music-hall performers.]

3309. TAGGART, TOM BERNARD. *Gaslight Gaieties: A Complete Gay Nineties Variety Show*. ed. and arranged by T. B. Taggart. N.Y.: Samuel French, 1949.

3310. WEBB, LAWRIE. *Best Music Hall and Other Jokes*. L: Wolfe, 1971. [Jacket by Richard Hook. Line ills. Derek Alder.]

XI. LITERARY AND ARTISTIC TREATMENT

"It was Mr. George Moore, I remember, who years ago broke to me, in conversation, the intelligence that the theatre was hopelessly played out, and that living art was to be found in the music-hall alone."

> William Archer, *The Theatrical "World" of 1895*. (London: Walter Scott, 1896) 98.

Archer believed the fad for music-hall among intellectuals an aberration, a typical paradox of the 1890s. But in the meantime many artists turned to the rude vigor of the halls for inspiration and new themes, and even now writers return to the period for color.

The following pages present only a sampling of the works that drew upon the music-hall, and no high level of quality can be demonstrated. Perhaps Priestley's *Lost Empires* and Osborne's *The Entertainer* are, respectively, the best novel and play to be set in that milieu. Walter Sickert was the only English painter of stature to return again and again to the music-hall for his subject matter (for Toulouse-Lautrec, see Supplement B). The cinema began as a novel appendage to music-hall bills, a brief flicker of news footage or coarse comedy at the end of an evening, and eventually usurped the popular audiences and even the theatres that had belonged to the older form. As if in recompense, the movies have often recreated the deposed variety stage. Charlie Chaplin, himself a symbol of film art, is the paradigmatic case: he was trained in the halls under Fred Karno's tutelage, and some of his earliest silent comedies, *The Rink* (1916) and *A Night at the Show* (1915), reproduce his stage sketches, while towards the end of his creative career, Chaplin returned to the music-hall in *Limelight* (1952) as a metaphor for his hero's decline. In our subsection on film, we include both works on music-hall themes and performers on the screen and articles and books devoted to the exploitation of cinema as a specialty presentation in the halls.

FICTION

Cross-references

See also Novels and Stories **406, 1453, 1944, 2743, 2746, 2837–38, 2841, 2979, 3704.**
Literary Studies **851.**

Novels and Stories

3311. BAMBRICK, WINIFRED. *Continental Revue*. L: Faber & Faber, 1946.

3312. BENNETT, ARNOLD. *Clayhanger*. L: Methuen, 1910. Repr. Harmondsworth: Penguin Books, 1954. [Chapter 10, "Free and Easy."]

3313. BENSON, EDWARD F. *The Male Impersonator*. L: Elkin Mathews and Marrot, 1929. [In which the title character does not appear.]

3314. BESANT, WALTER, and JAMES RICE. *Ready Money Mortiboy*. 3 vols. L: Guildford, 1872. Repr. from *Once a Week*. [2: 159–66, 260–74, Jewish music-hall prop.; 3:19, working-class audience at "North London Palace."]

3315. BLYTH, HARRY. *The Queen of the Air*. Glasgow: North British Publishing Co. [1888.] [About a trapeze artist.]

3316. BRADDON, MARY ELIZABETH. *The Cloven Foot, a Novel*.

N.Y.: Harper & Bros., 1878. [Chapters 4, 6–8, 14–16, 18 concern a music-hall dancer and her gruesome fate.]

3317. BRAHMS, CARYL and S. J. SIMON. *Trottie True*. L: Michael Joseph, 1946.

3317a. BURKE, THOMAS. *Victorian Grotesque*. L: Herbert Jenkins, 1941. [Tale of the vicissitudes of an eccentric comedian on the London halls in the 1870s; George Leybourne is a major character.]

3318. CAINE, HALL. *The Christian, a Story*. L: William Heinemann, 1897. [A serio-comic at the Alhambra is a leading character. See also, "'The Christian' and Music Halls," *Era*, 14 Aug. 1897, p. 19 [edit.]; 28 Aug. 1897, p. 18; 4 Sept. 1897, p. 18.]

3319. CATTO, MAX. *The Mummers*. L: Heinemann, 1953. Repr. L: World Distributors; Manchester: Consul Books, 1962.

3320. CHESTER, CHARLIE. *Overture to Anthem. A Novel about Show Business*. L: New English Library, 1977.

3320a. DISRAELI, BENJAMIN. *Sybil; or, The Two Nations*. 3 vol. L: Henry Colburn, 1845. Repr. Oxford: World Classics, 1926. [Ch. 10: a visit to a popular singing room "The Temple of the Muses."]

3321. FRANKAU, PAMELA. *Sing for Your Supper*. N.Y.: Random House, 1964. [Novel about seaside entertainers.]

3322. GISSING, GEORGE. "The Muse of the Halls," *English Illustrated Magazine*, Christmas 1893.

3323. HALL, ROBERT LEE. *Exit Sherlock Holmes,* N.Y.: Playboy Press, 1979.

3324. HAMILTON, COSMO. "Lame Dogs." In *Two Kings, and Other Romances*. L: Chatto & Windus, 1912.

3325. JACOB, NAOMI. *Straws in Amber*. L: Hutchinson, 1938. [Novel of two music-hall artistes separated by their careers.]

3326. JENKINS, JOHN EDWARD. *The Devil's Chain*. L: 1876. [Temperance novel about the Ratcliffe Highway.]

3327. KIPLING, RUDYARD. "My Great and Only." In *Abaft the Funnel*. N.Y.: B. W. Dodge, 1909. [Pp. 292–304.]

3328. LAWRENCE, D. H. *The Rainbow*. L: Methuen, 1915. [Chapter 7, "The Child": Will Brangwen's visit to the Nottingham Empire.]

3329. *The Loved and the Lost; or, The Music Hall Singer and the Stroller's Apprentice*. Serialized in N.Y. *Clipper*, 9 Oct. 1869 –8 Jan. 1870.

3330. MACKENZIE, COMPTON. *Carnival*. L: Macdonald, 1951.

3330a. "A Music-hall Squabble." *London Figaro*, 8 May 1877, pp. 3–4.

3331. NEVINSON, HENRY. "Little Scotty." In *Neighbours of Ours*.

Bristol: Arrowsmith, 1895. [Story of a London music-hall star.]

3332. PRIESTLEY, J. B. *The Good Companions.* L: Heinemann, 1929. [Adventures of a concert party in the early 1920s.]

3333. ———. *Lost Empires: being Richard Herncastle's Account of His Life on the Variety Stage from November 1913 to August 1914 together with a Prologue and Epilogue.* L: Heinemann, 1965.

3334. PRIOR, ALLAN. *Never Been Kissed in the Same Place Twice.* L: Cassell, 1978. [About a music-hall family.] Pub. in U.S. as *Never Been Kissed.* N.Y.: Harper & Row, 1979.

3335. REYNOLDS, GEORGE W. M. *The Mysteries of the Court of London.* L: John Dicks [1849–56]. [3rd ser., vol. 1, chapter 57, "The Recreations and Horrors of London Life" (Cider Cellar and 'Sam Hall'), pp. 277–79; chapter 75, "The Judge and Jury Society."]

3336. TABRAR, JOSEPH. "Just One Song." N.Y. *Clipper*, 2 Jan. 1886.

3337. THACKERAY, WILLIAM MAKEPEACE. *The History of Pendennis.* L: Bradbury & Evans, 1848–50. [Chapters 19, 30, 36, 39, 46, 55, *et al.* describe the Back Kitchen of the Fielding's Head in Covent Garden and Vauxhall Gardens.]

3338. ———. *The Newcomes.* L: Bradbury & Evans, 1854–55. [Chapter 1 is a classic account of a W. G. Ross performance at a hall like the Cider Cellars.]

3339. VINCENT, ADRIAN. *Song at Twilight.* L: New English Library, 1975. [About disillusioned artiste reflecting on his career.]

3340. WRIGHT, THOMAS. "Bill Bank's Day Out." In *The Savage Club Papers for 1868.* Ed. Andrew Halliday. L: 1868. [Pp. 214–30, includes a visit to the Alhambra.]

3341. ZANGWILL, ISRAEL. "The Serio-comic Governess." In *The Grey Wig.* L: Macmillan, 1903. [Pp. 446–563, a story of a convent-bred governess who becomes a music-hall singer. Zangwill's dramatized version *The Serio-comic Governess*, produced in N.Y. in 1904, was never printed.]

Literary Studies

3342. BOWEN, ZACK. "The Bronzegold Sirensong. A musical analysis of the 'Sirens' episode in Joyce's *Ulysses*." In *Literary Monographs 1*, ed. Eric Rothstein and Thomas K. Dunseath (Madison, Wisc.: 1967).

3343. ———. *Musical Allusion in the Works of James Joyce.* Albany, NY., 1974.

3344. HODGART, MATTHEW J. C. and MABEL WORTHING-
TON. *Song in the Works of James Joyce.* N.Y.: 1959.
3345. KEATING, PETER. *The Working Classes in Victorian Fiction.*
L: Routledge & Kegan Paul, 1971. [Chapter 6, "Rudyard Kipling
and the Cockney archetypes," pp. 139–66.]
3346. MacINNES, COLIN. "Kipling and the Music-halls." In *Rudyard
Kipling the Man, His Work and His World,* ed. John Gross.
L: Weidenfeld & Nicolson; N.Y.: Simon & Schuster, 1972.
[Pp. 57–61.]

POETRY

Cross-references

See also **1437, 1983, 2179–80, 2251, 2646, 2936, 3567, 3650,
3665–66.**

3347. ADLARD, J. "Poetry and the Stage-doors of the 'Nineties."
Review of English Literature 7, no. 4 (Oct. 1966): 50–60.
3348. BYWATER, ABEL. "Sheffield Cutler's Song." In F. W. Moorman, ed. *Yorkshire Dialect Poems (1673–1915) and Traditional
Poems.* L: Pub. for the Yorkshire Dialect Society by Sidgwick
and Jackson, 1916. [1837. Pp. 22–24.]
3348a. "Coster Ballads No. XI, 'The Music-hall Singer.'" *London
Figaro,* 13 July 1872, p. 435.
3349. CRAVEN, TOM. "Varieties." In *Tom Craven's Mixtures of
Recitations and Monologues.* L: Samuel French [n.d.]. Repr. in
Era, 3 Dec. 1910, p. 29.
3350. DAVIDSON, JOHN. *In a Music-hall and Other Poems.* L: Ward
and Downey, 1891.
3351. GILBERT, WILLIAM SCHWENCK. "'Musings in a Music-
hall,' by a Young Man from the Country." In Sidney Dark and
Rowland Grey, *W. S. Gilbert: His Life and Letters* (L: Methuen,
1923 [p. 18.]); and in *The Complete Bab Ballads,* ed. James Ellis
(Cambridge, Mass: Harvard University Press, 1970 [p. 66]).
3351a. HUME, WILLIAM ELLIOTT. "The Geordie tradition: from
Music Hall to Folk Song in Northumbria." *Poetry Review* 54
(1963): 148–53.

3352. KERMODE, FRANK. "Poet and Dancer before Diaghilev." *Puzzles and Epiphanies: Essays and Reviews 1958-1961.* 2d impression with corrections. L: Routledge & Kegan Paul, 1963. [Pp. 1-28, music-hall dancing and poetry.]

3353. LOCKER, FREDERICK, later LOCKER-LAMPSON. "The Music Palace." In *London Lyrics.* L: Kegan Paul, 1893.

3354. SYMONS, ARTHUR. "Prologue." In *London Nights.* L: L. C. Smithers, 1895. 2nd, revised ed. 1897. ["My Life is like a music hall."]

3355. WRATISLAW, THEODORE. "At the Stage-door." In *Orchids.* L: L. Smithers, 1893.

3356. ———. *Caprices.* L: Gay & Bird, 1893. ["The Music-hall"; "Etchings 3: At the Empire."]

DRAMA

Cross-references

See also Plays **1954, 2116, 2604, 2630, 2632, 3341.**

Plays on Music-Hall Themes

3356a. BOUCICAULT, DION[YSIUS LARDNER]. *After Dark: A Tale of London.* L: Samuel French, 1868. [E. W. Mackney appeared in the music-hall scene in the 1877 revival.]

3357. COWARD, NOEL. *Cavalcade.* L: William Heinemann, 1932. [Part 1, Scene 2.]

3358. ———. *Red Peppers.* In *To-Night at 8.30.* L: W. Heinemann, 1936.

3359. DISHER, MAURICE WILLSON. *Winkles and Champagne: Revue adapted from the Book.* Unity Theatre, L, 1944. Rev. *New Statesman* 27 (8 Jan. 1944); *Theatre World* 11 (Jan. 1944): 29.

3360. OSBORNE, JOHN. *The Entertainer.* L: Faber & Faber, 1957. [Allegedly based on Max Miller, though Osborne denies this.] Rev. K. Tynan in *Curtains* (N.Y.: Athenaeum, 1961), pp. 173-75.

3361. TEETGEN, W. "The Humours of a Concert Room (a Celebrated

Original Comic Dialogue). . . ." In *The Singer's Penny Magazine and Reciter's Album.* L: G. Drake, 1835.

3362. THEATRE WORKSHOP and CHARLES CHILTON. *Oh What a Lovely War.* L: Methuen, 1965.

3363. "Under the Rose." *Punch* 104 (1893): 9 Sept., pp. 112–14; 16 Sept., pp. 124–25; 23 Sept., pp. 136–37; 30 Sept., pp. 148–49; 7 Oct., pp. 160–61; 14 Oct., pp. 172–73; 21 Oct., pp. 184–85; 28 Oct., pp. 196–97; 4 Nov., pp. 208–9; 11 Nov., pp. 220–21; 18 Nov., pp. 232–33; 25 Nov., pp. 244–45; 2 Dec., pp. 256–57; 9 Dec., pp. 268–69; 16 Dec., pp. 280–81. Ills. Bernard Partridge. [A play about a respectable middle-class family: husband takes shares in the Eldorado music-hall; mother attends, scandalized; nephew clandestinely is an artiste. One scene takes place backstage and onstage.]

Literary Studies

3364. BROWN, G. E. "Music-hall references in John Osborne's 'Look Back in Anger.'" *Notes & Queries* 221 (1976): 310.

3365. CORVIN, MICHEL. *Le Théâtre nouveau en France.* Paris: Presses universitaires de France, 1963. [Pp. 67–72: emphasizes the music-hall techniques in the works of Samuel Beckett.]

3366. DAVISON, PETER. "Contemporary Drama & Popular Dramatic Forms." In *Aspects of Drama and the Theatre: Five Kathleen Robinson Lectures delivered in the University of Sydney 1961.* Sydney: Sydney University Press, 1965. [Pp. 143–97: connects Pinter, Beckett, Osborne, *et al.* to music-hall origins.]

3367. DUKES, ASHLEY. "The English Scene." *Theatre Arts* (N.Y.) 19 (Dec. 1935): 907-8. [Quotes Auden's statement, "The music hall, the Christmas pantomime and the country house charade are the most living drama of today."]

3368. FULLER, JOHN. *A Reader's Guide to W. H. Auden.* L: Thames and Hudson, 1970. [P. 77: on music-hall influence in Auden's plays.]

3369. HASSAN, IHAB. *The Dismemberment of Orpheus: Toward a Post-Modern Literature.* N.Y.: Oxford University Press, 1971. [P. 214: "If music is the formal analogy to Proust's art, vaudeville is the analogy to Beckett's.]

3370. HOWARD, HERBERT. *Notes on Some Figures behind T. S. Eliot.* L: Chatto & Windus, 1965. [Pp. 302-6, Eliot's interest in music-hall.]

3371. ISHERWOOD, CHRISTOPHER. *Lions and Shadows. An Education in the Twenties.* L: L. & V. Woolf, 1938. [P. 215: influence of music-hall on Auden's and Isherwood's plays.]

3372. SCHNEIDER, ULRICH. "'Everything in the Garden': ein Nachtrag zu H. Oppels Interpretation von Giles Coopers Drama." *Archiv für das Studium der neueren Sprachen und Literaturen* (Braunschweig) 215 (1978): 110-12. [Relates Giles Cooper's *Everything in the Garden* to Marie Lloyd's song of that title.]

PAINTING

Cross-references

See also **2311, 2314, 2320, 3552, 3572, 3590, 3632.**

3373. EMMONS, ROBERT. *The Life and Opinions of Walter Richard Sickert.* L: Faber & Faber, 1941. [Chapter 5, "The Music Halls," pp. 44-52.]

3374. LIECHTI, ROBERT. "The Music Hall on Canvas." *Call Boy,* Sept. 1971. [Sickert.]

3375. PICKVANCE, RONALD. "The Magic of the Halls and Sickert." *Apollo,* Apr. 1962, pp. 107-15. [Includes separately inserted section, "Songs Which Sickert Might Have Sung," chosen by Geoffrey Strachan.]

3376. ———. *Walter Richard Sickert 1860-1942.* L: Purnell & Sons, 1967. [Large plate of The Old Bedford; smaller ill. of the New Bedford.]

3377. *Spencer Frederick Gore 1878-1914.* [L] Anthony d'Offay [1974]. [Catalogue of an exhibition (28 March-3 May 1974) of Sickert's fellow music-hall lover, who specialized in Alhambra ballets. Several paintings of these are reproduced.]

3378. *Le Théâtre, le cirque, le music-hall et les peintres du XVIIIᵉ siecle à nos jours.* [Paris] E. Flammarion, 1926. [Preface by Camille Mauclair.]

3379. WYKES-JOYCE, MAX. " A Parrot, Twopenny Rice & the Moulin-Rouge." *Arts Review,* 2-16 Apr. 1964, pp. 6-7.

CINEMA

From the very beginnings of the cinema, music-hall performers rushed to record their stage acts (Little Tich, Harry Fragson), while others (Will Evans) tried to adapt to the new technique. Some, like Stan Laurel and Charlie Chaplin, developed their variety-trained talents into brilliant film comedy. In later generations, artistes like Gracie Fields, Will Hay, and the younger George Formby carried on successful film careers simultaneously with their music-hall performances. Eventually the great stars of the past received what Leslie Halliwell calls "biopic" treatment: Tommy Trinder portrayed George Leybourne in *Champagne Charlie* (Ealing, dir. Alberto Cavalcanti, 1945) and Vesta Tilley's life was romanticized in *After the Ball* (dir. R. Compton Bennett, 1950).

Music-halls themselves have proved popular settings for cinematic episodes. In some early cases, they provided a frame for variety acts, as in *A Music Hall Agent's Dream* (Gaumont, 1908; rev. *Motion Picture Herald,* N.Y., 15 Aug. 1908, 128) and *The Music Hall Singer* (Eclipse, 1912 rev. *Motion Picture Herald,* N.Y., XII, 1221, XIII, 13 July 1912 147). In later cases, they contained the climactic moments of the film, as in *The 39 Steps* (dir. Alfred Hitchcock, 1935); *Limelight* (dir. Charles Chaplin, 1952); and *The Entertainer* (dir. Tony Richardson, 1930).

On the Continent, variety theatres of the late nineteenth and earlier twentieth centuries were also exploited for their color and nostalgia value. The Moulin Rouge was glorified and glamorized in three films of that name (dir. E. A. Dupont, 1928; dir. Sidney Lanfield, 1933; and dir. John Huston, 1953) and in *French Cancan* (dir. Jean Renoir, 1955), probably the most authentic of the lot. A music-hall ambience helped create the atmosphere for three masterpieces of the German cinema: *Variété* (dir. E. A. Dupont, 1925); *Die Büchse der Pandora* (dir. G. W. Pabst from Frank Wedekind's play, 1928); and *Die Blaue Engel* (dir. Josef von Sternberg from the novel by Heinrich Mann, *Professor Unrath,* 1930) with a superbly tawdry recreation of a low dive.

Cross-references

General

3380. ANSTEY, F. (pseud. of Thomas Anstey Guthrie). "Animacules at the Alhambra." *Punch,* 24 Apr. 1907, pp. 290-91. [Charles Urban's Bioscope.]

3381. ANTHONY, BARRY. "Music Hall on Film." *Music Hall Records* 8 (Aug. 1979): 32-35.

3382. ARMSTRONG, ARTHUR COLES. "My Lady Kinema—the Eleventh Muse." *Stage Year Book* (1914): 33-38.

3383. "Army Life [cinematograph pictures]." *Era,* 13 Oct. 1900, p. 19.

3384. BARNES, JOHN. *The Beginnings of Cinema in England.* Newton Abbot: David & Charles, 1976. N.Y.: Barnes & Noble, 1976.

3385. "The Biograph at the Palace." *Era,* 20 Mar. 1897, p. 19.

3386. BRITISH FILM INSTITUTE. *British Music-Hall: a Catalogue of Music-Hall Turns.* L: BFI, 1966. (The Film as a Record of Contemporary Life, 1.)

3387. CHADWICK, STANLEY. *The Mighty Screen: the Rise of the Cinema in Huddersfield.* Huddersfield: Venturers, 1953.

3388. "A Chat with Charles Urban." *Era,* 1 Dec. 1900, p. 22. [Of Bioscope.]

3389. "A Chat with Mr R. W. Paul." *Era,* 25 Apr. 1896, p. 17. [Operator of the Animatograph.]

3390. "A Chat with Walter Gibbons." *Era,* 20 Oct. 1900, p. 22. [Of Bio-tableaux.]

3391. GIFFORD, DENIS. *The British Film Catalogue 1895-1970. A Guide to Entertainment Films.* Newton Abbot (Devon): David & Charles, 1973. [Complete list arranged both by year and alphabetical within year; separate title index.]

3392. HUNTLEY, JOHN. "B.M.H.S. uncover First British Film Scenario." *Call Boy* 5, no. 2a (June 1968): 1. [Percy Honri's *Mr Moon.*]

3393. LOW, RACHEL, and ROGER MANVELL. *The History of the British Film 1896-1906.* L: Allen & Unwin, 1948.

3394. LOW, RACHEL. *The History of the British Film 1906-1914.* L: Allen & Unwin, 1949.

3395. ———. *The History of the British Film 1914-1918.* L: Allen & Unwin, 1950.

3396. ———. *The History of the British Film 1918-1929.* L: Allen & Unwin, 1971.

3397. MALTIN, LEONARD. *Movie Comedy Teams.* N.Y.: Signet Books, 1970.

3398. MONTGOMERY, JOHN. *Comedy Films 1894–1954*. L: Allen & Unwin, 1954.
3399. ROBINSON, DAVID. *The Great Funnies, a History of Film Comedy*. L: Studio Vista; N.Y.: E. P. Dutton, 1969.
3400. SADOUL, GEORGES. *Histoire générale du cinéma*. Paris: De Noël, 1946. [1: 223 *et seq.* discusses the advent of the cinema as a music-hall attraction.]
3401. "The 'Theatrograph' in Court." *Era,* 18 July 1896, p. 7.
3402. "Variety is Charming." *Punch,* 3 Apr. 1897, p. 161. [The American Biograph at the Palace Theatre of Varieties.]

Works about Film Comedians That Emphasize Their Music-Hall Backgrounds

CHAPLIN, CHARLES SPENCER *

3403. CHAPLIN, CHARLES SPENCER. *Charlie Chaplin's Own Story*. Indianapolis: Bobbs-Merrill, 1916.
3404. ———. *My Autobiography*. L: Bodley Head, 1964. Harmondsworth: Penguin books, 1966. [Debut at Forester's Music-hall; work with Fred Karno.]
3405. ———. *My Life in Pictures*. L: Bodley Head, 1974. [Massive compilation of ills. from all sources, captioned by CC, with an intro. by Francis Wyndham.]
3046. ———. *Era,* 11 May 1901, 11 July 1903, 18 July 1903, 1 Aug. 1903, 18 June 1904, 22 Apr. 1906, 29 Apr. 1906, 29 June 1907, 14 Sept. 1907, 30 Apr. 1910.
3407. GIFFORD, DENIS. *Chaplin*. L: Macmillan; Garden City, N.Y.: Doubleday, 1974. [Pp. 9–27.]
3408. MANVELL, ROGER. *Chaplin*. Boston, Toronto: Little, Brown, 1974. [Chapters 2–3, pp. 3–85.]
3409. *Stage,* 1 May 1906.
* Raoul Sobel and David Francis' *Chaplin; Genesis of a clown* (L: Quartet Books, 1977) supersedes all earlier accounts of Chaplin's prefilm career in its attempts at establishing an exact chronology, exploding myths, and relating his comedy to traditional music-hall techniques.

BUSTER KEATON

3410. KEATON, BUSTER with CHARLES SAMUELS. *My Wonderful World of Slapstick*. L: Allen & Unwin, 1967. [Chapter 3: The

Keatons Invade Britain.]

STAN LAUREL [né Stanley Jefferson]

3411. McCABE, JOHN. *The Comedy World of Stan Laurel.* Garden City, N.Y.: Doubleday, 1974.
3412. [TURCONI, DAVIDE] "Stan Laurel." In *EDS* 6: 1280.

XII. RECORDINGS

Although sound recording arrived too late to enregister the voices of the first generation of music-hall performers, by the last decade of the century, most of the major artistes were represented in the catalogues of gramophone companies. Many of them failed to show up to advantage—"How can I be funny into a funnel?" (Dan Leno's complaint) illustrates the dismay of the performer at having to pare down an oversize personality and performance technique to accommodate an imperfect technology. Others, like Billy Williams and the elder George Formby, excelled at the intimate rendition required by the sound apparatus. But successful or not, these early recordings are valuable documents for the study of variety in its heyday.

The scope of the present work will not permit a discography of phonocylinders and discs prior to the era of the long-playing record. A listing of Harry Lauder's recordings alone would fill a brochure. The student will be able to find such listings in the books listed below, as well as in the journal *Music Hall Records* (from 1979 *Music Hall*), each issue of which provides well-researched discographies for at least two performers. We have, however, included a summary inventory of long-playing records, both re-releases of earlier pressings and recreations of earlier songs, for these works may be more easily available to a modern collector and student. In one case, that of Stanley Holloway, the performer has recorded both works he made famous in the halls (his "Sam Small" and "Albert" recitations) and interpretations of Victorian and Edwardian material in reasonably accurate versions.

Recordings

BOOKS AND ARTICLES

Cross-references

See also **77, 1967, 2031, 2140, 2155, 2162, 2249, 2388, 2498, 2562, 2965a.**

3413. ANDREWS, FRANK. "Music Hall Artists and Sound Recording; the Earliest to Record." *Music Hall Records* 2 (Aug. 1978): 8-12; 4 (Dec. 1978): 74-76.

3414. KOENIGSBURG, ALLEN. *Edison Cylinder Records 1889-1912.* Brooklyn, N.Y.: The Author, 1970. [Billy Williams, Jack Pleasants, Julian Rose, *et al.*]

3415. RUST, BRIAN. *British Music Hall on Record.* Harrow (Middlesex): General Gramophone Publications, 1979. [A comprehensive discography.] Rev. P. Gammond, *Gramophone,* Oct. 1979.

3416. ———. *Complete Entertainment Discography from the mid-1890s to 1942.* New Rochelle, N.Y.: Arlington House, 1973. [Written with Allen G. Debus. Josephine Baker, Maurice Chevalier, Maurice Farkoa, Gracie Fields, Will Fyffe, Yvette Guilbert, George Lashwood, Harry Lauder, Cissie Loftus, Julian Rose, Eugene Stratton, Vesta Tilley, Vesta Victoria, *et al.*]

3417. ———. *London Musical Shows on Records 1897-1976.* Harrow: General Gramophone Publications, 1977. [Written with Rex Burnett. Nora Blaney, Fred Emney, Sr., Maurice Farkoa, Sid Field, Bud Flanagan, George Formby, Sr., Louie Freear, Stanley Holloway, G. P. Huntley, Lupino Lane, Ethel Levey, Stanley Lupino, Tom McNaughton, Clarice Mayne, Billy Merson, Talbot O'Farrell, Ada Reeve, Ella Retford, George Robey, Harry Tate.]

3418. SENELICK, LAURENCE. "'All Trivial Fond Records': On the Uses of Early Recordings of British Music-hall Performers." *Theatre Survey* (N.Y.) 16, no. 2. (Nov. 1975): 135-49. [With a Research Note on Sound Collections.]

3419. STONE, CHRISTOPHER. "Jam Session 1897." *Daily Mail,* Dec. 1946.

DISCOGRAPHY OF LONG-PLAYING RECORDS

Cross-references

See also **2350, 3715, 3821.**

Original Performers: Anthologies

3420. *Daniel Farson Presents Music Hall.* (Fontana 680 943TL TFL 5043) (*Hetty King:* Ship Ahoy; *Albert Whelan:* The Jolly Brothers, the Preacher and the Bear; *Hughie Diamond:* I Love a Lassie; Stop Yer Tickling, Jock; He's a Bra' Bra' Highland Laddie; Keep Right on to the End of the Road; *Ida Barr:* Everybody's Doing It Now; Oh, You Beautiful Doll; *G. H. Elliott:* I Used to Sigh for the Silvery Moon; *Billy Danvers:* Kiss Me Goodnight; *Marie Lloyd Jnr:* I'm a Bit of a Ruin that Cromwell Knocked About a Bit.) [Music-hall veterans performing live before Chelsea pensioners.]

3421. *The Golden Age of the Music Hall.* (Rhapsody RHA 6014. Reissued as Delta TQD 3030). (*Gus Elen:* Wait Till the Work Comes Round; *Vesta Victoria:* Riding on a Motor Car; *Albert Chevalier:* My Old Dutch; The Fallen Star; *Marie Lloyd:* When I Take My Morning Promenade; The Coster Girl in Paris; *Dan Leno:* The Robin; The Tower of London; *Louis Bradfield:* The First Cigar; *George Robey:* Bang Went the Chance of a Lifetime; *Arthur Roberts:* Where's the Count?; *Henry Lytton:* When I Marry Amelia; *Little Tich:* The Territorial; *Florrie Forde:* Anona.)

3422. *Golden Voices of the Music Hall.* (Decca—Ace of Clubs ACL 1077). (*Ella Shields:* Burlington Bertie from Bow; The Army; *Tom Leamore:* Mick MacDougal; Percy from Pimlico; *Nellie Wallace:* The Blasted Oak; Three Times a Day; *Gus Elen:* It's A Great Big Shame; 'Arf a Pint of Ale; *Hetty King:* Tell Her the Old Old Story; Down Beside the Riverside; *Albert Whelan:* The Three Trees; The Preacher and the Bear.)

3423. *The Great Days of the Music Hall.* (Music for Pleasure MFP 1146) (*Mark Sheridan:* Hello, Hello, Who's Your Lady Friend; *Harry Champion:* I'm Henery the Eighth, I am; *Ella Retford:* Ship Ahoy; *Billy Merson:* On the Good Ship Wacki-Hicki-Doola; The Spaniard that Blighted My Life; *Vesta Victoria:* Waiting at the Church; Daddy Wouldn't Buy Me a Bow-wow; Poor John; *Charles Coborn:* The Man Who Broke the Bank at Monte Carlo; *Florrie Forde:* Down at the Old Bull and Bush; It's a Long Way to Tipperary.)

3424. *Hail Variety.* (Oriole MG 20033) (Forty artists, including Max Miller, Harry Champion, Ella Shields, Billy Williams, Marie Lloyd, Dan Leno, Gus Elen, Lily Morris, Albert Chevalier, Arthur Reece, Violet Loraine and George Robey, Little Tich, Gertie Gitana, Harry Lauder, Charles Austin, Harry Tate, Will Hay, Eugene Stratton, Florrie Forde, Albert Whelan, Charles Coborn, Tony Steele. Compère George Elrick.)

3425. *Let's All Go the Music Hall.* (Argo ZSW 535/6) (*Harry Claff:* Let's All Go to the Music Hall; *Trevor Crozier:* Sam Hall; *Robb Currie:* Beer, Glorious Beer; Auld Lang Syne; *Harry Fay and Company:* Jolly Company; *Alfred Lester and Buena Bent:* The Village Fire Brigade; *Primo Scala's Accordion Band:* The Man on the Flying Trapeze; *Sandra Kerr:* The Boy in the Gallery; *Bobbie Comber and Company:* Champagne Charlie; I Can't Tell You Why I Love You But I Do; Three Women to Every Man; *The Victor Chorus:* Paddle Your Own Canoe; *Gertie Gitana:* Nellie Dean; *Albert Chevalier:* 'E Can't Take a Roise out of Oi; *Maidie Scott:* If the Managers Only Thought the Same as Mother; *George Jackley and Leslie Sarony:* Excelsior; *Billy Merson:* The Night I Appeared as Macbeth; *Piccadilly Orchestra:* Cinderella Music; *London Orchestra:* Lancashire Clogs; *Domenico Possetti's Orchestra:* The Entry of the Gladiators; *Dawson's Musical Canaries:* Liebesträume; *Marie Kendal:* A Bird in a Gilded Cage; *Harry Champion:* I Enjoyed It; *Florrie Forde:* Kelly from the Isle of Man; *Creswell Colliery Band:* Rule Britannia; *Raymond Newell:* The Boys of the Old Brigade; *George Bastow:* Captain Ginjah O. T.; *Gus Elen:* Wait 'till the Work Comes Round; *Ella Shields:* Burlington Bertie from Bow; *Maurice Farkoa:* I Love You in Velvet; *Alice Lloyd:* The Nearer the Bone, the Sweeter the Meat; *Rosie Lloyd:* When I Take My Morning Promenade; *George Formby:* Toodle-i-oodle-i-oo; Twice Nightly; *Wilkie Bard:* The Cleaner; *Dan Leno:* Mrs. Kelly; *The Ridgeway Parade:* Watching the Trains Go By; *George Lashwood:* Riding on Top of the Car; *Charles Coborn:* It's So Simple; *Marie Lloyd:* Every Little Movement Has a Meaning of Its Own; *G. H. Chirgwin:* The Jocular Joker; *Little Tich:* One of the Deathless Army; *George Robey:* It's the First Time I've Ever Seen That; *Harry Lauder:* Roamin' in the Gloamin'; *Vesta Tilley:* Jolly Good Luck to the Girl Who Loves a Soldier; *Clarice Mayne:* Give Me a Cosy Little Corner; Put on Your Ta-ta, Little Girlie.) [Includes contemporary commentary read by actors like Stanley Holloway and Sandy Powell; songs are often cut.]

3426. *Music Hall to Variety. Volume One: Matinee.* (World Record Club. SH 148) (*Albert Chevalier:* My Old Dutch; *Clarice Mayne and "That":* Joshua; *George Bastow:* Captain Ginjah O. T.; *George Robey:* Archibald! Certainly Not; *Eugene Stratton:* Lily of Laguna; *Florrie Forde:* Down at the Old Bull and Bush; *Albert Whelan:* Whistling Bowery Boy; *George Formby:* The Grandfather Clock; *Billy Williams:* When Father Papered the Parlour; *Harry Champion:* A Little Bit of Cucumber; *Ella Shields:* Burlington Bertie from Bow; *G. H. Elliott:* Down Home in Tennessee; *Marie Lloyd:* Revue; *Fred Emney and Sydney Fairbrother:* A Sister to Assist 'Er; *Ada Reeve:* Foolish Questions; *Harry Fragson:* The Other Department, Please.)

3427. *Music Hall to Variety. Volume Two: First House.* (World Record Club SH 149) (*Harry Tate and Company:* Motoring; *Lily Morris:* Don't Have Any More, Missus Moore; *Flotsam & Jetsam:* Little Betty Bouncer; *Layton & Johnstone:* Here Am I Broken-hearted; *Will Hay and his Scholars:* Fourth Form at St. Michael's; *Leslie Sarony:* Don't Do That to the Poor Puss Cat; *Charles Penrose:* The Laughing Policman; *Norah Blaney & Gwen Farmer:* Second Hand Rose; *Tommy Handley & Company:* The Disorderly Room; *Sophie Tucker:* Me and Myself; *Billy Bennett:* Don't Send My Boy to Prison; *Douglas Byng:* Mexican Minnie; *Tom Clare:* The Fine Old English Gentleman.)

3428. *Music Hall to Variety. Volume Three: Second House.* (World Record Club SH 150) (*Horace Kenney:* A Music Hall Trial Turn; *Gracie Fields:* Rochdale Hounds; *Tessie O'Shea:* Two Ton Tessie; *Ronald Frankau:* I'd Like to Have a Honeymoon with Her; *Nervo & Knox, Naughton & Gold, Flanagan & Allen:* The Crazy Gang at Sea; *Nellie Wallace:* Under the Bed; *Stanley Holloway:* Runcorn Ferry; *Elsie & Doris Waters:* The Coronation Girls; *Max Miller:* Mary from the Dairy; *Florence Desmond:* Hollywood Party; *The Western Brothers:* Play the Game, You Cads; *Robb Wilton:* The Home Guard.)

3429. *Music Hall Top of the Bill.* (EMI World Records SHB 22 ST 221/222) (*Vesta Victoria:* Now I Have to Call Him Father; *Gus*

Elen: It's a Great Big Shame; If It Wasn't for the 'Ouses in Between; Wait Till the Work Comes Round; *Marie Lloyd:* That's How the Little Girl Got on; A Little of What You Fancy Does You Good; *Alec Hurley:* 'Arry, 'Arry, 'Arry; *Herbert Campbell:* Up I Came with My Little Lot; *Tom Costello:* I Made up My Mind to Sail Away; *George Lashwood:* Riding on Top of a Car; *Fred Emney & Sydney Fairbrother:* Mrs. Le Browning; *Harry Lauder:* Stop Yer Tickling, Jock!; *Victoria Monks:* Give My Regards to Leicester Square; If You Want to Have a Row Wait till the Sun Shines; *Whit Cunliffe:* A Wee Deoch an' Doris; *Lil Hawthorne:* Tessie; *George Formby:* I Had My Hands in My Pocket; *Maidie Scott:* The Bird on Nellie's Hat; *Eugene Stratton:* Little Dolly Daydream; *Kate Carney:* All Your Pals May Leave You; *Dan Leno:* The Beefeater; *Florrie Forde:* Oh! Oh! Antonio; *Ella Retford:* Mollie O'Morgan; *Mark Sheridan:* I Do Like to Be Beside the Seaside; *Wilkie Bard:* I Want to Sing in Opera; *Clarice Mayne & "That":* Nursie Nursie; *Little Tich:* The Best Man; *Vesta Tilley:* Jolly Good Luck to the Girl; *Billy Williams:* Kangaroo Hop; *Gertie Gitana:* My Dusky Princess; *Albert Whelan:* Yiddle on Your Fiddle; *The Two Bobs:* Waiting for the Robert E. Lee; *Beth Tate:* Take a Look at Me Now; *George Robey:* Mayor of Mudcumdyke.)

3430. *Oh, What a Lovely War.* (World Record Club SH 130) (*Courtland & Jeffries:* Oh! It's a Lovely War; Good-bye-ee; *Mark Sheridan:* Belgium Put the Kibosh on the Kaiser; *Edna Thornton:* Your King & Country Want You; *Gwendoline Brogden:* I'll Make a Man of You; *Murray Johnson:* Pack Up Your Troubles in Your Old Kit Bag; When the Moon Shines Bright on Charlie Chaplin; *Alfred Lester:* A Conscientious Objector; *Marie Lloyd:* Now You've Got Yer Khaki on; *Savoy Quartette:* Oh Boy' When You're Home on Leave; Over There; *Walter Jeffries:* When the War is Over, Mother Dear; *Renee Meyer:* Till the Boys Come Home; *Ernest Pike:* Roses of Picardy; *Lee White:* America Answers the Call; *George Grossmith and Haidee de Rance:* They Didn't Believe Me.)

3431. *Stars Who Made the Music Hall.* (Decca Ace of Clubs ACL 1170) (*Randolph Sutton:* When Are You Going to Lead Me to the Altar, Walter?; *Kate Carney:* Are We to Part Like This, Bill?; *Gus Elen:* Nice Quiet Day (The Postman's Holiday); *Hetty King:* Piccadilly; *Jack Pleasants:* I'm Shy Mary Ellen; *Florrie Forde:* Down at the Old Bull and Bush; *Charles Coborn:* The Man Who Broke the Bank at Monte Carlo; *George Jackley:* We All Went up the Mountain; *Lily Morris:* Why Am I Always the Bridesmaid?;

George Formby Jnr: John Willie, Come On; *Billy Bennett:* The League of Nations; *Billy Merson:* The Night I Appeared as Macbeth; *Tessie O'Shea:* Nobody Loves a Fairy When She's Forty; *Billy Russell:* On Behalf of the Working Classes, including We're Gonna Hang Out the Washing on the Siegfried Line.)

3432. *Top of the Bill.* (Fidelio ATL 4010) (*Harry Lauder:* I Love a Lassie; Same as His Father Did Before Him; *Little Tich:* The Gas Inspector. *Dan Leno:* Going to the Races; *Marie Lloyd:* Put on Your Slippers; Every Little Movement; *Eugene Stratton:* I May Be Crazy; Lily of Laguna; *Florrie Forde:* Has Anybody Here Seen Kelly?; Hold Your Hand Out, Naughty Boy; *Albert Chevalier:* My Old Dutch; 'E Can't Take a Roise out of Oi.)

3433. *The World of Music Hall.* (Decca PA 81) (*Leslie Sarony:* In the Twi-twi-twilight; *Florrie Forde:* She's a Lassie from Lancashire; Waltz Me Around Again, Willie; *Billy Danvers:* Kiss Me; *George Robey:* It's the First Time I've Ever Done That; *Marie Kendal:* Medley: Dorothy Dean; Kiss the Girl if You're Going to; When Liza got on the Donkey; Oh! said the Judge, Be Careful; Just Like the Ivy I'll Cling to You; Sweet Rosie O'Grady; Two Little Girls in Blue; A Bird in a Gilded Cage; I'll Be Your Sweetheart; *Albert Whelan:* Intro to the Three Trees; *Bobbie Comber:* Let's All Go to the Music Hall; *Max Miller:* Confessions of a Cheeky Chappie; *Marie Lloyd Jnr:* It's a Bit of a Ruin that Cromwell Knocked about a Bit; *Dick Tubb:* Ladies of the Naughty Nineties.)

Original Performers: Individuals

BILLY BENNETT

3434. *Almost a Gentleman.* (Topic 12T387) (Nell; My Mother Doesn't Know I'm on the Stage; Mandalay; I'll Be Thinking of You; Ogul Mogul—a Kanakanese Love Lyric; No Power on Earth; She Was Poor But She Was Honest; Family Secrets; Please Let Me Sleep on Your Doorstep Tonight; Christmas Day in the Cookhouse; The Club Raid; She's Mine; Mottoes; The Green Tie on the Little Yellow Dog.)

GUS ELEN

3435. *Gus Elen Sings.* (Privately issued for BMHS. Research and compilation by Douglas White. Notes on Gus Elen by John Moffat.) [Includes discography and filmography of GE on sleeve.] (If I Were King of England; It's a Marvel 'Ow 'E Does It, But 'E Do; The Pavement Artist; Me-mah; Don't Stop Me 'Arf a Pint o'Beer; Nature's Made a Big Mistake; The Publican; Pretty Little Villa down at Barking; I'm Going to Settle Down; Dick Whittington; The Coster's Pony; Mrs. Carter; 'E Dunno Where 'E Are; If It Wasn't for the 'Ouses in Between.)

GRACIE FIELDS

3436. *"Our Gracie." Gracie Fields Sings Her Most Popular Favorites.* (Point P-227) (That Lovely Weekend; Ave Maria; Walter, Walter, Lead me to the Altar; An Old Violin; He's Dead—But He Won't Lie Down; The Biggest Aspidistra in the World; Rose O'Day; The Bleeding Heart; The Thing-ummy-bob; Nighty-night Little Sailor Boy.)

3437. *Sing As We Go.* (London Ace of Clubs ACL 7914) (Sing as We Go; Grandfather's Bagpipes; I Love to Whistle; Danny Boy; I Never Cried So Much in All My Life; There is a Tavern in the Town; Medley; Little Old Lady; In Me 'Oroscope; The Sweetest Song in the World; Little Drummer Boy; When I Grow Too Old to Dream; Smile When You Say Goodbye.)

3438. *Stage and Screen. At the Holborn Empire 11th October 1933 plus Her Film Successes.* (World Record Club SH-170) (There's a Cabin in the Pines; Whiskers and All; The Punch and Judy Show; The Rochdale Hounds; May Morn; Out in the Cold Cold Snow; I Can't Remember; Sally; Stormy Weather; Fall in and Follow the Band; Happy Ending; My Lucky Day; Heaven Will Protect an Honest Girl; Sing as We Go; Love is Everywhere; Mrs. Binns' Twins; Danny Boy; Grandfather's Bagpipes; Annie Laurie; Wish Me Luck as You Wave Me Goodbye.)

3439. *The World of Gracie Fields.* (Decca SPA 82) (Sally; Come Back to Sorrento; Walter, Walter; Heaven Will Protect an Honest Girl; Bless This House; Shall I Be an Old Man's Darling; At the End of the Day; Little Old Lady; The Rochdale Hounds; Count Your Blessings; He's Dead but He Won't Lie Down; Oh! My Beloved Father; Now is the Hour.)

3440. *The World of Gracie Fields, Vol. 2.* (Decca SPA 125) [Recordings 1938-48.] (Sally; Sing As We Go; Pedro the Fisherman; Out in the Cold Cold Snow; In My Little Bottom Drawer; Red Sails in the Sunset; Turn 'Erbert's Face to the Wall, Mother; Lancashire Blues; The Kerry Dance; I Took My Harp to a Party; The Biggest Aspidistra in the World; Bluebird of Happiness; Ave Maria.)

FLANAGAN & ALLEN

3441. *The Best of Flanagan & Allen.* (EMI Starline SRS 5130)

(Underneath the Arches; Music Maestro Please; Home Town;
Maybe It's Because I'm a Londoner; Umbrella Man; How Do
You Do Mister Right; Home is Where Your Heart Is; Strollin';
Nice People; Hey Neighbor; Free; On the Other Side of Town;
Galloping Major; Goodbye Sue.)

3442. *We'll Smile Again.* (Ace of Clubs ACL 1196) (We're Gonna
Hang Out the Washing on the Siegfried Line; Let's Be Buddies; If
a Grey-haired Lady Says 'How's Yer Father?'; Don't Ever Walk
in the Shadows; The Smiths and the Jones; I'm Nobody's Baby;
Yesterday's Dreams; There's a Boy Coming Home on Leave;
Why Don't You Fall in Love with Me?; F.D.R. Jones; Don't
Believe Everything You Dream; What More Can I Say; Run,
Rabbit, Run; We'll Smile Again.)

GEORGE FORMBY

3443. *The Best of George Formby.* (EMI One-up OU 2072) (The Win-
dow Cleaner; Grandad's Flannelette Nightshirt; Riding in the
T.T. Races; In My Little Snapshot Album; I'm the Ukelele Man;
It's in the Air; Count Your Blessings and Smile; Mother What'll I
Do Now?; Leaning on a Lamp Post; Auntie Maggie's Remedy;
With My Little Stick of Blackpool Rock; Mr. Wu's a Window
Cleaner Now; Frigid Air Fanny; They Can't Fool Me; The Lan-
cashire Toreador; Our Sergeant Major.)

WILL FYFFE

3444. *I Belong to Glasgow.* (World Records SH 200)
3445. *On the Halls.* (World Record Club SH 43)

YVETTE GUILBERT

3446. *Les Belles années du music-hall no. 41: Yvette Guilbert.* (Pathé
EMI HTX 40246) [Accompagnement au piano: Irène Aitoff.] (Le
Fiacre; La Complainte des quatre z'étudiants; L'Hôtel du no. 3.;
Partie carrée entre les Boudin et les Bouton; Verligodin; La
Délaissée; D'elle à lui; Madame Arthur; Quand on vous aime
comme ça; L'Éloge des vieux; Les Vieux messieurs; Le Voyage de
Bethléem; La Passion du doux Jésus.)

3447. *Yvette Guilbert.* (Pathé DT 20001) (Le Voyage de Bethléem; Le
Miracle de Saint Berthe; C'est le Mai; La Passion du doux Jésus,
Ballade de Jésus-Christ; La Fille du roi Loys; Les Anneaux de
Marianson; La Délaissée.)

STANLEY HOLLOWAY

3448. *Champagne Charlie.* (World Record Club T325, ST325) [In

U.S.A. as *Tavern Songs of Old London* (Decca DL 4422). Over-orchestrated.] (Going to the Derby; My Lord Tomnoddy; Act on the Square, Boys!; If I Had a Donkey; The Workhouse Boy; Married to a Mermaid; A Motto for Every Man; Hey! Betty Martin; Shelling Green Peas; All 'round My Hat; Poor Old Horse; Champagne Charlie.)

3449. *'Ere's 'Olloway. Stanley Holloway with the Loverly Quartet.* (Realm CBS RM 52066) (Let's All Go down the Strand!; "My Word, You Do Look Queer!"; "Hello, hello! Who's Your Lady Friend?"; The Little Shirt My Mother Made for Me; You Can Do a Lot of Things at the Seaside; I Live in Trafalgar Square; And Yet I Don't Know; I'm Shy, Mary Ellen, I'm Shy; Oh I Must Go Home Tonight!; Sweeney Todd the Barber; Eving's Dorg 'Ospital; The Spaniard that Blighted My Life; My Old Dutch; Harry Champion Medley; It'll All Be the Same.)

3450. *His Famous Adventures with Old Sam and the Ramsbottoms.* (Angel Ang 650 19) (Albert and the Lion; Albert Comes Back; Runcorn Ferry; Albert and the Headsman; Jubilee Sovereign; Ann Boleyn; Marksman Sam; One Each Apiece; Sam's Medal; Sam Drummed Out; The 'Ole in the Ark; Jonah and the Grampus.)

3451. *"Join in the Chorus." English Music Hall Favorites.* (World Record Club T912, ST912) [In U.S.A. Vanguard VRS 9086.] (Join in the Chorus; Lily of Laguna; Any Old Iron?; A Bachelor Gay; While Strolling in the Park; The Honeysuckle and the Bee; Wot Cher! (Knocked 'em in the Old Kent Road); Down at the Old Bull & Bush; If I Should Plant a Tiny Seed of Love; Where Did You Get That Hat?; If You Were the Only Girl in the World; The Galloping Major; Two Lovely Black Eyes.)

3452. *Life in the Old Dog Yet.* (Argo ZDA 170) [Alan Cohen and his orchestra, Chris Hazell, piano.] (My Word, You Do Look Queer; The Battle of Hastings; Leanin'; St. George and the Dragon; Marksman Sam; The Parson of Puddle; Gunner Joe; Hand in Hand; And Yet I Don't Know; Albert's Re-union; Nature's Made a Big Mistake; The Magna Charter; Recumbent Posture; Life is What You Make It.)

3453. *The World of Stanley Holloway.* (Argo SPA 199) [Piano accompaniment by Michael Garrick.] (The Lion and Albert; Pick oop tha' Musket; Uppards!; Albert Comes Back; Beat the Retreat on Thy Drum; Brahn Boots; Good Old Yorkshire Pudden; Runcorn Ferry; With Her Head Tucked Underneath Her Arm; Three Ha'pence a Foot; Albert's Birthday; Old Sam's Party.)

SIR HARRY LAUDER

3454. *Harry Lauder, Esq. of Laudervale.* (Transatlantic XTRA 1097)
3455. *The Immortal Harry Lauder.* (RCA Camden CDN-130) (Wee Deoch an' Doris; Soosie Maclean; Wee Hoose 'Mang the Heather; Medley; End of the Road; etc.).
3456. *More Scotch Songs.* (Everest/Scala Sc-883) (She's the Lass for Me; The Message Boy; The Kilty Lads; Hey! Donal; Jean MacNeil; The Bounding Bounder or On the Bounding Sea; He Was Very Kind to Me; The Wee Hoose 'Mang the Heather; Foo' the nou'.)
3457. *Scotch Songs.* (Everest/Scala Sc-877) (Roamin' in the Gloamin'; I Love a Lassie; The Saftest of the Family; The Blarney Stone; A Wee Deoch an' Doris; MacGregor's Toast; When I Get Back to Bonnie Scotland; Breakfast in Bed on Sunday Morning.)
3458. *Sir Harry Lauder.* (Ember EMB 3404)

MAX MILLER

3459. *Golden Hour of Max Miller the Cheeky Chappie!* (Golden Hour GH 584) [Recorded live at the Holborn Empire, Edgware Road, 30 Nov. 1957; and at Star Sound Studios, 9 Sept. 1962.]
3460. *Max Miller in the Theatre.* (One-Up EMI OU 2075) [Recorded live at the Holborn Empire, 24 Oct. 1938.]
3461. *Max Miller. "You Can't Help Liking Him."* (Hallmark HMA 240) [Recorded at the Star Sound Studios, 9 Sept. 1962.]

RANDOLPH SUTTON

3462. *On Mother Kelly's Doorstep.* (Decca ACL 1266)

Recreations: Groups

3463. *Ave A Go wiv the Buskers.* (RCA Victor International FSP 104) (Glorious Beer; The Sunshine of Paradise Alley; She Told Me to Meet Her at the Gate; Nellie Dean; After the Ball; I Do Like to Be Beside the Seaside; Any Old Iron; Down at the Old Bull and Bush; Boiled Beef and Carrots; The Sunshine of Your Smile; Wot Cher or Knock'd 'em in the Old Kent Road; Far Far Away.)
3464. *Balmbra's Music Hall, Newcastle-on-Tyne.* (Decca EC 2-2073)
3465. *The Birth of Music Hall.* (World Record Club T797; ST 797) [Known in U.S.A. as *Anacreonticks* (Decca DL 4289). Orchestra conducted by Alfred Ralston. Good performances, grotesquely over-orchestrated.] (*Charles Young:* Champagne Charlie; *Benny Lee:* Pretty Polly Perkins; Work Boys Work; *Rita Williams*

Singers: Britannia Pride of the Ocean; *Alfie Bass:* Rat Catcher's Daughter; Villikins and his Dinah; Sam Hall; *Rita Williams:* Keemo, Kimo; *John Gower:* Anacreontic Song; Down among the Dead Men; *Benny Lee and Rita Williams:* Lost Child; *Pat Campbell:* Limerick Races.)

3466. *Charles Keeping's Cockney Ding Dong.* (Line Records L3032) [Chorus singing.] (Fall in and Follow Me; When There Isn't a Girl About; A Comical Cock; Wot Cher!; The D.C.M.; Liza, It's a Beautiful Starry Night; Memories; The Sunshine of Your Smile; My Old Dutch; It's a Great Big Shame; Jeerusalem's Dead; Pack up Your Troubles; Mademoiselle from Armentieres; The Moon Shines Tonight on Charlie Chaplin; It's a Long Way to Tipperary; Where Did You Get That Hat?; Come Inside Yer Silly Bugger; I'm Henery the Eighth; On Monday I Never Go to work; Don't Dilly Dally on the Way; They're Moving Father's Grave to Build a Sewer; I Speak the Truth; In the Shade of the Old Apple Tree; If Those Lips Could Only Speak; Feeding the Ducks on the Pond; Two Lovely Black Eyes; Glorious Beer; If It Wasn't for the 'Ouses in Between; Granny; Any Old Iron?; Boiled Beef and Carrots; I'm a Navvy; They're All Very Fine and Large; Down the Road; Knees Up Mother Brown.)

3467. *Daniel Farson's Music Hall.* (Philips 382065) [Known in U.S.A. as *Pubs, Pearlies & Pints. The Entertainers* (London International SW 99436). Recorded at the Waterman's Arms, East London.] (*Kim Cordell:* Maybe It's Because I'm a Londoner; Ta! Ta!; Sitting in the Shoeshine Shop; Bye bye Blackbird; *George Hiltteen:* Barrow Boy Song; *Rex Jameson:* Mrs. Shufflewick; *Tommy Pudding:* Put a Bit of Treacle on My Pudden, Mary Ann; *Rod Sparrow:* Oh Dear! What Can the Matter Be?; *Bob the Tray:* Mule Train; *Celia Hunt:* Don't Dilly-dally on the Way; Ship Ahoy!; Who Were You with Last Night?; Hello! Who's Your Lady Friend?; *Kerri Lane:* Bill Bailey Won't You Please Come Home?; *Tony Rayne:* Hard Hearted Hannah; *Hughie Diamond;* Scots Medley; *Ida Barr:* Come Up and See Me Sometime; Everybody's Doing It; Oh You Beautiful Doll; Recitation; *Sulky Gowers:* In a Shanty in Old Shanty Town.)

3468. *Duggie Chapman's Olde Tyme Music Hall.* (Saga Eros 8084) (*Ronnie Parnell:* Medley; *Kitty Gillow:* Following in Father's Footsteps; *Jean Barrington:* I'll Be Your Sweetheart; Peggy O'Neil; In the Twi-twi-twilight; Waiting at the Church; You Made Me Love You; The Sunshine of Your Smile; *George*

Raymonde: 'Till We Meet Again; *Buddy Smart and Peter Tracy:* Another Little Drink; There Is a Tavern in the Town; Goodbye-ee; *Tom Howard:* Roamin' in the Gloamin'; Lily of Laguna; My Old Dutch; Medley; Mammy.)

3469. *An Evening at Vauxhall Gardens in 1851.* (Rare Recorded Editions RRE 100)

3470. *The Good Old Days.* (CBS [S] 63077) [With Leonard Sachs.]

3471. *Keep Your Feet Still, Geordie Hinnie.* (Trailer LER 2020) [The High Level Ranters, with Johnny Handle and Tommy Gilfellon. Authentic performances of Tyneside music-hall songs.] (Keep Your Feet Still; The Pawnshop Bleezin; The Lambton Worm; Come, Geordie, Ha'd the Bairn; Geordie Black; Adam Buckham; Cushie Butterfield; The Neighbours Doon Belaa; Nannie's a Maizor; The Weshin Day; Last Neet; The Blaydon Races.)

3472. *Late Joys from the Player's Theatre, London.* (Decca SLK 4628) (Chairman: *Don Gemmell:* Covent Garden in the Morning; Oh! the Fairies!; Dear old Pals; *Stella Moray:* She Was Poor, But She Was Honest; Are We to Part Like This, Bill?; *Maurice Browning:* If It Wasn't for the 'Ouses in Between; *Margaret Burton:* The Honeysuckle and the Bee; *Patricia Rowlands:* When I Take My Morning Promenade; *Hattie Jacques:* The Bird on Nellie's Hat; Waiting at the Church; *John Rutland:* The Muffin Man; *Josephine Gordon:* I've Got Rings on My Fingers; *Joan Sterndale Bennett and Josephine Gordon:* He's Going There Every Night; *Robin Hunter:* Wot Cher! (Knocked 'em in the Old Kent Road); *Daphne Anderson:* Mother's Advice; *Clive Dunn:* My Old Dutch; *Joan Sterndale Bennett:* From Marble Arch to Leicester Square; *Bill Owen:* The Future Mrs. 'Awkins; *Dennis Martin, Brian Blades, Robin Hunter, David Jennings:* Goodbye Dolly Gray.)

3473. *Leonard Sachs—Old Time Music Hall.* (World Record Club 660 ST 667) [Known in U.S.A. as *An English Music Hall* (Capitol T10273).] (*Johnny Hewer:* Where Did You Get That Hat?; It's a Great Big Shame; *Rita Williams:* Don't Dilly Dally on the Way; Row, Row, Row; *Charles Young:* If Those Lips Could Only Speak; The Soldiers of the Queen; *Barbara Windsor:* Daddy Wouldn't Buy Me a Bow Wow; Soldiers in the Park; *Barney Gilbraith:* My Old Dutch; *Daphne Anderson:* I've Gone Out for the Day; *Rita Williams and Barbara Windsor:* I Don't Want to Play in Your Yard; *Four Singing Waiters:* Nellie Dean, Sweet Adeline.)

3474. *Mister Benjamin Hawthorne's Original Olde Tyme Music Hall.*

(Saga [S] SOC 1042)

Recreations: Individual Performers

3475. *'Alf & 'Alf: Songs of the British Music Hall.* (MGM SE-4381) [Merv Griffin and Arthur Treacher in London.] (When Father Papered the Parlour; The Ring Fell under the Sofa; She Pushed Me into the Parlour; Kitty the Telephone Girl; She's Going There Every Night; Gilbert the Filbert; I've Got a Loverly Bunch of Cocoanuts; I'm Henery the Eighth, I Am; My Old Dutch; Wot Cher (Knocked 'Em in the Old Kent Road); I'm Shy, Mary Ellen, I'm Shy; Who's Got the Suitcase.)

3476. *Beryl Reid Music Hall Singalong.* (EMI MFP 50174) (Fall in and Follow Me; The Honeysuckle and the Bee; Burlington Bertie from Bow; If You Were the Only Girl in the World; Oh! oh! Antonio; Moonstruck; Who Were You with Last Night?; Hold Your Hand out, Naughty Boy; I Live in Trafalgar Square; I'll Be Your Sweetheart; Only a Glass of Champagne; Don't Dilly Dally on the Way.)

3477. *Cockney London. Songs by Elsa Lanchester.* (Verve MGV-15015) [Accompanied by Ray Henderson.] (Our Threepenny Hop; When the Summer Comes Again; Her Golden Hair Was Hanging Down Her Back; He Didn't Oughter; Burlington Bertie from Bow; Put My Little Shoes Away; He Danced the Fandango All over the Place; At My Time of Life; When I Came to this House; Ta-ra-ra-Boom-de-ay; Mrs. Dyer, the Baby Farmer; The Old Kent Road; Won't You Buy My Sweet Blooming Lavender; The Fire Ship.)

3478. *Cockney Music Hall Songs and Recitations.* (Tradition TLP 1017) [Performed by Colyn Davies. Mainly broadsides and street ballads.] (They're Moving Father's Grave; The Cruel Gamekeeper; The Poor Young Man; The Captain's Apprentice; The Wind Was Weirdly Howling; The Hog's-eye Man; Villikins and his Dinah; Botany Bay; The Poor Young Girl; Georgie Barnvell; The Pig and Inebriate; Blow the Candles Out; Tim Turpin; Jack Hall.)

3479. *An Evening with Henry Russell.* (Nonesuch H-71338) [Clifford Nelson, baritone. William Bolcom, piano. Liner notes by Charles Hamm. Very authentic recreation.] (Cheer! Boys, Cheer!; Wind of the Winter Night; My Heart's in the Highlands; The Old Arm Chair; The Ship on Fire; A Life on the Ocean Wave; Woodman! Spare That Tree; The Dream of the Reveller; The Ivy Green; The Maniac.)

3480. *Heart-rending Ballads and Raucous Ditties.* (CBS SBPG-62405) [Sung by Julie Andrews.]

3481. *I Sing in a Pub. Kim Cordell.* (SEG 8449 Columbia/EMI) [45 rpm.] (Medley; Strollin'; The Boy I Love Is up in the Gallery; Maybe It's Because I'm a Londoner.)

3482. *I Sing in a Pub. Part II. Kim Cordell.* (Columbia/EMI SEG 8455) [45 rpm.] (Honeysuckle and the Bee; Wot Cher (Knocked 'em in the Old Kent Road); Underneath the Arches; Down at the Old Bull and Bush.)

3483. *John Foreman. . .The 'Ouses in Between.* (Reality RY 1004) [Excellent performance.] (The Four oss Sharrybang; If It Wasn't for the'Ouses in Between; Your Baby 'as Gorn dahn the Plug 'ole; Married to a Mermaid; Pretty Polly Perkins; Don't Go Down the Mine, Dad; The Hob-nailed Boots that Farver Wore; I Live in Trafalgar Square; Down the Road; If Those Lips Could Only Speak; The Amateur Whitewasher; Villikins and his Dinah; The Winkle Song; Captain Ginjah O.T.)

3484. *A Little Bit Off the Top: Dave and Al Sealey.* (Cosmotheka-Highway Records) (You Don't Want to Keep on Showing It, May; Billy's Wild Woodbine; Wait till the Work Comes Round; 'Arry, 'Arry, 'Arry; A Little Bit off the Top; Ragtime Waltz, *et al.*)

3485. *She Was Poor But She Was Honest. Nice, Naughty and Nourishing Songs of the London Music Hall and Pubs.* (Folkways FW 8707) [Sung by Derek Lamb with guitar augmented by banjo, violin, and voices.] (She Was Poor but She Was Honest; The Money Rolls in; Pickled Onions; Don't Cry Daddy; The Winkle Song; Roll-tiddly-ole; Pretty Polly Perkins; Botany Bay; The Hole in the Elephant's Bottom; The Landlady's Daughter; Slap Dab; Nine Inch Nails; My Daughter's Wedding Day; The Poor Young Girl; Villikins and his Dinah; Sweeney Todd the Barber; Barsted King of England; The Old Baby Farmer; I Don't Want to Play in Your Yard; They're Moving Grandpa's Grave to Build a Sewer; Thirty Years Ago today; Two Lovely Black Eyes; Do It No More; The End of My Old Cigar; The Little Shirt My Mother Made for Me; My Ma's a Millionaire; Wise Men Say; Any Old Iron; You Are a Marvel; Henery the Eighth; The Miner's Dream of Home.) [Low-key rendition of primarily street songs.]

3486. *Tessie O'Shea. Cheers.* (Command RS 33-872) [Originated and produced by Enoch Light.] (I've Got a Lovely Bunch of Cocoanuts; Maybe It's Because I'm a Londoner; It All Belongs to Me; Lily of Laguna; When You Come to the End of a Lollipop; It's Men Like You; I've Got Sixpence; Don't Have Any More,

Mrs. Moore; Two Ton Tessie; The Honeysuckle and the Bee; Joshu-ah; Hold Your Hand Out, Naughty Boy!)

3487. *This Is My Bag! Fifteen Great Songs of the Music Hall.* (Pye PKL 5548) [Sung by Roy Hudd.]

SUPPLEMENTS

"Many blessings may have been ordained by fate for the epoch of which the last expression is to be found in the notes of Verdi, but the artistic vocation was certainly not among them. Its own creation—the *café chantant*—an amphibious product, half-way between the beer-cellar and the boulevard theatre, fits it perfectly. I have nothing against *cafés chantants,* but I cannot give them serious artistic significance; they satisfy the 'average customer,' as the English say, the average consumer, the average bidder, the hundred-headed hydra of the middle class, and there is nothing more to be said."

Aleksandr Herzen, *My Past and Thoughts,* tr. Constance Garnett (N.Y.: Vintage Books, 1974) 662.

Despite the disdain of a Russian intellectual, even Herzen could not deny that the *café chantant* was a perfect embodiment of the nineteenth-century ethos. Because of the similarities and associations between the British music-hall and its Continental cognates, we considered it necessary to supply at least a cursory glance at those European forms.

However, a problem immediately arises, not present when investigating Britain. Very often in France, Germany, and Russia, the popular music-hall entertainment would merge with the literary cabaret, an independent subject of research which we could not begin to cover. We have therefore agreed to pick and choose the kinds of amusements granted coverage. In France, for instance, Aristide Bruant appears because his songs and cabaret were still firmly grounded in the life of the people, but the Chat Noir with its more precious recreations is omitted; in Germany, Karl Valentin, who appealed to the gross *Speisser* and the avant-garde artist alike, is cited, but not Frank Wedekind and the political cabarets of his time. Marinetti and the futurists appear under Italy, because of their interest in the ordinary variety theatre of their day; but under Russia, the literary miniature theatres of Nikolay Evreinov and Nikita Baliev have been ignored.

A note on foreign terminology is useful here. In Paris, boulevard cafés in which music could be heard were styled in the late eighteenth century *musicos,* a Dutch term, but by the Revolution they had already become known as *cafés chantants.* These were primarily outdoor entertainments; when they began to move inside, during the Second Empire, *cafés concerts* became the prevalent designation. These were the prestigious and well-established halls; smaller, more plebeian establishments were often known as *beuglants, bouis-bouis* or *bastringues. Cabaret,* which meant simply a tavern, did not take on its meaning of a night-spot providing smart entertainment until the last decade of the nineteenth century. It should be stressed that the *café concert* is the closest French equivalent of the Victorian and Edwardian music-hall, and was devoted wholly to song. The advent of variety entertainment brought new, sumptuous theatres, like the Folies-Bergère and the Casino de Paris; following the fashion for things English, the Olympia in 1892 adopted the title *music-hall* (the hyphen is *de rigueur* in French). The French *music-hall* is a *faux-ami* in translating the English term, however; with its elaborate production numbers, nudity, and sex appeal, it is closer to what an English speaker would call "revue."

Italy adopted French usage, with its *caffé concerto,* as did Spain with its *cafés cantantes.* However, in Italy, there seems to exist a distinction between a *caffé concerto,* where music plays during ordinary eating and drinking, and a *café chantant* [sic] where songs are sung. In any case, *varietà* soon ousted the older forms, and remains the usual term for a mixed bill of songs, comedy, specialty acts, and other turns. But in Europe, much more than in England, variety entertainments closely resemble circus shows, and the performances of acrobats, clowns, animal acts, and so on are interchangeable in both. Song, which remained an important feature of British music-hall even during the heyday of variety, on the Continent became relegated to cabaret or revue.

In Germany the close association of *Variété* and *Zirkus* held fast. Low singing-rooms were known as *Tingel-tangels,* a term already old-fashioned in the 1880s, while *Brettl* appears to have meant the popular stage in general. In 1900 Ernst von Wolzogen founded his literary cabaret and called it *Überbrettl* (or "Supergaff") on the analogy of Nietzsche's *Übermensch;* the name became a standard synonym for *Kabarett.* Russia has no indigenous nomenclature for its variety entertainments: *mjuzik-xoll,* an English loan, was common enough before the Revolution, but now is usually used in a pejorative sense as a coarse entertainment suitable only for the unreconstructed bourgeoisie or as the locale where Formalist theatrical experiments took place. The standard term is *estrada,* from the French *estrade,* a platform-stage, and can mean any form of variety show from recitations of poetry to circus acts.

SUPPLEMENT A
GENERAL FOREIGN

Cross-references

See also **179,239.**

3488. DAMASE, JACQUES. "Le Music-hall." In *Histoire des Spectacles,* ed. Guy Dumur. Paris; Gallimard, 1965. [Pp. 1543-55. Encyclopédie de la Pléiade.]
3488a. HOUDINI, HARRY [pseud. of Ehrich Weiss]. "European Music-halls and Managers." N.Y. *Dramatic Mirror,* Christmas

1905, pp. xxii-xxiii.

3489. FESCHOTTE, JACQUES. *Histoire du music-hall.* Paris: Presses Universitaires de France, 1965. (Série "Que Sais-je") [England, U.S., Italy, Germany, Russia, France.]

3489a. FIELDS, LEW. "European Music Hall." N.Y. *Dramatic Mirror,* 31 Jan. 1912, pp. 10-11.

3490. JACQUES-CHARLES. *Cent ans de music-hall: histoire générale du music-hall, de ses origines à nos jours, en Grande-Bretagne, en France, et aux U.S.A.* Génève-Paris: Jeheber, 1956. [Preface by Guy des Cars.]

3491. LESLIE, PETER. *A Hard Act to Follow: a Music-hall Review.* N.Y. and L: Paddington press, 1978. [Introduction by Pearl Bailey. Derivative; better on France than on England.]

3492. *The Orpheum Circuit of Continental Music-halls.* L [1912]. [A brochure on a plan to erect music-halls in various cities in France and Belgium.]

3493. OTTOLENGHI, VITTORIA. "Varietà." In *EDS.* [9: 1440-56. France by Luigi Ricci and Fiorenza Venzaga; Great Britain by Mollie Sands; United States by Bernard Sobel; Italy by Enzo Golino; Germany by Gisela Schwanbeck; Russia by Andrej Donatov and Genich Šluglejt.]

SUPPLEMENT B
FRANCE AND BELGIUM

Cross-references

See also General **331, 382, 1657–58, 1664-65, 1671-73, 1816, 2109, 2297-2325, 2560, 3378-79, 3488-93.**
Fiction **2300, 2306.**

General

3494. "About French Music Halls." *Era,* 4 Apr. 1885, p. 10; 1 Aug. 1885, p. 10.

3495. ACADÉMIE DU CIRQUE ET DU MUSIC-HALL. *Histoire du* *music-hall*. Paris: Editions de Paris, 1954. [By Edouard Beaudu, Pierre Bost, Robert Baze, Yves Brayer, Jacques Chesnais, Marcel Duvau, Paul Gilson, Dr Fernard Méry, Jean Texcier and Maurice Feaudierre dit Serge.]

3496. ADRIAN, PAUL. *Attractions sensationnelles. Les "Casse-cou" du cirque et du music hall*. Bourge-la-Reine (Seine): l'Auteur [1962]. [Limited to five hundred numbered copies.]

3497. *L'Assiette au Beurre* (Paris) 36 (7 Dec. 1901). [Ills. H. G. Ibels. Issue devoted to censorship in the music-hall.]

3498. AULNET, HENRI. *Le Music-hall moderne et les revues à grand spectacle*. Paris: Les Presses modernes, 1936.

3499. BACH, SIGISMUND FERDINAND. *Femmes du théâtre. Album absolument inédit*. Paris: Empis [1896]. [Prologue by Yvette Guilbert.]

3500. BATHILLE, PIERRE. *Maurice Donnay*. Paris: La Nouvelle revue critique, 1932.

3501. BEAUPLAN, R. DE. "L'Envers du music-hall." *L'Illustration* (Paris), 26 Mar. 1927, pp. 313-15.

3502. "A Belgium Café-chantant." N.Y. *Clipper,* 30 Apr. 1881, p. 93. [Alcazar.]

3503. BERCY, ANNE DE and ARMAND ZIWES. *A Montmartre le soir: cabarets et chansonniers d'hier*. Paris: Grasset, 1952.

3504. BERNARD, B. M. *Music Hall*. [Paris: 1949.] [Chiefly ills.]

3505. BERTAUT, J. *Les Belles nuits de Paris*. Paris: E. Flammarion, 1927. Repr. Paris: Tallandier [1956]. (Bibliothéque historie.)

3506. BIZET, RENÉ. "Dans la loge de Barbette." *Candide* (Paris), 14 Jan. 1926.

3507. ———. "La Danse au music-hall." *La Danse* (Paris), Feb. 1921.

3508. ———. *L'Époque du music-hall*. Paris: Ed. du Capitol, 1926.

3509. BONNAUD, DOMINIQUE. *Une Heure de musique avec Montmartre d'hier*. Paris: Aux Éditions cosmopolites, 1930. [Songs for one voice with piano accompaniment.]

3510. ———. MAURICE DONNAY and VINCENT HYSPA. *L'Esprit montmarteois. Interviews et souvenirs*. Joinville-le-Pont: Laboratories Carlier, 1938.

3511. BONREPAUX, GASTON. *Nos ancêtres les Gaulois. Les Pieds-noirs*. Monte-Carlo: Regain [1966]. [Chapter 4, "Le Pétomane," Pujol's tour of Algeria.]

3512. BOST, PIERRE. *Le Cirque et le music-hall*. Paris: Au Sans pareil, 1931. Rev. E. Gordon Craig, "The Paris Music Hall," *Saturday Review,* 13 June 1931, p. 867.

3513. *Bouis-bouis, bastringues et caboulots de Paris*. Paris: Tralin, 1861.

3514. BRACHARD, ADOLPHE D'HAENENSAR. *Guide des artistes du music-hall.* Bruxelles [Belgique]: L'Envers du théâtre, 1915.

3515. BRUANT, ARISTIDE. *Dans la rue. Chansons et monologues.* 2 vols. Paris: 1977. (Coll. "Les Introuvables." [Dessins de Steinlen. Réimpr. de l'ed. de Paris. First pub. 1889, 1896-97.]

3516. ———. *Sur la Route.* Loiret: Château de Courtenay, 1899. [Ills. Borgex. Songs and monologues.]

3517. BRUNACCI, GIORGIO. "Caffè concerto." EDS, 2: 1463-65.

3518. BRUNSCHWEIG, CHANTAL; LOUIS-JEAN CALVET and JEAN-CLAUDE KLEIN. *100 Ans de chanson francaise.* Paris: Ed. du Seuil, 1972. [Beautifully designed, extremely comprehensive encyclopedia with entries for famous songs, individual cafés-chantants, cabarets, music-halls, singers and composers.]

3519. "Café-chantant, a word for the music halls." *Era,* 21 Mar. 1885, p. 10.

3520. *Le Café concert 1870-1914. Affiches de la Bibliothèque du Musée des arts décoratifs du 10 octobre 1977 au 2 janvier 1978.* Paris: Musée des arts décoratifs, 1977. [Exhibition catalogue, text by Alain Weill.]

3521. *Cafés, bistrots et compagnie.* (Expositions itinérantes CCI No. 4). Paris: Centre du Création industrielle; Centre national d'art et de culture Georges Pompidou, 1977. [Exhibition catalogue.]

3522. "Les Cafés-concerts." *Le Figaro illustré* (Paris). Numéro spécial no. 75, June 1885.

3523. "Les Cafés-concerts." *Paris illustré* (Paris), 8 janvier 1886; 50 (1 août 1886): 129-50.

3524. "Cafés-concerts in Paris." *Era,* 10 Feb. 1900, p. 9.

3525. CANYAMERES, F. *L'Homme de la Belle Époque.* Paris: Éd. Universelles [1946]. [Preface by Gustave Fréjaville. La Goulue, pp. 77-86.]

3525a. CARADEC, FRANÇOIS and ALAIN WEILL. *Le Café concert.* Paris: Atelier Hachette/Massin, 1980. Rev. P. O'Connor, *TLS,* 11 July 1980, p. 784 [An excellent and concise survey by two of the finest modern experts.]

3526. CARCO, FRANCIS. *Les Humoristes.* Paris: Ollendorff, 1920.

3527. CENDRARS, BLAISE. *Le Plan de l'aiguille.* Paris: Au sans pareil, 1927.

3528. *Les Chansons et monologues illustrés.* 15 vols. Paris: Libres contemporaines [c. 1900]. [Scènes avec parlé, Chansons, Chansonettes, Romances avec musique (notée), Monologues comiques et dramatiques, etc. Créés, récités ou chantés par les principaux artistes des grands concerts parisiens.]

CHARLES, JACQUES. *See* JACQUES-CHARLES

3529. CHARNEUX, A., ed. *Un Procès de presse à propos du théâtre.* Namur: 1878. [Lawsuit of singer Judic and Humbert, manager of the Alcazar de Bruxelles vs. *L'Ami de l'Ordre.*]

3530. CHEVALIER, MAURICE. *Ma Route et mes chansons 1900-1950.* Paris: Julliard, 1950.

3531. ———. *The Man in the Straw Hat, My Story.* L: Odhams [1950]. [Adaptation of above.]

3532. ———. *Maurice Chevalier's Own Story, as told to Percy Cudlipp.* L: Nash & Grayson, 1930.

3533. COCTEAU, JEAN. "Le Numéro Barbette." *Nouvelle revue française* (Paris), 1 July 1926. Repr. as "Une leçon de théâtre" in *Antigone. Les Mariés de la Tour Eiffel.* Paris: Gallimard, 1928 [pp. 155-67].

3534. CODY, ÉMILE. *Cirque et music hall par A. Barrére.* [Paris] Souvenir du Cirque de Paris [n.d.].

3535. CONSTANTIN, MARC. *Histoire des cafés-concerts et des cafés de Paris.* Nouv. éd. rév. et augmentée. Paris: Renauld, 1872.

3536. ———. *La Lanterne magique, littéraire et artistique au cercle des variétés.* Paris: Panthéon contemporain, 1854.

3537. COQUIOT, GUSTAVE. *Les Cafés-concerts.* Paris: Librairie de l'art [1896].

3538. D'ALLEMAGNE, HENRY RENÉ. *Récréations et passe-temps.* Paris: Hachette [1906]. [Ouvrage contenant 249 ills. dans le texte et 132 gravures hors-texte dont 30 planches coloriées à l'aquarelle.]

3539. DAMASE, JACQUES. *Douze figures du music-hall.* Hollande: 1961.

3540. ———. *Les Folies du music-hall: histoire des music-halls à Paris de 1914 à nos jours.* Paris: Éd. "Spectacles," Trinckvel, 1960. [Preface by Bruno Coquatrix.] English trans. *Les Folies du Music-Hall: A History of the Music-hall in Paris from 1914 to the Present Day.* L: Anthony Blond, 1962. Repr. Feltham (Middlesex): Spring Books, 1970. [With a foreword by Noel Coward. Primarily pictures.]

3541. DAVIS, ESME. *Esme of Paris.* N.Y.: D. Appleton-Century, 1944. [Drawings by Constantin Alajalov.]

3542. "Death of Mme Judic." *Era,* 22 Apr. 1911, p. 15.

3543. DELVAU, ALFRED. *Histoire anecdotique des cafés & cabarets de Paris.* Paris: E. Dentu, 1862. [Avec dessins et eaux-fortes de Gustave Courbet, Léopold Flamencq et Félicien Rops.]

3544. *Les Demi-cabots. Le Café-concert—Le Cirque—Les Forains.*

Paris: Charpentier & Fasquelle, 1896. [Dessins de H. G. Ibels. Textes de Georges d'Esparbes, André Ibels, Maurice Lefèvre, Georges Montorgueil (pseud. of Octave Lebesque). O. Lebesque: "Le Café concert, " pp. 1-88; M. Lefèvre, "Les Gestes de la chanson, " pp. 89-148.]

3545. DENTU, E. *L'Eldorado et les cafés-concerts.* Paris: Dentu, 1889.

3546. DERVAL, PAUL. *Folies-Bergère. Souvenirs de leur directeur.* Paris: Éd. de Paris, 1954. English trans. *The Folies Berg*ère. L: Methuen, 1955. [Trans. Lucienne Hill, with a foreword by Maurice Chevalier.]

3547. DES AULNOYES, FRANÇOIS. *Histoire et philosophie du strip-tease. Essai sur l'érotisme du music-hall.* [Paris] Pensée moderne [1957]. [Préface d'Edmond Heuzé. Photographie de Roland Carré.]

3548. DONNAY, MAURICE. *Des souvenirs.* Paris: A.Fayard, 1933.

3549. ———. *J'ai vécu 1900.* Paris: A. Fayard, 1950.

3550. ———. *Mes Débuts à Paris.* Paris: A. Fayard, 1937.

3551. "Eloge du music-hall." *Le Populaire-Dimanche* (Paris), 7 Jan. 1951.

3552. FARGUE, LÉON-PAUL. *Pour la peinture.* Paris: Gallimard, 1955. ["Le Music-hall et Luc-Albert Moreau."]

3553. FOUQUIER, BARON. *Des Usages et de l'élégance.* Paris: Émile Paul, 1925.

3554. FRANC-NOHAIN, MAURICE. *De Paulus à Polin.* Paris: 1906.

3555. FRÉJAVILLE, GUSTAVE. *Au Music-hall.* Paris: Éd. du Monde nouveau, 1923.

3556. ———. "Baladines et bateleuses illustres." *Figaro artistique* (Paris), Nov. 1930, pp. 45-48.

3557. ———. [Figures du music-hall] *Triptyque* (Paris), Apr. 1931. [Little Tich, Damia, Barbette, etc.]

3558. ———. "Les Spectacles forains, le cirque, le music hall." In *Encyclopédie francaise.* Paris: Comité de l'Encyclopédie francaise [1935-in progress] [Vol. 16, chapter 4.]

3559. "French songs." *Era,* 16 June 1894, p. 15.

3560. FURSY [pseud. of H. Dreyfus]. *Chansons rosses.* 2 vols. Paris: Ollendorff, 1905. [Orné de 40 dessins de Grün. Musique notée.]

3561. ———. *Mon petit bonhomme de chemin: souvenirs de Montmartre et d'ailleurs.* Paris: Louis Querelle. 1928.

3562. GALLICI-RANCY. *Les Forains peints par eux-mêmes.* [Bordeaux] Music-hall Gallici-Rancy, 1903. [Préface de Paul Berthelot. Part 3: "Le Music-hall à la foire."]

3563. GOUDEAU, ÉMILE. *Dix ans de Bohème.* Paris: Librairie illustrée [1888].

3564. GRENET-DANCOURT, E. *Le Ventomane.* Paris: Paul Ollendorff, 1893. [Monologue comique, soupiré par X . . . Sociétaire de la Comédie-francaise. A spoof on both the pétomane and society monologues.]

3565. *Guide dans les théâtres.* Paris: Paulin et le Lechevalier, 1855.

3566. HARDEL, A. *Strass. En remontant les bas résillé du music-hall.* Paris: 1977. (Coll. "Entr'acte.")

3567. HAURIAC, MARCEL. *Météores. Poèmes.* [Moulins: Allier, 1955.] [Limited to one thousand numbered copies. 3: "Music Hall."]

3568. ———. "Music hall: rhythme et couleurs." *France illustrée* (Paris) 5 (1 Jan. 1949): 22. [About the Casino de Paris.]

3569. HELD, ANNA. *Mémoires. Une Étoile francaise au ciel de l'Amérique.* Paris: Nef de Paris, 1954. [Préface de Jacques-Charles. Highly unreliable and inaccurate.]

3570. HERBERT, MICHEL. *La Chanson à Montmartre.* Paris: La Table ronde, 1967.

3571. HOTIER, HUGHES. "Le Langage du cirque et du music-hall signums sociaux." *Le Cirque dans l'univers* (Paris) 88 (1er trimestre 1973): 29-32. [Excerpt from his book *Le Vocabulaire du cirque et du music-hall.]*

3572. HUISMAN, P. and M. G. DORTU. *Lautrec by Lautrec.* Trans. and ed. by Cornice Bellow. L: Macmillan, 1964. [Chapter 3, "Moulin-Rouge," pp. 66-93; Chapter 4, "Cafés-concerts," pp. 94-117.]

3573. IBELS. H. -G. "Le Café-concert et la chanson." In *Les Spectacles à travers les âges.* Paris: Editions du Cygne, 1931. [1: 289-315.]

3574. IBELS, JACQUES. *La Traite des chanteuses.* Paris: Librairie Felix Juven, 1906.

3575. IDZKOWSKI, M. "Variétés à Tabarin." *France illustrée* (Paris), 11 Apr. 1953, p. 516.

3576. ISOLA, Les Frères. *Souvenirs. 50 ans de vie parisienne.* Paris: Flammarion, 1948. [Recueillis par P. Andrieu.]

3577. JACQUES-CHARLES. *Le Caf' conc'.* Paris: Flammarion, 1966. (Coll. 1900 vécu.)

3578. ———. "De Dranem à Maurice Chevalier." In *Les Oeuvres libres,* 63, 289 (1951): 119-82.

3579. ———. *De Gaby [Delys] à Mistinguett.* Paris: 1933.

3580. ——. "Le Music-hall en France." In *Les Oeuvres libres,* 303 (1953): 164-224.

3581. ——. "Naissance du music-hall." In *Les Oeuvres libres, 304 (1952):* 97-164.

3582. ——. *La revue de ma vie.* Paris: A. Fayard, 1958.

3583. ——. *La Vie prodigieuse de Max Dearly.* Paris: Bejiat [n.d.].

3584. "The Jardin Mabille, and the Dancing-gardens of Paris." N.Y. *Clipper,* 14 May 1881, p. 121. ["Written by a Gothamite."]

3585. JOULLOT, EUGENE. *Histoires de théâtre de music-hall, suivies d'un dictionnaire humoristique d'argot théâtral.* Paris: Ed. universelles [1933].

3586. "Judic in America." *Era,* 31 Oct. 1885, p. 7.

3586a. JULLIAN, PHILLIPE. *Jean Lorrain ou Le Satiricon 1900.* Paris: Fayard, 1974. ["Music-halls," 139-42: a digest of Lorrain's jounalistic impressions of turn-of-the-century French variety.]

3587. ——. *Montmartre.* Oxford: Phaidon Press; N.Y.: E. P. Dutton, 1977. [Chapter 11, "Chat noir"; Chapter 13, "Moulin Rouge"; Chapter 14, "The Songs."]

3588. LANDRE, JEANNE. *Aristide Bruant.* Paris: Nouvelle société d'édition, 1930.

3588a. LAROCHE, ROBERT DE and FRANCOIS BELLAIR. *Marie Dubas.* Paris: Gandeau, 1980. Rev. P. O'Connor, *TLS,* 11 July 1980, p. 784. [Biography of great singing star with a list of her songs and recordings.]

3589. LAROUSSE, P. "Café chantant ou café concert." *Grand Dictionnaire universel du XIXe siecle,* vol. 3. Paris: Larousse, 1867.

3590. LASSAIGNE, JACQUES. *Toulouse-Lautrec e la Parigi dei cabarets.* [Milano] Fabbri [c. 1969]. English trans: *Toulouse-Lautrec and the Paris of the Cabarets.* N.Y.: Lamplight Publishing, 1975.

3591. "A Lecture on [French] Music-halls." *Era,* 30 Apr. 1898, p. 19.

3592. LEGRAND-CHABRIER. "Barbette avant et après son numéro." *L'Entr'acte* (Paris), 15 Jan. 1926.

3593. LEJAY, CHARLES. *Du Café-concert au théâtre chantant de Georgius.* Paris: M. Labbé, 1928.

3594. LEMARCHAND, L. "Paris's Most Famous Show: the Folies Bergere." *Saturday Review* 152 (25 July 1931): 11-15.

3595. LÉON-MARTIN, LOUIS. *Le Music-hall et ses figures.* Paris: Les Éditions de France, 1928.

3596. MacORLAN, PIERRE. "Music-hall." *Annales politiques et littéraires* (Paris) 90 (1 Mar. 1928): 224-25.

3597. MAHALIN, PAUL. *Les Mémoires du Bal Mabille*. Paris: Chez tous les libraires, 1864.

3598. MAINDRON, CHARLES ERNEST. *Les Programmes illustrés des théâtres et des cafés-concerts, menus, cartes d'invitation, petites estampes, etc.* Paris: Lamm, 1897. [Préface par Pierre Veber.]

3599. MARIEL, PIERRE and JEAN TROCHET. *Paris Cancan.* Bonn: Verlag des Europäichen Bücherei [1959]. [Text des historischen Teils Pierre Mariel. Text des modernen Teils: Jean Trochet. Übersetzung: Waldemar Sonntag, Sabine Weiler. Fotos: Daniel Frasnay und andere.] English trans: *Paris Can-can*. L: Alan Skilton, 1961. [Trans. Stephanie and Richard Sutton and ed. Alain de Moinerie. "Can Can Yesterdays" by Pierre Mariel, pp. 6-47.]

3600. MENETIÉRE, ALBÈRIC. *Les Binettes du café-concert.* Paris: Librairie central, 1869. [Sardonic chapters on individual types of performers and functionaries; list of principal Parisian cafés-concerts.]

3601. MÉRÉ, CHARLES. *Music-hall.* Paris: 1929. [A play.]

3602. MÉRODE, CLEO DE. *La Ballet de ma vie.* Paris: Pierre Horay, 1955. [Préf. par André de Fouquières.]

3603. MÉTENIER, OSCAR. *Le Chansonnier populaire.* Paris: Au Mirliton, 1893.

3604. MICHEL. G. *Un Demi-siècle des gloires théâtrales.* Paris: 1950.

3605. ———. *Une Journée de Cecile Sorel. Une Nuit de Mistinguett.* Paris: 1928.

3606. MILLANDY, GEORGAS. *Au Service de la chanson: souvenirs d'un chansonnier aphone.* Paris: Ed. littéraires de France, 1939.

3607. ———. *Lorsque tout est fini: souvenirs d'un chansonnier du Quartier Latin.* Paris: A. Messein, 1933.

3608. MISTINGUETT [pseud. of Jeanne Bourgeois]. *Mistinguett and her Confessions.* L: Hurst & Blackett, 1938. [Trans. and ed. Hubert Griffith.]

3609. ———. *Mistinguett, Queen of the Paris Night.* L: Elek Books, 1954. [Trans. Lucienne Hill.]

3610. ———. *Toute ma vie.* Paris: Julliard, 1954.

3611. "Mlle Judic." N.Y. *Clipper,* 26 June 1880, p. 105. [Portrait and biography.]

3612. *Mme Judic, a biographical sketch.* N.Y.: 1885.

3613. "Monsieur and Madame Maurice Chevalier." *Vanity Fair* (N.Y.), Aug. 1928.

3614. "Monsieur Thiers in a Music Hall." *Era,* 17 Nov. 1872, p. 4.

3615. MORAND, PAUL. *Paris to the Life. A Sketch-book.* L, N.Y.: Oxford University Press [1933]. [Trans. Gerard Hopkins. Written with Doris Spiegel.]

3616. MOULIN, JEAN-PIERRE. *J'aime le music-hall.* Lausanne: Ed. Rencontre, 1962.

3617. "The Music Halls of Paris." *Era,* 4 Dec. 1897, p. 22.

3618. *La Musique pour tous.* Paris [n.d.]. [Numéros speciaux. Ills. et musiques notées. 1. Les Dix derniers succés de M. et Mme. Xavier Privas; 2. Max Dearly. Ses dix plus amusantes créations; 3. Mayol. Les Dix plus jolies créations; 4. Montoya et ses dix chansons les plus jolies.]

3619. "A New Music Hall in Paris." *Era,* 25 Oct 1890, p. 16. [Casino de Paris.]

3620. NOHAIN, JEAN and F. CARADEC. *Le Pétomane 1857-1945.* Paris: Jean-Jacques Pauvert, 1967. English trans. L: Pop Universal, 1967; Los Angeles, Cal.: Sherbourne Press, 1968. [Trans. Warren Tute.]

3621. OTÉRO, CAROLINE. *Les Souvenirs et la vie intime de la Belle Otéro.* Paris: Éd. Le Calame [1926]. [Presentés et prefacés par Claude Valmart.]

3622. *Le Panorama.* 16 vols. Paris [1895?-1901]. [publié sous la direction de Rene Baschet. *Paris s'amuse:* part 1 (2 fascicules): "Les Cafés-concerts, théâtres, cirques, palais de glace, " etc. Photos by Reutlinger, etc.]

3622a. PAPICH, STEPHEN. *Remembering Josephine. A Biography of Josephine Baker.* Indianapolis and N.Y.: Bobbs-Merrill, 1976. [Somewhat maudlin and sentimental account.]

3623. *Paris at Night. Sketches and Mysteries of Paris High Life and Demimonde. Nocturnal Amusements. How to Know Them! How to Enjoy Them!! How to Appreciate Them!!!* Boston: Boston and Paris Pub. Co., 1875.

3624. "Paris Music Halls." *Era,* 3 Sept. 1892, p. 15; 25 Sept. 1892 p. 17; 10 Dec. 1892, p. 16. [Good reportage of current bills.]

3625. PAULUS [pseud. of Paulin Habans]. *Trente ans de café-concert.* Paris: Société d'Éditions et de Publications [n.d.]. [Souvenirs recueillis par O. Pradels. Includes sixty songs of the period with music.]

3626. "Paulus at the Trocadero." *Era,* 12 Sept. 1891, p. 17.

3627. PIÉCHAUD, M. "Le Café-concert n'est plus." *France-Illustration,* 31 Jan. 1948.

3628. POIRET, PAUL. *En habillant l'époque.* Paris: B. Grasset, 1931.

3629. POUGIN, ARTHUR. *Dictionnaire historique et pittoresque du théâtre et des arts qui s'y rattachent. Poétique, musique, danse, pantomime, décor, costume, machinerie, acrobatisme, jeux antiques, spectacles forains.* . . . Paris: Firmin-Didot, 1885. [Ill. de 350 gravures et de 8 chromolithographies. Beuglant, p. 97; Boui-boui, p. 108; Cafés-concerts, pp. 130-33; Cafés-spectacles, p. 134; Musicos, p. 533.]

3630. "Queer Songs, Queer Face." N. Y. *Sun,* 6 Dec. 1891. [Paulus.]

3631. RAGEOT, G. "Music-hall." *Revue politique et littéraire* (Paris) 67 (6 July 1929): 408-10.

3632. RAVENNES. "Lautrec, peintre du cirque et de music-hall." *Comoedia* (Paris), 4 Dec. 1924.

3633. RENIEU, LIONEL. *Histoire des théâtres de Bruxelles depuis leur origine jusqu'à ce jour.* 2 vols. Paris: Duchartre & Van Buggenhoudt, 1928. [Préface de Auguste Rondel. "Bibliographie des théâtres & concerts de Bruxelles," 1: [13]-57; "Complément de la bibliographie théâtrale et table alphabetique de tous les journaux de théâtre et de cinéma qui ont paru à Bruxelles," 2: [1189]-1206.]

3634. RIMELS, LUCIEN. *Du caf' conc' au Concert Mayol.* Paris: Éd. L. M. E., 1949-50.

3635. RIVOLLET, ANDRÉ. *De Menilmontant au Casino de Paris.* Paris: Bernard Grasset [1927].

3636. ———. *Maurice Chevalier vypravuje.* Prelozil: Václab Vitinger. Praha: L. Mazáč, 1931. [Illustroval (after Paramount) Slavomir Kittner.]

3637. ROMI. *La Chanson du café chantant au microsillon. Gros succés et petits fours.* Paris: SERG, 1967.

3638. ———. *Petite histoire des cafés-concerts parisiens.* Paris: Jean Chitry [1950].

3639. ROUBAUD, LOUIS. *Music-hall.* Paris: Querelle, 1929. [Illustré par Be'Cau.]

3640. RUDORFF, RAYMOND. *Belle époque.* L: Hamish Hamilton, 1972.

3641. SAINT-YRE, MARTIN [pseud. of Tristan Rémy]. "Les Origines circassiennes d'Edith Piaf." *Le Cirque dans l'univers* 63 (4e trimestre 1966): 21-24.

3642. SALLES, JACQUES. *L'Empire, un temple du music-hall.* Paris: SFP, 1975.

3643. SAUVAGE, MARCEL. *Les Mémoires de Josephine Baker.* Paris: Correa, 1949.

3644. ———. *Voyages et aventures de Josephine Baker.* Paris: Seheur, 1931.

3645. *Scènes parisiennes. Album de la jeunesse.* Paris: Maison

Martinet-Hautecoeur frères [c. 1845].

3646. SCHWAB, FREDERICK A. "Parisian Cafés-concerts." In *The Music of the Modern World*. N.Y. [1895]. [Ed. Anton Seidl. 1: 185-87.]

3647. SHERCLIFF, JOSÉ. *Jane Avril of the Moulin Rouge*. L: Jarrolds, 1952. [With 14 ills. by Toulouse-Lautrec.]

3648. SOTHEBY'S. *Catalogue of Designs for Costumes and Decors: the Casino de Paris, 1920-1935, the Collection of Wilfrid Piollet, Paris. Designs for Operas, Cabarets and Music Hall, the Property of Various Owners*. [L: Sotheby's, 1970].

3649. STRONG, ROWLAND. *Where and How to Dine in Paris, with Notes on Paris Hotels, Waiters and their Tips, Paris Theatres, Minor Theatres, Music Hall, Racing round Paris, etc.* L: Richards, 1900.

3650. SYMONS, ARTHUR. *Colour Studies in Paris*. L: Chapman & Hall; N.Y.: E. P. Dutton, 1918. ["Songs of the Streets" (Bruant), pp. 67-73 (1895); "At the Ambassadeurs/to Yvette Guilbert," p. 89 (poem, 1894); "Yvette Guilbert," pp. 91-101 (1900); "La Melinte: Moulin-Rouge," pp. 105-6 (poem, 1892); "Dancers and dancing," pp. 107-18 (1897.]

3651. ———. *Plays, Acting and Music*. L: Duckworth, 1903. ["Yvette Guilbert," p. 117; "The Paris Music Hall," p. 123.]

3652. TEXCIER, JEAN. "Paris qui chante." *Le Crapouillot* (Paris) 29 (1965): 74-78. [Special issue on "Belle Epoque."]

3652a. [Théresa.] *London Figaro*, 9 June 1877, p. 13.

3653. TOWERS, EDWARD J. "English Girls and Continental Music Halls." *Era*, 14 Nov. 1885, p. 10. [On white slavery.]

3654. VERNE, MAURICE. *Aux Usines du plaisir: la vie secrète du music-hall*. Paris: Ed. des Portiques, 1929.

3655. ———. *Musée de volupté: le secret des nuits électriques*. Paris; Ed. des Portiques, 1930.

3656. VERNILLAT, FRANCE and JEAN CHARPENTREAU. *Dictionnaire de la chanson française*. Paris: Librairie Larousse, 1966. [Exemplary small biographical dictionary with entries on cafés-chantants, music-halls, etc.]

3657. VESQUE, MARTHE. "Folies-Bergère." *Le Cirque dans l'univers* (Paris) 26 (2e trimestre 1957): 20-21. [Capsule history 1869-85 with special reference to specialty acts.]

3658. VEUILLOT, LOUIS. *Les Odeurs de Paris*. Paris: Ed. Palme, 1867.

3659. VITU, A. C. J. *Paris l'été*. Le Jardin Mabille. Paris: 1847.

3660. ———. and J. FREY. *Physiologie du Bal Mabille*. Paris [1850?].

3661. WARNOD, A. *Bals, cafés et cabarets*. Paris: E. Figuiere, 1918.

3662. WEBER, LOUISE. *La Goulue. Danseuse & dompteuse. Mes débuts—les Bals publiques—Souvenirs retrospectifs—L'Art de dresser les fauves.* [Nice: G. Mathieu, 1920?] [Ghostwritten autobiography of the Moulin Rouge star.]

3663. WEILL, ALAIN. *100 Years of Posters of the Folies Bergère and Music Halls of Paris.* N.Y.: Images Graphiques; L: Hart-Davis, Macgibbon, 1977. [Well-informed letterpress.]

3664. WITTKOWSKI, G. -J. and L. NASS. *Le Nu au théâtre depuis l'antiquité jusqu'à nos jours.* . . . Paris: Daragon [1909]. [Chapter 10, "Les Temps modernes," pp. 174-272.]

3665. XANROF, LEON. *Chansons sans-gêne.* Paris: Ondet, 1890.

3666. ———. *Mesdames, en scène?* Paris: Ernest Flammarion, n.d. [Poems and sketches by Yvette Guilbert's favorite lyricist.]

3667. ZEVAES, ALEXANDRE. *Aristide Bruant.* Paris: La Nouvelle revue critique, 1943.

Fiction

3668. BRUANT, ARISTIDE. *Les Bas-fonds de Paris.* 3 vols. Paris: Rouff, 1897.

3669. ———. *Fleur de pavé.* Paris: Tallandier, 1920.

3670. ———. *Fleurs de Montmartre.* Paris: J. Tallandier, 1929.

3671. ———. *Les Princesses du trottoir.* Paris: Ferenczi, 1925.

3672. COLETTE, SIDONIE GABRIELLE [pseud. of COLETTE WILLY]. *L'Envers du music hall.* Paris: Flammarion, 1913. Repr. with Dessins en couleurs d'Henri Mirande. Gravés sur bois par Hermine Mayeras. Paris: Ferenczi & fils, 1929. English trans. *My Apprenticeship and Music Hall Sidelights.* L: Secker & Warburg, 1957. Repr. Harmondsworth: Penguin Books, 1967.

3673. JACQUES-CHARLES. *Le Journal d'une figurante, roman de moeurs de music-hall.* Paris: Gallimard [c. 1933].

3674. KNAPP, BETTINA L. *Le Mirliton. A Novel based on the life of Aristide Bruant.* Paris: Nouvelles éditions Debresse, 1968.

3675. LE TARARE, JEAN-PAUL. *Moi, un nain.* Paris: Éd. Denoël, 1938.

Periodicals

3676. *L'Album musical.* Paris. No. 1- . 1901-. Monthly.

3677. *La Lanterne de Bruant.* Paris. 1897-99. [Directed by Aristide Bruant.]

3678. *Le Mirliton.* Paris: 1885-94. [Directed by Aristide Bruant.]

3679. *Le Music Hall illustré.* Paris. 1913- .

3680. *La Musique pour tous.* Paris. No. 1- . Juillet 1905- . Monthly.
3681. *Paris plaisirs. Mensuel esthétique, humoristique et théâtral.* Paris. No. 1- . Juin 1921- . Monthly.
3682. *Paris qui chante. Revue hebdomaire illustrée des concerts, théâtres, cabarets-artistiques, music-halls.* Paris. No. 1- . Jan. 1903- . Weekly.

SUPPLEMENT C
ITALY AND SPAIN

Cross-references

See also **288, 1757–58, 1760–61, 1763, 3489, 3493.**

3683. BEERBOHM, MAX. "In an Italian Music Hall." *Saturday Review* 104 (21 Dec. 1907): 758–59, supplement.
3684. BRAGAGLIA, A. G. *Il Teatro della rivoluzione.* Roma: Edizioni Tiber, 1929.
3685. CANGIULLO, FRANCESCO. *Caffè concerto: alfabeto a sorpresa.* Milano: Poesia [1919]. [On futurism.]
3686. ———. *Le Novelle del varietà.* Napoli: 1938.
3687. ———. *Le Serate futuriste: romanze storico vissuto; con guidizi di Marinetti, Ojetti, Borgese, Simoni, Lippartini, Goll.* Napoli: Editrice Tirrena, 1930.
3688. CAVALIERI, LINA. *Le Mie varietà.* Roma: 1936.
3689. CERVELLATI, ALLESSANDRO. *Il Circo e il music-hall. Catalogo della Mostro patrocinata dal Comune di Bologna.* [Bologna: Tamari, 1962.] [Museo civico, 22 dec. 1962–22 gen. 1963.]
3690. ———. *Music-hall.* Bologna: Cappelli [1945].
3691. CHESHIRE, DAVID F. "Futurism, Marinetti and the Music Hall." *Theatre Quarterly* 1, no. 3 (July–Sept. 1971): 54–58.
3692. DE ANGELIS, RODOLFO. *Caffè concerto.* Milano: 1940.
3693. ———. *Storie del café-chantant.* Milano: Il Balcone, 1946.

3694. DESDIVIZES DU DÉZART, GEORGES NICHOLAS. *Entre Camarades*. Paris: 1901. ["Le Théâtre populaire à Madrid," pp. 273-78.]

3695. *Ettore Petrolini as Seen by the British Press*. L: Little Theatre, 1933.

3696. *Ettore Petrolini vu par la presse française*. Paris: Théâtre de Pontinière, 1933.

3697. FALCONI, DINO and ANGELO FRATTINI. *Guida alla rivista e all'operetta*. Milano: Academia, 1953.

3698. FERRARI, D. "'De Profundis' per l'avanspettacolo." *Tempo libero* (Roma), maggio 1969.

3699. "Futuristic Fun. (Notice from 'The Daily Iconoclast' for November 21st, 1923.)" *Punch*, 3 Dec. 1913, p. 476. [Marinetti at the "Pallidrome Theatre of Varieties.")

3700. JARRO [pseud. of Giulio Piccini]. *Attori, cantanti, concertisti, acrobati. Ritratti, macchiette, anedotti, memorie umoristiche di Jarro*. 3. ed. cor. e amen. Firenze: R. Bemporal, 1898.

3701. ———. *Viaggio umoristico nei teatri*. 3. ed. con molte aggiunte. Firenze: R. Bemporad, 1908.

3702. KIRBY, MICHAEL, ed. *Futurist Performance*. . . . N.Y.: E. P. Dutton, 1971. [With manifestoes and playscripts trans. from the Italian by Victoria Nes Kirby. 3: "The Variety Theatre" Manifesto, pp. 19–27.]

3703. LONGMAN, STANLEY VINCENT. "The Modern *Maschere* of Ettore Petrolini." *Educational Theatre Journal* (Washington, D.C.), Oct. 1975, pp. 377–86.

3704. LOPEZ-MARIN, ENRIQUE. *Music-hall*. Madrid: 1905. [Novel.]

3705. MALADACEA, N. *Memorie*. Napoli: 1933.

3706. MARINETTI, FILIPPO TOMASSO. "'The Meaning of the Music-hall." *Theatre Quarterly* 1, no. 3 (July–Sept. 1971): 59, 53.

3707. ———. "The Variety Theatre." *Daily Mail*, 21 Nov. 1913. [First pub. *Lacerba* (Firenze), 1 ott. 1913. Repr. *The Mask* (Firenze), Jan. 1914, pp. 188–89.]

3708. MOROSI, ANTONIO. *Il Teatro di varietà in Italia*. Firenze: Calvetti, 1901.

3709. PEREIRA, ANTONIO. "Los Cafés cantantes." *La Vanguardia española* (Barcelona), 2 Feb. 1971.

3710. PETROLINI, ETTORE. *Gastone*. Bologna: L. Cappelli, 1932.

3711. RAMO, LUCIANO. *Storia del varietá*. Milano: A. Garzanti, 1956. (Serie per tutto, pp. 84–85.)

3712. SYMONS, ARTHUR. "A Spanish Music-hall." *Fortnightly*

Review 51 (1892): 716–22. Repr. in *Cities and Sea Coasts and Islands*. L: W. Collins, 1918.

3713. *Teatro, circo y music-hall*. Barcelona: Argos, 1967.

3714. "Le Théâtre léger en Italie. Du Café chantant à la revue musicale." *Vie italienne* (Paris) 6 (1966).

3715. VAZQUEZ MONTALBAN, MANUEL. *100 años de cancio y music hall*. Barcelona: 1974. [Includes four 10" long-playing records.]

3716. VIVIANI, R. *Dalla Vita alle scene*. Bologna: 1928.

3717. ———. "Eden Teatro e la Boheme dei comici." *Teatro* (Torino) 1 (1957).

SUPPLEMENT D
GERMANY, AUSTRIA-HUNGARY, THE NETHERLANDS, AND CZECHOSLOVAKIA

Cross-references

See also **1908, 3489, 3493.**

General

3718. BAB, JULIUS. *Das Theater der Gegenwart*. Leipzig: J. J. Weber, 1928. [Pp. 95–97: on the origin of cabaret.]

3719. BAUER, BERNHARD ADAM. *Komödianten—Dirne? Der Künstlerin Leben und Lieben im Lichte der Wahrheit*. Wien: Fiba-Verlag, 1927. [Mit 6 farb. Kunstbeil.]

3720. BUCHNER, EBERHARD. *Berliner Variétés und Tingeltangel: Grosstadt-Dokumente Vol. 22*. Berlin & Leipzig: H. Seeman, 1905.

3721. CERVENY, J. "Cervena sedma." *Česky život* (Praha), 1948, no. 3.

3722. COLMAN, FRED A. and WALTER TRIER. *Artisten (Ernstes und heiteres Variété)*. Dresden: P. Aretz [1928].

3723. DOKTOR, COR. *Flick-Flack. Anecdotes en verhalen uit het Nederlandsche Variété-leven.* Hengelo (O.): Loek, 1947. [Geillustreerd met fotos door den schrijver en door teekeningen en "penseelstrekn" van Roland Wagter.]

3724. ———. *Variété.* Amsterdam: Jacob van Kampen, 1948. [Met illustraties von Roland Wagter (en fotos). De wijze Jacob, 14.]

3725. FREY, HERMANN. *Immer an der Wang lang . . . Allerlei um Hermann Frey.* Berlin: Dionysos Verlag [1944]. [Mit Bildern von H. Zille.]

3726. GAČS, JUDIT. *Rodolfo, illusioniste hongrois.* Budapest: Minerva, 1973.

3727. "The German Music Hall War." *Stage Year Book* (1909): 74–76.

3728. "German Variety Artists." *Era*, 9 Apr. 1910, p. 16.

3729. GOBBERS, EMIL. *Artisten, Zirkus und Variété in alter und neuer Zeit.* Düsseldorf: Droste [1949]. [Mit einem Vorwort und Nachtrag von F. Brecher.]

3729a. GÜNTHER, ERNST. *Geschichte des Variétés.* Berlin: Henschel, 1978.

3730. GUTTMANN, RICHARD. *Variété. Beiträge zur Psychologie des Pöbels.* Wien-Leipzig: Deutsch-Österreich Verlag. 1919.

3731. HAAS, ALEX DE. *De Minstrel van de Mesthoop: liedjes, leven en achtergronden van Eduard Jacobs, pionier van het Nederlandse cabaret 1867–1914.* Amsterdam: Uitgeverij de Bezige Bij, 1958.

3732. HABER, S. *Tingel-Tangel: Berliner Kneipenstudien.* Berlin: 1871.

3733. [HERCÍKOVA, IVÁ. comp.] *Začalo to Redutou.* Praha: Orbes, 1964. [Doslav napsal Jan Císar.]

3734. HILDENBRANDT, FRED. *Variété.* Frankfurt/M.: M. Uzielli [1919]. [Mit (farbigen) Steinzeichnungen Emil Hölzl. Herausg. von der Frankfurter Werkstatt. Edition of 50 copies signed by illustrator.]

3735. JARETSKI, H. J. J. "Frauen vom Variété." *Die Woche* (1926): 276.

3736. KERR, ALFRED. *Eintagsfliegen oder die Macht der Kritik. Die Welt im Drama.* Vol. 4. Berlin: Fischer, 1917. [Pp. 327–49: on "Brettl" and Wolzogen's "Überbrettl."]

3737. KOLLER, JOSEF. *Das Wiener Volkssängertum in alter und neuer Zeit; Nacherzähltes und Selbsterlebtes, mit Biographien . . .* Wien: Gerlach [1931].

3738. *Kuenstler-Adressen-Nachweis. Ausgabe für Variété, Kabarett, Zirkus, Bühne, Musik und Tanz mit Anschriften der Agenten*

Direktionen. Berlin-Stahnsdorf: Künstler-Adressen-Archiv, Ch. Mewis [1948].

3739. LOGGEM, MANUEL VAN. "Lachen is gemeen." *Samenspel* (Marssen), no. 6, 1973.

3740. *Die Mädchen vom Variété und Ihre Partner.* Leipzig: 1933.

3741. MOELLER VAN DEN BRUCK, ARTHUR. *Das Variété.* Berlin: Bard, 1902. [Umschlagzeichnung von Louis Morin. Schlussvignette von Fidus.]

3742. MOHOLY-NAGY, LASZLO. "Theater, Circus, Variety." In *The Theater of the Bauhaus,* ed. with an introduction by Walter Gropius. Trans. by Arthur S. Wensinger. Middletown, Conn.: Wesleyan University press, 1961. [Pp. 49-70.] Repr. in *Total Theater, a Cultural Anthology,* ed. E. T. Kirby, N.Y.: E. P. Dutton, 1969.

3743. NEUMANN, ERNST. *Variété Sterne. Ein Künstlerheft Blätter.* Berlin: Verlag der Lust, 1910.

3744. OSTAIJEN [or OSTAYEN] PAUL VAN. *Music-hall; een programma vol charlestons, grotesken polonaises en dressuur nummers.* Den Haag: Daamen, 1955. [Intr. Gerrit Borgers. Poetry, originally published in 1916.]

3745. OSTWALD, HANS. *Berliner Tanzlokale. Grossadt-Dokumente, vol. 4.* Berlin & Leipzig: H. Seeman, 1905.

3746. OTTO, HERMANN WALDEMAR. *Artisten-Lexikon: Biographische Notizen über Kunstreiter, Dompteure, Gymnastiker, Clowns, Akrobaten, Spezialitaten, etc. aller Lander und Zeiten.* 2d ed. Düsseldorf: E. Lintz, 1895.

3747. POLLARD, PERCIVAL. *Masks and Minstrels of New Germany.* Boston: Luce, 1911.

3748. RICHARDS, P. [pseud. of Richard Pichler]. *Variété. Humour. Heiteres vom Brettl.* Berlin-Halensee: Reflektor, 1914. [Mit zahlreichen Karikaturen des Verfasser.]

3749. RICHTER, L. "Das Berliner Couplet der Gründerzeit." In Carl Dahlaus, ed., *Studien zur Trivialmusik des 19. Jahrhunderts.* Regensburg: Bosse, 1967. [Pp. 199-217.]

3750. ———. *Der Berliner Gassenhauer: Darstellung, Zeugnisse.* Leipzig: Deutscher Verlag f. Musik [1968].

3751. ———. "Parodieverfahren im Berliner Gassenlied." *Deutsche Jahrbuch der Musikwissenschaft.* Leipzig: Edition Peters, 1959. [Pp. 48-81.]

3752. SALTARINO, Signor [pseud. of HERMANN WALDEMAR OTTO]. *Das Artistentum und seine Geschichte.* Leipzig: W. Backhau, 1910. [Conjuring and acrobats.]

3753. SCHAEFFERS, WILLI. *Tingeltangel: ein Leben für die Kleinkunst.* Hamburg: Broschek, 1959. [Aufgezeichnet von Erich Ebermayer.]
3754. SCHULTZE, PAUL. *Paul Schultze Agentum für Variete und Zirkus.* [Berlin: Friedrichstr. 204, 1927.]
3755. SIEMSEN, H. "Variété." *Weltbühne* 21 (1925): 870.
3756. SUHR, W. "Die Welt der Artisten." *Universum*, 1927, no. 15.
3757. TICHÝ, FRANTIŠEK. *Cirkus a Variété.* Praha: Odeon, 1967. [Color studies.]
3758. TOMÉK, VÁCLAC VLADIVOJ, Ritter von. *Ze starých paržských santánci: bujný a pestry život v zaslych šantánech s jeho pikantteriemi.* Praha: Vysehrad [1929].
3759. ULRICH, WALTER. *Bibliographie der Deutschen Circus und Variete. Literatur abgeschlossen mit ersten Halbjahr 1966.* Wien: 1966.
3760. *Variété und Zirkus.* Dresden: Haus Bergmann, 1935. [Vorwort von Paula Busch. Ausgabe 1935 der Bergmann-Zigarettenfabrik Dresden.]
3761. ZAHN, PETER VON. *Hinter den Sternen. Eine Geschichte des Showbusiness.* Stuttgart: Goverts, 1967. [Unter Mitarb. von H. Oelbermann und H. A. Seeberg.]

Karl Valentin

Clown and revue-artiste; b. Valentin Ludwig Fey, Munich, Germany, 4 June 1882; d. Feb. 1948.
3762. *Buchbinder Wanninger.* Stuttgart: Reclam, 1978. Ausw. und Nachwort von Rudolf Goldschmit.]
3763. *Der Feuerwehrtrompeter. Monologe und Couplets.* 3. Aufl. München: Piper, 1977.
3764. *Gesammelte Werke.* 13. Aufl. München: Piper, 1977. [Mit einer Erinnerung v. Ernst Buschor u. einem Essay v. Kurt Tucholsky "Der Linksdenker."]
3765. *Das grosse KV Buch.* 3. Aufl. München: Piper, 1977. [Hrsg. von Michael Schulte.]
3766. *Das KV Buch.* München: Knorr & Hirth, 1932. [Erstes und einziges Bilderbuch über KV über ihn und Lisl Karlstadt. Mit Vorwort und ernsthafter Lebensbeschreinbung und Bildunterschriften von ihm selbst, sowie zwei Aufsätzen von Tim Klein und Wilhelm Hausenstein.]
3767. *Mono- und Dialogue.* Piper-Sprechplatte, No. 3. München: Piper, n.d.
3768. *Der reparierte Scheinwerfer, Szenen und Dialogue.* 3. Aufl. Mün-

München: dtv, 1977.

3769. *Riesenblödsinn. Eine Auswahl aus dem Gesamtwerk.* Frankfurt: Fischer, 1975.

3770. *Sturzflüge im Zuschauerraum. Der gesammelten Werke anderer Teil.* 3. Aufl. München: Piper, 1977. [Vorw. Kurt Horwitz.]

3771. *Tingeltangel—Das Oktoberfest.* München: Piper, 1977.

3772. *Trompeten-Unterricht und andere Lachstücke.* Piper-Sprechplatte, No. 5. München: Piper, n.d.

Secondary Materials

3773. APPIGNANESI, LISA. *The Cabaret.* L: Studio Vista, 1975. [Pp. 149–53.]

3774. BRECHT, BERTOLT. "KV." In *Schriften zum Theater 1. Gesammelte Werke*, vol. 15. Frankfurt: Edition Suhrkamp, 1967. [p. 39.]

3775. BUDZINSKI, KLAUS. *Die Muse mit der scharfen Zunge. Vom Cabaret zum Kabarett.* München: List, 1961. ["KV," pp. 176–78.]

3776. CALANDRA, DENIS. "Valentin and Brecht." *The Drama Review* (N.Y.) T–61 (Mar. 1974): 86–98.

3777. DIETL, EDUARD. *Clowns.* München: Markus, 1967. [KV, pp. 54–74.]

3778. FEUCHTWANGER, LION. *Erfolg. Drei Jähre Geschichte einer Provinz.* Berlin: Kiepenheuer, 1930. ["Der Komiker Hierl und sein Volk," 1: 259–68.]

3779. GRAF, OSKAR MARIA. *An manchen Tagen, Reden, Gedanken und Zeitbetrachtungen.* Frankfurt: Nest, 1961. ["München verlor etwas Unwiederbringliches. Zum Tode des grossen Komikers KV."]

3780. GRUNAUER BURG, GUSTI. *Passiert is was. Valentiniaden.* Munchen: Heimeran, 1959.

3781. HAUSENSTEIN, WILHELM. *Die Masken des Komikers KV.* München: Heimeran, 1948.

3782. HOPPE, HANS. *Das Theater der Gegenstände. Neue Formen szenischer Aktion. Theater unserer Zeit.* Vol. 10. 2. Aufl. Bensberg: Schäube, 1971. [KV, pp. 29–39.]

3783. HORWITZ, KURT. "Erinnerung an KV." *Neue Zürcher Zeitung*, 16 Nov. 1958.

3784. KONIG, HANNES, ed. *Das Bilderbuch vom KV.* München: Wilhelm Unverhau, 1975.

3785. MAYER, HANS. *Bertolt Brecht und die Tradition.* Pfullingen: Neske, 1971. [KV, pp. 27–29.]

3786. SCHULTE, MICHAEL. *Alles von KV. Monologue und Geschichten.* München: Piper, 1978.

3787. ———. *KV in Selbstzeugnissen und Bildokumenten.* Reinbeck: Rowoblt, 1968.
3788. ———. and PETER SYR. *KVs Filme. Alle 29 Filme, 12 Fragmente, 347 Bilder, Texte, Filmographie.* München: Piper, 1978.
3789. VALENTIN-BÖHEIM, BERTL. *"Du bleibst da, und zwar sofort!" Mein Vater KV.* 2. Aufl. München: Piper, 1972.
3790. ———. ed. *Die Jugendstreiche des Knaben Karl.* 6. Aufl. München: Piper, 1977.
3791. WOLTER, KARL KURT *KV—privat.* München: Olzog, 1958.

Fiction

3792. BUSCH, PAUL. *Die Comtesse vom Variété. Kunstler-Roman aus Theaterleben.* Breslau: Rekord-Verlag, 1921. (Rever-Bücher, 4)
3793. DELBRUCK, JOACHIM. *Variété. Roman.* Berlin: Ullstein, 1916.
3794. HESSLET, DOLLY. *Das Nummerngirl vom Eden-Variete. Ein Roman teils vor, teil hinter den Kulissen.* Wien, Leipzig: Amonesta-Verlag [1933]. (Frauenschicksals-Romane.)
3795. KNESCHKE-SCHÖNAU, MARTHA. *Der Sprung aufs Brettl.* Dresden: Verlag Deutscher Buchwerkstätten [1919]. (Residenz-Bücher, 105.)
3796. LORENZ-LAMBRECHT, HEINZ. *Variété.* Haarlem [c. 1940]. (Avonduurlectuur, 25). [Abridged version of *Barbette und die Bestien. Roman.* Berlin: E. Zander (1938). (Die neue Reihe). Repr. 1940.]
3797. MANN, HEINRICH. *Professor Unraht, oder Das Ende eines Tyrannen.* München: Albert Langen, 1905. [Filmed as *Die Blaue Engel.*]
3798. MUUSMAN, CARL [pseud. of Edvard Högbert and Ole Clausen]. *Artistblod. Romantiserade skildringar ur det skandinaviska teater-variete-, och cirkuslifet.* Stockholm: Victor Lundins Bokförlag, 1905. [Illustr. af Carsten Ravn. Swedish trans. of: *Artistblod (1–7). Romaner og Fortaellinger fra Cirkuslivet.* Med illustr. af Carsten Ravn. Köbenhavn: A. Christiansens Förlag, 1905-7.]
3799. RAFF, FRIEDRICH. *Peter Tingeltangel. Roman.* Bewerkt [naar het Duitsch] door de V. Jr. (S. de Vries Jr.). Rotterdam: Voorwaarts, 1929.
3800. STEINMANN, HERBERT. *Unter Zirkuskuppel und Variété-himmel. Artistenschicksale zwischen Leben und Tod.*

[Erzählungen.] Berlin [c. 1942] [Stencilled]

Periodicals

3801. *Artistik. Internationales Fachblatt für Variete, Zirkus, Kabarett.* (Berlin) 1954–in progress.
3802. *Entre. Tidskrift för teater, film, danse, musik, cirkus och variete.* (Stockholm) 1953–54.
3803. *Vestriček.* Červene sedmy. Ròc. 1– . 1919–1920. Praha: Červená sedma.

SUPPLEMENT E
RUSSIA AND EASTERN EUROPE

Cross-references

See also **3489, 3493.**

General

3804. ABRAMSKIJ, I. "Istočniki sovetskoj estrady." *Sovetskaja Estrada i Tsirk* 8 (1976). [Sources of Soviet Variety.]
3805. ALEKSEEV, ALEKSEJ GRIGOR'EVIĆ. *Ser'ëznoe i smešnoe: polveka v teatre i na estrade.* Moskva: Iskusstvo, 1972. [Serious and Comic: Half a Century in the Theatre and Variety. Entertaining memoirs of a famous compère.]
3806. [ARDOV, VIKTOR EFIMOVIĆ] *Razgovornye žanry estrady i cirka; zametki pisatelja.* Moskva: Iskusstvo, 1968. [Spoken Genres of Variety and Circus; a writer's observations.]
3807. *Estrada* [Variety]. Moskva: Goskul'trosvetizdat, 1955.
3808. *Estrada* [Variety]. Ed. S. A. Voskresenskij and M. Pando. Moskva-Leningrad, 1928.
3809. *Estrada. Repertuarnyj sbornik dlja armejskoj i flotskoj xudožestvennoj samodejatel'nosti. Vypusk pervyj.* Moskva: Voennoe izdatel'stvo Ministerstvo Oborony SSSR, 1963. [Variety. Collection of pieces for military and naval artistic amateurs. First Part.]

3810. *Estrada. Repertuarnyi zbirnyk.* Kiev: Mystetstvo, 1967. [Variety: collection of pieces. In Ukrainian.]

3811. *Estrada. Sbornik stixotvorenij, monologov, rasskazov, romansov i t.p., prigodnyx dlja čtenija s estrady.* [St. Peterburg]"Teatr i iskusstvo," 1910–11. [Variety: collection of poems, monologues, stories, ballads etc., suitable for recital on a variety stage.]

3812. FILLER, WITOLD; RYSZARD MAREK; GRONSKI and JERZY WITTLIN. *Alfabet Polskiej Rozrywki.* Wyd. 1. Warszawa: Wydawn. Artystyczne i Filmowne, 1974.

3813. GERSHUNI, JU. *Sovetskaja Estrada.* Leningrad: 1959. [Soviet Variety.]

3814. KADYROV, MUXSIN. *Iskusstvo mašxarabozov i kizikči. Ferganšij tradicionnyj teatre.* Tashkent: Fan, 1971. [The Art of Maskharabozes and Kizikchas: Traditional Ferghan Theatre.]

3815. [KUKARETIN, VASILIJ MIXAILOVIČ, comp.] *Estradnye žanry v agitbrigade.* Moskva: Iskusstvo, 1965. [Variety genres in the Agitbrigade. Ed. N. V. Kaminskaja and S. S. Nikol'skij.]

3816. KUZNECOV, EVGENIJ. *Iz prošlogo russkoj estrady.* Moskva: Iskusstvo, 1958. [From the Past of the Russian Music-Hall. The best all-round history of Russian music-hall.]

3817. LAWINSKI, LUDWIK. *"Aczkolwick," popowiadania z 1000-ca i jednej nocy.* L: Gryf Publications, 1963. ["Sprawa Igo Syma," by Aniela Lawínska, pp. 85–89.]

3818. MASSLER, S. "Teatrul român de revistá." In *Teatrul* (Bucharest), no. 3, 1972. [Romanian Music-Hall.]

3819. *Mastera estrady—samodeijatel'nost.* 2 vols. Moskva: Iskusstvo, 1971–75. [Amateur Masters of Variety. Ed. E. G. Prilutskaja.]

3820. MONAXOV, N. F. *Povest' o žizn'.* Leningrad: Bol'šoj dramatišeskij teatr, 1936. [Literaturnaja redakcija i vvodnaja stat'ja S. S. Mokul'skogo. Xudožestvennaja redakcija S. Ja. Abašidze. (A Story about Life. Literary editor and introduction: S. S. Mokulsky, designed by S. Ya. Abashidze.) Memoirs of a performer.]

3821. NEST'EV, IZRAIL' VLADIMIROVIČ. *Zvëzdy russkoj estrady (Panina, Vjal'ceva, Plevitskaja): očerki o russkix estradnyx pevit-sax načala XX veka.* Moskva: Soveckij kompozitor, 1970. [Stars of Russian Variety (Panina, Vyaltseva, Plevitskaya): Sketches of Russian Music-Hall Singers at the Turn of the Century. Contains a six-inch recording.]

3822. *Russkie narodnye guljan'ye po rasskazam A. Ja. Alekseeva-Jakovleva, v zapisi i obrabotke Evg. Kuznecova.* Leningrad-Moskva: Iskusstvo, 1948. [Russian Popular Amusements as told by A. Ya. Alekseev-Yakovlev, recorded and adapted by Evgeny

Kuznetsov. Memoirs of a famous showman.]

3823. ŠAPIROVSKIJ, EMIL' BORISOVIČ. *Konferans i konferans'e.* Moskva: Iskusstvo, 1970. [Compèring and Compères.]

3824. ———. *Maski i obrazi estrady.* Moskva: Sovetskaja Rossija, 1976. [Masks and Images of Variety.]

3825. SIDEL'NIKOV, V. *Russkoe narodnoe iskusstvo i estrada.* Moskva: 1950. [Russian Popular Art and Variety.]

3826. *Slovo s estrady: repertuarnyy sbornik.* Moskva: Iskusstvo, 1975. [Word from Variety: a collection of pieces. Ed. M. L. Stel'max and A.N. Strel'cov.]

3827. SMIRNOV-SOKOL'SKIJ, N. *Sorok pjat' let na estrada: fel'etony, stat'i, vystupleniya.* Moskva: Iskusstvo, 1976. [Forty-five Years in Variety: Feuilletons, Articles, Introductions.]

3828. UTJUSOV, L. *Spasibo, cerdce. Vospominanija, vstreči, vdumki.* Moskva: Vserossiiskoe Teatral'noe Obščestvo, 1976. [Thanks, heart. Reminiscences, encounters, reflections.]

3829. UVAROVA, E. D. "Estrada i xudožestvennaja kritika." *Sovetskogo Estrada i Cirk* 2 (1976). [Variety and Criticism.]

3830. ———, ed. *Russkaja sovestskaja estrada 1917–1929. Očerki, istorii.* Moskva: Iskusstvo, 1976. [Russian Soviet Variety 1917-1929. Sketches for a history. Includes: "The Special Character of Variety Art," by A. N. Anastas'ev; "Basic Tendencies in the Development of Soviet Variety in the '20s," by A. N. Anastas'ev; "Variety during the Civil War," by V. V. Frolov; "Spoken Genres," by V. V. Frolov, O. A. Kuznecova, M. I. Zil'berbrandt, E. D. Uvarova, and E. Ja. Dubnova; "Variety Singing," by M. I. Zil'berbrandt; "Variety Dancing," by N. E. Šeremet'evskaja; "Circus Genres in Variety," by N. N. El'sevskij; "Miniature Theatres" by E. D. Uvarova; and "Variety Puppetry," by N. I. Smirnova.]

3831. ———, ed. *Russkaja sovetskaja estrada 1930–1945. Očerki istorii.* Moskva: Iskusstvo, 1977. [Russian Soviet Variety 1930-1945. Sketches for a history. Includes: "Music-halls," by Ju. A. Dmitriev; "Variety and Miniature Theatres," by E. D. Uvarova; "Spoken Genres," by V. V. Frolov, O. A. Kuznecova, M. I. Zil'berbrandt, and E. D. Uvarova; "Literary Variety," by E. Ja. Dubnova, M. I. Zil'berbrandt and V. V. Frolov; "Puppets in Variety," by N. I. Smirnova; "Song in Variety," by M. I. Zil'berbrandt; "Jazz in Variety," by V. B. Fajertag; "Dance in Variety," by N. E. Šeremet'evskaja; "Circus Artistes in Variety," by Ju. A. Dmitriev; and "Variety during the Great Patriotic War," by O. A. Kuznecova.]

3832. *Voobrazennyy koncert. Rasskazy o masterax sovetskoj estrady.*

Leningrad: Iskusstvo, 1971. [Imaginary Concert. Tales of Masters of Soviet Variety. Ed. A. Beilin.]

3833. XOL'MSKAJA, Z. "Vospominanija." In *Russkij provincial'nyy teatr.* Moskva: 1937. ["Reminiscences," in Russian Provincial Theatre.]

Periodicals

3834. *Artist i scena.* Moskva: 1910–12. [Illjustrovanyy žurnal dramy, opery, operety, farza, teatra-varieté, cirka, sporta i kinematografa.]

3835. *Artističeskij Mir.* Moskva: 1912–18. [Žurnal teatra, iskusstva-varieté, cirka, sporta i kinematografa.]

3836. *Cirk i Estrada.* Moscow. 1925–30. [Ninety issues in all.]

3837. *Sovetskaja Estrada i Cirk.* Moskva. July 1963– . Monthly.

3838. *Varieté i cirk.* Moskva. 1912–17. [Illjustrovannyy žurnal.]

3839. *Vestnik Teatra. Cirk i Var'eté.* Moskva. 1912.

SUPPLEMENT F
AFRICA AND ASIA

Cross-references

See also **1741, 1816, 2325, 3074.**

3840. BARBOR, H. R. "Arab Music-hall." *Saturday Review* 147 (30 Mar. 1929): 427–28.

3841. "A Chat with Luscombe Searelle." *Era,* 21 July 1894, p. 14; 4 Jan. 1896, p. 13. [S. African mgr.]

3842. "A Chat with Mr. Ernest Searelle." *Era,* 1 Feb. 1896, p. 18. [S. African mgr.]

3843. "The Empire, Johannesburg." *Era,* 9 Mar. 1895, p. 20.

3844. "Empire, Johannesburg, opening." *Era,* 29 Dec. 1894, p. 11.

3844a. "New Music Hall for Johannesburg." N.Y. *Dramatic Mirror,* 10 June 1904, p. 16.

Supplements

3845. STODEL, JACK. *The Audience is Waiting.* Cape Town, S.A.: Timmins, 1962.

ADDENDA

General Studies. Historical.
3846. PERTWEE, BILL. *Pertwee's Promenades and Pierrots: One Hundred Years of Seaside Entertainment.* Newton Abbot: Westbridge Books, 1979.

London. Collins' Music Hall.
3847. BRAHAM & SONS, Ltd., W. & F. C. *Collins Music Hall: the World's Oldest Music Hall Islington Green, N. 1: a Catalogue of the Famous Collection of Autographed Photographs, Old Playbills, Mementoes etc. . . . to be sold . . . on Tuesday 23rd April, 1963 . . .* [L: 1963.]

London. London Pavilion, Piccadilly.
3848. SAVE LONDON'S THEATRES CAMPAIGN. *Going . . . Going . . . The Fight for a Theatre.* L: Save London's Theatres Campaign [1979]. [London Pavilion. Reproduced typescript.]

Collective Biography.
3849. MASON, DAVE. "Kate? George? Tom? Alec?" *Music Hall* 9 (Oct. 1979): 58-60. [On difficulties of ascertaining vital data on music-hall performers.]

Alec Hurley.
3850. BARKER, TONY. "Alec Hurley." *Music Hall* 9 (Oct. 1979): 44-53. [With discography.]

Addenda

Sir Harry Lauder.
3851. *Newsletter of the Sir Harry Lauder Society.* Portobello, Scotland: 1979–.

Ella Shields.
3852. "Ella Shields Centenary." *Call Boy* 16, no. 3 (autumn 1979): 14.

Harry Tate.
3853. TATE, HARRY, Jr. "My Father and I." *Call Boy* 16, no. 3 (Autumn 1979): 4–5.

Wee Georgie Wood.
3854. [Obit.] *Times,* 16 Nov. 1979, p. vi.

Song and Music Studies. General.
3855. SPAETH, SIGMUND. *Read 'em and Weep; the Songs You Forgot to Remember.* Garden City, N.Y.: Doubleday, Page, 1927.
3856. ———. *Weep Some More, My Lady.* Garden City, N.Y.: Doubleday, Page, 1927. [Although primarily devoted to nineteenth-century popular song in the U.S., both give information on American versions of music-hall numbers.]

Jokes, Monologues and Sketches.
3857. "CUE." [pseud.] *Diversion! The Entertainers' Budget of Comedy, Recitations, Monologues, War Humour, Trench Tales, etc.* L: W. Paxton [c. 1917]. (Paxton's Edition #15053.)
3858. *Francis and Day's Jokelets, as performed by the Mohawk, Moore & Burgess' Minstrels.* L: Francis, Day & Hunter, n.d.
3859. ST CLAIR, F. V. *Recitations, Monologues, Short Stories, Humorous Readings, Parodies and Gags, a True Guide to the Stage, and Other Useful Information.* Revised ed. L: W. Paxton [c. 1917].

Long-Playing Records. Original Performers: Anthologies.
3860. *On the Halls.* (EMI. SHB 43) [*James Fawn:* Tablets; *Hamilton*

3860. *On the Halls.* (EMI. SHB 43) [*James Fawn:* Tablets; *Hamilton Hill:* A Bird in a Gilded Cage; *Lillie Langtry:* On the Margate Boat; *Herbert Campbell:* No Show Tonight; *Harry Randall:* Oh the Business; *Kate Carney:* Liza Johnson; *Ernest Shand:* In a Case like That, Don't Wait; *Lil Hawthorne:* Lucy Lu; Mamie May; *Vesta Victoria:* Riding on a Motor Car; It Ain't All Honey and It Ain't All Jam; *Malcolm Scott:* Encyclopaedia Britannica; *Wilkie Bard:* O, O, Capital O; Sea Shells; *Alec Hurley:* What a Kid 'E Is!; *Marie Lloyd:* The Coster Girl in Paris; Woman's Opinion of Man; Every Little Movement Has a Meaning of Its Own; *Alf Gibson:* I've Got to Get Back to Work; *George Lashwood:* Oh! Blow the Scenery on the Railway!; *Ellaline Terriss:* I Wants Yer Ma Honey; *Jack Pleasants:* Watching the Trains Come In; I'm 21 Today; *Morgan Wilder:* On Strike; *Hetty King:* I'm Going Away; Oh Girls, Why Do You Love the Soldiers?; *Happy Fanny Fields:* The Double Dutch Fusiliers; *Sam Mayo:* Bread and Marmalade; *George Formby:* John Willie's Ragtime Band; *Bransby Williams:* The Green Eyes of the Little Yellow God; *Ada Reeve:* Nobody Knows, Nobody Cares; *Tom Foy:* The Fool of the Family; *Victoria Monks:* Victoria Monks' Love Song; *Harry Weldon:* Sleuthy the Dread of the Heads; *Beth Tate:* Billy; *Olga, Elgar and Eli Hudson:* The Sunshine of Your Smile; *Will Evans and Company:* Building a Chicken House.]

Long-Playing Records. Original Performers: Individuals.
3861. *Gus Elen. You Have Made a Nice Old Mess of It.* (Topic 12T396) [The Golden Dustman; 'E Dunno Where 'E Are; Mrs. Carter; If It Wasn't for the 'Ouses in Between; Me-riah; 'Arf a Pint of Ale; The Pavement Artist; Wait till the Work Comes Round; The Publican; The Coster's Pony; Dick Whittington; Nature's Made a Big Mistake; Don't Stop my 'Arf a Pint of Ale; I'm Going to Settle Down; Pretty Little Villa down at Barking.]

Long-Playing Records. Recreations: Individual Performers.
3862. *Cosmotheka—Wines and Spirits.* (Highway SHY 7001) [Al and Dave Sealey. Good Little Girl; The 'Ouses in Between; The Baby's Name; Little Dolly Daydream; Down the Road; Up Went My Little Umbrella; The Golden Dustman; The Ragtime Ragshop; The Kangaroo Hop; Hitchy Coo; Johnny; Robin Redbreast; Music Box Tune; Only Come Down for the Day; Timothy Let's Have a Look at It; Just Like the Ivy.]

Addenda

SUPPLEMENT D. Germany. Periodicals.
3863. *Der Artist.* Central-Organ zur Vermittlung des Verkehrs zwischen Directoren und Künstlern der Circus, Varietebühnen, reisenden Theater und Schaustellungen. (Düsseldorf) Weekly. 1883–? [Ed. M. C. Krauss.]

INDEX OF AUTHORS

Numbers refer to item classification, not to pages.

Index of Authors

Arthur, Thomas, 2781
Ashton, Ellis, 2510, 2561, 2594, 2677, 2775a
Askwith, George, 1795
Aubrey, Crispin, 962
Aulnet, Henri, 3498
"Autolycus," 952
Aza, Bert, 2218

B. M., 769
B., W. N., 3198
Bab, Julius, 2309, 3718
Bach, Sigismund Ferdinand, 3499
Baedeker, Karl, 390
Bagueley, Wilfred, 1200
Bailey, Peter, 81–83
Baker, Roger, 1722
Ballantine, William, 326
Ballantyne, Evelyn, 179, 3487a
Bamberger, Louis, 327
Bambrick, Winifred, 3311
Barbor, H. R., 3840
Bard, Wilkie, 1918–19
Barke, Ellen, 877
Barker, Felix, 705
Barker, Kathleen, 179a, 1051–53
Barker, Tony, 1967, 2038, 2092, 2140, 2154–55, 2162, 2213, 2388, 2498, 2562, 2965a, 3850
Barnes, Horace, 391
Barnes, John, 3385
Barnes, Peter, 1954
Baron, Alec, 1849
Barret-Zemganno, Jean, 1657
Barrett, Vernon E., 1888
Bason, Fred, 327a
Bathille, Pierre, 3500
Baudez, Jean, 1727
Bauer, Bernhard Adam, 3719
Baumann, H., 1
Baylis, Lilian, 879
Baze, Robert, 3495
Bear Gardens Museum, 84
Beaudu, Édouard, 3495
Beauplan, R. de, 3501
Beavan, John, 770, 2220
Beaver, Patrick, 85
Bedford, Paul, 328
Beecham, Henry, 84
Beerbohm, Max, 180–90,329, 911, 1914, 2163, 2310, 2374, 2512, 2563, 2646, 2799, 2824–25, 3199, 3683
Behrman, S. N., 330

Index of Authors

Brandreth, Gyles, 2514
Bratton, Jacqueline S., 964–65, 3200
Braun, Eric, 2221
Braydon, J. L., 1492
Brayer, Yves, 3495
Brecher, F., 3729
Brecht, Bertolt, 3774
Brent, Peter, 2595
Brereton, Christopher, 1015
Brewer, Charles, 1841
Bridges-Adams, W., 97
Brien, Alan, 3069
Bristow, Eugene, 2144
Britannia Extension Service, 98
British Film Institute, 3386
Britton, A. [pseud.], 99a
Broadbent, R. J. 334, 1110
Broadwood, A., 3201
Brookfield, Charles H. E., 335
Brophy, John, 3202–3
Brough, Peter, 1778
Brown, G. E., 3364
Brown, Ivor, 100, 196, 2596, 3204
Browne, C. Elliott, 101
Browne, Matthew, 197–98
Bruant, Aristide, 3515-16, 3668–71
Brunacci, Giorgio, 3517
Brunschweig, Chantal, 3518
Buchner, Eberhard, 3720
Buckman, David, 966
Budzinski, Klaus, 3775
Bullock, J. M., 3199
Burke, Thomas, 102, 397–99, 3317a
Burnand, Francis C., 199, 336
Burnett, Rex, 3417
Burnley, James, 1257
Burton, Percy, 1798
Busby, Roy, 1892
Busch, Paul, 3792
Bussey, Harry Findlater, 337
Butt, Alfred, 1799
Byl, Arthur, 2311
Bywater, Abel, 3348

C. J. S. T., 1111
Caffin, Caroline, 200
Caine, Hall, 3318
Calandra, Denis, 3776
Calthrop, Dion Clayton, 201
Calvet, Louis-Jean, 3518
Camp, Jack, 338

Index of Authors

Clifford, Charles, 1767
Clunn, Harold P., 402
Coborn, Charles, 1494, 2045, 2074–91
Cochran, Charles Blake, 88, 95, 2105–16, 3199
Cocteau, Jean, 3533
Codey, Émile, 3534
Cole, Walter, 1782, 1909
Colette, Sidonie Gabrielle (Colette Willy), 3672
Collier, Constance, 2516
Collier, John W., 527
Collins, Jose, 2120
Collinson, W. E., 205
Colman, Fred A., 3722
Combes, William H., 1614–15
Compton-Rickett, Arthur, 156
Connolly, Charles, 1617
Constantin, Marc, 3535–36
Conway, Harold, 2204
Cooke, Dutton, 2877
Cooper, Joe, 2256
Coquatrix, Bruno, 3540
Coquiot, Gustave, 3537
Corderoy, E., 1421
Corvin, Michael, 3365
Costanduros, Mabel, 2219
Cotes, Peter, 106, 1804, 2722, 2853, 3070
Couderc, Pierre, 1664
Court, Alfred, 1665
Coveney, Michael, 403, 723
Coward, Noël, 3199, 3357–58, 3540
Cowell, Emilie Marguerite, 2145
Cowen, John, 1422
Craig, Edward Gordon, 139, 206, 339, 1423
Craven, Tom, 3297, 3349
Cross, John E. 2598
Crow, John, 207
Crowther, Bosley, 2276
Croxton, Arthur, 107
"Cue," 3298, 3857
Curl, James Stevens, 641
Curtis, C. V., 567
Curwen, J. Spencer, 1424
Cutts, Randle S., 1168

D'Alcorn, H., 3103
D'Allemagne, Henry René, 3538
Damase, Jacques, 3488, 3539–40
Damer, John, 518
Darewski, Herman, 340
Dark, Sidney, 341
Dauven, L.-R., 2057

Index of Authors

Dubnova, E. Ja., 3830–31
Dukes, Ashley, 3367
Duncan, Isadora, 1635
Duncan, John, 2523
Dunville, T. E., 1904, 2153
Duvau, Marcel, 3495
Dwight, Thomas, 1717a
Dyer, James Somers, 2944
Dyos, Harold James, 538

E. F. S., 2410
Earl, John, 554
Earl, Michael, 742
East, John M., 412, 2358, 2723–25
Edgar, Marriott, 2346–48
Edwards, G., 3211–12
Elder, T. C., 2502
Elen, Gus, 1909, 2157–61
Eliot, Thomas Stearns, 213, 2601
Elkin, Robert, 413
Ellery, Channing, 2988
Elliot, William George, 342
Elliott, Walter, 3199
Ellis, Don, 1114
Ellis, S. M., 497
El'sevskij, N. N., 3830
Elvin, Joe, 1904, 2179–80
Emery, Rongy, 623
Emmons, Robert, 3373
Ervine, St. John, 214, 2854, 2978
Evans, Will, 2188–89

F. L. M., 2855
Fairbrother, Sydney, 2195
Fairlie, G., 2186
Fajertag, V. B., 3831
Falconi, Dino, 3697
Fargue, Léon-Paul, 3552
Farson, Daniel, 119, 2602–4
Feaudierre, Maurice (Serge), 3495
Feest, Leonard J., 698
Felstead, Sidney Theodore, 1893
Ferguson, Rachel, 2605
Fergusson, Sir Louis, 743, 1894
Ferrari, D., 3698
Ferrari, Gustave, 2313
Feschotte, Jacques, 3489
Feuchtwanger, Lion, 3778
Field, Sid, 2200–2201
Fields, Fanny, 2212
Fields, Gracie, 2215–18

338

Index of Authors

Guest, Ivor Forbes, 1640–42
Guilbert, Yvette, 2296–2308
Guitry, Sacha, 2567
Günther, Ernst, 3729a
Guthrie, Thomas Anstey. *See* Anstey, F.
Guttmann, Richard, 3730

Haas, Alex de, 3731
Habans, Paulin. *See* Paulus
Haber, S., 3732
Haddon, Archibald, 121, 223, 354, 1506a, 2414, 2568
Hale, Philip, 2124, 2903
Hall, Edward Hepple, 1435
Hall, Lillian A., 1897
Hall, Owen (J. Hickory Wood), 2539
Hall, Robert Lee, 3323
Hall, Stuart, 224
Hamilton, Cicely, 879
Hamilton, Clayton Meeker, 2315, 2415
Hamilton, Cosmo, 2267, 2316, 3324
Hand, Charles, 1809
Hands, Charles E., 1436
Hannon, Sir Patrick, 2991
Hardel, A., 3566
Harding, Frank, 420
Hardy, C. Graham, 2955
Hardy, Harold, 1572a
Harrison, Brian, 1437–38
Harting, Hugh, 439
Hassan, Ihab, 3369
Hastings, Macdonald, 122
Hatton, Joseph L., 226, 355–56, 3128
Hauriac, Marcel, 3567–68
Hausenstein, Wilhelm, 3781
Haverly, C. E., 3215
Haweis, H. R., 1439
Hayman, Joe, 3299
Hayward, Arthur L., 3216
Hayward, Edward, 227
Haywood, Steve, 962
Headlam, Stuart Duckworth, 1440–42
Held, Anna, 3569
Heppner, Sam, 2114
Herbert, Michel, 3570
Hercíkova, Ivá, 3733
Hertz, Carl, 1708
Hesselt, Dolly, 3794
Hester, Wallace, 2970
Heuze, Edmond, 3547
Hibbert, Henry George, 123, 123a, 123b, 228, 357, 835, 1811
Hildenbrandt, Fred, 3734

Index of Authors

Hiley, Michael, 1718b
Hill, Desmond, 2230–32
Hill, Jenny, 2327–28
Hillerby, Brian, 1286
Hodder, Edwin, 881
Hodgart, Matthew J. C., 3344
Hogan, Michael, 2219
Högbert, Edvàrd, 3798
Holden, W. H., 421
Holdworth, Peter, 1262
Hole, Donald, 1442a
Hole, J., 1280
Holland, D. J., 1916
Hollingshead, John, 125–26, 229–30, 358, 477, 1508–10, 3286
Holloway, Stanley, 2345
Holt, Hazel, 308, 309
Honri, Baynham, 1391
Honri, Peter, 976, 1391, 1858, 1898, 2350, 2608, 2699
Hopkins, Tighe, 231
Hoppe, Hans, 3782
Horwitz, Kurt, 3783
Hosie, Ian, 2362
Hotier, Hugues, 3571
Hotten, John Camden, 2879
Houdini, Harry, 3489a
Hough, Tom Hitch, 1236
Howard, Cecil, 2943
Howard, Diana, 3
Howard, Herbert, 3370
Hoyland, Eric, 1741
Hudd, Roy, 310, 3272a
Hudson, Derek, 359
Huisman, P., 3572
Hume, William Elliott, 3351a
Hunt, G. W., 3131, 3218
Huntley, John, 3392
Husk, W. H., 127
Hutton, Laurence, 2882

Ibels, André, 3544
Ibels, H.-G., 3497, 3573
Ibels, Jacques, 3574
Idzkowski, M., 3575
Iliffe, Richard, 1200
Image, Selwyn, 1444–45
Imeson, W. E., 3291
Irving, Gordon, 128, 1299–1300, 1336, 2442–44, 3300
Irving, Henry, 232, 1573
Isaacs, Sidney Charles, 1512
Isherwood, Christopher, 3371
Isola, Les Frères, 3576

342

Index of Authors

McNamara, Brooks, 1394
Macneice, Louis, 2251
MacOrlan, Pierre, 3596
Macqueen-Pope, Walter James, 115, 133-36, 370-72, 2610, 3199
Macrae, F. G. H., 1058
Mahalin, Paul, 3597
Maindron, Charles Ernest, 3598
Mair, G. H., 245
Maladacea, N., 3705
Maltin, Leonard, 3397
Malvern, Gladys, 2459
Manchester Central Library, 1147
Mander, Raymond, 311-12, 432-33, 979
Mandle, W. F., 137
Mann, Heinrich, 3797
Mann, Roderick, 2206
Manning, Harold, 1241
Manton, Henry, 1454
Manvell, Roger, 3393, 3408
Mar, Helen, 2379
Mare, E., 2501
Marek, Ryszard, 3812
Margetson, Stella, 138-39
Mariel, Pierre, 3599
Marinetti, Filippo Tomasso, 3706-7
Marks, Edward B., 2934
Marriott, R. B., 3049
Marsh, Janet, 605
Marshall, Ernest, 434
Marshall, Michael, 2349
Marston, John Westland, 2881a
Martin, Denis, 2632
Martin, Roy, 2326
Martinetti, Paul, 1909, 2710
Mason, Dave, 3849
Massler, S., 3818
Masson, David, 435
Matthews, Brander, 247
Matthews, J. B., 2882
Matthews, William, 436
May, Betty, 1684
May, David, 980
May, Phil, 313
Mayer, David, 2784
Mayer, Hans, 3785
Mayes, Ronald, 677
Mayne, W. M., 2938
Melling, John Kennedy, 468
Mellor, Geoff J., 1018-19, 1262, 2531
Menétière, Albéric, 3600
Méré, Charles, 3601

Index of Authors

Nash, Jolly John, 2747
Nash, Paul, 2571
Nass, L., 3664
Nerman, Einar, 314
Nest'ev, Izrail' Vladimirovič, 3821
Nettel, Reginald, 3235
Neumann, Ernst, 3743
Nevill, Ralph, 442–43
Nevinson, Henry, 3331
Newman, Alexander, 2660
Newton, Henry Chance ("Carados"), 144–45, 373, 444, 492, 1465, 2737
Nicholls, Harry, 2756–59
Nicholson, Herbert, 573
Nicholson, Renton, 2760–61
Nicholson, Watson, 1547
Nicoll, Allardyce, 146–47
Nielsen, Jens Røgind Hauge, 3236
Noble, Peter, 2207
Nohain, Jean Marie, 1761, 3620
Norgate, Matthew, 2869, 3054
Northedge, Richard, 756
Nutkins, Harry, 1733
Nuttall, Jeff, 2796

Oates, Arthur, 1724
O'Connor, T. P., 3086
Ohard, Prof., 1686
O'Malley, F. W., 445
"One of the Audience," 1131
"One of the Old Brigade," 446
Orens, John Richard, 1465a
O'Rourke, Eva, 476
Orwell, George, 2727
Osborne, John, 258, 2728, 3360
Ostaijen (or Ostayen), Paul van, 3744
Ostwald, Hans, 3745
Otéro, Caroline, 3621
Otto, Hermann Waldemar (Signor Saltarino), 3746, 3752
Ottolenghi, Vittoria, 3493
"Owl," 2962

Page, Philip, 3199
Page, Will A., 2465a
Palmer, John, 260
Palmer, Tony, 3239
Papich, Stephen, 3622a
Park, A. J., 167
Parker, Derek, and Julia, 1646
Parker, John, 1906
Parks, John Gower, 148
Partridge, Eric, 3202–3

Index of Authors

Rageot, G., 3631
Raleigh, Cecil, 1550
Ramo, Luciano, 3711
Randall, Alan, 2261
Randall, Harry, 2787–89
Randall, Henry, 1909
Raven, Simon, 2318
Ravennes, 3632
Ray, Trevor, 447
Raymond, J., 1672
Redfern, John, 3050
Reece, R., 1471
Reeve, Ada, 2797–98
Relph, Harry (Little Tich), 2556–59
Rémy, Tristan, 1673, 1734, 1763, 1907, 3641
Rendle, Thomas Macdonald, 377
Renieu, Lionel, 3633
Renton, E., 1395
Reynolds, Charles and Regina, 1712
Reynolds, Frank, 1623
Reynolds, George W. M., 3335
Reynolds, Harry, 153
Reynolds, Walter, 1551
Ricci, Luigi, 3493
Rice, James, 3314
Richards, Denis, 884
Richards, Grant, 378
Richards, Nellie, 1909
Richards, P. (Richard Pichler), 3748
Richardson, Sir Benjamin Ward, 560
Richardson, John, 379
Richter, L., 3749–51
Rickards, Harry, 2810
Ridge, W. Pett, 380–81
Rigby, Reginald, 268
Rimels, Lucien, 3634
Ritchie, T. Ewing, 449–50
Rivollet, André, 3635–36
Roberts, Arthur, 2818–19
Roberts, J. E., 2907
Roberts, Peter, 885
Roberts, R. A., 1764, 1904
Robey, Edward, 2873
Robey, George, 1904, 2834–50
Robinson, David, 987, 2366, 2925a, 3051, 3399
Robinson, J. W., 3031
Robson, Joseph P., 2785
Rochdale Museum, 2336
Rochdale *Observer,* 2337
Roger-Marx, Claude, 2320
Rohmer, Sax (A. H. Ward), 2558

Index of Authors

Scott, Christopher and Amoret Scott, 3246a
Scott, Clement, 275, 383, 1473, 2884, 2943
Scott, Harold, 155, 3191
Scott, Margaret (Mrs. Clement), 384
Scott, W. S., 156–57
Seaman, L. C., 158–59
Seaton, Ray, 2261, 2326
Secombe, Harry, 384a
Seldow, Michel, 1713
Senelick, Laurence, 104, 160, 1908, 2629, 3183, 3248, 3418
Šeremet'evskaja, N. E., 3830–31
Serge (Maurice Feaudierre), 3495
Shand, John, 276
Sharpley, Anne, 2576
Shaw, Chris, 1724
Shaw, George Bernard, 277–81, 1554
Shears, E. M., 1719, 1736
Sheppard, Thomas, 1276
Shercliff, José, 3647
Sherek, Henry, 1839
Sheridan, Mark, 1904
Sheridan, Paul, 854
Sherrin, Ned, 2630
Sherry, Sam, 1649a
Sherson, Erroll, 453
Short, Ernest, 161–63
Sidel'nikov, V., 3825
Siemsen, H., 3755
Silva, Mario de, 1737
Simon, S. J., 3317
Simmons, E. Romayne, 1916
Simpson, Harold, 2308
Sims, G. R., 385, 472, 509
Sitwell, Sacheverell, 3294
"Slapkins, The Rev. Joseph" (Alfred Allinson), 283
Sloman, Charles, 2927, 3158
Sluglejt, Genich, 3493
Smirnova, N. I., 3830–31
Smirnov-Sokol'skij, N., 3827
Smith, Arthur, 1626
Smith, Bessie, 284
Smith, Morris, 1098
Snaith, Stanley, 464
Sobel, Bernard, 3493
Soldene, Emily, 2928–29
Somerset, Lady Henry, 1749
Sotheby's, 3648
Soutar, Robert, 1973
Southworth, J. G., 164
Spaeth, Sigmund, 3855–56
Spain, Geoffrey, 1398

Index of Authors

Theatre Workshop, 3362
Thomas, Dylan, 3254
Thompson, Lydia, 1651
Thompson, Paul, 1402
Thorne, Guy, 1479
Tich, Mary. *See* Powell, Mary Relph
Tichý, František, 3757
Tiller, John, 1652
Tilley, Vesta, 2974–80
Timbs, John, 456
Titterton, W. R., 292
Tomék, Václav Vladivoj, Ritter von, 3758
Tomkin, W. G. S., 480
Toole, J. L., 1573
Toole Stott, Raymond, 7, 1714
Towers, Edward J., 3653
Townsend, George Henry, 631
Trevor, Charles T., 2920
Trewin, J. C., 734
Trier, Walter, 3722
Trochet, Jean, 3599
Trussler, Simon, 1725a
Truzzi, Marcello, with Massimiliano Truzzi, 1737a
Tucker, Henry, 1653
Turconi, Davide, 3412
Turner, E. S., 1480
Tynan, Kenneth, 2210, 3360

Ulrich, Walter, 3759
Unthan, Carl Hermann, 1770a
Utjusov, L., 3828
Uvarova, E. D., 3829–30

Valentine, J., 1571
Valentine, Karl, 3762–72
Valentine-Böheim, Bertl, 3789–90
Valerio, Edith, 2322
Van Vechten, Carl. *See* Vechten, Carl Van
Vaunce, Sidney, 2238
Vazquez Montalban, Manuel, 3715
Vechten, Carl Van, 1917, 2323
Venzaga, Fiorenza, 3493
Verne, Maurice, 3654–55
Vernillat, France, 3656
Vesque, Marthe, 3657
Veuillot, Louis, 3658
Vicinus, Martha, 104, 171, 1627
Vincent, Adrian, 3339
Vitu, A. C. J., 3659–60
Viviani, R., 3716–17
Vizetelly, Henry, 2764

Index of Authors

CROSS-INDEX OF
LONDON MUSIC-HALLS

Albion Saloon. *See* Wilton's Music Hall
Albion Theatre. *See* Queen's Theatre
Alhambra Theatre. *See* Alhambra Palace
Alhambra Theatre of Varieties. *See* Alhambra Palace
Ancient Hall of Rome. *See* Trocadero Music Hall
Apollo Music Hall. *See* Queen's Theatre
Arches, The. *See* Player's Theatre
Argyll Rooms. *See* Trocadero Music Hall
Artichoke Public House. *See* Foresters Music Hall

Balham Music Hall. *See* Balham Empire
Barnard's Theatre, Woolwich. *See* Woolwich Empire
Battersea Palace of Varieties. *See* Battersea Palace
Bedford Arms Tavern and Tea Garden. *See* Bedford Theatre
Bedford Music Hall. *See* Bedford Theatre
Belmont's Sebright. *See* Sebright Music Hall
Berners Hall. *See* Islington Palace
Boar and Castle Public House. *See* Oxford Theatre
Bow Music Hall. *See* Bow Palace
Bower Music Hall. *See* Bower Theatre
Bower Operetta House. *See* Bower Theatre
Bower Saloon. *See* Bower Theatre
British Saloon. *See* Winchester Music Hall
Bromwich Theatre. *See* Variety Theatre

Cambridge Music Hall. *See* Royal Cambridge Music Hall
Canterbury Arms Public House. *See* Canterbury Music Hall
Canterbury Hall. *See* Canterbury Music Hall
Charing Cross Music Hall. *See* Player's Theatre
Coliseum Theatre. *See* London Coliseum
Collins' Theatre of Varieties. *See* Collins' Music Hall
Corinthian Bazaar. *See* London Palace
Coronation Pleasure Ground. *See* Grecian Theatre
Crowder's Music Hall. *See* Greenwich Hippodrome

357

Cross-index of London Music-halls

Dalston Circus. *See* Dalston Theatre
Dalston Theatre of Varieties. *See* Dalston Theatre
Deptford Empire Theatre of Varieties. *See* New Cross Empire
D'Oyly Carte's New Theatre. *See* Palace Theatre
Dubourg's Theatre of the Arts. *See* Trocadero Music Hall
Duchess of Kent's Theatre. *See* Woolwich Empire

Eagle Public House. *See* Mile End Empire
Eastern Empire. *See* Bow Palace
Eastern Opera House. *See* Pavilion Theatre
Empire, Islington. *See* Islington Empire
Empire Music Hall, Islington. *See* Islington Palace
Empire Music Hall, Newington. *See* Montpelier Palace
Empire Theatre, Woolwich. *See* Woolwich Empire
Empire Theatre of Varieties. *See* Holloway Empire
Empress Music Hall. *See* Empress Theatre of Varieties
English's Music Hall. *See* Sebright Music Hall
Euston Music Hall. *See* Regent Theatre
Euston Palace of Varieties. *See* Regent Theatre
Euston Theatre. *See* Regent Theatre

Falstaff's Club. *See* Evans' Music-and-Supper Rooms
Frederick's Royal Palace of Varieties. *See* Wilton's Music Hall

Gatti-in-the-Road. *See* Gatti's Palace of Varieties
Gatti's Charing Cross Music Hall. *See* Player's Theatre
Gatti's Music Hall. *See* Gatti's Palace of Varieties
Gatti's-over-the-Water. *See* Gatti's Palace of Varieties
Gatti's-under-the-Arches. *See* Player's Theatre
Golden Horse Public House. *See* Lord Raglan Music Hall and Public House
Grand Harmonic Hall. *See* Winchester Music Hall
Grand Hotel. *See* Evans' Music-and-Supper Rooms
Grand Theatre, Islington. *See* Islington Empire
Grand Theatre of Varieties. *See* Grand Theatre
Grapes Public House. *See* Winchester Music Hall
Great Mogul. *See* Winter Garden Theatre
Grecian Saloon. *See* Grecian Theatre
Greenwich Palace of Varieties. *See* Greenwich Hippodrome

Harwood's Music Hall. *See* Variety Theatre
Hengler's Grand Cirque. *See* London Palladium
Hippodrome, Poplar. *See* Poplar Hippodrome
Hoxton Variety Theatre. *See* Variety Theatre
Hungerford Music Hall. *See* Player's Theatre

Islington Hippodrome. *See* Collins' Music Hall
Islington Palace, High Street. *See* Islington Empire

Kilburn Vaudeville Theatre. *See* Kilburn Empire

Lansdowne Arms Public House. *See* Collins' Music Hall

358

Lansdowne Music Hall. *See* Collins' Music Hall
London Colosseum and National Amphitheatre. *See* Dalston Theatre
Lusby's Music Hall. *See* Mile End Empire
Lusby's Summer and Winter Garden. *See* Mile End Empire

Marlow's Music Hall. *See* Bow Palace
Middlesex Music Hall. *See* Winter Garden Theatre
Mogul Music Hall. *See* Winter Garden Theatre
Mogul Saloon. *See* Winter Garden Theatre
Mohawkes Hall. *See* Islington Palace
Montpelier Music Hall. *See* Montpelier Palace
Montpelier Tavern. *See* Montpelier Palace
Mortimer's Theatre. *See* Variety Theatre
Moy's Music Hall. *See* Victoria Palace

National Hall. *See* Holborn Empire
National Skating Palace. *See* London Palladium
National Standard Theatre. *See* Shoreditch Olympia
New Battersea Empire. *See* Battersea Palace
New Bedford Palace of Varieties. *See* Bedford Theatre
New Bedford Theatre. *See* Bedford Theatre
New Concert Hall, Islington. *See* Islington Palace
New Cross Empire Theatre of Varieties. *See* New Cross Empire
New Eldorado. *See* Poplar Hippodrome
New Grand Theatre of Varieties. *See* Grand Theatre
New Kilburn Empire. *See* Kilburn Empire
New King's Theatre. *See* Variety Theatre
New Lyric Music Hall. *See* Foresters Music Hall
New Lyric Theatre. *See* Foresters Music Hall
New Middlesex Theatre of Varieties. *See* Winter Garden Theatre
New Oxford Theatre. *See* Oxford Theatre
New Portable Theatre. *See* Woolwich Empire
New Prince's Theatre. *See* Poplar Hippodrome
New Queen's Theatre. *See* Trocadero Music Hall
New Standard Theatre. *See* Shoreditch Olympia
New Victoria Palace. *See* Royal Victoria Hall and Coffee Tavern
North London Colosseum Theatre. *See* Dalston Theatre

Old Mahogany Bar. *See* Wilton's Music Hall
Old Vic. *See* Royal Victoria Hall and Coffee Tavern
Olympia, Shoreditch. *See* Shoreditch Olympia
Oriental Palace of Varieties. *See* Camberwell Palace
Oriental Theatre, Poplar. *See* Queen's Theatre
Oxford Music Hall. *See* Oxford Theatre

Palace Theatre, Bow. *See* Bow Palace
Palace Theatre of Varieties. *See* Battersea Palace
Palace Theatre of Varieties, Westminster. *See* Palace Theatre
Palladium Theatre. *See* London Palladium
Paragon Music Hall. *See* Mile End Empire
Parthenon Palace of Varieties. *See* Greenwich Hippodrome

Cross-index of London Music-halls

Philharmonic Hall. *See* Islington Empire
Portman Theatre. *See* West London Theatre
Prince's Theatre, Poplar. *See* Poplar Hippodrome

Queen's Arms Palace of Varieties and Public House. *See* Queen's Theatre
Queen's Music Hall. *See* Queen's Theatre
Queen's Theatre of Varieties. *See* Queen's Theatre

Raglan Music Hall. *See* Lord Raglan Music Hall and Public House
Regent Theatre of Varieties. *See* Sebright's Music Hall
Rising Sun Public House. *See* Sun Music Hall
Rose and Crown Palace of Varieties. *See* Greenwich Hippodrome
Royal Albion Subscription Theatre. *See* Trocadero Music Hall
Royal Albion Theatre. *See* Trocadero Music Hall
Royal Alfred Theatre. *See* West London Theatre
Royal Alhambra Palace. *See* Alhambra Palace
Royal Alhambra Theatre. *See* Alhambra Palace
Royal Canterbury Theatre of Varieties. *See* Canterbury Music Hall
Royal Coburg Theatre. *See* Royal Victoria Hall and Coffee Tavern
Royal Eagle Music Hall. *See* Eagle Tavern Music Hall
Royal English Opera House. *See* Palace Theatre
Royal Foresters Music Hall. *See* Foresters Music Hall
Royal Holborn Empire. *See* Holborn Empire
Royal Holborn Theatre of Varieties. *See* Holborn Empire
Royal Marylebone Theatre. *See* West London Theatre
Royal Music Hall. *See* Holborn Empire
Royal Pavilion West. *See* West London Theatre
Royal Standard Hotel. *See* Victoria Palace
Royal Standard Music Hall. *See* Victoria Palace
Royal Standard Music Hall, Battersea. *See* Battersea Palace
Royal Standard Public House and Pleasure Gardens. *See* Shoreditch Olympia
Royal Standard Theatre. *See* Shoreditch Olympia
Royal Surrey Gardens Music Hall. *See* Surrey Music Hall
Royal Trocadero and Eden Theatre. *See* Trocadero Music Hall
Royal Trocadero Music Hall. *See* Trocadero Music Hall
Royal Victoria Theatre. *See* Royal Victoria Hall and Coffee Tavern
Royal West London Theatre. *See* West London Theatre

Sebright Arms Public House. *See* Sebright Music Hall
Seven Tankards and Punch Bowl Public House. *See* Holborn Empire
Shepherd and Shepherdess Gardens. *See* Grecian Theatre
South London Music Hall. *See* South London Palace of Varieties
Standard (Washington) Music Hall. *See* Battersea Palace
Stangate Music Hall. *See* Bower Theatre
Stangate Theatre. *See* Bower Theatre
Strand Musick Hall. *See* Gaiety Theatre
Surrey Gardens Theatre. *See* Surrey Music Hall
Surrey Music Hall, Southwark. *See* Winchester Music Hall

Theatre of the Arts. *See* Trocadero Music Hall
Theatre of Varieties, Hoxton. *See* Variety Theatre

Theatre Royal, Alhambra. *See* Alhambra Palace
Theatre Royal, Woolwich. *See* Woolwich Empire
Three Cups Public House and Music Hall. *See* Bow Palace
Tivoli Theatre, Bow. *See* Bow Palace
Town Hall, and Temple of Varieties. *See* Hammersmith Palace of Varieties
Town Hall, Hammersmith. *See* Hammersmith Palace of Varieties
Turner's Music Hall. *See* Windsor Castle Music Hall and Public House

Varieties Music Hall. *See* Variety Theatre
Victoria Palace Theatre. *See* Victoria Palace
Victoria Theatre. *See* Royal Victoria Hall and Coffee Tavern

Walworth Empire. *See* Montpelier Palace
Washington Music Hall. *See* Battersea Palace
West Kent Theatre. *See* Woolwich Empire
West London Stadium. *See* West London Theatre
Weston's Music Hall. *See* Holborn Empire